Myth and Mind

HARVEY BIRENBAUM

*the gods work in and out of one another
as of us*   —C.S. Lewis

UNIVERSITY
PRESS OF
AMERICA

On the cover:
APOLLO AND DAPHNE,
*marble statue by
Gian Lorenzo Bernini,
1622 - 1625*

Copyright © 1988 by

University Press of America,® Inc.

4720 Boston Way
Lanham, MD 20706

All rights reserved

Printed in the United States of America

Library of Congress Cataloging-in-Publication Data

Birenbaum, Harvey.
Myth and mind / Harvey Birenbaum.
p. cm.   Bibliography: p.
Includes index.
1. Myth. 2. Mythology. 3. Consciousness. I. Title.
BL304.B58   1988   291.1'3—dc19   87-29439 CIP
ISBN 0-8191-6756-8 (alk. paper).
ISBN 0-8191-6757-6 (pbk. : alk. paper).

All University Press of America books are produced on acid-free
paper which exceeds the minimum standards set by the National
Historical Publications and Records Commission.

for

TANYA AND JOSHUA

CONTENTS

    Acknowledgements   vii
    PREFACE   xi

Part I: SEEING

ONE   THE IMAGE-ING MIND
- Images   3
- Seeing with the mind   4
- Subjective substance   5
- The visionary image   7
- The charm of weirdness   12

TWO   FELT LOGIC
- Styles of the mind   14
- Keeping the world in line   16
- The sense of qualities   19
- How images think   22
- The logic of quality   23
- Mythic thought   25
- Qualitative form in myth   29
- The shape of life   31

THREE   THE MEANING OF WONDER
- The problem of meaning   34
- Nonlinear values   36
- The realization of wonder   41
- Strangeness and intimacy   43

FOUR   THE QUALITATIVE WORLD: ITS FORM
- The motif   49
- 1. Space   52
  - Here and there   52
  - Extraordinary space   53
- 2. Time   58
  - Shapes of time   58
  - An anatomy of time   59
  - The experience of infinity   62
  - Transitional time   65

FIVE   THE QUALITATIVE WORLD: ITS OPERATION
- 3. Causation   67
  - Magical cause   67
  - The foregone conclusion   69
  - Traps of commitment   71
- 4. Identity   74

	Characterization	74
	Levels of identity	75
	The self dispersed	76
	Ambiguous identity	80
	The identity of god	82
	Sharing identity	86
	The linear element	87
	The Mercator principle	91

Part II: MEETING

SIX	THE VIEW FROM THE PSYCHE	
	The psychic organ	95
	Self and other	96
	Conscious and unconscious	96
	A myth of resistance	99
	Jung: the objective view	104
	Jung: the subjective view	106
	The impact of consciousness	109

SEVEN	THE DEFINITION OF MORTALITY	
	Myth as confrontation	113
	The quotient of mortality	117
	Creation	118
	Cosmology and sacrifice	120
	Myth of the sexes	123
	Hero and monster	129
	Tragic myth	136
	Fairy tale	138

Part III: BEING

EIGHT	THE MYTHIC TRUTH	
	How myth is	145
	Functional theories	152
	Making belief	155
	Intrinsic images	158
	Projection	159
	Projecting the universe	163
	Modes of projection and modes of belief	165

NINE	MYTH IN NATURE	
	Participating members	168
	Saving the environment	170
	Playing the field	171
	The limits of subjectivity	174
	The physical universe revisited	178

ACKNOWLEDGEMENTS

I am very grateful to James Freeman (in anthropology) and John Lamendella (in linguistics), colleagues who read much of the manuscript and made helpful suggestions, and to Thomas Leddy (in philosophy) who reviewed the section on metaphor. My typist for this project, P.J. Nosek, was generous and energetic in her work. Gabriel de la Llata very kindly helped with the diagrams. Some portions of the book were researched and written while I held a Fellowship from the National Endowment for the Humanities. A small grant from the San Jose State University Foundation helped cover publication expenses.

The following museums, agencies and persons have kindly given me permission to reprint photographs from their collections: DEPARTMENT OF LIBRARY SERVICES, AMERICAN MUSEUM OF NATURAL HISTORY (*Bear Mother*, p. 124, Neg. 321824). ASIAN ART MUSEUM OF SAN FRANCISCO: THE AVERY BRUNDAGE COLLECTION (*Kaliya Krishna*, p. 132). MRS. WILLIAM BASCOM, KENSINGTON, CA. (*Nail Fetish*, p. 161). TRUSTEES OF THE BRITISH MUSEUM (*Garuda*, p. 77.; *Thunderbird*, p. 78; *Fiddle-shaped Figurines* p. 84; *Changes of Urizen, Urizen in Fetters*, p. 100; *Los Consumed*, p. 101); *Hariti*, p. 125). FIELD MUSEUM OF NATURAL HISTORY, CHICAGO (*Transformation Mask*, Neg. 1318, p. 78). ISTITUTO CENTRALE PER IL CATALOGO E LA DOCUMENTAZIONE, ROMA (Bernini's *Daphne and Apollo*, cover and frontispiece, series E, negs. 58487, 59498). LOS ANGELES COUNTY MUSEUM OF ART (*Uma Mahesvara*, gift of Mr. & Mrs. Harry Lenart, p. 128; *Geb & Nut, Sarcophagus*, purchased with funds provided by Mr. & Mrs. John Jewett Garland, p. 129; *Chamunda*, unrestricted funds, p. 144; *Master of Animals*, from the Nasli M. Heeramaneck Collection of Ancient Near Eastern Art, Gift of the Ahmanson Foundation, p. 173). THE LOWIE MUSEUM OF ANTHROPOLOGY, UNIVERSITY OF CALIFORNIA, BERKELEY (*Tlingit Rattle*, p. 77; *Bear Kachina*, p. 161). THE METROPOLITAN MUSEUM OF ART, all rights reserved. (*Eagle-headed Winged Being*, gift of John D. Rockefeller, Jr. 1913 [31.72.3], p. 77; *Cypriote Female Figures*, The Cesnola Collection, purchased by subscription, 1874-1876 [74.51.1545, .1547, .1549, .1544], p. 84; *Yashoda & Krishna*, purchase, Lita Annenberg Hazen Charitable Trust Gift, in honor of Cynthia Hazen and Leon Bernard Polsky, 1982 [1982.220.8], p. 124; *Virgin and Child*, gift of Mr. & Mrs. Frederick B. Pratt, 1935 [44.85.3], p. 125; *Theseus and the Minotaur*, Stuart Tray Collection, p. 133; *Xipe Totec*, the Michael C. Rockefeller Memorial Collection, Gift of Nelson A. Rockefeller, 1978 [1978.412.108], p. 160; *Slit Drum*, Director's Fund, 1975 [1975.93], p. 160. MUSÉES NATIONAUX, PARIS, The Louvre. (*Piombino Apollo*, p. 150). MINISTRY OF CULTURE, GREECE (*Poseidon of Artemision; Athene*, p. 2; *Apollo of Piraeus*, p. 150; *Apollo at Olympia*, p. 151). MERLE GREENE ROBERTSON (*Sarcophagus of Pacal*, p. 54). THE PIERPONT MORGAN LIBRARY (Plates from William Blake's *First Book of Urizen, Copy B*, Morgan Library no. 63139: *Los*

Howled, p. 101.) DUKE OF SUTHERLAND COLLECTION, on loan to the National Gallery of Scotland (Titian's *Diana and Actaeon*, p. 94). THE UNIVERSITY MUSEUM, UNIVERSITY OF PENNSYLVANIA (*Herakles & Nemean Lion*, p. 133).

Quotations of the following material is reprinted with permission as indicated: from *The Tao of Physics* by Fritjof Capra, c 1975. Reprinted by arrangement with Shambhala Publications, Inc., 314 Dartmouth St., Boston, MA 02116; and Gower Publishing Company Ltd. (U.K.). / from *The Philosophy of Symbolic Forms*, Vol. 2: *Mythical Thought* by Ernst Cassirer. Reprinted by permission of Yale University Press. / from *The Sacred and the Profane* by Mircea Eliade, copyright 1957 by Rowohlt Taschenbuch Verlag GmbH; copyright 1959 by Harcourt Brace Jovanovich, Inc. Reprinted by permission of Harcourt Brace Jovanovich, Inc. / from "Burnt Norton" in *Four Quartets* by T.S. Eliot, copyright 1943 by T.S. Eliot; renewed 1971 by Esme Valerie Eliot. Reprinted by permission of Harcourt Brace Jovanovich, Inc. / from *The Tibetan Book of the Dead* by W.Y. Evans-Wentz. Reprinted with permission of Oxford University Press. / from *The Interpretation of Dreams* by Sigmund Freud. Translated from the German by James Strachey. Reprinted by permission of Basic Books, Inc.; and Unwin Hyman Ltd. (U.K.), London. / from "The Cool Web" by Robert Graves. Reprinted with permission of A.P. Watt Ltd. on behalf of the Executors of the Estate of Robert Graves. / from *The Complete Grimm's Fairy Tales*, translated by Margaret Hunt and James Stern. Reprinted by permission of Pantheon Books, a Division of Random House, Inc. / from *The Collected Works of C.G. Jung*, trans. F.R.C. Hull, Bollingen Series XX, Vol. 5: *Symbols of Transformation*. Copyright (c) 1956. Reprinted by permission of Princeton Univ. Press. / from *Metaphors We Live By*, by George Lakoff and Mark Johnson. Copyright 1980 by The University of Chicago. Reprinted by permission of The University of Chicago Press. / from *The Savage Mind* by Claude Lévi-Strauss. English translation copyright 1966 by George Weidenfeld and Nicolson Ltd. Reprinted with permission of The University of Chicago Press. / from *Black Elk Speaks* by John G. Neihardt, copyright John G. Neihardt, published by Simon & Schuster Pocket Books and The University of Nebraska Press, with permission of Hilda Neihardt Petri, Trustee. / from *The Metamorphoses* by Ovid, translated by Horace Gregory. Copyright 1958 by The Viking Press, Inc. Copyright renewed c 1986 by Patrick Bolton Gregory. Reprinted by permission of Viking Penguin, Inc. / from *Language, Thought and Reality: Selected Writings of Benjamin Lee Whorf*, edited by John B. Carroll. Reprinted by permission of the publisher, MIT Press. / from *The Philosophy of "As If"* by Hans Vaihinger. Reprinted by permission of Barnes & Noble Books, Totowa, N.J., and Associated Book Publishers (U.K.) Ltd.

PREFACE

Mythology has been studied by anthropologists, psychologists, sociologists, folklorists, philosophers, historians, classicists, linguists, theologians of particular religions, and scholars of comparative religion. Within each field, camps have divided and factions splintered. Mythology has provided the field for many a skirmish and ambush and for testing out many a new deadly weapon. Occasionally, whole armies have been wiped out. Sometimes, insurgent bands have bravely ignored the fact that they were living under conquest. Victory celebrations have been frequent, even while new attacks have had to be repulsed. As soon as peace is established for our times, time and again, a fresh array of enemies arises demanding unceasing struggle. There has been little infiltration but much propaganda. Slogans have been as deadly as bombshells.

In the broadside of one sentence, a recent writer sets aside "the erratic Harrison, the factual Rose, the Jungian Kerenyi, the repetitive Eliade, [and] even the brilliant but in this field totally misguided Robert Graves . . ." At the start of an important brief campaign, Claude Lévi-Strauss, who has been a major influence on scholars dealing with the myth in modern times, laments the slackness of his fellow anthropologists in the field and rallies his cohorts with a solid trouncing of presumptuous amateurs: ". . . precisely because the interest of professional anthropologists has withdrawn from primitive religion, all kinds of amateurs who claim to belong to other disciplines have seized this opportunity to move in, thereby turning into their private playground what we had left as a wasteland."[1]

I don't mind belonging to the feckless horde of amateurs. Even if everyone who is not a specialist of some kind is an amateur, the very diversity of factions suggests that an outside voice may be of some use. Being an amateur, moreover, gives me license to hear good sense in some writers whom the dominant authorities of the day have declared dated or otherwise inconsiderable. In the preface to my favorite book on myth, Heinrich Zimmer calls himself a "dilettante of symbols," reminding us that a dilettante is, after the Italian, "one who takes delight."[2] An amateur is, of course, after the French, a "lover," and while lovers are not celebrated for their discretion, they have been known to enter a depth of relationship unsuspected by their solemn observers.

I come to the study of myth from the triple perspective of a struggling literary theorist, a person who has found myth-study of great value in his own life, and a teacher. I have been attracted, therefore, to the work of those specialists who have been able to help me best in these three roles.

In the study of literature, I have found that a comprehension of mythic form illuminates the differences between imaginative reality and the reality of everyday life, clarifying sharply, moreover, the ways in which meaning happens in the arts. The arts are all, in a way, mythic (as I shall eventually try to show), and much of what I say about myth is true of them as well.

As for the personal value of myth, I have found, like quite a few other people in our age, that an awareness of traditional myth has helped to orient me amid my own experience. Every seeker after "life's meaning" enacts the timeless quest of the typical mythic hero, after his Golden Fleece or his Holy Grail, his elixir of immortality or his supernal bride, and the basic patterns of myth are maps of life's course. Myth suggests what kind of meaningfulness we might count on within institutions and what kind we can count on without them.

In the classroom, thirdly, I have tried to find ways of conveying this kind of meaningfulness to others. Many people come to the study of myth with either a religious or a skeptical point of view, both of which seem to preclude an actual "mythic" way of seeing things. For the practical reasons of pedagogy, I have welcomed whatever help I could get in making this strange alternative seem plausible. Accordingly, I have brought together a sampling of the many insights that have contributed to our current understanding of myth. I have tried to represent briefly the major contributors (or combatants), but instead of summarizing them all directly in an analytical survey, I have introduced them within a framework that I hope will be in itself a useful thinking tool.

In looking at the theories of different disciplines, I have had the impression that they do not disagree quite as much as they think they do. Perhaps it would take an outsider to appreciate their common ground. The specialist might consider my combinations of sources undiscriminating. I suppose I have been a bit of a scavenger, picking at the scraps I could use (or, to follow my original metaphor, the bones of the slain). The value of a philosophical position lies not in its premises, I think, but in its ability to cope with reality. Accordingly, I would presume to offer here a perspective and some principles that might reconcile differences, that might even make lovers of some weary foes.

Of course, I have my favorites. I have found the assistance I have needed especially in the work of the philosopher Ernst Cassirer and the psychiatrist Carl Jung, and in some writers who have been influenced by them. Along with the German theologian Rudolf Otto, Cassirer and Jung both developed, with different kinds of detail, the point of view that myth is, first of all a condition of consciousness and, secondly, a valid way of representing recurrent human experience.[3] It is this dual perspective that I think still calls out for insistent clarification and that I will dwell on in the following pages. In the language of philosophy, this approach to myth is *phenomenological* and *ontological*. It looks for the significance of myths in the quality of experience that they present to us (their phenomenology) and in the kind of reality (the ontology) that they make up or possess as we understand them through that experience.

It is important, as the anthropologist Clifford Geertz states, "that our formulations of other people's symbol systems must be actor-oriented."[4] Surely, we would not like strangers to interpret our own actions without appreciating the viewpoint from which we act. It must be a pointless exercise to analyze another culture's works as though they were simply fossilized bones or strata of rock. Social scientists, eager to prove they are indeed scientists, speak all too often in the third person about the human race, looking at life forces as though they were isolated entities. To deal with the *actor*, however, is to deal with his experience, with his consciousness. It is to imagine what it is like to *be* the actor in the process of acting, alive as a self unto himself. To do this, we need some appreciation for the nature of consciousness itself--some consciousness of consciousness--and that requires more intuition (literally, "looking within") than methodology, more of what we all have than what we need to be trained in.

When we experience, with imaginative penetration, the images of another culture, we open dimensions of consciousness our own culture has kept closed. Our culture establishes the environment and the horizons of consciousness for us, the full range of what we take to be possible. If we entertain myth as a way of seeing life, then, we take quite seriously the experience of a radically different kind of culture from our own. The more ways we experience in which the mind can be conscious of itself, the more basic is the level of consciousness that we come to know, the consciousness with which we face the rest of the world, go out to it, and bring it back to us.

Intuitively, without thinking about it, people from earliest human times seem to have had a sense of something profoundly special about the phenomenon of consciousness and have felt a need to keep aware of its reality, as an order distinct from objectively observed facts. That is one telling reason why myth, religion, and the arts exist at all. All three of these ways of formulating experience nourish a sense of urgency and awe about the way they deal with life. We usually dress up to go to a place of worship or to the concert hall and a mysterious hush envelopes us in either place, even some fear of expressing our own ordinariness, as in coughing or laughing too loud. In religion, of course, this special attitude lies in the aura of sacredness or sanctity that its symbols are meant to cultivate and preserve.

It is only from the direction of *thinking* that this specialness seems odd or hard to grasp, or simply ridiculous or pretentious. And it is in thinking about myth that we have difficulty coping with it. The most important points about myth may be the simplest, yet they often seem the hardest to talk about. Then we have to arrange our thoughts into systems in order to get back to what in itself is very natural. But also even then we will have little success if we cannot shake down our minds to the basic level of consciousness. From that level we can rise to meet the words and concepts half-way and find some truth in that act of meeting.

Obviously, definitions can simplify the organization of our thoughts. We ought to be cautious about them, however, and not only because their own kind of organization may well be simpler than the facts themselves. A definition purports to tell us what something is in itself, but as often as not--at least in academic and philosophic matters--it is really just an action by which the speaker stakes his claim over a certain territory, telling us what it is he proposes to discuss. For the anthropologist, myth will be a function of ritual, for the psychologist it will be an expression of unconscious drives, for the sociologist a program of social patterns, for the theologian an attempt to reach God. Under such circumstances, the quarrels over who is right obviously can go on forever.

Although we cannot give an absolute definition of myth, we can supply a define-it-yourself kit with all the parts that should be needed. The customer can select according to his needs or use all the components, perhaps in this arrangement:

1. impossible or unrealistic stories, probably with
2. miraculous or supernatural elements, possibly through
3. the presence of deities, suggesting
4. a religious framework, implying
5. the probability of belief or ritual adherence, sharing therefore
6. communal acceptance, derived in part from
7. the justification of cultural standards, based upon
8. purported explanation of natural phenomena, derived from
9. primeval, impersonal origin, followed by
10. traditional evolution within the society, perhaps upon the basis of
11. archetypal, or at least typal, form, conveying
12. representative power, a capacity to capture and magnify typical situations, that may have
13. transcultural applicability, conveyed through
14. subjective expressiveness, establishing
15. a special imaginative reality.

Conservative anthropologists will be wary of the last five items. Some will require the third, fourth, or fifth. Numbers seven and eight are sometimes included in functional definitions of myth (see Chapter 8), but they talk about what the myth does rather than what it is. By omitting most terms between three and nine, we can include fairy tales. By speaking only of the last five, we can further extend the word to include literary mythmaking. The last two alone suggest a still broader conception of myth, as any subjective reality, which I shall discuss in my penultimate chapter.

Myth, in other words, makes an excellent example of Wittgenstein's notion of a class of entities unified by "family resemblances," which "overlap and criss-cross" the way that "build, features, colour of eyes, gait, temperament, etc. etc." characterize the members of a family without all such traits needing to appear in the same form in all members.[5] We can recognize the category without the generalization of a uniform definition, knowing that different sorts of what we call myth are like some of the other sorts, that some are like some others in some ways and like still others in other ways, and that none have to satisfy a definition just because it applies to different members of the group.

Far along into the book, in Chapter 7, I will offer a "working definition" that grows out of my own context. I prefer, usually, to think I am describing what I am talking about rather than defining it. From the start, I am interested in myth as an activity of the imagination coping with its own experience. Myth is, as I will explain the term, a *nonlinear* narrative. It is archetypal, in my use of the word, because it reflects the very basic structure of the psyche, a structure which has enormous implications for our sense of life and which stirs within us, inevitably, the most powerful sorts of feelings. This "structure" is simply the psyche's division of itself into conscious and unconscious tendencies while establishing its sense of being a *self* radiating amidst an *other* world.[6]

The central part of the book, called "Meeting," explores this view of archetypal form. It is preceded by "Seeing," which explains the concept of "nonlinear logic" and shows how through it myth establishes a subjective reality that reflects accurately the nature of human experience. The third part, "Being," argues that myth demonstrates a way of existing, or a kind of truthfulness, which may be considered the most basic dimension of its meaning.

4

Since I am exploring myth through such broad concepts, I will blithely ignore some distinctions that a more scholarly approach might well observe. Although I refer to the need, I do not attempt to treat concretely the important influence of economic and cultural contexts on shaping a body of myth--a main concern of ethnologists. But after all, you do need to know the species before you can identify the individual, the theme before the variation, the archetype before the type.

I may treat in the same breath an indubitable myth, a folktale, and a modern novel or poem, since I am more interested in what they all have in common--that sense of the archetype--than in what distinguishes them. Myth and folk tale overlap significantly, the one leading back to religion, ritual, and metaphysics, the other to art, entertainment, and our pleasure in one another's company. Yet their psychological material and their methods are essentially the same, and they both cultivate a sense of life's mysteries. What is probably the most fertile and the most familiar type of traditional narrative, the tale of heroic quests or adventures, is often poised ambiguously between the two, at least in the shape it has come down to us. As for "literature," even down to modern times, the traditional style derived from the old oral sources has continued to inspire most of the literary works we regard as "world masterpieces," the major exceptions being works of satire and social realism. From Homer and the Biblical authors to Sophocles to Shakespeare to Blake to Melville to Joyce, Kafka, Eliot, Mann, Lawrence, and Hesse--all of them conscious and sophisticated artists--great writers have continued to compose highly crafted and styled works on the bases of archetypal form.

The relation between myth and religion is also ambiguous, but it can be, to be sure, a more troublesome one. Much of what must certainly be called myth can be defined as the narrative and pictorial content of religion. Whenever deity is imagined with a concrete form, whenever the facts of existence are accounted for through story, whenever gods and men are portrayed in direct interaction, whenever a condition of life beyond death or before natural existence is dramatized with local color, we are engaged in myth.

We should be cautious in two ways. First of all, this does not mean that such images are untrue. They have a special kind of truth, one, I maintain, that has nothing exactly to do with belief and one that permits all the possible contradictions among them. It is the main purpose of my book to explore what that kind of truth might be. Secondly, it does not mean that, in describing the mythic content of religion, we are exhausting the subject of religion, or even discussing it fairly in its own proper terms, or implying anything at all about its value or lack of value. When I talk about the mythic content of a religion, let the phrase be understood: "whatever else can be said on the subject as well." Images that have a mythic truth may conceivably have a literal truth at the same time. Any implications of this "mystery," certainly any application of it, I gladly leave to every reader.

The most important effect that the study of myth can have, I believe, is that it can help develop a significant flexibility of mind. After a first study of myth, more often than not, believers and nonbelievers alike find their convictions or inclinations clarified. Beliefs and skepticisms alike may seem more meaningful, their relation to one's life more sure. That is precisely because myth and consciousness illuminate each other-- and this thought is the main premise of my book.

5

The relation of myth and mind is a matter of ultimate responsibilities, and responsibility is how we acknowledge what is real. Although anyone can see that myth always presents its own version of reality, by studying its features with close attention, we can reach, in fact, some further insight into what *is* real, what truth actually consists of, what existence--in the most basic and the broadest sense--may mean. More specifically, the relation of myth and mind provides a useful model for the idea, which modern scientists continue to explore, that reality consists of organized energy. Far from being mere pretty old fables or antiquated

TEN	THE PSYCHO-MYTHOLOGY OF EVERYDAY LIFE	
	Common myth	183
	The forms of common myth	185

any belief, any system of beliefs (185), one's world view, personality (186), self and other, time (187), the future, the present, the past (188), history, the arts, self-expression, assertions (189), description (190), the sciences (191), explanation, generalization (192), negation, photographic reality (193), any perception (194), figures of speech (195), prophetic truth (196), system and chaos (197), the fine world and the gross, the linear world (198)

	The ordinary and the archetypal	199
ELEVEN	SYMBOLIC CONSCIOUSNESS	
	Inside and out	207
	In the end	210
APPENDIX I: ABOUT CONSCIOUSNESS		
	Trying to say what it is	214
	The fundamental flow	215
	The subject: parallel terms	217
	Descriptions of consciousness	217
	Being conscious of consciousness	218
	The polarization of eneregy	219
	Problems with the word "consciousness"	223
APPENDIX II: MYTHS, FICTIONS, METAPHORS		
	Myth or fiction?	225
	Myths and metaphors	227
	Notes	232
	Bibliography	261
	Index	268

fallacies, or priestly deceptions, myth may provide a view of the universe that can satisfy the very sophisticated needs of our time.

Myths can be thought of as paradigms--exemplary illuminations of life that are meaningful because they are concrete and particular; they are suggestive instances, fraught with nuance. But also, the study of myth is itself paradigmatic. The process pursued in the following text should suggest broader implications about the ways that human beings operate in the world because of the minds that they have. Quite dramatically, the study of myth suggests some basic points about how we find ourselves in nature and in our selves, but also, I have found, it leads to an especially useful view of how we find our way in the world of culture, among the symbols, assumptions, conceptions of ourselves, perspectives, and *versions* of truth that make up the intangible but intensely vivid kind of reality we negotiate together and alone every day.

The emphasis on myth's special "versionary" truth can be extended from the study of traditional, or archetypal, myth to what I have called in Chapter 10 "common myth." By a change of key, myth becomes the whole range of realities that mind constitutes for us to live by, through, and in, now as always. But all these more-or-less subjective forms of truth, which I have surveyed and sketched out in an undoubtedly crude sampling, can be understood further in relation to the archetypal conception that has been the book's main concern. We have then a principle of culture that allows both for relativism and for a definitive kind of truth at the same time, understanding each in relation to the other. Thus, by addressing the variety of questions that the study of myth has raised for me, I have wandered further than I had thought to go and have come back to the main point by doing so. And that, of course, is the manner of myth, as it is also the manner, I trust, of mind.

PART ONE

SEEING

To see or to perish *is the very condition laid upon everything that makes up the universe, by reason of the mysterious gift of existence. And this, in superior measure, is man's condition.*
--Teilhard de Chardin

THE POWER OF THE IMAGE

(above) **Poseidon** *(or Zeus) of Artemision, between 460-450 BC*

(right) **Athene,** *clay head from Olympia, about 490 BC*

CHAPTER ONE

THE IMAGE-ING MIND

*The lord whose oracle is in Delphi neither
speaks out nor conceals, but gives a sign.*
— Heraclitus

IMAGES

We think first of the Greeks; we know them best: Troy, after nine years of siege, wavering; Hector's body dragged around its walls as Achilles proudly satisfies his aching grief. Herakles, monument of brawn, drawing a river from its course to purge the reeking Stables of Augeas; and Herakles climbing his burning pyre with a poisoned tunic eating into his flesh. The confident Oedipus, swathed in ignorance, extinguishes the weird Sphinx with easy cleverness. Watching the petrifying Gorgon in his shield, Perseus slashes off the monstrous head. Actaeon, luckless hunter, having chanced upon a virgin goddess, is suddenly a deer, torn down in mute terror by his own fine dogs. The Titan Prometheus in immortal agony, bound down upon a mountain, his liver pecked by fierce birds because he stole us fire. Sisyphus rolling his boulder up-hill miserably everafter. Over a dark river, a ferry to that dreariest, most democratic afterlife.

Frozen among the stars, vague figures that don't quite fit the spare patterns of the constellations. But haunting the mind, images of strained passion, grotesque predicaments, unlikely possibilities as real as nightmares, what cannot be that cannot help but be. Men and women, children and parents released to work out their will on one another. Absurdly confident young men, unaware that they should be afraid, stepping forth into monstrosity.

Perhaps we remember from the Norse myths Loki, redolent with malice, encouraging the grateful blind old beggarwoman to join in nature's game and toss a fatal sprig of mistletoe, apparently so harmless, at Balder, the beautiful man whom everybody loves. Or Odin, suspending himself head downwards on the tree of life, god sacrificing god to god, paying his eye to learn life's mysteries.

And from the Celtic lands the images of Arthur. The child sent to help his foster brother: why bother riding home when a good sword sits useless in the rock? And older Arthur, his proud table now abandoned for a higher goal, the Grail, sees that this world of strength and decency and splendor will help him little when he is alone. The lovers, obsessed with one another hopelessly, letting the world crumble about them: Lancelot and Guinevere, Isolde and Tristan.

The Image-ing Mind

From all quarters come the images: Quetzalcoatl, Mexico's white god, the feathered serpent, running from a world now mastered by the one art he neglected to teach men, the art of war. Or Raven, troublemaker of the Eskimos, at once a man and bird, a hero, deity, a foolish demon; or his African cousin Spider, who weaves a web between the earth and sky to tangle both gods and humans.

From India, young Krishna teasing the goatherd girls who love him to ecstatic distraction; as they clamor to dance with him in the night forest, he is nowhere. On the battlefield of Kurukshetra, Krishna as charioteer reveals his divine nature to Arjuna that the war of life may proceed: the most blessed and the most horrific are as one in him. Shiva, as the Lord of Dance, poised in his statuettes forever still but swirling through the universe in continual creative death. And the Buddha-to-become sitting by the Bo tree, waiting through seductions and destructions, unarms the demons of the world by waiting.

[margin note: Dionysos]

Or, since myth includes the narrative part of all religions, from the Bibles: so strong are the associations for us that we need only flash the names. Cain and Abel, Lot's wife, Joseph and his brothers, Moses descending from Mt. Sinai; the Annunciation, Resurrection . . . and the mind is captured by the startling scenes that arise immediately.

We see these pictures with imagination's eye, we seem to hear their voices, dimly; and rather strangely, we can even feel their presence. Not only seen and heard, they are felt images. Some of the images may seem pacified briefly with a name or a slogan--greed or lust or envy--but the images of myth have more subtlety than words will capture, more life. When I look back at my descriptions, I think I have trapped the myths into statements about them. When I look in my mind toward the images themselves, I find it harder still--but more important--to say what they *are*, what kind of reality they can have, and what meanings can be true to their reality.

What we take to be true, how far do we know it to be true? When we see, do we really know what we see? Do we know anything we do not see? What we imagine, how does it exist? Do we see what we imagine? What does the mind want with what cannot be true? What is the mind, that it should imagine? We feel we know what we mean. What can we know by feeling?

Where is the land of myth? In the mind, of course, but in what space? How is it there, what substance does it have? Why is it as it is because of what it is? If its nature is mind's nature, how is it mind-like? Is it the landscape of the mind?

Is there anything in the mind that is not myth?

SEEING WITH THE MIND

We come to terms with reality most simply and most richly when we merely comprehend it, take it in, allowing our faculties to penetrate its nature and trace its implications. Unlike abstract analysis, or that kind of thinking which must prove its point, this is a concrete and integrated

Seeing with the Mind

activity of mind. We see the tree and say, "Yes, this is a tree. Thus do its branches and thus do its leaves." Perhaps we do most of our actual thinking with a kind of "felt logic," through which we realize unities, relationships, proportions, differences, and similarities, in and among whatever we may perceive, as we perceive it.

Traditional myths reveal their meaning only as they reveal their nature, and they reveal their nature to me only as I, a conscious self, experience them. As we may say more obviously of dreams, I must *have* them in order to know them, not merely observing them as though they were concrete objects and analyzing them "objectively" but entering into them subjectively. Dreams and myths--and works of art--are organized *experiences* of life. I must interpret a myth, therefore, as such a *having* of the experience, not just as the doing of an act, or the appearance of a fact, or a pattern out in space.

In my experience then, the myth is not just the fossil of some creatures that flourished in the past. As such it would be an object outside me. As I dwell upon it, it *is* me, in *my* experience for the time, as it fills my mind with its own world of characters in action and in passion, all traversing the space of their destinies. So to know it, I will know it in relation to *my* being, in relation to the nature of my own mind, and in relation to my wish to know.

Who am I, however, to expect that what I see when I look at myth has anything to do with the remote tribal cultures that produced it? Living in the twentieth century, in a practical industrial culture that is dominated by its commercial and scientific achievements, in a democratic society, which mingles so many ways of life together: can any single person feel sure he understands anything at all, let alone something so remote from our common ways of thought as mythology? Can reflection show me anything that is not personal, that is not, in fact, my own "reflection?" The answer to such a challenge lies again in the very nature of the mind imagining, even in the mind imagining the skeptical question. Mind, in some shape or form, is the stuff of myth, and mind explored will find out its own solution. Looking together at how our minds work, we see to what extent they must be working alike. We get some notion, also, how much about ourselves must be due to the nature of mind itself.

If myth is an activity *of* the mind, and we inevitably know it *through* the mind, then the mind trying to understand must stay aware of its own operation as it tries to understand. It may turn out that its own light is the light it seeks.

SUBJECTIVE SUBSTANCE

Whatever else we can say about myth at the start, we can also observe with little trouble that it is certainly not rational or logical in ordinary terms. A realm of magic and miracle, gods and demons, it hardly describes the world we know around us. We can readily agree, even insist, that it is nonrational and imaginary--but if we call it "irrational," sadly lacking in good reason, we prejudice ourselves against

The Image-ing Mind

it. We need to see what myth is, instead of what it is not. The god drawing the sun behind his chariot across the sky to give us day, the dying youth become a flower, the monster yielding his overwhelming life to a hero armed with magic: reason may have no use for such propositions, but surely they came into existence in some way and continue to exist in some way as we think about them. If we want to understand what they mean, therefore, we must come to see *how they exist.*

The existence of myth is, of course, imaginative. We usually think of imagination as a faculty that produces only false worlds. But if we try to isolate in our minds how much we know through direct perception alone and then reflect on what is left in our picture of reality, we can get a glimpse of how much we must imagine to be true. "What would we know of others if we did not imagine things?" asks Gaston Bachelard.[1] What, we may add, would we understand of ourselves? How could we undertake a business, a marriage, or a vacation? And beyond our imagination's filmy re-creation of the past or its sketches of the future, how could we detect patterns of meaning in that past which drive us to see that future just as we desire or fear it? How else could the physicist comprehend the molecule, the astronomer the nebulae, the paleontologist the body that once fleshed out a skeletal fossil?

"One has never seen the world well," Bachelard writes, "if he has not dreamed what he was seeing . . ." Myth is such a way of dreaming about the world. The mythmaker sees the world by imagining it, because the images that he sees figure forth the qualities he experiences in the world. His image-ing eye sees the world in concrete shapes and incidents. In them patterns unfold that may remind us all of life's own features. Though the result is not rational in the more "realistic" or objective sense, it is bound to have both its own kind of reality and, accordingly, its own kind of truthfulness.

The imaginative truth of myth reminds us, in other words, that experience has, so to speak, its own kind of substance. We have a strange disinclination to take the world of experience quite seriously.[2] We contrast it with the "real world," focusing upon *what* we are experiencing as we attempt to look *through* our actual experience of it. From this point of view, experience itself seems transparent and insubstantial, or else it is only an instrument for handling the real substances of the world, a means to an end.

Our reluctance to take experience seriously in itself is a strange attitude for the reason that "experience" means *having* our lives. If we do not see it, that is probably because it is what we see *with*--and because it so familiar to us. It is so close that it is our very selves at the same time that it is our unity with the entire universe beyond. It is what puts us *in* the world, as we experience it.

Similarly, the word "subjective" (*merely* subjective, we say) commonly means *personal* or *idiosyncratic,* what comes from one's particular point of view or one's own personality and can therefore have no general validity. Any *merely* subjective statement is of dubious value. But "subjectivity" also means *the quality of experience*. As such, it is the

6

essential nature of our being. It is the only instrument in the orchestra, although we all play upon it our own variations and our own favorite themes.

Subjectivity, as experience, is always real in its own right. It is in its own way whole and substantial: *whole* because it fills the universe, from wherever we are, with the flow of our being, and *substantial*, of substance, because it strikes us intensely with its nature. The red reddens our vision (we don't just *know* that it is red), the pain really hurts, a fantasy of floating in the sky is a very real fantasy, and the game of make-believe really makes belief transpire, so that it can ultimately become a living force at least as creative or as destructive as any other. Beliefs sustain lives and beliefs kill. It is for good reason that we speak of "coming up against feelings" that "stop us dead," that overwhelm us and "carry us away." Of course, there is no stopping some ideas imbued with passion, such as the idea of one's own importance--or one's nation's.

If we want to "see" what myth is, then, we can start usefully with its integral involvement in the human mind. We can say that it is made out of experience and therefore shares the subjective "substance," the reality, of the experienced universe. The *qualities* of living are its stuff. In fact, in mythical thinking, qualities are often regarded as objects in themselves. The American Indian hero Raven puts on his bird-nature as a cloak. The sun puts on his light. The native doctor sucks the illness out of his patient. The stuff of experience is malleable, therefore, and it is readily molded into imagery. [3]

THE VISIONARY IMAGE

The interest in psychedelic and visionary experience that was widespread in the 60's made us familiar with the way in which images that are encountered directly, without the conscious mind intervening, are totally real in their own right. Recording an experience under LSD, Alan Watts describes the sight of objects around him as being enmeshed in his own capacity for perceiving them. Their substance is his substance, as body and as mind, as an individual and as part of the universe.

> Sometimes the image of the physical world is not so much a dance of gestures as a woven texture. Light, sound, touch, taste, and smell become a continuous warp, with the feeling that the whole dimension of sensation is a single continuum or field. Crossing the warp is a woof representing the dimension of meaning--moral and aesthetic values, personal or expressive form . . . I feel that the world is *on* something in somewhat the same way that a color photograph is on a film, underlying and connecting the patches of color, though the film here is a dense rain of energy. I see that what it is on is my brain--"that enchanted loom," as Sherrington called it. [4]

The Image-ing Mind

Images may come to us as parts of the world around, as figures of spirit, as memories, or "simply out of nowhere." Yet when they are experienced whole-heartedly, as it were, a revelation of our own nature comes to us through their very existence as images. Our feelings respond to their form with complex subtlety, so that we feel an intimacy with their being and an extraordinary knowledge of their presence.

The visionary, or seer, is one who *sees* habitually with his own whole being alive to the world. The visions he may have demonstrate what is substantial in the world of experience and show how he is to relate himself to it. The classic account of American Indian vision experience is *Black Elk Speaks*, the autobiography of an Oglala Sioux as recorded by John G. Neihardt, a poet who composed epics on Indian life. The book preserves an extremely sensitive, articulate, and moving account of a young boy's visions but also of the futility of his calling as his race perishes around him in the years that follow. At the age of nine, Black Elk is summoned by two men bearing down from the clouds. Leaving his body in a coma, he is carried to the sky, where he takes part in an elaborate series of pageants sponsored by magnificent horses who are Grandfathers "older than men can ever be--old like hills, like stars." They are the Powers of the World, the oldest of whom gives him symbolic gifts of life and death.

> Now there was a wooden cup in his hand and it was full of water and in the water was the sky.
> "Take this," he said. "It is the power to make live, and it is yours."
> Now he had a bow in his hands. "Take this," he said. "It is the power to destroy, and it is yours."
> Then he pointed to himself and said: "Look close at him who is your spirit now, for you are his body and his name is Eagle Wing Stretches." [5]

Black Elk sees himself growing backwards and forwards through time:

> Now I knew the sixth Grandfather was about to speak, he who was the Spirit of the Earth, and I saw that he was very old, but more as men are old. . . . I stared at him, for it seemed I knew him somehow; and as I stared, he slowly changed, for he was growing backwards into youth, and when he had become a boy, I knew that he was myself with all the years that would be mine at last. When he was old again, he said: "My boy, have courage, for my power shall be yours, and you shall need it, for your nation on the earth will have great troubles. [6]

The nature of his power is explained not through words but through vivid scenes in which he is the main actor.

The Visionary Image

I looked below me where the earth was silent in a sick green light, and saw the hills look up afraid and the grasses on the hills and all the animals; and everywhere about me were the cries of frightened birds and sounds of fleeing wings. I was the chief of all the heavens riding there, and when I looked behind me, all the twelve black horses reared and plunged and thundered and their manes and tails were whirling hail and their nostrils snorted lightning. And when I looked below again, I saw the slant hail falling and the long, sharp rain, and where we passed, the trees bowed low and all the hills were dim.

. . . . .

Then the black horse riders shouted "Hoka hey!" and charged down upon the blue man, but were driven back. And the white troop shouted, charging, and was beaten; then the red troop and the yellow.

And when each had failed, they all cried together: "Eagle Wing Stretches, hurry!" And all the world was filled with voices of all kinds that cheered me, so I charged. I had the cup of water in one hand and in the other was the bow that turned into a spear as the bay and I swooped down, and the spear's head was sharp lightning. It stabbed the blue man's heart, and as it struck I could hear the thunder rolling and many voices that cried "Un-hee!," meaning I had killed. The flames died. The trees and grasses were not withered any more and murmured happily together, and every living being cried in gladness with whatever voice it had. Then the four troops of horsemen charged down and struck the dead body of the blue man, counting coup; and suddenly it was only a harmless turtle.

You see, I had been riding with the storm clouds, and had come to earth as rain, and it was drouth that I had killed with the power that the Six Grandfathers gave me. So we were riding on the earth now down along the river flowing full from the source of waters, and soon I saw ahead the circled village of a people in the valley and a Voice said: "Behold a nation; it is yours. Make haste, Eagle Wing Stretches!" [7]

Although Black Elk keeps his vision to himself for eight years, he retains a clear knowledge of its details and its intense effect upon him. He could "feel the meaning with a part of me like a strange power glowing in my body":

for nothing I have ever seen with my eyes was so clear and bright as what my vision showed me; and no words that I have ever heard with my ears were like the words I heard. I

The Image-ing Mind

did not have to remember these things; they have remembered themselves all these years. [8]

In adolescence, he becomes ill with fear until, when he is 17, he reveals the experience to a medicine man who tells him he must carry out his mission. Then, under Black Elk's own direction, the people of the tribe duplicate his vision in a great horse dance.

In all religions, the prophets and mystics teach out of the intensely known imagery of their own revelations. Occasionally, visionary artists crystallize such experience in poetry or painting. For an example of the visionary within European civilization, we can glean from the prolific independent mind of William Blake, both painter and poet of visions, as well as a profound interpreter of them. On October 1, 1800, while he was living in the village of Felpham on the south coast of England, he wrote to Thomas Butts back in London. The letter contains this account, in verse, of an experience that is the stuff of myth:

> To my Friend Butts I write
> My first Vision of Light,
> On the yellow sands sitting.
> The Sun was Emitting
> His Glorious beams
> From Heaven's high Streams.
> Over Sea, over Land
> My Eyes did Expand
> Into regions of air
> Away from all Care,
> Into regions of fire
> Remote from Desire;
> The Light of the Morning
> Heaven's Mountains adorning:
> In particles bright
> The jewels of Light
> Distinct shone & clear.
> Amaz'd & in fear
> I each particle gazed,
> Astonish'd, Amazed;
> For each was a Man
> Human-form'd. Swift I ran,
> For they beckon'd to me
> Remote by the Sea,
> Saying: Each grain of Sand,
> Every Stone on the Land,
> Each rock & each hill,
> Each fountain & each rill,
> Each herb & each tree,
> Mountain, hill, earth & sea,
> Cloud, Meteor & Star,
> Are Men Seen Afar.

The Visionary Image

I stood in the Streams
Of Heaven's bright beams,
And Saw Felpham sweet
Beneath my bright feet
In soft Female charms;
And in her fair arms
My Shadow I knew
And my wife's shadow too,
And My Sister & Friend.
We like Infants descend
In our Shadows on Earth,
Like a weak mortal birth.
My Eyes more & more
Like a Sea without shore
Continue Expanding,
The Heavens commanding,
Till the Jewels of Light,
Heavenly Men beaming bright,
Appear'd as One Man
Who Complacent began
My limbs to infold
In his beams of bright gold;
Like dross purg'd away
All my mire & my clay.
Soft consum'd in delight
In his bosom Sun bright
I remain'd. Soft he smil'd,
And I heard his voice Mild
Saying: This is My Fold,
O thou Ram horn'd with gold,
Who awakest from Sleep
On the Sides of the Deep.
On the Mountains around
The roarings resound
Of the lion & wolf,
The loud Sea & deep gulf.
These are guards of My Fold,
O thou Ram horn'd with gold!
And the voice faded mild. [9]

It is not possible to speak of such experiences simply as imaginary, even though we wish to stress the power of their images. The distinction between real and unreal objects vanishes. We cannot say what is inside, what is outside. All we can know confidently, and all we need to know, is that the *experience* is real and the images are tremendously powerful.

THE CHARM OF WEIRDNESS

The three examples in the last section demonstrate the kind of *perceptive imagination* that produces myths, expressing itself spontaneously in forms and shapes of life, with a kind of truth that compels attention and teases the intellect. It is easy to see how, if he had lived in earlier times, without a writer to tell his story to, Black Elk's adventure could have been passed on over generations to become tribal tradition.

Because they are mythic in quality, these passages also illustrate certain features of the mythic imagination that we ought to appreciate before we become a little more analytical for a while. Some of the most important effects of myth's nonrational nature are so obvious that study is likely to pass them by without noticing. When we enter the world of a myth responsively, we sense these qualities in its atmosphere. They are inherent features of the mythic spirit. It is hard to say whether they belong to the myth in its simplest sense, as the basic scenario of events, but they are potentialities of the material realized when the myth comes to life in the imagination--whether in story-telling, art, or ritual enactment. They are aspects of myth *and* they are ways we experience a particular myth, for through them mythic images express their proper aura.

<u>Charm</u>. The images of myth draw the interest of our imagination and make us wish to enter the spell of a special reality ("special" meaning both unique and preferred). There is charisma in style and place as well as in characters. The story is not only *about* magic; its way of engaging us is magical. To know the myth is to know the power of its aura, its prestige.

<u>Weirdness</u>. This reality is importantly *different*, with at least a touch, probably, of the frightening, the grotesque, the unsettling. We should feel disoriented, more *or* less, as we submit to myth's charm. If we are *disarmed*, we are delighted but we are also vulnerable. Myth needs weird people, places, and events, weird ways of having things happen, and it needs the full sense of their weirdness. "Understanding" must not clear away this feeling.

<u>Familiarity</u>. The same old stories, the same old patterns. If it's done well, if the imagination has integrity, we should find ourselves *wanting* to watch them awesomely reappear. And, when the weirdness strikes us, we may start to suspect that what is most weird is a strangely familiar feeling about certain emotions that we can't quite place. We are watching distant memories of our selves at play in fancy dress.

<u>Preposterousness</u>. Though we enjoy the spell, we cannot completely forget our common sense, for we need to appreciate how far away from it we are going. The joy of myth mocks reason, reminds us how little our intelligence understands, so myth keeps emphasizing its own absurdity. We keep wanting to "know better" (even, I would think, if we live in the forest and myth is our native lore), but the charm catches us and frees us from "the truth."

The Image-ing Mind

<u>Perversity</u>. Therefore, it needs to go the other way. Although it endlessly repeats familiar formulas, it refuses the vagueness of the familiar world. It needs to show an *other* kind of truth.

<u>Extravagance</u>. Everything is so much, so utterly, what it is--and more so. The mythic imagination wants to go on and on, to squander its wealth, to have it all ways at once. It is preposterous because it pays more than it needs to, beyond reason. It is exuberant in the fresh vitality with which it finds out the familiar themes. It rejoices in its own geometry.

<u>Elegance</u>. In its own way, it follows its own contours. There is a rightness in the movement with which it carries out its forms. It comes to its own fulfillment with a capacity for grace. The beauty of the myth is as much part of its meaning as beauty is in any kind of art. Its sense of form enables the engaged imagination to trace emotions sensitively, usually with suggestive understatement. The charm of myth negotiates its dance.

<u>Authenticity</u>. Although its world is fantastic and its terms extreme, myth's sensitivities are true. It is not simply fantasy, which is soothing or sensational; true myth has *heart*, which requires integrity, a willingness to feel vulnerable even if we are going to live happily ever after. If the myth works, it does not simply rehearse the familiar forms, it recreates them with sensibility, with voice or consciousness, with presence, with the imagination that sees.

<u>Authority</u>. It seems to speak for itself, absolutely and definitively. The point is obvious in traditional cultures, where divine sanction is likely to dramatize this quality of the myth. But even when modern authors work deliberately with mythic images and forms, they seem to find in them, according to their own authenticity, an impersonal voice-- racial perhaps, mystical perhaps, but somehow a phenomenon *given* in our world, something like a fact of nature even though we know it has taken its shape and body through the life of a culture. Modern reinterpretations of myths always remind us that there is something disturbingly *there*, which we want a way of relating to.

It is especially because of factors like these--its charm, its weirdness, and so forth--that we cannot deal with myth simply as structures or as plots, let alone as teaching devices or intellectual experiments. What makes myth *myth* involves these qualities. We know them when we pay attention to the qualitative nature of myth as a kind of experience. It is important, therefore, that our descriptions of myths be able to account for them, that our theories be true to their power.

CHAPTER TWO

FELT LOGIC

What was joy in ages when one believed in devils and tempters? What was passion when one saw demons lying in wait nearby?   --Nietzsche

STYLES OF THE MIND

We have two ways of experiencing, two ways of interpreting, two ways of expressing. Poets and pragmatists have clashed since early times, mystics and magistrates, irresponsible dreamers and narrow realists. In truth, everyone requires both ways to survive humanly--we dream, play, and love; we plan, work, and pay--and though we specialize ourselves as our cultures, our friends, or our personalities encourage us to do, our fuller nature calls for a more generous accounting. In fact, we can easily see at work here two basic directions in which consciousness itself can move.

The two styles or modes of consciousness have been described variously by various writers and designated with different paired terms. Such sets of names are bound to overlap in their range, each suggesting aspects of the others but with somewhat different kinds of relationship within each pair. I prefer the words "linear" and "nonlinear." They are abstract, but they seem to me to cover an especially broad range and refer equally well to the sense of reality, to the special kind of logic, and to the languages of expression that go along with the distinctions. Since "nonlinear" is a negative term, saying what something is *not* rather than what it *is*, I try to use the word "qualitative" in contexts where it works clearly.

Both "linear" and "nonlinear" (or "qualitative") refer to forms of continuity or organization, how parts of anything are related to each other or take on larger shape together. "Linear" indicates organization along a line, from one point to another over a clear surface within a stable dimension of being, like the painted dashes of a highway, leading from one town to the next over the surface of ground. Here everything holds together for reasons that are apparent to the intellect. We are likely to think in the linear mode when we remain detached from the situation in order to observe it, analyzing its parts in an objective manner.

We perceive nonlinear reality subjectively, with the participation of our feelings. In our dreams most clearly, we see things as we feel them. We make the world *look like what it feels like*, so that the person we fear occurs to us misshapen and leering, the place we long to be

Styles of the Mind

appears in heavenly pastels. The images of our dream are not meant to show the way things *are*; they are meant to express our experience of things. We naturally expect them to be subjective. Yet they speak with a kind of subjective accuracy that it is important for us to credit and to understand. In dreams we see nonlinearity in its purest state, but it is the characteristic form of the arts and of myth as well. It is also implicit in much of the casual operation of our minds: in daytime fantasy, in the half-conscious busy-work of talking to ourselves, and in much of what we call common sense.

Linear thinking is rational in three main senses: it explains, and it plans, and it is objective. It tries to understand things by finding what makes them work. Its sense of action is purposeful or goal-oriented. We leave point A on the line, Chicago, in order to get to point B, Los Angeles, and we are well aware of the car, train, or plane that gets us there. As for objectivity, rational or linear thought inquires into a *given* reality; one assumes that we view the universe as it is in itself, with ourselves merely incidental features of it. Linearity relates our consciousness, therefore, to a consistent, continuous, and unique order of reality, to which all other "rational" statements have equal relevance.[1] It is dualistic because it tells us something is always itself in contrast to its opposite, which is always *its* self.

Nonlinear reality is, by contrast, spontaneous. Energy flows because it is its own nature to do so, pleasure proliferates its own opportunities: we desert Chicago impelled by an inner urge, lured by the spell of romance, or magnetized by the distant unknown. We express what the world looks like from the center of consciousness where we experience it.

The nonlinear is the rhythm of nature, which *is* and which *grows* and dies and also perpetuates itself, all spontaneously, whereas the linear mode is the deliberate activity introduced to the world by human intelligence. According to a well-known contrast, the linear is *mechanical*--composed of separate parts joined together; the nonlinear is *organic*--growing parts out of parts, all of which implicitly depend on one another. The linear mind sees reality through distinctions, knowing things by what they are not and choosing between alternatives that always seem contradictory. You are "born into the world alive . . . either a little liberal or else a little conserva-tive" (as the Gilbert and Sullivan song has it); *you* make mistakes while *I* have accidents; the wicked are inexplicable but *we*, behaving naturally, need to be understood. This distinction between the linear and nonlinear is, as we shall see, itself the work of the linear mind, which deliberately withdraws from nature in order to cope with it. The nonlinear, in contrast, tends to integrate all things, even the nonlinear, into its unity.

As I'll be using the terms, then,--and that is rather loosely--<u>the linear</u> is: objective, rational, purposeful, mechanical, dualistic, analytic.

<u>The nonlinear:</u> subjective, nonrational, spontaneous, organic or natural, holistic, integrative (or synthetic, as opposed to analytic).

Felt Logic

The distinction corresponds, more or less, to the specialization that has been discovered between the left (linear) and the right (nonlinear) hemispheres of the brain.[2]

KEEPING THE WORLD IN LINE

There can be little doubt that modern Western culture--from the Renaissance and Reformation and then, with much greater impetus, from the "Age of Enlightenment" of the 17th and 18th Centuries, and with still greater force from the Industrial Revolution--has favored increasingly the linear sense of reality and linear forms of expression. The nonlinear side will not let itself be expunged, but it has been relegated to the fringes, the underground, the unconscious. A concern with the organic nature of life must belong to the *counter*-culture, a minority voice of opposition. Our penchant for linear thinking is more basic than historical develoments, however. It is ingrained in our culture on the elementary level of the sentence structure and vocabulary with which we speak in daily life.

Benjamin Whorf is best known, along with Edward Sapir, for the argument that a society's vision of reality is built into its language, which therefore places limits upon our personal perception. In the "give-and-take between language and the culture as a whole" there develops a "'thought world' [which] is the microcosm that each man carries about within himself, by which he measures and understands what he can of the macrocosm."[3]

> We are inclined to think of language simply as a technique of expression, and not to realize that language first of all is a classification and arrangement of the stream of sensory experience which results in a certain world-order, a certain segment of the world that is easily expressible by the type of symbolic means that language employs.[4]

Whorf shows that in the Indo-European languages, including English, intangible qualities of experience are necessarily transformed into linear representations.

> We express duration by "long, short, great, much, quick, slow", etc.; intensity by "large, great, much, heavy, light, high, low, sharp, faint," etc.; tendency by "more, increase, grow, turn, get, approach, go come, rise, fall, stop, smooth, even, rapid, slow"; and so on through an almost inexhaustible list of metaphors that we hardly recognize as such, since they are virtually the only linguistic media available. The non-metaphorical terms in this field, like "early, late, soon, lasting, intense, very, tending," are a mere handful, quite inadequate to the needs.[5]

Keeping The World In Line

This is a clear matter of grasping relations as though they were objects and occupied linear space--as though they could, in fact, be "grasped," as though this fact were a "matter." Our most natural expressions perform this process habitually and unconsciously.

> This has gone so far that we can hardly refer to the simplest nonspatial situation without constant resort to physical metaphors. I "grasp" the thread of another's arguments, but if its "level" is "over my head" my attention may "wander" and "lose touch" with the "drift" of it, so that when he "comes" to his "point" we differ "widely," our "views" being indeed so "far apart" that the "things" he says "appear" "much" too arbitrary, or even "a lot" of nonsense!"[6]

Languages of some nonliterate cultures, like the American Indian Hopi which Whorf analyzes in depth, can avoid this distortion of reality by remaining closer to the form and rhythm of direct experience. Our own sense of reality is rooted in "two grand COSMIC FORMS, space and time; static three-dimensional infinite space, and kinetic one-dimensional uniformly and perpetually flowing time," time itself being subdivided into past, present, and future.[7] This structure is, of course, reflected thoroughly in the structure of our language, and our language in turn keeps us seeing things in such terms. We do not only talk in our language, to express ourselves, we also think in it (or it thinks in us) to figure things out, even when our thoughts are rambling and fragmentary.

The Hopi mind, however, comes to the world and away from it on a very different basis, and the distinction it makes in both language and world-view is a distinction between the objective reality and the subjective, or, in Whorf's terms, between the "MANIFESTED and MANIFESTING (or, UNMANIFEST)."

> The objective or manifested comprises all that is or has been accessible to the senses . . . the subjective or manifesting comprises . . . all that we call mental--everything that appears or exists in the mind, or, as the Hopi would prefer to say, in the HEART, not only the heart of man, but the heart of animals, plants, and things, and behind and within all the forms and appearances of nature in the heart of nature, and by an implication and extension which has been felt by more than one anthropologist, yet would hardly ever be spoken of by a Hopi himself, so charged is the idea with religious and magical awesomeness, in the very heart of the Cosmos itself. The subjective realm . . . embraces not only our FUTURE . . . but also, all mentality, intellection, and emotion, the essence and typical form of which is the striving of purposeful desire, intelligent in character, toward manifestation. . . .[8]

Felt Logic

Time is expressed in Hopi as a process, one of "latering" or "durating," rather than as the sequence of three hypothetical states into which we divide it.[9]

"English compared to Hopi," Whorf concludes in another essay, "is like a bludgeon compared to a rapier."[10] Reading his account of this "primitive" language, I found myself wishing, whimsically, that Whorf's essays had been written by a Hopi analyzing English rather than the other way around. But of course we do not have the language to see life fluidly and directly in the Hopi manner for the same reason that we are analytical. Because the Hopi *can* see his world so clearly, he is not likely to analyze it. We objectify the world in order to look at it, until what we supposedly wanted to see is no longer there.

In some work more recent than Whorf's, Dorothy Lee, an anthropologist, has used the terms "lineal" and "nonlineal" to compare our own language habits with the Trobrianders', emphasizing our dependence on the *line* itself to organize the world: "In our own culture, the line is so basic, that we take it for granted, as given in reality."[11]

> When we see a *line* of trees, or a *circle* of stones, we assume the presence of a connecting line which is not actually visible. And we assume it metaphorically when we follow a *line* of thought, a *course* of action or the *direction* of an argument; when we *bridge* a gap in the conversation, or speak of the *span* of life or of teaching a *course*, or lament our *interrupted career*.[12]

We insist on understanding events in chronological order, so that causes and influences can become clear, and we especially like to see events build up to a climax.[13] We assume, of course, that such order is a given fact of reality or at least an essential ingredient in thinking about things. The natives of the Trobriand Islands, however, think in terms of overall patterns of organization and experience rather than of moving progressions, and they place value in events themselves rather than translating them into factors affecting other factors. Lee's comparison of the Trobriand approach to pregnancy (a linear phrase!) and ours makes a particularly suggestive example. If we expect any aspect of life to lead somewhere, this is surely it. We make it "a period of mounting tension and drama."

> A pregnancy is not formally announced since, if it does not eventuate in birth, it has failed to achieve its end; and failure to reach the climax brings shame. In its later stages it may be marked with a shower; but the shower looks forward to the birth, it does not celebrate the pregnancy itself. Among the Trobrianders, pregnancy has meaning in itself, as a state of being. At a first pregnancy, there is a long ceremonial involving "preparatory" work on the part of many people, which merely celebrates the pregnancy. It does not anchor the baby, it does not *have as its purpose* a more comfortable

time during the pregnancy, it does not *lead to* an easier birth or a healthy baby. It makes the woman's skin white, and makes her be at her most beautiful; yet this *leads* to nothing, since she must not attract men, not even her own husband.[14]

The Trobrianders' village is not a line or a circle of huts but a "*kway* which means *bump* or *aggregate of bumps*." [15] Their language does not string one item or experience artificially after another with *ands* or distinguish past, present, and future. Rather they represent events as experience that always *is* and interrelated events as parts of one whole. Thus we might say (if we were involved in their lives with our language mentality), "You go and get the coconut and bring it here so we can plant it, and then it will start to grow"--as though we first perceived the person addressed, then the thought of the act of going and then another action of identifying the coconut that is to be got, which is then to be brought, after which its purpose can be realized . . . etc., etc. The Trobriander, however, sees and expresses a unified process, which translates exactly: "Thou-approach-there-coconut thou-bring-here-we-plant-coconut thou go thou-plant our coconut. This-here it-emerge sprout."[16] The expression is nearly as integral as the process and as the experience of the process.

THE SENSE OF QUALITIES

We can bring out further implications of the difference between linearity and the nonlinear if we look at similar distinctions that some other writers have made. Carl Jung contrasts

> two kinds of thinking: directed thinking, and dreaming or fantasy-thinking. The former operates with speech elements for the purpose of communication, and is difficult and exhausting; the latter is effortless, working as it were spontaneously, with the contents ready to hand, and guided by unconscious motives. The one produces innovations and adaptation, copies reality and tries to act upon it; the other turns away from reality, sets free subjective tendencies, and, as regards adaptation, is unproductive.[17]

The philosopher Susanne Langer provides a parallel distinction that is especially valuable for understanding myth and art, between two types of expression that make up the realm of culture: *discursive* symbolism (which *discourses* on, or talks *about* its topic), like history, the sciences, philosophy, or any act of explanation; and *presentational* symbolism (which *presents* itself before us, requiring a direct encounter), like the arts, mythology, and dreams.[18] The lecture, the essay, or the textbook tell us *about* reality; the painting, the drama, the creation story tell us *of* it by giving us their own reality to experience. This "symbolic reality" will itself fascinate us with its own charm, which we will honor in museums,

Felt Logic

elegant theaters, and anthologies. It should be clear that in Langer's use (and mine) "symbolism" is the activity--all the activity--of human culture, and it is also the full range of culture's products.

After surveying a list of alternative choices offered mostly by fellow neurologists and psychologists, Joseph Bogen settles on the terms *propositional* and *appositional*. [19] The one faculty makes propositions about reality, the other "thinks" by apposing impressions--setting them side by side, that is--so that their implicit relationship can emerge.

The word I prefer, "qualitative," I have from the literary theoretician Kenneth Burke, who, in a somewhat different context and with a different emphasis, contrasts *qualitative progression* with *syllogistic progression* (movement according to *syllogism*, or logical formula). [20] In treating the consciousness of myth, a subject on which he is the principal philosopher, Ernst Cassirer stresses that "We must take the qualities of mythical experience on their immediate qualitativeness." [21]

The term "qualitative" has the advantage over "appositional" that it refers not simply to the relation between elements set side-by-side but also to what we experience directly within each element that seems to give it its significance. Its "quality" is its redness and roundness, its particular degree of apparent hardness and smoothness, the *nature* of its substance which makes it characteristic to us. We grasp not just the identity for which we substitute a name, "apple" or "cherry," but the thing in itself *as we experience it*. It is in this way, qualitatively, that we know spontaneously what we see, and it is this way that imagination plays with its images, organizing them with felt coherence. When we deal imaginatively with language, as the poet does, we play with the qualities of words, their sounds and rhythms and their feeling in the throat.

I can get nourishment from an apple even if I pay no attention to its taste. The painting I must *see*. When I look at the painting of an apple, I take in a web of qualities that make up the whole painting: the framed rectangle in relation to all the internal shapes, the painted-canvas textures, the relation of apple qualities to paint qualities, the roundnesses and squarenesses, the flatnesses and thicknesses, the symmetries and contrasts, the unification of all into patterns, and a good deal more. It is only to the extent that I take in its qualities, giving my consciousness over to them, that I can *know* the painting, and it is only to that extent that I have the ghost of a chance of enjoying it. And if I do not enjoy it (in the secondary sense of "making use of it" as well as in the more common sense of "taking pleasure in it"), I cannot care about it, no matter how many meanings I know it is supposed to have. Without the experience, the physical painting does not become a work of art.

Within myths specific images stand out and recur worldwide as natural symbols, compelling the mind with their suggestive power: the "heavenly" bodies, mountains, fire, bodies of water, trees, flowers, roads and paths and the deep forest, particular forms of creaturely life, most commonly serpents and birds.[22] We are aware of the qualities of such images in different ways at once.

The Sense of Qualities

example:	serpent	star
context:	earth (containment)	sky (distance)
functioning:	sloughing skin	light
contrasts:	lack of legs	multiplicity (contrast sun)
direct qualities:	sinuousity, suddenness	flickering, permanence
suggested quality:	secrecy	inaccessibility
associations:	water	fire
human response:	fascination, fear	aspiration, desire

The "meaning" of an image is the interaction of such qualities as we relate to them in the context of a particular story, with the accent of a particular culture. The meaning of a story, therefore, is, qualitatively, the combined effect of the images interacting.[23]

The images of myth are not just static pictures, however. They are complicated patterns of gods, heroes, spirits, demons, and humbler folk too, in fantastic settings, and the patterns are in continual action. Thoughts and passions flash through the characters, who struggle among each other, loving, hating, pursuing, escaping, destroying, and exulting. A qualitative reading of myth takes in these dynamic aspects of the experience as the imagination *makes belief*. The importance of the hero's journey lies in the yearning of his search as he dares what obviously cannot be done in order to find out what apparently cannot be known. What the monster means *is* the absolute sense of danger that he presents to the populace, combined with the ultimate limit of his power before the hero's integrity. These are qualities we perceive as the tale unfolds. As Actaeon is torn down by his dogs, the horror of how he dies complements the dazzling vision of the naked goddess whom he has chanced upon. The gulf between mortal and deity is defined by both the beauty and the pain, and by the austere judgment which is outrageous yet somehow natural and even fitting.

Qualitative perception develops meaning by linking one element to another with their common attributes. The mind may go from apple to cherry to strawberry to blueberry to Huckleberry Finn on his raft to Tom Sawyer painting his fence (eating an apple?) all without explanatory words, purely on the basis of immediately perceived qualities-- "immediate" because there are no "mediate" or middle terms, logical connections, to interpret the situation for us.[24]

Felt Logic

HOW IMAGES THINK

Qualitative continuity must be the means by which lower animals "think," orienting and directing themselves without language to mediate their experience and without, presumably, self-awareness. It is also the language of the human unconscious, where we are more available to our animal nature, and we can see it operating in dreams and fantasies as well as in the free association the analyst will invite us to perform from the couch. It carries us along that drift of images on the threshold of our minds, bubbling from the depth below.

An extensive analysis of nonlinear logic occurs in one place we might well expect to find it, Sigmund Freud's book *The Interpretation of Dreams*--but Freud's views will require some strong qualification. The dreamer puts forth images that express aspects of his or her feelings through concrete, implied linkages: a powerful, confident image of Father merges with the policeman who caught one speeding the day before, or a scene with Mother blends into one with a sexually provocative young woman. Because they are concrete, naturally, such images cannot make the kinds of linear logical distinctions that the conscious mind specializes in. They do not say, "My Father was *not* as kind as he pretended to be" or "My mother must have been *either* a saint *or* a slut and I cannot decide which" or "Mother left Father *because* I was slow on the potty," although these are the kinds of emotional perplexity that the unconscious is likely to harbor.

> What is reproduced by the ostensible thinking in the dream is *subject-matter* of the dream-thoughts and not the *mutual relations between them*, the assertion of which constitutes thinking. [25]

The analyst's job, then, is to help make conscious, linear translation.

Dream excels, of course, in expressing the naturally appositional "relation of similarity, consonance or approximation--the relation of 'just as'." If our dream wants to show us that things or persons are alike, it can do so either by "identification" or by "composition."

> In identification, only one of the persons who are linked by a common element succeeds in being represented in the manifest content of the dream, while the second or remaining persons seem to be suppressed in it. . . . In composition, where this is extended to persons, the dream-image contains features which are peculiar to one or the other of the persons concerned but not common to them; so that the combination of these features leads to the appearance of a new unity, a composite figure. [26]

How Images Think

Either the blending or the isolating of figures can express the qualities that are significant to the dreamer. But apposition of images--setting them next to each other--must also express more problematic relationships. Dreams "reproduce *logical connection by simultaneity in time*."[27] They can indicate cause only by spending more time on the result, making the result a "principal clause" of a sentence, as it were, or by mere emphasis, or by showing things transforming into another, the cause into its consequence.[28] "The alternative either-or cannot be expressed in dreams in any way whatever."[29] Most important, perhaps, is the expression of negatives.

> The way in which dreams treat the category of contraries and contradictories is highly remarkable. It is simply disregarded. "No" seems not to exist so far as dreams are concerned. They show a particular preference for combining contraries into a unity or for representing them as one and the same thing. Dreams feel themselves at liberty, moreover, to represent any element by its wishful contrary; so that there is no way of deciding at a first glance whether any element that admits of a contrary is present in the dream-thoughts as a positive or as a negative.[30]

In other words, qualitative expression will not seem very logical to the linear consciousness. However, the translation of a dream into objective terms is bound to lack the deeper powers of penetration that a dream does possess by virtue of the fact that it is a dream. The dream is ambiguous because it is sensitive to the ambiguities of life. It is frustrating because it mirrors frustration.

THE LOGIC OF QUALITY

The possibility that we might be basically irrational is for most of us a fearful and humiliating danger, and we strain the resources of our minds to keep ourselves and others assured that we are consistent and purposeful, "reasonable" and fair. Is there any height we are prouder of attaining than a position of objectivity? There we can feel invulnerable and unjudgeable. Reason means control, power, authority. In the dark corners of irrationality, chaos seems to await us. We must believe in these presences, surely, in order to fear them. Yet such a belief itself must be the essence of irrationality.

In our fear of the irrational, we hasten to condemn the properly nonrational as well. There is, however, a nonlinear logic as well as the linear sort. While linear logic is a principle of the intellect dealing with the relationships among *things*, nonlinear logic reflects the structure that life takes on. That is why it is organic, and that is why comprehending it is a matter of *seeing*. We trace the natural relations among events in life and see that life's forms increase not by adding but by growing, each part flowing from the last, all parts sensing one another in a web of being.

Felt Logic

Living things exist not for further purpose but to perpetuate their existence; they luxuriate in what is delicate and passing, even their power and their ferocity poised on the verge of nonexistence; their existence culminates not in any grand achievement but in age and weakness. All this is the organic principle of mortality at work in its own way, through gratification and through the gradual progress toward death. Sensing this, we notice our own minds participating in the process. Consciousness too is organic, and the logic of living form which it mirrors reveals its own nature.

In his treatment of dream logic, Freud speaks for the linear intellect with the intellect's assumption that only its own terms are clear and fully meaningful. After all, Freud is the analyst and his job is analysis. The unconscious tries to express "dream-thought," he assumes, but it lacks the means to do so. However, in making his objective survey of the subject, Freud pays little attention to what he must have dealt with intuitively in actual practice: the qualitative communication that occurs when images are combined. He is bound by a linear criterion of logical relationships and their formulation in sentence grammar. If we put side-by-side (or in sequence) two images or thoughts that are mutually exclusive--like two attractive women (in a man's dream), the juxtaposition itself is likely to produce a new kind of effect: a frustration of potentials that cannot move, probably, and that call for a choice. Can reasoning tell us more?

When he explains how dreams show images simultaneously in order to express their logical relationship, Freud compares the method to that of the two paintings by Raphael in which the philosophers and the poets of different ages are shown together as though they were contemporaries.

> It is true that they were never in fact assembled in a single hall or on a single mountain-top; but they certainly form a group in the conceptual sense.[31]

We have no difficulty grasping what that conceptual sense is. Such paintings suggest a timelessness about the life of genius. They portray a spiritual community among great minds that transcends both time and space. The painting is not hampered, as Freud suggests, by an inability to express time; rather it exploits the qualities of the artist's medium to convey a positive insight. Similarly, when our dream-mind simply puts forth a cause together with its effect, we can feel the impact directly, as we might feel the consequence of similar facts in real life. Putting together contradictory facts is, of course, the language of paradox--like "the lonely crowd" or "the wisdom of babes"--which can tell us something significant by holding the conflict in tension or by frustrating our expectations.

We are familiar with qualitative continuity as the technique of the motion picture, especially as it was developed in its earlier days, before sound, when it was dependent on visual connections. If we are shown a shot of a marksman followed by a view of a running man, we do not

The Logic of Quality

need to be told that the first will have an effect on the second or what that effect will be. The impact is all the stronger for the fact that we must *realize* the event immediately. The film addresses our sensibility our capacity to understand life through our feelings; we do not have to think it all out.

In all of Freud's instances of dream logic, the language of imagery speaks eloquently *through the effects it produces*. Every poet, every artist understands this process and revels in it. To comprehend the Mona Lisa, we do not need to explain the painting but to look at it. The nonlinear imagery is much closer to the actual nature of life, with its infinitely complex flow of relationships, than the deliberate categories of logical analysis can be. These cannot help but oversimplify our experience in the process of clarifying it. "The image, poetic or mythic," writes Alan Watts, "is closer than linguistic categories to events themselves, or to what I would rather call natural patterning."

> We pay for the exactitude of factual language with the price of being able to speak from only one point of view at a time. But the image is many-sided and many-dimensioned, and yet at the same time imprecise; here again, it is like nature itself.[32]

Thus the richness of dreams, of art, and of myth. They exist as fact does, not as idea. Their concreteness keeps them suggestive and preserves their subtlety. Qualities merge and blend and contrast and complement in all directions and to all degrees. Much is true in one way and untrue in another, or true in many ways at once. We find ourselves close to the sensibility that Philip Wheelwright describes as our "liminal" or "threshold" existence.

> To be conscious is not just to be; it is to mean, to intend, to point beyond self, to testify that some kind of beyond exists, and to be ever on the verge of entering into it although never in the state of having fully entered. The existential structure of human life is radically, irreducibly liminal.[33]

Dreams and myths and the subjective elements of art arise from a level of experience that is not explicit, not cut and dried and labeled, but flowing with impressions in an endless context.

MYTHIC THOUGHT

The basic principle of qualitative logic is continuity of nature overriding (or subsuming) differences in identity. I experience my son (in part) qualitatively as an extension of myself, *as my son*, although I know he is a separate person. The poet's metaphor blends the stirring of love with a flow of poignant music so that emotion and art coalesce into

Felt Logic

one imaginative whole. The shock of sudden lightning seen and thunder heard fuse in a relation more basic than cause and effect, a relation that reveals identity on a new level, reinforcing the reality of what happens in passing events.

Qualitative thinking flows naturally, of course, outside our rationalistic civilization, just as it typifies our own mind-work in childhood and in dreams, when natural sublogical rhythms prevail.[34] Both traditional cultures and our own pragmatic one have areas of rational and areas of nonrational expression, just as both have tendencies toward individualism and tendencies toward communal identity. *The main difference is where each attributes meaningfulness--a base of reality and a standard of interpretation where each feels, so to speak, its center of gravity.* In traditional cultures, the nonrational is granted essential validity, so thought can easily follow the qualitative form of direct experience. The French anthropologist Claude Lévi-Strauss, who describes mythic thought as "a system of concepts embedded in images,"[35] collects many good examples from which I shall borrow three, using them towards a different end. They show how the logic in myths grows out of the more fundamental "mythic thinking" inherent in the culture.

1. On Mota, a Melanesian island, children are identified with a particular fruit or animal that their mother happened upon while she was pregnant.

> In such a case, a woman takes the plant, fruit or animal back to her village and asks about the significance of the event. It is explained to her that she will give birth to a child who will resemble, or actually be, the object. She then returns it to the place where she found it and, if it was an animal, builds it a shelter out of stones. She visits and feeds it every day. When the animal disappears, it is because it has entered her body, from which it will reappear in the form of a child.
>
> The child may not eat the plant or animal with which it is identified under the pain of illness or death. If it is an inedible fruit which was found, then the child may not even touch the tree on which it grows. Ingestion or contact are regarded as a sort of auto-cannibalism. The relation between the person and the object is so close that the person possesses the characteristics of the object with which he is identified. If, for example, it was an eel or sea-snake which was found, the child will, like these, be weak and indolent, if a hermit crab, it will be hot-tempered; or again, it will be gentle and sweet-tempered like the lizard, thoughtless, hasty and intemperate like the rat or, if it was a wild apple which was found, it will have a big belly the shape of an apple.[36]

In our more linear world, we may very well identify ourselves with the image of another person (the spitting image of his old man) or with groups (an all-American boy) or even with animals (he's a wildcat, a

Mythic Thought

mouse). Under pressure of such labels, we can come to experience ourselves, quite nonrationally, even irrationally, through images fixed to our consciousness with a qualitative bond. They are more than nicknames, more than metaphors, as they enter into our personalities and weigh upon the course of our lives. The Mota example is far more intense, more literal, and more systematic. Most importantly, it provides a qualitative conception of cause and effect that is not counteracted by a conscious explanation of what must be objectively true.

Before the Mota child is given the animal's attributes, we should notice, the animal is made human. The eel is indolent, the hermit crab's temper is violent while the lizard's is gentle and sweet, the rat is thoughtless. Logically, if one process is possible, so is the other. If the animal can be human, the human can be animal. We are simply borrowing back the qualities we have loaned out. In doing so, however, something strange happens to our sense of human identity. Our world is linked to nature with a bond that is beyond question because it is beyond reason.

2. According to some American Indian peoples, diseases are caused by specific animals and cured by specific plants, so that men, animals, and plants are involved in a three-way drama of suffering and recovery, life and death.

> Vexed with men, animals sent them diseases. Plants, who were friends of men, retorted by supplying remedies. The important point is that each species possesses a specific disease or remedy. Thus, according to the Chickasaw, stomach disorders and pains in the legs come from snakes, vomiting from dogs, aches in the jaw from deer, pains in the abdomen from bears, dysentery from skunks, nose-bleeding from squirrels, jaundice from otters, disturbances of the lower part of the abdomen and the bladder from moles, cramp from eagles, eye diseases and somnolence from owls, pain in the joints from rattle-snakes, etc. [37]

We can guess a concrete association of some of these illnesses with qualities perceived or imagined in the animals--stomach aches and leg pains coming from snakes crawling leglessly on their own stomachs, dysentery from the bad smell of skunks, troubles of the eye and sleepiness from the owl's watching at night. The concrete qualities are transferred directly to the human recipient, the sickness being not the work of micro-organisms but the condition itself. Cause is not separated from the experience, in other words, but must be expressed as a function of it.

It follows, qualitatively, that animals being our enemies, plants are our friends, since plants and animals contrast in the obvious ways at the same time that they share the qualities of life. The Indians, of course, have know an extraordinary range and number of valid herbal medicines. So the extension of their grateful relation to the plant world apparently extends itself into the animal world by a simple equation:

Felt Logic

$$\frac{\text{cause}}{\text{cure}} = \frac{x}{\text{plant}}$$

and x must equal animal. The imagination is not "thinking" in abstract formulas, however, but in concrete ones, filling out analogies through that principle of continuity overriding identity. Another way to express the process is to say that the animal world provides a mirror in which we may see a reversed image of what we perceive directly among the plants.

3. Particularly important to the structure of myth is the logic of sacrifice, for this central ritual act conveys the continuity through mankind, nature, and deity. The ritual itself, and the myths that go along with it, are based, as Lévi-Strauss observes, on a principle of substitution through continuity. One kind of "victim," in some circumstances, can replace another because the focus of attention rests upon their common feature: life taken as life offered. Lévi-Strauss quotes from a study of the Nuer people of Africa:

> When a cucumber is used as a sacrificial victim Nuer speak of it as an ox. In doing so they are asserting something rather more than that it takes the place of an ox. They do not, of course, say that cucumbers are oxen, and in speaking of a particular cucumber as an ox in a sacrificial situation they are only indicating that it may be thought of as an ox in that particular situation. And they act accordingly by performing the sacrificial rites as closely as possible to what happens when the victim is an ox. The resemblance is conceptual, not perceptual. The "is" rests on qualitative analogy. And the expression is asymmetrical, a cucumber is an ox, but an ox is not a cucumber.[38]

In all sacrifice, the same principle of continuity gives the ritual its significance. The priest embodies the people as a whole; their identity in themselves is suspended and conveyed through him. The offering itself is a symbol that embodies the common life of the people or their sins, which are being offered up for them by the priest. The smoke of the burnt offering or the flowing blood of the slain beast carries to the gods the human qualities that it has taken on. Through the symbolic act of death, the people attain a consciousness of a renewal, their lease on life confirmed by death experienced and survived. The principle of symbolic continuity operates in a partly similar manner in the sacrament of the Eucharist, where God's body and the bread wafer become one--with necessary literalness for Catholics--and enter thus into the body of the communicant.

QUALITATIVE FORM IN MYTH

An especially clear example of qualitative logic occurs in a myth of the birth of Attis, who is one of a group of sacrificial youths in related myths from the Near East that are associated with the cycle of agricultural fertility. All these youths (notably also Adonis, Tammuz, and Osiris) are beloved by their corresponding versions of the Mother Goddess, and all die violent deaths. They are known as the "dying gods." The goddess mourns for her beloved boy and some form of rebirth ensues, expressing the new life of springtime vegetation.

Like many of the central figures of myth, Attis is the result of a miraculous conception between a linear (or human) and a nonlinear (or "mythic") parent, usually a maiden and a god. In this instance the father is a wild bisexual being named Agdistis, proud and violent, itself the offspring of Zeus and a rock that had taken on the Great Mother's form. His violence toward gods and men is finally brought to an end by Dionysos, the god associated with wine and intoxicated ecstasy.

> There was a certain spring to which Agdistis came to assuage its thirst when it was overheated with sport and hunting. Dionysos turned the spring-water into wine. Agdistis came running up, impelled by thirst, greedily drank the strange liquor and fell perforce into deepest sleep. Dionysos was on the watch. He adroitly made a cord of hair, and with it bound Agdistis's male member to a tree. Awakened from its drunkenness, the monster sprang up and castrated itself by its own strength. The earth drank the flowing blood, and with it the tornoff parts. From these at once arose a fruit-bearing tree: an almond-tree or--according to an other tale--a pomegranate tree. Nana, the daughter of the king or river-god Sangarios (Nana is another name for the great goddess of Asia Minor), saw the beauty of the fruit, plucked it and hid it in her lap. The fruit vanished, and Nana conceived a child of it.[39]

Dionysos, like Christ, turns water miraculously to wine. As a result of drinking the wine, Agdistis is made to shed "his" blood together with "his" male sexuality. The blood (and genitals) produces a fruit tree. Nana, who is both maiden-princess and mother-goddess at the same time, absorbs the fruit in her lap and conceives the child Attis. We can trace a qualitative progression as follows:

water -----> wine -----> blood -----> fruit (semen)

Through the intervention of nonlinear forces (the god Dionysos), water becomes more and more potent until it issues forth as life. Water itself is often felt to be the source of life. Wine is a fluid of vegetation that enters the body and transforms consciousness. Then we move up

Felt Logic

the scale from mineral to vegetable to animal as the red wine becomes red blood. The qualities of wine are paradoxical: it brings violence and also creative excitement or inspiration. Similarly, blood is a naturally two-sided symbol of mortality, signifying both the richness of life and the violence of death (blood shed). In castration, furthermore, blood and seed become identified with one another, so that the vital quality of blood becomes actively potent as the victim becomes sterile in death. Thus blood becomes the fruit, which is succulent and nourishing (sensual and life-giving, like the act of love) but which also decays when it is ripe, so that it may leave seed.

Although the fruit is vegetable, therefore, it has all the symbolic qualities it needs to bear life. Because of its place in the sequence, it contains within it, in fact, all the associations of water, wine, and blood, the sense of life that the imagery has accumulated. In the linear terms of biology, of course, the fruit is still not human seed. But the difference between fruit and semen highlights the nonlinear nature of the miracle, the extraordinary identity of the child that is to be. Thus each image gives way to the next in a process that we can summarize in this way:

$$\text{thirst} \rightsquigarrow \text{birth}$$

The misdirected thirst (as of a beast for mere water) is channeled creatively by the god, so that it issues forth into heroic life by means of a human sexual union--with a difference.

After Attis reaches adolescence, however, Agdistis, still untamed and unrepentant, though now apparently more female, conceives a passion for him. As the boy is about to be married to a mortal princess, Agdistis drives him mad by playing on the syrinx-pipes. Then Attis performs the act which formed the central symbol of his worship in one of the important "mystery religions" of the ancient world. He castrates himself, crying "Unto thee, Agdistis!" and he dies, as violets spring from his blood.

The castration of Agdistis leads to the castration of Attis through the sequence of qualitative transference. In neither case is castration merely a linear act of grotesque violence, however--although it may be that as well. It is also, as in the Christian Crucifixion, a paradoxical symbol of rebirth. The punishment of the parent, which is actually an act of enforced procreation, is repeated in its qualitative form upon the child as an act of love. Consequently, it signifies fertility, confirmed in the violets of spring, even though castration is logically the very opposite. The sexual dedication of Attis to Agdistis is celebrated by his worshippers with their own self-mutilation in ecstatic frenzy. They join together in sacrifice, along with Attis, to affirm the basic rhythm of nature: out of death comes life, as out of winter, spring. For the religious celebrant, fully immersed in the experience: out of ecstatic chaos comes the order of life and his own part in it as a living being.

Such leaps of qualitative logic as we see in this myth carry forward the "streams of consciousness" of our everyday fantasies. They are common also in the reasoning of children, who may very well expect the world to make sense qualitatively. Once, when my son was four years old, he threatened his eight-year-old sister with knocking her head "into the mouth of God." The image is a powerful one by mythological standards and expressed his feelings with precision, but the boy dramatized the image by imagining God's response: "He'll say 'Yuk'." Undaunted, his sister lectured him with a linear distinction: "God doesn't eat people; he makes them." Then she reflected for a moment and generously corrected her hasty assumption. "Guess it could be that he eats them. We make chocolate cake and eat it." An image emerged out of her own world of desire (the children get as little chocolate cake as religious training) and reminded her of the organic rule of appetite. Eating and devouring is living and dying, the rhythm of mortality.

On another occasion, my wife explained to the boy the current "ecological" meaning of "organic": "You can put the apple core in the soil outside. Whatever rots is good for the earth." His nonlinear mind immediately extended the idea to the proper basis of myth: "We're good for the earth then too. When we die, we are." With such an eager student, Momma went on: "Plastic bags are not good for the earth. They don't rot." Then again, the immediate qualitative leap: "What eats dies. Paper bags have mouths and you put food into them. They eat, so they die. Plastic bags too." The images took over, with their own logical energy, and a mythical world was going of itself. If his mind had not been fascinated by the image, he would certainly have "known better"; bags are familiar enough inanimate useful objects. But "he stuck very tenaciously to this idea," my wife reported, "explaining patiently to me, since I didn't seem to understand, that 'the hole at the top is the mouth.'"

THE SHAPE OF LIFE

The nonlinear idiom of mythic imagination conveys a sense of *shaped life*, of a life so fully contained within its own sharp outlines that it is irrelevant to *real* life. We often hear of myth *applying* form to life in order to *give* life meaning. We hear this said of the artist as well and the philosopher. Form, it is assumed, is arbitrary and reality itself chaotic. But in spite of life's infinite variability, in spite of the profusion of accidents that fall around us, upon us, and through us, in spite of how little we understand, even though we muddle up our own lives and twist ourselves about in the lives of others, still life has form for us quite naturally in countless ways. Birth and death, the succession of the generations, the process of growth and aging, the pairing of the sexes and the configuration of the family, the basic shape of the body and the rhythms within it--these are all ways we simply *have* form as living animals. All around us we know things by recognizable size, shapes, colors, and textures, as well as the regular changes in the seasons, the alternation of night and day. And as we live, we can see some basic aspects of living itself, as a process, that become principles of form in myth:

Confrontation. We set ourselves against the world, we address it, we face it.

Focus. We limit our attention to manageably perceived features of the world.

Felt Logic

<u>Polarization</u>. We divide the world into opposites we can choose between.

<u>Intention</u>. We find ourselves caught up in rhythms of expectation and fulfillment (or failure).

<u>Recurrence</u>. We find stability in the repetitions nature gives us and we pick out among events similar patterns that may or may not occur by chance.

<u>Transformation</u>. Stages of life, phases of emotion, aspects of perception, personal relationships--all pass and alter, often in predictable rhythms, but also in ways that provide continuity in difference, complementarity in unity, self-transcendence, and self-exhaustion.

Of course, myth, like all story-telling and art, shows form in ways that life does not have it naturally--in selfcontained wholes of action, in clear-cut characters, in obsessive coincidences and contrasts. What the mythmaker, the artist, the imagination does is to transpose, dislocate, or extend the natural forms of life to areas where they are not readily apparent. It is as though we were looking at different levels or dimensions at the same time and seeing disproportionate facts brought into alignment. We have the experience of life's continuous, interflowing energies while we isolate its repetitive features into stylized units of story. We exaggerate some aspects of life, blur some, and let others drop out of sight altogether. "Reality" is distorted but in a way that is true to its importance rather than its appearance. In a fundamental way, life then seems more natural--or, rather, we are reminded of how natural it is. Culture itself appears more clearly an expression of nature. In myth, form seems intrinsic, rising by itself through the act of imagining life, beating out the rhythms felt in the life imagined.

In myth (and often in the arts), therefore, form is not significant primarily as the form *of* anything but rather *as form itself*. What form expresses at its deepest level is simply a fundamental coherence. Through patterns of wholeness, symmetry, and recurrence, the myth constitutes in our minds a sense of *meaningfulness* in being alive rather than conveying a meaning about life. We often find, in fact, that the more outrageously artificial the form of a story becomes, the more familiar its motifs, the more we enjoy the sheer coherence of it all, and that response itself goes a long way to explain and justify all of myth's nonlinear features.

Even an aspect of artistic form like rhyme, which may seem mechanical and arbitrary, has power in its mere nonlinearity. A Vietnamese Buddhist student of mine wrote about the ritual she had been told to perform in order to remove a curse. Her story reminds us of the magical nature of words--their power as subjective substance, but it also suggests something important about the origin of rhyme. In a moment of rare anger, she had told a favorite cousin that she wished he would die. So she placed three strands of her hair together with three blades of grass, lit a candle, and prayed. Then she felt safe: "the prayer that I said not only made sense, it also rhymed, so I was assured that it was not made up by other people but by God."

We think mythically, then, it terms of life's inherent forms, and when form comes to seem important for its own sake, we are focused on

The Shape of Life

the importance of existence, pure and simple, for its own sake. However, existence always occurs as something existing in itself, and form comes to us as forms of imagined beings, not as geometrical abstractions.[40] Although it is misleading to say that myth (and other kinds of symbolism) gives life form, therefore, we can say that *a* myth (etc.) gives reality *a* form. When we say it provides *form*, we think of form as structure, but *a form* has substance, or body.

Myth provides embodiment for elusive aspects of experience, and that embodiment heightens, sharpens, and transforms our way of being ourselves in the world. It reminds us that in its more elusive way, our experience is substantial as well. But also, it summons (so to speak) the energies of life into our presence so that we can meet them in a familiar guise. Myth conjures nature with its repetitive, incantatory rhythms at the same time that it conjures subliminal fears, desires, and intuitions. Thus we meet nature, the nature of our world, through our being rather than our intelligence. When this happens, myth certainly adds forms to the world, human forms in the spirit of nature, so that, held in forms, the energies we participate in can be more consciously of man as they are of the sky, the earth, and the animals that "people" the world along with us.

CHAPTER THREE

THE MEANING OF WONDER

The man who cannot wonder, who does not habitually wonder . . . is but a Pair of Spectacles behind which there is no Eye.   --Carlyle

THE PROBLEM OF MEANING

Where is the "meaning" of a myth? Is it hidden inside? Is it transformed by a code? Is it resolved at the end? Is it lost with the lives of its original users?

Since we naturally focus on what we are talking *about*, we fail to appreciate a very important aspect of any symbolic expression: every statement is a state of mind. All language, therefore, has an implicit dimension of drama. The use of language in the theatre demonstrates the point well. When we listen to an actor's speech in a play, we are not just learning about a character and his problems, we are getting a sense of his experience. We are getting to know what it is like to be this imaginary person at this moment in his fictitious life. The play *consists of* the various characters' experience as it combines with the experience of all the others. We in the audience have our own experience of receiving this blend, which playwright, director, and actors work together to sustain and convey. In this progression of consciousness, our minds build up the play's dramatic meaning. This is meaning that *happens*, through an arrangement of felt experience.

Dramatic meaning is as dramatic in myth as it is in drama itself. We understand subjectively, grasping the myth by imagining it to be true. That is simply a way of saying "by making believe" but taking the expression quite seriously. When we imagine the image, its reality becomes our state of mind, and it is precisely in this way, qualitatively, that it communicates.

The two commonest ways of reading myth that most of us were brought up on, and that have kept us from taking myth seriously in its own terms, are based, then, on linear fallacies. In fact, contemporary theorists on the subject regularly do regard them as naive, but for most people the old assumptions linger. The idea one is most likely to produce to explain myth is to say that it is primitive science, early man's pathetically ignorant attempts to explain events in the physical universe, like the apparent movement of the sun and moon, changes in the seasons, the existence of the world, the appearance of the human race as we know it, and the eventuality of death. This interpretation was actually propounded by the most influential writer who ever studied myth, J.G. Frazer, whose brilliant multi-volumed work *The Golden Bough* nevertheless stimulated

The Problem of Meaning

endless speculation about the symbols of myth and ritual and fascination with their nonrational patterns.

The second way we are likely to (mis)interpret myths, particularly if we consider them one at a time, is by looking for moral lessons. To be sure, archetypal stories often are told in a form that suggests moral implications. The royal confidence of Oedipus looks suspiciously like arrogance, because it is based on spectacularly false assumptions. The story of Arachne, who boasted she was a better weaver than the goddess Athene, can obviously be taken as a warning against pride. "Cinderella" obviously favors docile and patient virtue through the successful example it provides. Yet moral readings are always linear and dualistic in their logic: do *this* and don't do *that*, dividing life into the good, which is to be pursued, and the bad, which is to be left behind, each irrevocably opposed to the other.

Similarly, myths themselves often do imagine the way nature works and therefore do seem to be explaining it. The image of Helios, the Greeks' sun god, driving his chariot across the sky does seem to show what makes the daylight come and go. We *are* given an interpretation of seasonal rotation in the Persephone story: she spends one division of the year in Hades with her abductor-husband (the cold, dead time of the year) and the rest above the earth (when life renews itself). Yet myth cannot be so emphatically and exuberantly imaginative simply in order to explain anything. Such a richly nonrational language must do more than address such clear rational questions as why? or how?

Such moralistic and pseudo-scientific interpretations let us feel intellectually unperturbed as we tie onto the myth a neat label and dispose of it. We are left feeling somewhat superior to the ancients who seem to have had simple-minded ideas about the world, or who expended such bizarre efforts of imagination to reach rather ordinary philosophical conclusions. But, of course, we appreciate any aspect of another culture--its manners, its morals, or its gods--by sensing (and not merely analyzing) the positive human phenomenon it represents. What makes us do anything we do? In spite of the inevitable degree of our ignorance and error, sometimes enormous, there is always some force of life working to realize itself.

In the mythmaking process, rational explanation and moral advice may not be the distinct faculties we usually consider them. It is a significant commonplace, in fact, that tribal art does not distinguish function from form, or use from beauty. Tools well made by hand *are* beautiful tools, and dwellings erected with caring express the human spirit and the group's ways with pride and grace. Similarly, there is no separation between the spiritual and the worldly, the ritual act and the practical one. At the colossal ring of ancient stones at England's Stonehenge, we are told by the guide and guidebook that huge rocks were drawn over 200 miles and erected upright, or set over at a twenty-foot height, not for inexplicable or romantic religious practices or old superstitions but to serve as a calendar and observatory, the arrangement being ideal for marking the sun in solstice. But no such distinction need be, or perhaps can be, made. Such a need to choose results from modern linear assumptions. In early

The Meaning of Wonder

times, to deal with the sun, the stars, the turning of the year could not but be as religious a project as a practical one. No matter how practical such ceremonies may have been, they must have been motivated by powerful nonrational drives in order to take such monumental form.

We do not simply do things. We do them *in the way that we do them*. The imagery of Helios may present a reason for the sun's apparent motion, but instead of asking whether it is correct or incorrect, we may want to ask *why* it explains the event as it does. What, in other words, does myth achieve by being mythic? What can myth do that science cannot? Instead of saying it argues with naive logic, we need to let it be nonrational and ask what that can mean. Like most things in life, myth has many causes. A rain dance may be intended *in the short run* to induce rain, but *in the long run* it serves two other kinds of purpose: on the one hand, social cohesion and, on the other hand, collective but personal self-expression. As Gregory Bateson observes, making a similar point in relation to the ecology of evolution: "surely the mountain lion when he kills the deer is not acting to protect the grass from overgrazing." [1] In the short run, the predator merely satisfies his hunger, but at the same time, beyond his own felt drives, the field of nature, in which he thrives, is sustained. Unlike the lion's hunger, the short-run reasons for myth and ritual (being careful not to marry your mother) strike us justly as rather insubstantial and even simple-minded. It is far more likely the reasons of the long run, with their organic coherence, that keep myth and ritual alive through the ages. They certainly can tell us better why myth and ritual took shape in the kind of forms that they did and why they continue to interest us.

NONLINEAR VALUES

Even if the Greeks telling and hearing mythic tales did think explanatorily or ethically with the linear sides of their minds, they were doing something a good deal more complex, subtle, and intriguing with their imaginations in the process. For the world of myth--heroes and demons, Hades and Paradise--is not simply "imaginary," or unreal. It is *imaginative*--alive to the senses and sustained with pleasure. The pleasure of imagining is essential, in fact, to the mythmaking impulse, and so is another feature of imagination, the sense that our emotions have a kind of rightness that demands respect in spite of those logical, practical, or ethical considerations which look at them askance. Being imaginative, therefore, myth celebrates certain values which imagination inspires and enhances. These include personal energy, self-exploration, openness to emotions, willingness to take chances, and the perception of beauty.

Myths often emphasize the very aspects of life that our ethics or our sense of decorum will teach us to shun, such as the grotesque and the violent, the painful, the impractical, the self-indulgent. We may not want to see a place for them in our personalities, and we may not know how to accommodate them morally. "Civilization," writes Northrop Frye, "tends to try to make the desirable and the moral coincide." [2] Myths, like dreams, often oblige us, on the other hand, to imagine just what we

36

would prefer to forget. They often seem to have a neutralizing effect on the thinking or judging mind, allowing us simply to imagine extraordinary events--while the dramatic images channel our feelings--and to wonder at the visions we imagine. When we read, for example, that one generation of Greek deities has killed off its forebears, we can only frustrate ourselves if we insist on knowing why they did it or whether they should have done it or whose side we are on. We do sense symbolic implications qualitatively, however: the rising present kills off the past; an advanced civilization suppresses its roots; each generation thrives at the expense of its parents; independence, asserting one-self, means violating one's bond to others. In these instances, we are tracing principles in life that are being illustrated or we are suggesting parallel examples. The bizarre qualities of the imagery make us particularly aware of the non-linear way these aspects of life run on, simultaneously familiar and strange, powerful and elusively subtle.

A myth itself is a context for insight rather than the vehicle of a message. It is not essentially for communication in any ordinaray way but for expression, experience, and (as Chapter 7 will show) confrontation. Insight is understanding that comes necessarily in the midst of experience. As our imagination plays upon the myth's imagery, we seem to *see into* the nature of life, we get "hunches" about existence. We talk most appropriately about what such symbolis*m expresses*, therefore, rather than about what it *means.* The myth has implications rather in the way that historical events do, without anybody intending them to, but just because of the forces that they bring into play--although, unlike an event in history, the myth *is* an expression of experience, which exists with its own shape in a symbolic world, as a shape with a concentrated, significant effect.

The implications I suggested for the myths of divine patricide suggest an insight that freedom depends upon violence in the way that an adolescent rebels against his family out of a need to feel his own being. However, the violence of these myths seems quite natural and quite horrible at the same time. We sense that the gods' world is evolving into a clearer, "more human" order, but we also feel that such an evolution is a costly and painful process, even an ugly one. In other words, the energy of the tale concentrates upon a tragic effect, a kind of effect that prevents judgment--a realization that the horrible and the desirable are the same, implicated at the least in each other and bound together.

In such a way, the aspects of life that ordinarily seem to us undesirable often become the essential features of a story, the key perhaps or the turning point in a hero's quest. The mythic character goes typically in the wrong direction in order to get to the right place, finding security through danger, heaven through hell, abandoning those values that can be taught in order to find those that grow from within. These values tend to reflect the wholeness of life rather than its divisibility and the sense in which the positives (as we generally regard them) may be said to grow out of the negatives. They are elusive to the rational and conventional mind, so that the qualitative and strange form of myth's images is the natural way to express them. We can say that such values are *reflexive*,

The Meaning of Wonder

because their logic seems to turn back on itself, and in this sense too we can call them "nonlinear values."

The values of myth are nonlinear also in the sense that they remind us of that age-old theme of mysticism, the "integration of opposites," which undercuts all sorts of dualistic assumptions. The conscious mind orients itself by splitting our experience into such polarities as evil and goodness, the feminine and the masculine, strength and weakness, the human and the divine, the body and the spirit, the comic and the solemn, the obscene and the sacred, and so forth, but in the unconscious flow of energy, all opposites meet and take meaning from each other. This state of pre-logical oneness may constitute a definition of God, as it did for the early Greek philosopher Heraclitus: "God is day night, winter summer, war peace, satiety hunger." [3] An authority on the Mexican Nahua Indians compares Western compromise, which "achieves comfort," with Nahua *equilibria*, a balance of opposites "which achieves meaning." [4] Compromise is expedient and comfortable, it helps life to *work;* but meaning lies in integrity, integration, balance, unity, the natural state that seems so perversely ambiguous and paradoxical but is simply primordial, prior to the differentiation of linear logic. [5]

Reflexive and nondualistic values are familiar, therefore, in the sayings of visionaries and the formulations of theology. Their basic logic, their sense of reality, is epitomized in such expressions as Yeats' "Nothing can be sole or whole / That has not been rent"; Blake's "The road of excess leads to the palace of wisdom"; Jesus' dictum "the first shall be the last" and the Christian doctrine of the Fortunate Fall, which celebrates the Expulsion from Eden on the grounds that it made possible redemption through Christ; Lao Tzu's "Those who know do not tell, / Those who tell do not know"; or the Bhagavad Gita's praise of "the inaction that is in action and the action that is in inaction." [6] The point in all instances expresses the view that the linear wisdom of the ego, of the world, or of society--whether power, intelligence, prestige, wealth, or righteousness--cannot lead to the more natural and simple values of living that clarify and exalt the spirit.

It is this same logic that is dramatized in the mythic hero's need to descend to the underworld, to face down the monster of death, in order to know the real quality of life and affirm its power. In many archetypal narratives, especially those we call tragedies, the hero must commit acts ordinarily regarded as sinful or make disastrous mistakes or succumb to apparent weakness in order to achieve real integrity. Heinrich Zimmer has explored this theme in his deeply insightful and eloquent book *The King and the Corpse*, particularly in discussing a beautiful legend of John Chrysostom, who is said to have arrived at sainthood by committing crimes and then living as a beast in horror of himself. [7]

An example from religious history shows how a human passion for nonlinear logic can manifest itself in real life. It shows, as well, how such principles, which can be subjectively meaningful in themselves, run up against linear facts that do not bend to meet them. In 1665, a Jewish mystic named Sabbatai Zevi proclaimed himself Messiah with the support of a young prophet named Nathan of Gaza. Over the years, in states of ecstatic illumination, he had been practicing ritual violation of traditional religious laws as a holy act of liberation. (The Age of the Messiah was expected to transcend the old laws, and Jesus, of course, had also discarded them.) Sabbatai inspired thousands of enthusiasts, many of whom sold off their property expecting to be moved imminently to the Holy Land. The following year the messiah travelled to Constantinople to demand the Sultan's kingdom, which included Palestine. He was, however, imprisoned, and, to save his life, he himself accepted Islam. His conversion naturally disillusioned many, but for others it fed new fuel to the movement, for it was seen as evidence of his sacrificial need to immerse himself in evil in order to bring redemption, to turn life inside out in order to clarify it. Sabbatianism flourished on this basis as an important, though often underground, heretical sect within Judaism down through the nineteenth century. The messiah's abandonment of his people provided a substantial myth on a compelling spiritual, or psychological, basis, as believers continued to expect his return over the generations. [8]

To take now a very different kind of example, a work of archetypal fiction whose images have become fixed in our imagination: Mary Shelley's novel *Frankenstein*--mythically subtitled *The Modern Prometheus*--is a good example of how a writer's conventional (linear) morality can distort the mythic imagery that imagination provides. Shelley's scientist, Victor Frankenstein, is driven by the mythic impulse toward mystery as well as the one toward creation. In fact, he justifies his zealous study of cadavers with the logic of the mystics: "To examine the causes of life, we must first have recourse to death." [9] However, he has the scientist's compulsion to demystify the mystery, to master it intellectually and make use of it, rather than the truly mythic motivation, which, as we shall see, is merely to experience it and preserve its power.

Desperate to recreate nature, therefore, Frankenstein produces a "monster," an image of Nature perverted, who himself cries out:

> Accursed creator! Why did you form a monster so hideous that even *you* turned from me in disgust? God, in pity, made man beautiful and alluring, after his own image; but my form is a filthy type of yours, more horrid even from the very resemblance. [10]

As this outburst shows, the creature is a very sensitive and idealistic being, articulate and even eloquent, responsive to beauty, delighted with the powers he perceives in good people and outraged by evil, eager to learn, and much more eager to love and be loved. He spies enthralled upon a human family:

> Night quickly shut in, but to my extreme wonder, I found that the cottagers had a means of prolonging light by the use of tapers, and was delighted to find that the setting of the sun did not put an end to the pleasure I experienced in watching my human neighbours. In the evening the young

The Meaning of Wonder

> girl and her companion were employed in various occupations which I did not understand; and the old man again took up the instrument which produced the divine sounds that had enchanted me in the morning. So soon as he had finished, the youth began, not to play but to utter sounds that were monotonous, and neither resembling the harmony of the old man's instrument nor the songs of the birds; I since found that he read aloud, but at the same time I knew nothing of the science of words or letters.[11]

It is his sensitivity, actually, which makes the monster act in a monstrous way, for when he sees how "natural" people respond to his appearance, with horror and violence, he is tortured with anguish and a passion for revenge in order to release his pain. The author's imagination expresses through him a poignant psychological dilemma, and he becomes an image of very human violence himself. He is not simply evil but tragic: "Satan had his companions, fellow devils, to admire and encourage him, but I am solitary and abhorred.[12] His monstrosity is the fact that the world has no place for his innocence.

Shelley herself creates *his* creator, Victor Frankenstein, as a relatively superficial, pathetic figure who condemns the evil he has produced without at all comprehending it.[13] Yet she asks us to admire him as a "glorious spirit," while she obliges the monster to destroy himself with justified self-loathing. Her book's point of view, in other words, strikes a tone of righteousness that cannot assimilate the myth she has engendered. What remains compelling is the image of an evil that brings suffering to self and others because it is branded evil not only by its own creator but by its creator's creator as well.[14] Shelley is like her scientist: she too cannot own the thing she has made even though she is compelled by its pathos. The book itself is the monster that it describes. She actually refers to it, albeit jocularly, as her "hideous progeny."[15] What remains fascinating in it, nevertheless, is not the maker's moral stamina but the image of evil bound fiercely to the life that is its source, human in its desires and its violence alike and leading the imagination deeper and deeper into a futile dilemma.

To the linear mentality (including Freudian psychology) the nonlinear features of myth are, of course, illusion, or mental toys. In particular, images of transcendence in myth are fantasies of wish-fulfillment or escapism. If a hero ascends to the gods or lives happily ever after or purges his land of evil, he expresses, we may be told, an immature reluctance to accept reality. Such images of fulfilllment, however, can be seen also as definitive statements of potentiality. They reveal what human nature strives for, and that is to say they reveal our true nature dissolving the linear considerations that conceal it. "Potentialities not only *will* be or could be; they also *are*," writes Abraham Maslow, who was the leading theorist of the "Human Potential" movement. "The human being is simultaneously that which he is and that which he yearns to be."[16]

Of course, a stable goal or ideal can measure for us where we are. But the images of transcendence suggest more than that: a sense of self

Nonlinear Values

freed from guilt and anxiety, from defensiveness and the fear of death, in a state of sufficiency that requires no justification, no pursuit of continually receding goals of progress, no perpetually renewable gratifications. What we long to be is ourselves, natural beings existing graciously. What impels the quest for this "miracle" is the restless feeling we are not at home in the practical house of civilization. And that is why the hero's journey is said to be circular: back, down, and up at the place he has never left to begin with.

THE REALIZATION OF WONDER

The familiar mythic image of the sun-chariot focuses our attention on the sun itself, standing out from the rest of nature, not in its fahrenheit but its magnificence. The image of the chariot underscores the subtle phenomenon of the sun's movement. Associating the sun with a god stresses its utter brilliance in quality and its overwhelming importance to the world. As the fire of god, it is all our light, our warmth, the preparer of our food, but an energy also that brings agonizing disaster. The image of divinity grasps the very "mystery" of this paradox, that creative and destructive powers are one--touching at once the essence of mortal life and something quite beyond it.

A mythic image of the sun, as we have seen, is not about the sun of the physical universe *in itself*, but the sun of the universe *experienced*, the sun in the *human* universe.[17] Myth accurately perceives this universe--with subjective accuracy; about this universe it always speaks the truth, as our dreams speak truly in portraying unresolved emotions. The languages of astronomy and physics cannot deal with the sun's magnificence or the *feeling* that its ambivalent power is mysterious, and if they could, they would only explain it. The myth captures it, it heightens our consciousness of the sun as being *what it is to us*. When Carl Jung visited an African tribe to study the psychology of its rituals and myths, he observed that this particular people, the Elgonyi, worshiped the sun only at the moment of its dawning. Then, after the frightening darkness of the forest night, it seemed most precisely extra-ordinary, recreating the whole world with daylight.[18]

In the mode of mythical thought, as Cassirer states, ordinary logic and attention to facts are suspended. The force of the images takes over as "thought is captivated and enthralled by the intuition which suddenly confronts it."[19] This is the faculty of "charm." A mythic image like the sun-chariot puts forth a proposition that is qualitatively effective because it is indeed preposterous. Being out of the ordinary, extra-ordinary, its logic conveys the extraordinariness of virtually all facets of reality as we experience them directly and keenly in themselves. The absurd, as Existential theology affirms, is another name for the miraculous. In myth everything is miracle--"impossibility"--because the last fact that linear thought can deal with is the fact that anything should exist at all, most of all that crown of absurdity, the consciousness that thinks so.

The one most important feature of myth--and the one we are most likely to shrug our shoulders at--is the response of wonder which it

The Meaning of Wonder

arouses. Not just an incidental quality that goes along with the stories, the sense of wonder is always the underlying and overriding qualitative "meaning" and theme, what it is about, and what myth can convey only through its own properly mythic style. In nonlinear fashion, the myth can treat the literally "wonder"-full universe meaningfully--and even analyze it--but only by evoking it. This is no subject to be understood objectively in abstractions, but only through the actual experience. The myth is a device to stimulate wonder. Like all qualitative symbols, its subject is the state of mind that it produces. Its image is *dynamic*, working on consciousness as consciousness plays upon the forms, figures and configurations of the imagery. Symbols are always forms for consciousness to entertain, as the sense of their significance fills out the patterns.[20]

The imagination thrives on play, and play is a freeing of the spirit from objective and pragmatic sense. Even though one drive of the mind may take the process quite seriously, perhaps by "believing" in it as theology, the imagination, producing myth *as myth*, luxuriates in its own free activity.[21] Theology attributes a linear validity to myth, treating it as history in a geographical world. In some cultures, or at some periods within a culture, myth has been freer from theological translation than in others. That is to say, it is more clearly cultivated because of its value *as myth*. Then the sense of wonder at nature and at humanity's place in the scheme of things comes forth as delight in the consciousness imagining.

Myths, then, have to be understood not so much for specific meanings as for the state of consciousness which they induce. That is their real content, their real significance or import. (Both of these words, "significance" and "import," have the virtue of blending together "meaning" and "importance.") From our sophisticated culture, we can still appreciate this spirit of myth to the extent that we yield to the images, *imagining their truth*, and letting what is substantially the same state of mind arise in ourselves.

A creation myth from Colombia bursts into an extra-ordinary play of images:

> Seen from below, from Ahpikondía [Paradise], our earth looks like a large cobweb. It is transparent, and the Sun shines through it. The threads of this web are like the rules that men should live by, and they are guided by these threads, seeking to live well, and the Sun sees them.[22]

Conceiving the apparently solid earth now as a cobweb, we abruptly turn linear space and substance inside-out into nonlinear intangibility. The Sun, who is the creating Father, penetrates this world with the implicit brilliance of the sun blazing on any cobweb, and this delicate, intricate, and sparkling mesh is also humanity's way of life--not simply moral strictures but the efforts of men "seeking to live well." We sense life at once from earth, from Paradise, which is below, and from the sun above, so that the combination of perspectives itself becomes a web of life's substance. The play of images is theological in its subject, but it is sacred in

The Realization of Wonder

the act of imagination that weaves its images together with such beauty, releasing a fundamental sense of living unity through its particular collocation of pictures and points of view.

It is difficult, in a discursive style, to convey the importance of wonder. It is the child's element, we are all born to it. We know it again whenever life feels eminently right to us and we are glad to share existence with the universe. The inner self continually seeks out this feeling but settles over and again for adulterated substitutes. So committed to linear self-determination do we become as we "mature" that, typically, we fail to see meaning *or* importance in it. It does not sound sophisticated, it is not a theory or belief that we can claim to hold, it leads nowhere, we cannot easily convey it to someone who feels sensible and practical. It is ephemeral and passes. It is merely childish, just a mood, romantic. Because wonder implies a loss of self-consciousness, when we return to "ourselves," and become self-conscious once again, we are no longer geared to understand or care. Nevertheless, it is in the state of wonder that life feels clearly right to us and awakens us to our own existence.

STRANGENESS AND INTIMACY

Myth deals with horrors in life and intricate ironies, but like the child for whom it has not yet all become old hat, mythic vision sees its life as both fresh and strange. If myth strikes us as weird, with its outlandish images clothing feelings that are not so unfamiliar as all that--like Narcissus perishing of love for his own image in the water--the weirdness is really much to the point. Lévi-Strauss, whose Structuralist methodology is extremely rational, writes:

> When an exotic custom fascinates us in spite of (or on account of) its apparent singularity, it is generally because it presents us with a distorted reflection of a familiar image, which we confusedly recognize as such without yet managing to identify it.[23]

The distortion is itself a functional aspect of the mythic communication. Seeing life strange, we see it fresh; seeing it fresh, we see it as it is. Within and without, our sophisticated world has fallen into the background: just our tree in our garden, just our feelings in our mind--until we cease to see them because they are so common. Most of the world becomes peripheral. Shrugging off the strangeness of myth, we remain oblivious to both the world and our selves. But when we feel the fascination of the strange, we may sense the essential strangeness of whatever is, especially of our selves.

"A myth," writes Richmond Hathorn, "is a tissue of symbolism clothing a mystery."[24] He is drawing on a distinction between "problem" and "mystery" propounded by the French philosopher Gabriel Marcel:

The Meaning of Wonder

> A problem is something which I meet, which I find complete before me, but which I can therefore lay siege to and reduce. But a mystery is something in which I myself am involved, and it can therefore only be thought of as "a sphere where the distinction between what is in me and what is before me loses its meaning and its initial validity." [25]

A problem, in Marcel's terms, is a difficulty that can be solved. It has a linear cause that explains it, and we find out a linear solution. On the other hand, a mystery is an aspect of reality that it is appropriate only to confront, appreciate, and wonder at. (Not, however, to wonder *about*.) The phenomenon of death is in this sense a mystery, the persistence of evil or suffering, the sudden appearance of extreme happiness, the strength of love, and certainly the fact of existence itself. The strangeness of myth separates such primal aspects of life from the mesh of facts and casts them up to stare us in the face. [26]

As a central point in his philosophy, the Jewish theologian Martin Buber developed a conception similar to Marcel's that is also very valuable for the study of myth. He makes what is now a famous distinction between two ways one can relate to another person, to nature, and to the universe. "I" ordinarily experience all three as "It," objectively, in the third person, as things that are important in the way they are useful to me in my world. I relate to other people according to their roles in my life: as my wife or my children, as students, colleagues, salespersons, or presidents of the United States. Nature and the universe I see as just what happens to be out there. I observe and analyze it, and drive on through it with my eye on my destination. Such objectivity is necessary and wholly desirable for millions of practical reasons, but it does not give to life, in the double sense, *significance*.

Truly significant is the rarer mode of relationship, when "I" confront a member of my world in the second-person singular, as what was once in English the familiar form of address "Thou." Then I experience the other person as a self; the particular birch or blue jay as the center of its own life, being completely itself; the universe, my total home, as infinitely alive. "Thou" is (thou *"art"*) the beloved; this experience is the mode of love and art and worship.

There are three aspects of the "I-Thou" relation that can help us understand the style of myth. First of all, it supports our impression that myth is not just a tale once believed in and now exploded, but rather the natural and appropriate expression of a condition of consciousness. This condition, moreover, we can now see more clearly as one that is profound; it is, in fact, the sense of a profundity in life and the source of life's meaningfulness. "Meaning" in life is not, therefore, abstract philosophy. It is the function of a state of consciousness. When we want to know life's meaning, we usually yearn to feel its meaningfulness.

Secondly, "I-Thou" consciousness implies a way of relating to other beings or things, a relationship that depends on how we experience them. And in this experience, what is addressed as "thou" is not seen to be concrete and finite, like a thing, but rather open-ended or infinite, as our own consciousness is.

> When *Thou* is spoken, the speaker has no thing for his object. For where there is a thing there is another thing. Every *It* is bounded by others; It exists only through being bounded by others. But when *Thou* is spoken, there is no thing. *Thou* has no bounds. [27]

Thirdly, in this state of mind, our relation with nature or the universe is mutual, just as our relation with people is. In the consciousness of "Thou," we experience whatever we confront as having individuality that faces us. The tree or the starry night-sky utters to us its nature. It speaks forth as we let ourselves absorb it and realize what it is, in the bark and branch of the one, in the sparkling patterns of the other. We let it be itself without needing it to serve our purposes; we allow ourselves intimacy with it and sense it as being alive with its own personality. This is what the child does with his or her dolls--a point that was explained to me nicely by my son, when he was nine. "Do you know," he asked me, "why kids say 'My Teddy bear is alive'?" I thought he would say, "Because they're lonely and want someone to love them," but his answer was more subtle: "Because they feel they love their Teddy bear and they think that anything they love must be alive. They feel that way but it's just cloth." [28] The child's feeling of participating, *with love*, in the object's reality brings it to life for him--and that was apparently the case with the ancient shepherd facing the stellar constellations, the woods alive with nymphs and sylphs, and the whole "mysterious" universe vibrant with deity. "Myth lives entirely by the presence of its object," writes Cassirer, "by the intensity with which it seizes and takes possession of consciousness in a specific moment." [29] The world of myth is thoroughly alive, even in its dealings with death, because it sustains a perfect flow between "I"--the self--and whatever "I" dwell upon. [30]

The relevance of Buber's formulation to myth has been developed by a pair of scholars, the Frankforts. They elaborate on the insight that mythmaking peoples retain, as they continue to absorb their culture, this natural propensity for the experience of "thou." It is simply a receptivity, an openness to the intense and intimate sense of life that impels the mythic imagination. This attitude, of course, is another way of describing the capacity for wonder.

> The world appears to primitive man neither inanimate nor empty but redundant with life; and life has individuality, in man and beast and plant, and in every phenomenon which confronts man--the thunderclap, the sudden shadow, the eerie and unknown clearing in the wood, the stone which suddenly hurts him when he stumbles while on a hunting trip. Any phenomenon may at any time face him, not as "It," but as "Thou." In this confrontation, "Thou" reveal its individuality, its qualities, its will. "Thou" is not contemplated with intel-

The Meaning of Wonder

> its qualities, its will. "Thou" is not contemplated with intellectual detachment; it is experienced as life confronting life, involving every faculty of man in a reciprocal relationship. Thoughts, no less than acts and feelings, are subordinated to this experience.[31]

To know the world as "Thou," therefore, *is* to know it mystically.

The chief deity of the Huichol Indians is Tatewarí, "our Grandfather Fire." He has utilitarian value as the actual fire that one builds:

> We believe in him. Without him, where would we get warmth? How could we cook? All would be cold. To keep warm Our Sun Father would have to come close to the earth. And that cannot be so.[32]

However, he is known in himself as a presence, intimately, in the way that only myth can express:

> Imagine. One is in the Sierra, there where we Huichols live. One walks, one follows one's paths. Then it becomes dark. One is alone there walking, one sees nothing. What is it there in the dark? One hears something? It is not to be seen. All is cold. Then one makes camp there. One gathers a little wood, food for Tatewarí. Once strikes a light. One brings out Tatewarí. Ah, what a fine thing! What warmth! What light! The darkness disappears. It is safe. Tatewarí is there to protect one.[33]

In their rituals, the Huichols make use of peyote to open themselves to the sense of divinity. As they do, they experience the peyote itself as Thou, keenly personal.

> Peyote, like maize, can read one's thoughts and can punish one for being false or evil. . . . The peyote rewards or punishes a man according to his inner state, his moral deserts.

If one ingests the improper form of peyote, one is treated in a particularly critical manner.

> If one comes there not having spoken of one's life, if one comes not having been cleansed of everything, then this false hikuri will discover it. It is going to bring out that which is evil in one, that which frightens one. It knows all one's bad thoughts.[34]

The "bad peyote" is experienced as an accusing demon. In either case, the emergence of such a personal deity in the hallucinogenic state suggests the ancient confrontations with Dionysos, who is at once the grape, the wild power of nature, and the enormous nonrational drive that he releases from within the human spirit. The plant taken into one's body naturally becomes oneself. In that realm where such a plant merges also with the special state of mind that it produces, myth arises of its own accord.

Today, in our world, in moments of extreme feeling, we may lapse unconsciously into such a mode of experiencing and interpreting the world. We do so most often, unfortunately, out of irritability or a sudden sense of helplessness, cursing the machine that spitefully will not start or the bad weather on a weekend. We joke to lighten our feelings but we have entered the outer range of "I-Thou" consciousness, which, in its negative phases, conjures demons as well as sprites and sky gods. If--to elaborate on one of the Frankforts' examples--I stub my toe on an unseen rock and thoughtlessly exclaim "God damn you," I am in roughly the state of mind that a jungle native might experience. Momentarily and unaware, I inhabit a universe in which my god is ready to confront a devil in the stone and cast him into hell in order that my dignity might be restored. My sudden sharp though minor pain, coming out of carelessness, has made me feel a little foolish as well as hurt, and I need someone to be angry at. Only a willful opponent can account for such a predicament. My momentary myth is trivial but it expresses with vivid precision my state of mind.[35] "Damn *it*," strangely, may sound a little less blasphemous to some ears, but it is far weaker in expression, and this is just because it lacks the sense of confrontation that the Frankforts emphasize. There is a curious revelation in the fact that spontaneous mythic sensibility remains alive for us most clearly in the quite traditional practice of "cursing."

Finally, a third conception (after Marcel's and Buber's) may help to elucidate the sense of wonder still further. The anthropologist Victor Turner describes ritual practices as a way for people to suspend their awareness of themselves as social creatures and experience themselves on an absolute level of their common humanity, in a state that he calls *communitas*. In initiation rituals, the initiate loosens the bonds of the highly structured society and enters a threshold, or *liminal*, condition, where he or she lives for the time without ordinary roles to play in ordinary time. One ceases to regard oneself as a specific personality but lives as a *human self* according to the manner made possible by one's particular culture. All those who share the experience together are bonded in a state of profound fellow-feeling, which extends beyond them to encompass the rest of humanity as well, in what is often described as cosmic or mystical ecstasy, in harmony with nature, under the patronage of the gods. A continuing condition of *communitas* is institutionalized in monasticism and utopian societies, it is induced in all forms of worship, it is sought after in the arts, and it is perverted in social or political movements that seek power or prestige through an exclusive kind of unity. However, one of Turner's most valuable insights about this condition is that it is not a reaction against society or a contradiction of it; *communitas* provides,

The Meaning of Wonder

rather, a form of "anti-structure" that balances the ordinary structure of society, constituting at least as important a dimension of group life as the more obvious kinds of structure.[36]

Turner draws upon Buber's work to support and interpret his own, quoting for example: "The *We* includes the *Thou*. Only men who are capable of truly saying *Thou to* one another can truly say *We with* one another".[37] *Communitas* is, therefore, implicitly mythogenetic, conducive, that is, to mythic expression. A sense of the presence of deity is an important feature of this state; here all procedures and accoutrements are felt to be sacred. The *liminal* transition, furthermore, characterizes the situation of the archetypal hero, who leaves his familiar linear world to risk the ultimate threats against humanity. The process of initiation prefigures (or commemorates, or simply parallels) the mythic journey, indicating its basic narrative form. Clarifying the subjective basis of ritual, Turner provides a principle, therefore, that helps interpret mythic narrative--its personages, settings, and events--in terms of the qualities of consciousness that it evokes and that it relates to one other. In the communal sharing of myth, we can see a society's cultivation of the profound *communitas* experience that is also a running commentary on its daily life. The whole body of myth dramatizes "anti-structure" and justifies it as the very heart of society's structure of social distinction, role-playing, custom, and law, which are more clearly functional perhaps but no more meaningful or vital.

CHAPTER FOUR

THE QUALITATIVE WORLD: ITS FORM

In the gift of water, in the gift of wine, sky and earth dwell.   --Heidegger

THE MOTIF

In one of the most richly mythic and most poetic of the Grimm's fairy tales, "The Juniper Tree" (in some texts called "The Almond Tree"), a good woman wishes for a child as she stands beneath the tree in her courtyard. Soon she becomes pregnant with a son whose own life is mysteriously bound up with the tree's. His growth in the womb is described through the annual cycle of vegetation.

> Then she went into the house, and a month went by and the snow was gone, and two months, and then everything was green, and three months, and then all the flowers came out of the earth, and four months, and then all the trees in the wood grew thicker, and the green branches were all closely entwined, and the birds sang until the wood resounded and the blossoms fell from the trees, then the fifth month passed away and she stood under the juniper tree, which smelt so sweetly that her heart leapt, and she fell on her knees and was beside herself with joy, and when the sixth month was over the fruit was large and fine, and then she was quite still, and the seventh month she snatched at the juniper-berries and ate them greedily, then she grew sick and sorrowful, then the eighth month passed, and she called her husband to her, and wept and said: "If I die, then bury me beneath the juniper tree." Then she was quite comforted and happy until the next month was over, and then she had a child as white as snow and as red as blood, and when she beheld it she was so delighted that she died.[1]

The mother's delivery and her death are evoked suggestively as a natural process, while we are also made aware, with delicate pathos, that the human realm, being conscious, remains distinct from the rest of nature. The boy, as the tale evolves, is butchered by his stepmother and served by her to his father in a soup. His half-sister, however, carries his bones beneath the tree, and he is reborn out of its boughs in the form of a wonderful bird.

The Qualitative World: Its Form

> Then the juniper tree began to stir itself, and the branches parted asunder, and moved together again, just as if someone were rejoicing and clapping his hands. At the same time a mist seemed to arise from the tree, and in the center of the mist it burned like a fire, and a beautiful bird flew out of the fire singing magnificently, and he flew high up in the air, and when he was gone, the juniper tree was just as it had been before, and the handkerchief with the bones was no longer there.[2]

After the stepmother has been destroyed, he resumes his own shape, to be reunited with his father and sister.

The most common sign of nonlinear form in myth is its basic vocabulary of motifs. A motif can be identified for practical purposes simply as *any detail that recurs*: a kind of character, a kind of place or structure, animal, or plant, or any feature of the narrative process as it unfolds, such as symmetry and repetition.[3] In our very brief account of "The Juniper Tree," both the ideal mother dying and the wicked stepmother succeeding her are among the most familiar motifs of fairy-tales. The symbolic tree of life is a myth motif of the first importance. In this instance it has been associated with the mythic theme of animism, which attributes spirit to elements of nature. The miraculous bird arising out of fire is familiar as the phoenix. The slaughtered child served to his father occurs in the famous Greek myth of the brothers Atreus and Thyestes but elsewhere as well.

Before the bird drops a millstone on the stepmother's head, it receives a climactic series of three gifts in exchange for its magic song. From a goldsmith it receives a chain, which it gives to the father. From a cobbler it gets red shoes, which go to the sister. A group of millers hoist up to the bird a heavy millstone, which it carries aloft with extraordinary ease until it drops the weight upon the agonized stepmother. The association of bird and inspired song is a motif of mystical origin. It occurs here in an especially suggestive form since the bird's song *is* the boy's story; it is, in fact, the "myth" itself.

The grouping of incidents in units of three (often with a fourth to cap the series) is, of course, extremely common, as are groupings in seven and twelve. With qualitative vision, we may suspect that the quantity in the number is not as important as the fact of set pattern in itself. We have seen (at the end of Chapter Two) that the sense of form has power and meaning in itself. Three is the minimum number for a climax--beginning, middle, and end--but any recognizably artificial unit of groupings, in person, events, or accoutrements, serves most of all to sever the action from linear continuity.[4] Such material is emphatically qualitative. It exists as formed substance, as rhythmic stuff belonging to the whole texture of the tale, and not to the linear world around us. In its rhythmic way, myth moves its fiction towards music, which is an art of pure *quality*, testing the rhythms and tensions of consciousness itself.

There are at least two reasons behind the motif-formation of mythic narration. The first is its affinity with ritual, which operates

The Motif

necessarily through set patterns of recurring action in such a way as to produce a satisfaction through the process unfolding. Rituals clearly separate their reality from that of linear everyday life and they do so through activities that are rhythmical, symmetrical, and self-contained-- in a word, geometrical. They develop a definite sense of form, therefore, and a sense that meaning accrues as one follows the coherence of the forms. They are, accordingly, climactic as well, leading to a state of reconstitution, which is experienced as a rediscovery of wholeness found in the midst of life's apparent formlessness.

The second reason is the process of oral transmission. The impetus of mythic narrative evolved before writing or in cultures that never developed it, and many of the features of myth result from the story-telling process itself. Traditional story-telling maintains its continuity through the centuries by the regular use of set phrases, in a formulaic manner of expression, and set events, or themes of action, which are well-loved for both their familiarity and their special status. Events recur in clusters of elements that immediately suggest one another and require other well-known elements in order to work themselves out. As Milman Parry and Albert Lord showed, when they made an intensive study of the Balkan oral epic, these features allowed story-tellers to remember their stock of tales and to recreate them spontaneously in a tradition that could remain stable while it still depended upon continual limited change.[5]

The major reference work for contemporary folklorists is Stith Thompson's *Motif-Index of Folk Literature*, which, in 2,500 pages, categorizes a stupendous range of motifs with world-wide samples of their occurrence.[6] Thompson lists more than 1,200 variations on the taboo motif, which are organized under 72 sub-divisions of ten categories. The basic structure of the fairy tale has been analyzed by the Russian folklorist Vladimir Propp, using a number of charts and tables. He sees all versions of the heroic tale as variations on a single sequence of "functions," or units of action, that result from either an initial piece of villainy or the realization of some *lack* that needs to be filled.[7] Propp lists 151 characteristics of his basic tale,[8] distributing the action among seven character types: villain, donor (of magical help), helper, princess, dispatcher (who assigns the hero his task), hero, and false hero (such as a brother who claims the true hero's prerogatives).[9]

Identifying, classifying, and interrelating motifs is only a start at understanding them, however. To go further, we need to consider what they express by virtue of *being motifs*, by reducing life, that is, to non-linear structures, and we need to consider what they all add up to. We will see that they reflect the human mind in its own make-up. But first, it will be useful to see the kind of reality which they help build. Because motifs represent life in an obviously artificial or *different* form, woven together they constitute their own kind of reality. A myth or folktale transpires in a universe that we cannot confuse with the ordinary one all around us. The hero and the gods walk through space and time made out of mind, so of course the parts will hold together with peculiar gravities and magnetisms. According to the philosophical categories of our own

The Qualitative World: Its Form

culture, we can differentiate the two kinds of *seeing*--the experiential and the physical, or the subjective and objective--into four aspects of reality: space, time, causation, and identity.[10]

1. SPACE

Here and There

Linear space and time are characterized by a simple and rigid principle of continuity that fixes them into the world. San Francisco and London and the moon are all in different places, yet they exist in the same *space*. One is over in this direction while the other is up that way, but I can get from one town to another and to the moon (with the help of a few rockets) by going through this single realm of space in a steady, uninterrupted flow, all places of which seem to be "here" when my body coincides with them. I can set up fences and boundaries and see where ocean starts and land ends, but space runs through them all; it is "occupied" but indivisible. Within space, places remain dependably stable. I can count on London being where it was last year, and even if an earthquake utterly shatters San Francisco, the place where it had been would remain the same place.

"Euclidean space," writes Cassirer, referring to the linear space interpreted by Euclid's geometry, "is characterized by the three basic attributes of continuity, infinity, and uniformity. But all these attributes run counter to the character of sensory perception."[11] As we actually perceive space, we get to see only arbitrary portions of it at a time, with an expanded awareness of some areas, usually those nearby. On the level of simple personal subjectivity, in fact, space is manifold. *There* is a different kind of space from here, for once I get there, it turns into *here*. *There* is always someplace else, and *else* is a space of its own. Nonetheless, we spend much of our time nonlinearly *there*. In memory, I place myself *there* where I walked in the woods last month or I fantasize about lying *there* on an ideal tropic beach, while I am working *here* in winter. Obviously, in this sense, anyone can be *here* and *there* at the same time, and, as a matter of fact, you can be *there* only while you still are *here*-- otherwise, *there* will turn into *here*. Of course, *here* is subjective also, since it is always changing from one place to another as we move around. It depends upon our point of view, like right and left, which change with the way we face.

Less tangibly, we can think of states of mind as occupying different kinds of space, with their own manners of orientation, their own horizons. The verbal state of mind I am completely absorbed in as I write has its own rather tight kind of space. Love is a kind of space far less congested than the space of anger or frustration. There is a gentle climate in the space of love.

In my imagination and in my dreams, I go with absolutely zero effort from one space to another, leaping like a cosmic kangaroo, for different kinds of space are discontinuous, and one kind can be overlaid upon another with no trouble at all. In a dream, my childhood house can be the same as my present home 3,000 miles away, and it can also be a palace and a prison and a college classroom. A continuity does exist among these places but I must sense it in the feeling that I have about them all which makes them one. And aside from fantasy, I can actually be physically in a place that I experience as *there*--when I am travelling, for example, or when I am lost. On vacation, I am suspended pleasantly in a special *distant* place while the less fortunate souls serving me are *here* in their own world alongside me. Exile, similarly, is not just physical removal from one's homeland. It is the experience of residing against one's will in a state of *there*ness, and that is, of course, part of the punishment of imprisonment as well.

We can see good examples of this theme in the visual arts. In tribal arts, and in medieval carvings and tapestries, everything is *here*. *There* (like Heaven or Hell) is represented as a distinctly separate state that is here in itself. The modern Western style of painting that begins with the Renaissance conveys through perspective the steady transition that roots *there* to *here*, making the distance *there*. We then have a continuous unified scheme of space, in which the observer occupies an arbitrary position. The world is then clearly everything outside that we happen to be *in*. In modern fantasy fiction, when we have gone through the looking glass or through the galaxies, we know we are *there* in a bizarre imaginary place, on vacation from reality. In most kinds of myth, on the other hand, *there* is real, so when we are there, we are already *here* in a new way. We do not awaken from it or escape in a space ship. We reckon with it, and it affects the way we are here on all levels at once.

Extraordinary Space

In myth, the universe consists typically of a *here* for humankind between two forms of *there*, one for gods above and one below for demons and the dead. These realms usually seem to be lands that have no *land*, and they are commonly separated from linear space by bounded waters like the Greek river Styx. Interpreting their subjective basis, the mythologically oriented literary theorist Northrop Frye calls these heavens and these hells the limits of desire and of repugnance.

> The conception of a heaven above, a hell beneath, and a cyclical cosmos or order of nature in between forms the ground plan, *mutatis mutandis*, of both Dante and Milton. The same plan is in paintings of the Last Judgment, where there is a rotary movement of the saved rising on the right and the damned falling on the left.[12]

The principle of gravity is here emotional, attracting and repelling us according to feelings we already have, and this image of the cosmos, out of both *linear* time and space, is significantly *cyclical* instead. In the mythic dimension, human action is always pointing in a circle.

The Qualitative World: Its Form

Mayan world-tree, *in shape of cross. Sarcophagus cover of Pacal, 7th-century ruler of Pallenque, who is shown being swallowed by death at roots of the tree while a sacred bird sings in the heavens above.*

Space

The fundamental form of process is cyclical movement, the alternation of success and decline, effort and repose, life and death which is the rhythm of process.[13]

Myth expresses the nature of life continually perpetuating itself, so action is always here and everywhere at once. The subjective circle leads us always where we are. In adventure tales, the mythic hero descends to the underworld or a symbolic form of death, then, conquering, returns as a savior to the world he left.

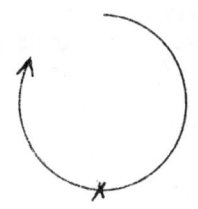

In *The Hero with a Thousand Faces*, an invaluable introduction to the study of myth, Joseph Campbell analyzes this pattern as the three-part movement: departure, initiation, and return.[14]

One of the most important things that a mythic hero does is to travel, and his journey in itself necessitates a special kind of world for him to explore. Mythic space, in other words, is constituted by the process of traversing it. In the common ritual of pilgrimage, heroic space is recreated. One seeks out a specific geographical place, but its meaning transcends geography, and one travels roads that lead out of the world itself. Such seeking leads clearly, of course, where it must go, but, as in the hero's journey, the effort of the "quest" and the sense of a re-orientation in space make the arrival fully meaningful and important, so that one is clearly *there* in body's space at journey's end.[15]

Mircea Eliade, a leading scholar of comparative religion, uses the clear terms "sacred" and "profane" to contrast the two modes of space (and of time).

> For religious man, space is not homogeneous; he experiences interruptions, breaks in it; some parts of space are qualitatively different from others. . . . For religious man, this spatial nonhomogeneity finds expression in the experience of an opposition between space that is sacred--the only *real* and *real-ly* existing space--and all other space, the formless expanse surrounding it.[16]

The temple or the church is not just on an acre or ten of land, it is the House of God amid the universe. The architecture of great places of worship, often overwhelming in its scope, creates a sense of God's space. That is space itself experienced as one whole. An important motif of nonlinear space, within the "middle world" of earth, is a point said to be

The Qualitative World: Its Form

the center of the world, called by mythologists (in the Greek word) the *omphalos*, or navel. Such a place, like the Greek oracle at Delphi, or often a mountain or a tree, is an image (sometimes, like Delphi, with a geographical location) experienced as a link between the human world and the divine--or the linear and the nonlinear. It is the navel that marks our relation to the subjective source of life. At the climax of his great vision, the young Sioux Indian Black Elk finds himself atop the highest mountain in view.

> . . . and round about beneath me was the whole loop of the world. And while I stood there I saw more than I can tell and I understood more than I saw; for I was seeing in a sacred manner the shapes of all things in the spirit, and the shape of all shapes as they must live together like one being.[17]

He identifies this marvelous vantage point as Harney Peak in the Black Hills, but notes explicitly, for his author's benefit, that "anywhere is the center of the world." [17] Also, Black Elk receives a portable world-tree. The fourth Grandfather speaks:

> " . . . Behold, the living center of a nation I shall give you, and with it many you shall save." And I saw that he was holding in his hand a bright red stick that was alive, and as I looked it sprouted at the top and sent forth branches, and on the branches many leaves came out and murmured and in the leaves the birds began to sing. And then for just a little while I thought I saw beneath it in the shade the circled villages of people and every living thing with roots or legs or wings, and all were happy.[18]

The center of the world, not surprisingly, always sits among the people whose myths we are in and gives them ("us") a privileged position near the spiritual roots. "'Our World' is Always Situated at the Center." [19] Naturally, "I" and "we" subjectively *are* the perspective from which life is seen, while all the rest of nature and humanity spreads out around us, as our setting and environment, the context of all our experience.

In our modern lives, without a sense of sacredness to take for granted, we still relate to certain symbolic places in a way that lifts them out of the mere three dimensions. Our home, certainly, becomes a space expanding past its walls and acreage, the mere *house*.

> There are [as well other] privileged places, qualitatively different from all others--a man's birthplace, or the scenes of his first love, or certain places in the first foreign city he visited in youth. Even for the most frankly nonreligious man, all these places still retain an exceptional, a unique quality; they are the "holy places" of his private universe, as if it were in such spots that he had received the revelation of a reality

other than that in which he participates through his ordinary daily life. [20]

Wherever we have an intense or intimate ("I-Thou") experience, space takes on "mythical" dimensions. Even as we go about the routines of life, our feelings constantly assimilate the world about us, evoking a subjective environment in which we always live.[21]

In fairy tales, characters are freed from spatial linearity by an ability to fly, or by seven-league boots or magic carpets. Then they move not simply fast or even extremely fast, but like mind itself, instantaneously, propelled just by will in a world of infinite possibilities. The spatial relation among characters within a myth is also malleable. The size of dwarfs and giants is significant, of course, in relation to the ordinary folk. They express, Jung suggests, "the queer uncertainty of spatial and temporal relations in the unconscious."[22] Undoubtedly, and more concretely, they echo our childhood sense of ourselves in contrast to our parents, when the difference in size controlled critically the emotional space we lived and moved in.

If we think of life in general--and consciousness in particular--as a field of energy, we sense at once that energy is a tendency to go someplace. Jean-Paul Sartre, accordingly, sees imagination as a natural process of putting mental impulses, or intuitions, into space. He draws on a German psychologist, Flach, who suggested specific thoughts to subjects in an experiment and studied images that these thoughts aroused. Through these "intuitive images," as Flach called them, the relationships among ideas become spatial schemes.

> Here is an example: when we asked, what do you understand by altruism, the subject had the representation of a direction, the fact of going towards another thing which is not given.[23]

"These determinations of psychological space" notes Sartre, "are none other, in fact, than impressions of movement apprehended imaginatively."[24] The mind consists of urges in all directions. These overflow in the imagery of myth to fill a universe of (or *with*) conscious space.

Thus we surround ourselves with a world to live in, which as conscious beings, we cannot do without. It is a powerfully suggestive universe, for, though *there* is linearly no place, yet it is subjectively the measure of all places. Memories and fantasies define our expectations; our goals define the place we are. Myths of paradise or houses of the dead have lit up or shadowed men's dwellings, reflecting poignantly upon the way they pass their days.

The Qualitative World: Its Form

2. TIME

Shapes of Time

Space and time are interwoven. Much of what is true of space seems true of time. The experience of linear time is abstract, however, compared to our sense of space. We have to intellectualize about it, to posit that endless progression of particular times which we cannot see or otherwise experience directly but which *must* link us solidly to the train of past and future (must or *else*; "else" being a logical kind of *there*). Linear time has no immediate reality, no matter how much we swear by it. In fact, as we have seen in the passages from Dorothy Lee, the very idea of time as a line applies to time the apparent qualities of space.[25] "You cannot, absolutely cannot think of time," emphasizes Julian Jaynes, "except by spatializing it."[26] (When I speak of space "going on in all directions," I apply time terms to the space, imagining myself, as what Jaynes calls the "analog I",[27] going outward from a place *here* in a progression of steps.) In the technocratic-Watergate jargon left over from the 1970's, there seems to be an increased desire to make something physical, and hence more easily manipulated, out of "this point in time."

Yet we do not only swear but live by linear time and break it up in orderly sequences of minutes, years, millenia, and set our clocks together ticking us along in harmony. I may need to scurry to keep up, but my five o'clock is your five o'clock, and we all want to get into the same traffic jam to keep life from getting a good deal more messed up than it already is. From the moment of birth to the moment of death, we are made of series of events elapsing from one clearly demarcated (and artificially fenced-off) point to another, and we co-ordinate our sequences according to the intersecting lines of other persons and events.

From the fifth Century B.C., when Sophocles wrote his tragedies, to the time I study them, time has moved in a solid continuity from what I call year to year. I can travel steadily over the world to Athens, where he lived and wrote. However, although I can visit also what now remains of the ancient city of Thebes, in no way but my mind can I reach the Thebes in which Sophocles' Oedipus lived out his mythic agony, and lives it out again and still again, forever killing his father, marrying his mother, tearing out his eyes, whenever the play is read or seen or recollected. Sophocles himself, of course, had no other way to get there.

We must remember that, for a nonliterate culture, historical time can be at all possible only within living memory, so the vast nonlinear expanse is very close, just as the familiar world of space is circumscribed by an unknown expanse that is *virtually* reachable: if one just went a little further away from home, into the forest or out to sea.

The time of the myth (or of any kind of fiction) is *discontinuous*, free of history. While the incidents of the story pass along in sequence, they also are both timeless and simultaneous. I can even scramble up the sequence in my mind, imagining the hero's death before his birth. If we remember that the individual events all are images, we can see them laid out, as it were, upon a table or painted on a canvas. We think of linear

Time

time as though it followed a line in space, but qualitative time--as in dreams and myths--takes on even stronger spatial qualities. As in the three-step climax of the fairy tale, time takes on a closed or outlined sense of form, typically a cyclic shape revolving on itself within a single area. As a form, therefore, time has space-like stability, staying itself. It is also like space in its character of simultaneity. All space is at once, and we can see all myths as patterns of motifs overlaid on one another. We see the meaning in the pattern as a whole, taking it in at one view.

It is obvious in daily life how malleable subjective time can be. It speeds or slows, stops and leaps, according to anxieties and pleasures, busyness and boredom. The drunk man's time and space have their unique and spectacular characteristics. Late or busy, sleepy or hungry, we fold time around us in a curved world. Jung points out that "Any kind of excitement, no matter in what phase of life, displays a tendency to rhythmic expression . . ."[28] Especially in fairy tales, like "The Juniper Tree," images and events can turn back and round upon themselves in cyclic and repetitive structures. They can loop in circles and in circles within circles, like the refrain of a song. As in music and poetry, rhythm itself establishes a qualitative order. It breaks up the linear flow of time and events into a structured reality, with marked stages and a self-contained shape or outline.

The linear mind seeks always new information and it values original contributions to the culture. The basis of traditional culture, however, lies in "getting it right," which is to say: re-creating, with variations, the chief patterns of life according to the culture's accustomed images. For the linear mind, "more of the same" is *superfluous*, just as it has made "redundant"--literally "redounding" or "overflowing"--mean "excessive" or "out of a job."[29] But qualitatively, "more of the same" intensifies and builds experience to its peaks, or simply keeps one where one wants to be. Thus a child can repeat the same song, the same prank, almost endlessly.

> To the Hopi, for whom time is not a motion but a "getting later" of everything that has ever been done, unvarying repetition is not wasted but accumulated. It is storing up an invisible change that holds over into later events.[30]

An Anatomy of Time

All the time of myth is qualitative; its density fluctuates with the story-line. However, just as underworlds and heavens are the most familiar types of qualitative space, we know the realm of nonlinear time first of all as afterlife. It is also once-upon-a time and ever-after. Eliade compares "profane" time with, in a Latin phrase, *illud tempus*--"*that* time" or "those days."[31] *In illo tempore* ("in those days"), there was a "time" before the world began, and time when the gods made world and men, or when giants (*not* dinosaurs) stomped upon the earth, or our fathers and mothers lived peacefully and creatively in a Golden Age or short-lived Eden. All myth takes place *then*, in those days, which are

The Qualitative World: Its Form

not, however, merely very *old* days but a different *kind* of time. Australian aborigines consciously recognize the special nature of mythic time as *alcheringa*, or "dream time." Being discontinuous, mythic time cannot have come before linear time. Not being linear, it cannot have the quality of before-ness. Imagination merely lets it be *as though* before, in order to get linear time off to a start, emerging from the background of an absolute world of meaning.

"The good old days" is mythic time *in illo tempore*, but so is that utopian day "come the revolution," when tyranny will be overthrown and we will all live like brothers. "All *fulfilled* time," writes another historian of religion, "is mythical."[32] Like nonlinear space but more clearly, nonlinear time interprets our present lives. All fantasies are made of such nonlinear "time," reflecting wishful commentaries on real experience. Daydreams, that is, like the dreams of night, release energy from our frustrations. "If only . . ." is a way of saying "but I can't."

The Structuralists, adapting terms introduced by the linguist Ferdinand de Saussure, often make a useful distinction between "synchronic" and "diachronic" relations to time.[33] The "diachronic" moves steadily along (horizontally, as it were) and corresponds to the story of a myth unfolding in one direction. The "synchronic" is reversible and stoppable and can be grasped all at once (vertically). It refers to the meaning of the myth, which takes in all the "time" of the narrative in a single perception:[34]

diachronic

synchronic

Properly, the vertical runs down at every point along the horizontal. It can be imagined more meaningfully, I think, as the side view of a moving circle (or the circumference of a cylinder):

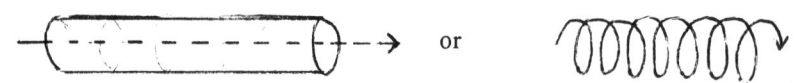

We can, however, combine the distinctions of Eliade and Saussure into a scheme that we can represent in four parts with two sub-divisions:

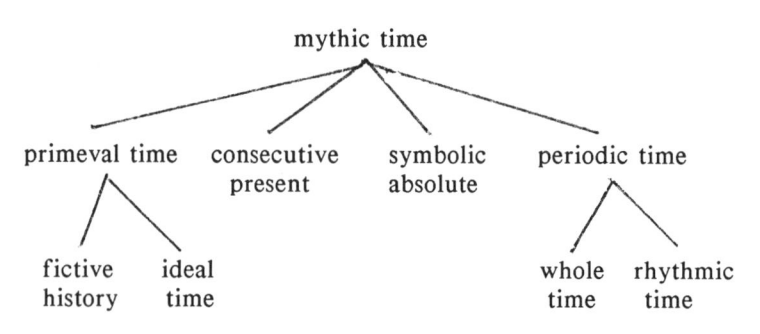

mythic time

primeval time   consecutive   symbolic   periodic time
                  present   absolute

fictive   ideal   whole   rhythmic
history   time   time   time

Time

Within a given myth, time takes place in all these ways at once. We hardly need think about them as we read, but noticing the differences can keep us from irrelevant commentaries and conclusions.
1. Primeval Time, *illud tempus*. The story all took place *then*. This time is both:
    a. Fictive History. A fiction experienced as truly in the historical past. If it did not make us feel a continuity with the past, it would not evoke the nostalgia for the glorious olden days of a traditional culture, which is an important part of the mythic experience.
    b. Ideal Time. The sense of a different kind of time, psychic or spiritual perhaps, in which the events are only said to have elapsed. This time is experienced with a true quality of *duration*, or unfolding, but it is discontinuous from history.
2. The Consecutive Present. As I read a story, almost any kind of story, I imagine it unfolding *now*, as I make my way through it. Or, to put it differently, within the imaginary world, I am *then*, but move along progressively as though each moment were a new time *now*.
3. The Symbolic Absolute. "Synchronic" time, without duration, in which the total pattern of events coheres as a statement always true. The significance of the statement is always implicit in each part; each part is shaped the way it is (as in a painting) because of its capacity to contribute to the whole. It is paradoxical, and perhaps perverse, to consider simultaneity a form of time. Literary critics sometimes speak, in fact, of spatial time to describe an overview of "time" laid out all at once. However, we become aware of the symbolic *as* absolute in its relation to the time through which it continually occurs. Furthermore, since it demonstrates aspects of life, it has to be thought of as *occurring*, and therefore as elapsing.
4. Periodic Time. Time in myth elapses with a clear sense of form, under the control of narrative motifs. Clearly, events constitute time rather than occurring in it. Time is therefore qualitative, felt to be shaping itself, freeing itself into the imitation of space. Lévi-Strauss writes, "it is as if music and mythology needed time only in order to deny it."[35] But the periodic is still felt to be a form of time. The word "periodic" has a double meaning:
    a. Whole Time. The period is a self-contained, discontinuous unit, an epoch, a statement. We follow out a story, pleasurably, with a sense of its growing self-fulfillment. Then it has become a complete world, with no beyond but "ever-after." The whole tends to become a microcosm, drawing on a sense of the symbolic absolute, so that its whole little world conveys something about the whole world-at-large in regard to its wholeness.
    b. Rhythmic Time. Formed time occurs periodically, through recurrence. Myths recur, motifs recur, and there are motifs of recurrence. Repetitive events progress in the same "place," carrying the present with them. Periods of time overlap, therefore, rather than succeed one another. In what is called "incremental repetition," a form repeats itself with variations that lead up to a climax, like the bird's three songs (the

The Qualitative World: Its Form

same) and gifts (appropriately varied) in "The Juniper Tree", or, in the nursery tale, the wolf's huffing and puffing first on the hut of straw, then the cottage of sticks, and finally the impregnable house of bourgeois brick. In such a series, each event implies the other two and therefore contains them, so that all three can be said to exist at all three stages of time. The idea of straw or sticks or brick is contained in the other two. But also, such sequences give the sense of a necessary limit that can be reached only through stages, so that the internal rhythm of the story is needed in order to produce the whole. The form, in other words, is like the incantation of a spell. Naturally, the climactic rhythm makes the most clearly self-fulfilling form.

<u>The Experience of Infinity</u>

When we think about linear space, we expect infinity to be an endless extent of constant places or a straight line with always more and more ahead and more and more behind.

<--->

But mythic infinity is always here. Similarly, all mythic time is now, not an endless sequence of passing moments, and it is, therefore, all eternal. From Creation to Last Judgment, time is a circle, and the circle is only an expanded dot. To the native of the Trobriand Islands,

> climax in history is abominable, a denial of all good, since it would imply not only the presence of change, but also that change increases the good; but to him value lies in sameness, in repeated pattern, in the incorporation of all time within the same point. What is good in life is exact identity with all past Trobriand experience, *and all mythical experience.*[36]

There is a fundamental truth about the way our psyche experiences life in this refusal to abandon the moving present. Western mystics and Eastern teachers of enlightenment have always emphasized the psychological fact that the mind fully absorbed in its present experience is a timeless mind, and that this timelessness is not merely distraction, a *lack* of time, but an enormously positive state with a characteristically absolute sense of reality. For this timeless mind, death and change cannot be cataclysmic, and anxiety, the fear of what is *going* to happen, does not drown the clarity or intensity of being. T.S. Eliot explores this nonlinear sense of timeless time, and its paradoxes, in the most celebrated modern poem of religious experience in English, *The Four Quartets*. Near the beginning of this complex quest through images of his family's and his culture's past, he affirms the eternal present around which the quest itself revolves:

> At the still point of the turning world. Neither flesh nor fleshless;
> Neither from nor towards; at the still point, there the dance is,
> But neither arrest nor movement. And do not call it fixity,
> Where past and future are gathered. Neither movement from nor towards,
> Neither ascent nor decline. Except for the point, the still point,
> There would be no dance, and there is only the dance.
> I can only say, *there* we have been: but I cannot say where.
> And I cannot say, how long, for that is to place it in time.[37]

Whorf the linguist provides a psychological interpretation of the theme:

> If we inspect consciousness we find no past, present, future, but a unity embracing complexity. EVERYTHING is in consciousness, and everything in consciousness IS, and is together.[38]

It is certainly one of the chief functions of both ritual and myth to affirm and reaffirm the roots of human time in presentness. Just as one enters completely an open-ended and unbounded precinct of space within a church or temple, similarly one enters into absolute time on a sabbath or any other holy days (or even secular *holi*days), in times of any commemorative ceremony, in meditation or in prayer. The bustle ceases; instead of straining to become, we let ourselves simply *be* and acknowledge the utter reality of our consciousness. In ritual and in the recital of myths, the distinction between the present and the past becomes irrelevant.

> He who recites or performs in the origin myth is thereby steeped in the sacred atmosphere in which these miraculous events took place.[39]

> What is involved is not a commemoration of mythical events but a reiteration of them. [Then] one is no longer living in chronological time, but in primordial Time, the Time when the event *first took place*.[40]

One starts out feeling the specialness of *time then*, but the separation dissolves until it is *now* that is special and being is itself the all.

In recreating primeval time through the play of imagination, myth becomes, as the German novelist Thomas Mann has written similarly, "a making present of the past."

The Qualitative World: Its Form

> For life in the myth, life, so to speak, in quotations, is a kind of celebration, ... it becomes a feast.

And a "feast is an abrogation of time, an event, a solemn narrative being played out conformably to an immemorial pattern . . ."[41] At the time Mann composed these phrases, for a lecture on Sigmund Freud, he was at work on one of the major works of modern mythic fiction, *Joseph and his Brothers*. At the beginning of this massive novel, Mann undertakes a quest for the source of life, probing backwards and deeper into time to little avail.

> For the deeper we sound, the further down into the lower world of the past we probe and press, the more do we find that the earliest foundations of humanity, its history and culture, reveal themselves unfathomable.[42]

Then he locates his source not in history but in a myth which achieves "the dissolution of time in mystery."[43] Here *mystery* is a name for that substratum of life that eludes our linear logic and our linear languages with their limiting categories of past, present, and future.

> For the essence of life is presentness, and only in a mythical sense does its mystery appear in the time-forms of past and future.[44]

And this mystery

> is, always is, however much we may say it was. Thus speaks the myth, which is only the garment of the mystery.[45]

Then Mann proceeds to recreate one of the familiar legends of our tradition, out of the primeval aeons into a vividly present narrative.
    It is one of the paradoxes of myth, as it is of life, that this sense of timelessness must be sought and must be experienced through the passing sense of time and the unfolding processes of life. Eliot's quest involves him in this realization.

> Time past and time future
> Allow but a little consciousness.
> To be conscious is not to be in time
> But only in time can the moment in the rose-garden,
> The moment in the arbour where the rain beat,
> The moment in the draughty church at smokefall
> Be remembered; involved with past and future.
> Only through time time is conquered.[46]

The complex sense of mythic time, therefore, with its blend of the absolute and the passing, of the historical and the symbolic, provides a flexible and subtle tool with which human consciousness can be captured in its shifting aspects.

Transitional Time

Since the earliest stages of human life, undoubtedly, the flow of time has been parceled out into patterns of recurrent rituals, perhaps to make mere endurance more bearable but also to let one identify oneself with the progression of life by finding meaning in life's essential repetitiveness. There are (still with us) festivals of midwinter and of spring, celebrating a "death and rebirth" in the turning of the seasons, and there may be weekly sabbaths and daily prayers. In completely secular life we celebrate personal cycles of birthdays and anniversaries. In traditional cultures, stages of life are demarcated by transitional rituals (*rites de passage*, is the anthropological term, contributed by Arnold van Gennep), at birth, puberty, marriage, and death. The most important of these, for the study of myth, is the adolescent ritual of an initiation into the adult life of the society--which we know in the western religions as confirmation and Bar Mitzvah. The initiation ritual provides the central pattern of a symbolic death and rebirth around which most mythology revolves, as the initiate dies to his old identity so that he may be reborn into his new. Van Gennep showed that such rituals express in human action the rhythms of nature: "The universe itself is governed by a periodicity which has repercussions on human life, with stages and transitions, movements forward, and periods of relative inactivity."[47] Only the dramatic periods of transition have "meaning," therefore, and they are celebrated at set times which mark their specialness.

One reason why mythic time is discontinuous is that it exists similarly only in critical time, only that is, at these turning points of life which give it its form and clarify its nature. In an influential book called *The Hero*, Lord Raglan charted the typical hero's career into a series of episodes and features:

1. The hero's mother is a royal virgin;
2. His father is a king, and
3. Often a near relative of his mother, but
4. The circumstances of his conception are unusual and
5. He is also reputed to be the son of a god.
6. At birth an attempt is made, usually by his father or his maternal grandfather, to kill him, but
7. He is spirited away, and
8. Reared by foster parents in a far country.
9. We are told nothing of his childhood, but
10. On reaching manhood he returns or goes to his future kingdom.
11. After a victory over the king and/or a giant, dragon, or wild beast,
12. He marries a princess, often the daughter of his predecessor, and

The Qualitative World: Its Form

    13. Becomes king.
    14. For a time he reigns uneventfully, and
    15. Prescribes laws, but
    16. Later he loses favour with the gods and/or his subjects, and
    17. Is driven from the throne and city, after which
    18. He meets with a mysterious death,
    19. Often at the top of a hill.
    20. His children, if any, do not succeed him.
    21. His body is not buried, but nevertheless
    22. He has one or more holy sepulchres.[48]

The hero exists only to have been born in an extraordinary manner, to make his nature known in childhood (Arthur drawing his sword Excalibur from the stone), to meet his monster, to claim his bride, to meet or to transcend death. There is not, as there is for us linear folk, any time between. It is "uneventful" (see items 9, 14), and in narrative terms that means nonexistent. Time for the hero only turns, it does not pass. His whole existence is a death and rebirth, a continual miracle which he repeats in a cycle of such cycles, like the church calendar. He expresses a rhythm of life that is always true, so he no more belongs in time than any other kind of symbol does, a flag or a cross or a uniform, except that they are visual and static images, whereas rhythm is dynamic, a process, and it must unfold. Like any other kind of rhythm, however, it creates a time of its own in the hollows of its rise and fall.

CHAPTER FIVE

THE QUALITATIVE WORLD: ITS OPERATION

*From the conception the increase,
From the increase the swelling,
From the swelling the thought,
From the thought the remembrance,
From the remembrance the desire.
. . . .
The word became fruitful . . .*
     --Maori creation chant

3. CAUSATION

Magical Cause

   The first axiom of linear causation is that everything has a specific cause within the same order of reality. Parents produce children, ideas beget ideas, forces clash with forces to produce impact, wishes lead to disappointments, you must sow if you will reap, and so forth. The second axiom is that all events make up an unending sequence of events begetting events: every effect is itself a cause of other events. Every babe a potential parent in its turn. The third is that physical causes precede any others; any feelings, ideas, or behavior seem less strange when they are rooted in matter. And, of course, there is "nothing can be made out of nothing," although Shakespeare's *King Lear* disposed of that one rather nicely, and "what is done cannot be undone," which is, in fact substantiated by *Macbeth* as a psychological truth.
   In myth, as we have seen, to deprive events of their strangeness is to deny them their reality. The most important kinds of mythic cause are magic and miracle. Magic is performed by a specialist with a technique and often with appropriate equipment; it is a technology of nonlinear cause. The magician, no less than the physicist, may have had decades of training, either by a predecessor or by the supernatural forces that preside over his field of operation. He works with particular animals, objects, garments, verbal formulas (spells), and other symbols--all of which are not what they seem and which are, therefore, carriers of nonlinearity. Often they show up of their own accord as special human beings need them. What distinguishes magical technology from the scientific variety is that, typically, magic brings forth its effects by a qualitative transference rather than by physical force. You bind your victim and your voodoo doll with a common nature, so that what you perform to the identity of one will transfer to the identity of the other. Metaphor, it has

The Qualitative World: Its Operation

been said, is itself a form of magic, and magic a form of metaphor. They are both, that is to say, forms of qualitative logic.[1]

The miracle is super-magic, because it needs no intervening cause of either linear or nonlinear form between the wish and the fulfillment. Even the magician does something to get what he wants. When we are surprised to get what we want without effort, however, we say it is a miracle. The commands of deity also strike us as miraculous. When I turn on the light switch, a stream of electrons is transmitted along a continuity of wires, leading to a brilliant glow at the end, but when the Old Testament God says "Let there be light," there *is* light, by God. His words are His wish and there seems to be no time and no cause between His realization of a lack and its fulfillment. The emphasis is on *total* power, on the mystery (in Marcel's sense) of power itself.[2] Thus the miracle strikes us properly with awe. It makes a revelation about the universe that is humbling to our own capacities, speaking forth the overwhelming forces amidst which our little linear lives unfold. The Hindu gods are often surprised by their own miraculous powers, which simply play out, spontaneously, their own nature. Thus Brahma in a rage creates the god of anger without any intention to do so or any forethought; transported in a flash of sexual desire, he finds Love standing before his eyes.

In terms of mythic language, the most important aspect of both miracle and magic is simply that they do break drastically the linear sequence of causality. In doing so, they break down our familiar sense of a consistently objective world and let another order of reality break *through*. Where it comes from is not very far.

As we encounter them in myth, magic and miracle are simply nonlinear occurrence seen--with surprise--from linear expectations. In the presence of the extraordinary and the strange, we are given notice, first of all, that usual assumptions are no longer working. We are transported instantly across boundaries of the linear world, out of familiar time and cause into an order of events that has its own spontaneous coherence and its own efficacy. In this process of imagination, consciousness expands to the proportions of the magic. *We* are acted upon magically, but, of course, it is our own minds that are the magicians, our own minds discovering their own natural vitality. Cassirer makes a similar point:

> Magic is a dramatic expression of human consciousness feeling its own power. It is an overestimation in practical terms, we might wish to insist, but still a proud exploration of human prerogatives. [3]

The source of the "other world" is our own nature, or, at least, our subjective nature. Through the logic of magic, in the state of wonder, mind liberates itself from the train-tracks of common sense and the disillusionment of alleged maturity. It comes into its own, following its own subjective sense of order with its boundless (and therefore undivided) energy. The impact of this process is a sense of life's integrity, an ap-

The Foregone Conclusion

In mythic logic, what looks like cause is more subtly something else. Events may be involved in each other with qualitative links that reflect each other's features. In "The Juniper Tree," the millstone that kills the stepmother is her own burden of guilt. Cause is not simply what makes later events happen but what substantiates them or gives them a background out of which to emerge.[4] If a hero like Oedipus is abandoned to die in infancy, that is so he can survive his murder and return astonishingly to his people as a visitation from the beyond. The point is exactly to break linear sequence and introduce the heroic order. Thus, cause may be not what makes events happen but what makes them possible. To put it the other way around, "effect" may be interpretations of their causes, bringing out their implications.

In creation myths, the perfect nonlinear order is interrupted to make room for the world as we know it. The specific causes, therefore, evoke familiar qualities of life.

> In the beginning of days Wulbari and man lived close together and Wulbari lay on top of Mother Earth, Asase Ya. Thus it happened that, as there was so little space to move about in, man annoyed the divinity, who in disgust went away and rose up to the present place where one can admire him but not reach him.
> He was annoyed for a number of reasons. An old woman, while making her *fufu* outside her hut, kept on knocking Wulbari with her pestle. This hurt him and, as she persisted, he was forced to go higher out of her reach. Besides, the smoke of the cooking fires got into his eyes so that he had to go farther away.
> According to others, however, Wulbari, being so close to men, made a convenient sort of towel, and the people used to wipe their dirty fingers on him. This naturally annoyed him. Yet this was not so bad a grievance as that which caused We, the Wulbari of the Kassena people, to remove himself out of the reach of man. He did so because an old woman, anxious to make a good soup, used to cut off a bit of him at each mealtime, and We, being pained at this treatment, went higher.[5]

In order to live, man gets himself into problematic situations, making his mark at the expense of the world. Here his simple peskiness alienates him from God, because it consists of conscious intentions to make his own lot easier.

The process of thinking in motifs, by which mythic narratives develop, itself prevents linear movement. Just as they control time and

The Qualitative World: Its Operation

space with their clear outlines, motifs take on patterns of relationship among themselves that preclude ordinary cause. In the three-step movements of "The Juniper Tree," the death of the stepmother results from the momentum gained in the climactic build-up, and it results from her own crazed spirit, for she runs out to her doom to escape the anguish building up in her as her daughter and husband receive their rewards. And this accumulation reflects in reverse the good mother's process of dying through her fruition--dying, in fact *of delight*--as the juniper tree ripens through the year; the second mother must be wicked as the mirror-image of the first.

Motifs are units of imaginary experience, cells that link to one another as their content calls up association with other cells.[6] By analogy with modern design, we can think of them as *modular*, coming in preset forms that combine in varying ways to make up larger structures for different situations. Or, in another image, we can think of the process of image-thinking as a game of dominoes. Each piece, or "tile," overlays one of its values on the next, so that a unique pattern evolves through continual transitions, each move directing the next. As such fairly stable units, joined together and used again and again, the motifs can be static, of course, but when mythic imagination uses them spontaneously and speaks their language fluently, they can be as easily dynamic and alive with feeling. Being made out of the malleable stuff of imagination, unlike dominoes, they can reflect the nature of the mind imagining. Life comes to them in a number of ways:

--They seem to provide unending possibilities for variation, especially from one culture to another.[7]

--They can combine with each other in different ways.

--They become absorbed into the main flow of the narrative.

--Most importantly, they can be realized, or imagined, with different degrees and qualities and nuances of feeling.

In motifs events come packaged, as it were, and this fact sets clear limits on the range of motivations or deliberate actions that can cause events. A certain start requires a certain finish, a build-up requires a climax, and practical reasons will not easily fit preset rhythms. The occurrence of one incident immediately implies a whole set of other incidents that go along with it. If a maiden is beset with a dragon, certainly a wandering hero will come to save her, and if he saves her, he is a little more than likely to marry her. If a god seduces a girl, their child will kill a monster or achieve a great quest.[8] It is a foregone conclusion that the hero will be heroic. It is true, he undergoes a test of his capacities, but the test really *manifests* his nature as a hero; it does not present a linear challenge that can be answered "yes" or "no," "pass" or "fail." He is born miraculously a hero, he reveals himself heroically in childhood, he slays heroic, weds heroic, and either dies heroic or ascends, most heroically of all, directly to the skies. He has magic weapons or supernatural helpers, but they do not cause his success as instruments in themselves. They can be only his, and that is because they, again, manifest his nature as the hero. They are symbolic extensions of his own magical--heroic--being.

Causation

Our sense of time grows in good measure from our sense of cause. What results must come after; consequence implies subsequence. But where there is a foregone conclusion, we have the curious situation of result preceding cause on the level of logic. The virgin's sacrifice to a dragon is controlled by the fact that she is destined to "later" marry a hero. Which "fact" comes first? Linear time is at any rate dissolved into the circularity of the pattern of *apparent* cause, which is really not "cause" at all.[9]

There is as little room for suspense as for linear cause in the principle of the "foregone conclusion." When adversity strikes, one can tell immediately in which cases it will turn into a blessing; bad happens so that it *can* turn good. When a hero begins in prosperity, you know he must be tested by tribulation; the cause of his joy is, then, his suffering to come. Yet, in spite of this circular logic with its evident predictability, tension builds up rhythmically and imagination is gratified emotionally as it takes part in the unfolding of events, letting the coherent shapes of feelings work out their natural course.

Traps of Commitment

There is a class of plot motifs that are especially provocative in the way they structure experience and limit cause. They propose some form of personal commitment, such as an oath or a promise, that absolutely requires an ironical conclusion, so that the end turns the linear intention completely inside out. The characters look straight ahead with ordinary human logic only to find they have made their lives impossible. One common form, familiar in folk tales, is the *wish trap*. A character gets what he wished for but has to suffer implications of the wish itself that he would not have foreseen. One wishes for eternal life, then has to linger on forever in a grotesquely debilitated body with a senile mind. Jonathan Swift uses this traditional motif in *Gulliver's Travels*, extending it to an entire nation trapped in endless senility.

The reverse of this pattern is the *curse trap*, in which one's rage or righteousness rebounds upon oneself. As king, Oedipus curses the murderer of his predecessor with promise of dire punishment, only to find that he alone is the culprit. In the *blasphemous vaunt*, one boasts of one's presumed superiority over the gods and is stricken to a subhuman condition. In Greek myth, this is the specialty of women. Arachne boasts that she can weave better than Athene, and she is turned into a spider to weave forever after. Cassiopeia says she is more beautiful than the sea-nymphs, and her daughter must be sacrificed to a monster from the sea that is sent to plague their land. (Perseus rescues the girl, Andromeda, and marries her.) Niobe asserts that she and her fourteen children are worthier of worship than Latona and her two children Diana and Apollo, so she must lose her entire family, then turn to stone in her grief.

Familiar also are the trap structures of the vow and the extremely important taboo. In the *vow trap*, Jephtha (of the Old Testament) swears that, if he wins his battle, he will sacrifice to God the first creature

The Qualitative World: Its Operation

whom he meets on his return home, then finds he must sacrifice his beloved daughter. A medieval English play of Abraham and Isaac has Abraham trick himself into a similar promise.

> Ah, Lord God, almighty King,
> What manner beast will make thee most fain?
> If I had thereof very [*true*] knowing,
> It should be done with all my main
> Full soon anon.[10]

The naivete is ironic, and the irony is pathetic.

The *taboo*, of course, must always be broken.[11] It is a temptation that brings out humanity's inevitable curiosity, in Adam and Eve's apple or in Pandora's box. The Prince in Grimm's tale "Faithful John," is left with his dead father's command that he not enter one special room, and there he finds a portrait of the beautiful bride whom he *must* seek out. In full nonlinear fashion, the hero's destiny, and therefore his nature *as a hero*, is usually made possible by his violation of the law. This implication of the motif was recognized by the Christian doctrine of *felix culpa*, the "Fortunate Fall": if Adam had not fallen, mankind could not have been saved.

In a variation of the taboo paradox, the *trap of control*, a parent must fail to inhibit the heroic child. The future Buddha's father will not let him see signs of old age, illness, death, or the life of monks. Life breaks in, the boy sees all; and leaves his father's palace on his great spiritual quest. Parzival's mother tries to protect her son, in a forest retreat, from seeing knights, since knighthood had taken her husband's life. A band arrives and the naive child is off to adventure, breaking his mother's heart. A final motif in this group of inverted commitments is the *oracle* or *prophecy resisted*, and the most famous illustration is again Oedipus. The hero cannot help but try to block the prophecy that he will kill his father and marry his mother; however it is precisely his effort to prevent the prophecy that in fact fulfills it, playing him into the trap of his destiny. The disaster of Oedipus does not grow from a fortuitous "error of judgment," a flawed character trait (royal pride), or an impetuous action (forcing a chariot off the road)--as conventional Aristotelian interpretations usually have it. The disaster is simply--and terribly--a structure unfolding, an "infernal machine"[12] that is all too human.

The taboo works by commandment and gives the hero an idea he cannot resist; often the idea is not important in itself, only the intolerable test of blind obedience. The oracle, on the other hand, works by instilling fear and throws the hero into anxiety. Both trap the mind in its own consciousness, then leave it all the more poignantly caught in its consciousness of the trap itself. A command is a challenge and therefore a test. Ordinary persons nicely do as they are told, demonstrating thereby what a hero is not. In an interesting inversion of the Orpheus theme, Sisyphus is said to have cheated death by having his wife leave his body unburied; thus he had to come back to punish her. As Albert Camus tells the tale, Sisyphus was testing his wife's love by reverse psychology.

He ordered her to cast his unburied body into the middle of the public square. Sisyphus woke up in the underworld. And there, annoyed by an obedience so contrary to human love, he obtained from Pluto permission to return to earth in order to chastise his wife. But when he has seen again the face of this world, enjoyed water and sun, warm stones and the sea, he no longer wanted to go back to the infernal darkness.[13]

Sisyphus' wife, therefore, failed his test by obeying him.

All of these motifs are closed structures of action, in which cause is predetermined by the given formula. It is clearly *the nonlinear form* in itself which communicates to us. Each of them dramatizes life as a game with self-defeating rules to play by. The players are limited by their situation within the structure, but that should be no surprise, for surely mortality is fraught with limits. Consciousness is not merely an open window to the world, but the organ of an organism built of living sensitivities. Consciousness, moreover, is in itself a predicament. It is a tool that hammers the hand, a telescope that brings the eye closer; it is a mirror at least as truly as it is a window. All the traps of commitment prove the unsuspected substantiality of consciousness. It is not only a medium in which we live, but also obstacle and burden, support and goal. It is structure and mechanism that we can know only in its own terms.

In many of these "traps," a person's word turns out to have a magically binding force (as it does in our lives when we ritually swear an oath or just give somebody "our word"). In the magnificent and enormous Hindu epic *The Mahabharata*, the five Pandava princes, joint heroes of the main plot, are living in disguise as beggars when one of them, Arjuna, wins a princess, Draupadi, in an archery contest. When they return to their hut, they call their mother to see what prize they have obtained that day. Before she sees them, she replies, as a good mother should, "Now you share that together!"[14] --and Draupadi becomes the wife of all five. "The word of a guru is Law, and of all gurus the mother is the first."[15] Because she is the mother, her word is not *just* a word, it has substance, it is numinous. Her motherhood has substance and her word is an extension of that utter reality. As in all word magic, including the laws of the land as well as popular superstition--as well as the Word of the Creator, language is absolute. It is as real as any thing.

In the traditional cultures without writing, in which myths were born and also came of age, thinking through motifs provided a natural method for the elaboration of tales and for their transmission through the ages.[16] The motif-language is not just a kind of shorthand or memory technique, however, for the qualitative nature of these "packaged actions" allows them to express consciousness directly while capturing views of concentrated experience.

Nonlinear causation, in fact, reflects a kind of logic within the nature of our feelings. We have often seen love and hatred turn into each other. Rage expended leads to clearer insight. In despair, we wish to die, but having cried our tears, we find calm again and perhaps a new

The Qualitative World: Its Operation

energy emerging. As tragic myth and drama most frequently demonstrate, pride in our powers leads not only to a fall but to humiliation. And humiliation endured passes to humility, with surer sense of strength in apparent weakness. Western and Eastern religions alike are based upon such psychological patterns, as we saw in the discussion of "Nonlinear values." Christianity is built of paradoxes like "the first shall be last" and death is the way to life. Hindus and Buddhists stress the logic of detachment: power comes not as the linear mind expects it, through accumulation, but through giving up our dubious conviction of what we need.

4. IDENTITY

Characterization

Everyone knows that myth personifies nature and forces in life, but the word suggests merely a rhetorical figure of speech unless we re-imagine the process as person-ifying (or of *personing*) nature. Through its stories about heroes, their helpers, their enemies, and their gods, myth brings forth the sense of living presence in the world and the dynamic quality of forces within or among ourselves. The primary form of image in myth is, therefore, character. Not character, of course, in the sense that we are used to it in modern literature--as the illusion of a real person. In myth character clearly *is* a kind of image, presenting us with *person*-like beings (humanoid conceptions) who are meant to be imagined, who can exist only as they are imagined. By imagining them we bring them to a kind of life, a life where they serve us in a way they could not if they were more like us than they are. By retaining both the elasticity and the clarity of imagination, they express all the better the nature of mind imagining. The schematic, or simplifying, nature of mythic characterization emphasizes specific features of life at the expense of one kind of truthfulness but it still permits very definite sensitivity to life's essential quality of having identity.

Character is primarily important, therefore, because it gives the story-images their full sense of *presence*, life's being in itself *as self*, being *here*. And among characters we sense the poised tensions that give life its vitality. Mythic characters assert notably a charisma, which occurs in both positive and negative, attractive and repellent, forms. This is the foundation of their significance, because of the relationship it demands from us, a kind of commitment we make if we participate in the story through the innocence of imagination. Knowing life through the story is a matter of *being with a self*, of *being set before an other*. This charisma is one aspect of the *charm* of myth, the very power which entices us away from logic.

A good example of the power that mythic "personification" exerts is the use of the word "man" in its generic reference to *humanity*: the family of *man*, *man* finds *his* nature through *his* mind, and so forth. Identifying the species with the same word we use for the male human certainly enhances male prestige; however, the generic meaning may have come first and may have expressed mankind's *mental* nature.[17] If this is so, the sexist drift occurs in calling males *men* rather than the other way around. In any case, the word continues to posses a peculiar *mythic* vitality that a more abstract and fair-minded substitute is not likely to have. Unlike "*the* horse" or "*the* dog," the word "man" characterizes being human as being a self, with an individual presence but a shared identity. Neutral words like "humanity" or "people" look at us in sum from the outside, impersonally. "Man" conveys our being from within, with a concrete dramatic feeling, embodied. As myth, it expresses something of the nature of *being* human. We may well feel that that advantage is not too much to sacrifice on behalf of social justice, but we should be aware perhaps that the cultural question is not only one of gender power.

Levels of Identity

In linear terms, I am the person I am, you are a separate person; we have parallel identities, similarly human and equally real, while remaining distinct and unique at the same time. I perceive you and you go on perceiving me back. I go my way and forget about you; you go your way, forgetting about me. All of us have different identities, with different personalities and varying qualities of consciousness. But all of us have the *same kind* of identity.

Although I may go through many changes in my life, and though I forget much that happens to me, I remain the same person that I always was. I try to imagine a time when "I" will cease to be, and although I cannot do that (my mind can find no "time" or "space" in which not to be), I easily imagine my same self up to the point of departure. Consciousness has run continuously through my life (self as time as space), with an indescribable but recognizable sense of being a person. At the center of my consciousness (omphalic spatialization), I look back in time (visual linearity) and anticipate a future, and I talk back and forth with all of you under the firm unthought conviction that you are listening. If you speak and I respond, I assume it is your words I am hearing, your thoughts I am digesting, and your minds I am trying to reach.

In the subjective world that I carry with me, however, I might well be talking to myself when I address my words to you, while I convince myself of something that I hope is true, or try to amuse myself, or scold myself for faults that are more obvious in your derelictions. Our conversation goes on and on while I am locked in a dramatic struggle with an image composed partly of my sense of you and partly of some aspect of me, hovering unseen and unacknowledged in the mythic space between us. And heaven knows who you are talking to.[18]

Such a mythic antagonist as I then am dealing with has a different kind of identity from my self or your self as a person. "He" is me and "he" isn't, he is there and he isn't. His being is tenuous and I cannot get rid of him. In dreams and myths and literature, we deal with person-images who have different kinds of identity from us as people. Whatever else we may want to affirm about such an existence will be at least a nonlinear affirmation.

In plays and novels, we relate differently to characters who are created of a realistic mold, complete with personal ambiguities, and those who are more clearly symbolic in both their function and their style. This second kind do not exist in quite the same manner, although they may be equally important and imaginatively valid. Their ontology, or existence, depends upon their stylization. Within a myth or dream or work of literature, "characters" may also relate to one another in a variety of ways, with different qualities of being. One important way to see the whole symbolic world in each instance is to see it as a network of such interrelations.

In "The Juniper Tree," the little boy has a more fundamental kind of existence than his pair of mothers, the one loving and sacrificial, the other monstrously malign, but the two seeming like the halves of one whole. When the boy becomes a bird, he enters a new realm of being-- not just a biological change in species but a change in symbolic status. In fact, we cannot quite say that he *becomes* the bird. The bird *is* a bird, and it is a special order of animal-being, a bird that can sing symbolic songs and can carry a millstone in mid-air until he drops it with more accuracy than a bombardier. He has a spiritual or psychic existence *and* he is materialized in the imagination as a bird. Yet, we know it somehow *is* the boy too, and to the boy it will return. When the boy is reborn, he, exists now, in a way, on a different plane than he did originally, because he has incorporated the bird-stage into his being. Throughout the tale, we experience the mysterious unstated relation between the child's existence and that of the tree. The tree feels like a character also with a hovering presence. It exists as a being of its own order while permeating all. An embodiment of the rhythm of nature and an image of spreading growth, of death and renewal, it seems timeless with protective strength, unifying the mother and the child in its gradual fruition.

Although the style of characterization in myth and mythic literature is usually very simple, repetitive, and "unrealistic," it still therefore expresses strong implications about the nature of human identity. Because of its conventional flatness, it conveys implications about our general nature rather than portraying particular case studies. And though its outlines may be simple, they can be drawn with exquisite sensitivity, depending on the storyteller's skill, a sensitivity that evokes appropriately the qualities of consciousness all people share. Thus hero tales can always be seen as explorations of the nature of identity.[19] They demonstrate and they analyze what it is to be a self--not a personality (in the sense of the rounded product we see, from outside, in a film or a novel) but a process of experience, reflecting its own being from within.

The Self Dispersed

Freud's view of dreams, and after him the dominant view of modern psychology, rests upon the premise that everything within the

Identity

NONLINEAR IDENTITY: *the human bird.* (above left) **Eagle-human divinity** *pollinating sacred tree. Assyrian wall panel from Palace of Ashurnasinapal, 9th century BC.* (above right) **Garuda**, *bird-person vehicle of Hindu god Vishnu, shown here as winged youth. India 11th or 12th century.* (below) **Raven Rattle.** *Tlingit Indian, Northwest Coast. On the back of a hawk, a man extends his tongue into a raven's beak. According to one interpretation, a shaman is receiving his power from the raven-deity; according to another, Raven is stealing a shaman's art by tearing out his tongue, a parallel to Prometheus stealing fire from the gods.*

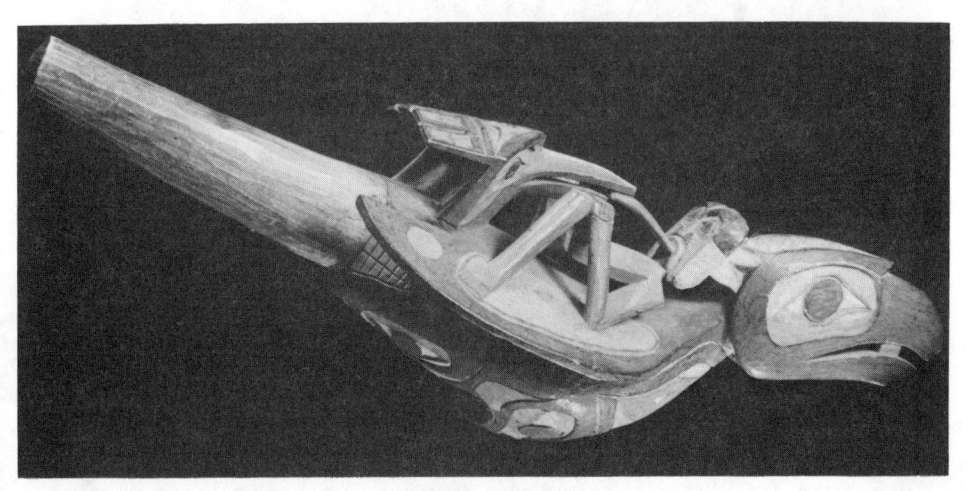

The Qualitative World: Its Operation

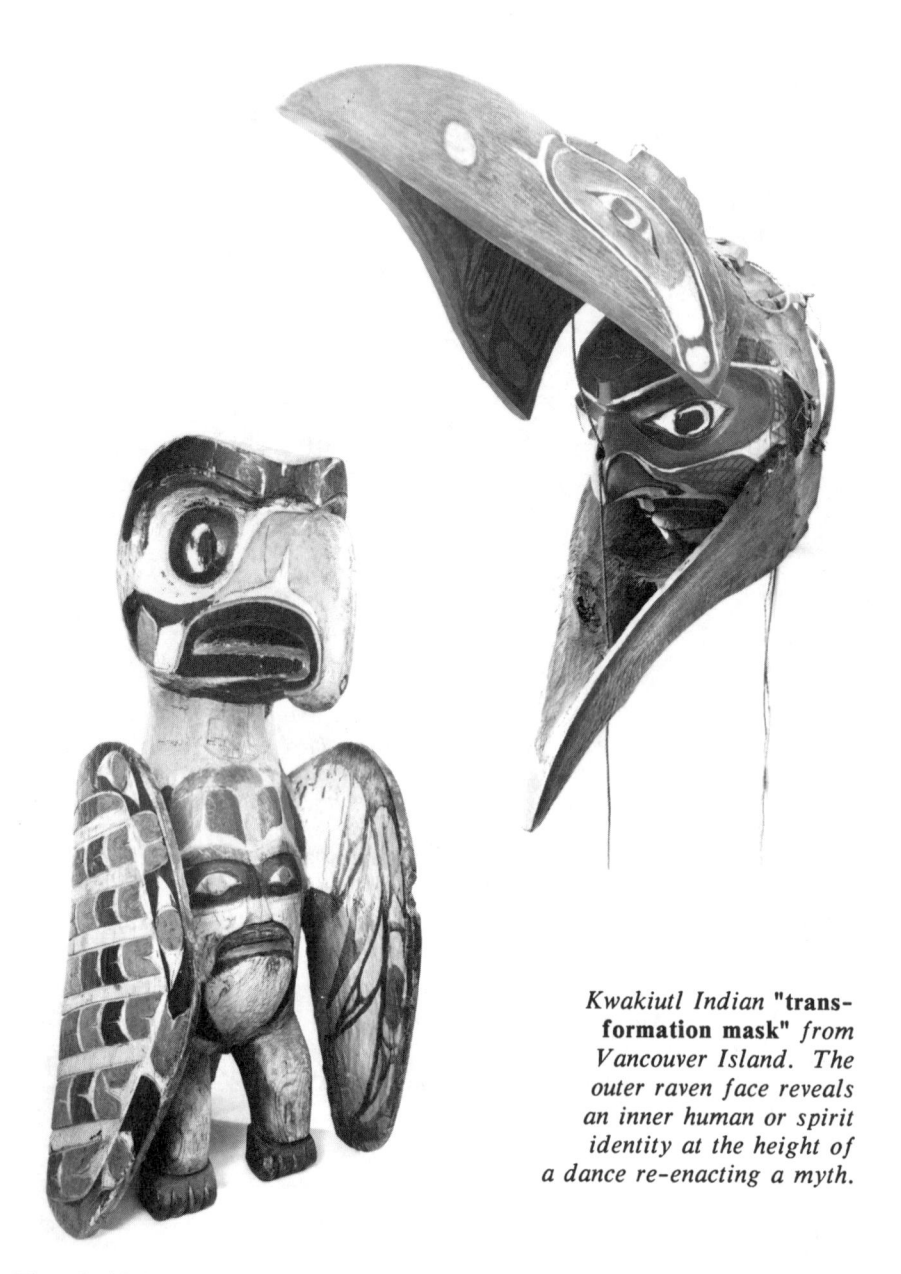

Kwakiutl Indian "**transformation mask**" *from Vancouver Island. The outer raven face reveals an inner human or spirit identity at the height of a dance re-enacting a myth.*

Thunderbird, *whose wings create the thunder, with a simultaneous human identity. Haida Indian carving.*

Identity

world of one's dreams expresses aspects of one's own largely unconscious experience. If I have a dream in which you seem to appear, the image of "you" figures forth an aspect of me. It focuses the feelings I have about you that is first of all a feeling I have about myself. "Every dream deals with the dreamer himself. Dreams are completely egoistic."[20] The dream world is entirely *endopsychic*, within the psyche of the self.

The same principle applies to myth. It is the factor that controls the arrangement of identity, for it distributes among the individual figures aspects of consciousness. "The whole dream," writes Jung, "takes place in the individual's own psyche."[21] As a result, just as all the "persons" in my dream are me, so all the persons of the myth refer to one unifying self; and if they are all one, it follows that they are all each other as well. In the myth of a hero, "at a pinch, all the characters are interchangeable."[22] A single sense of self permeates them all and encloses them. In "the world of mythical imagery," Frye writes, "everything is potentially identified with everything else, as though it were all inside a single infinite body."[23] Cassirer stresses the more basic feature of mythic logic which underlies this principle: in myth, any whole and its parts are always interchangeable.[24] That is because their truth lies in their qualities and not in their identities.

Since all the figures within a myth are aspects of the self, the whole myth adds up to the representative human personality. Consciousness itself is dynamic, full of active tendencies that we often find in conflict with one another, as though they were indeed separate persons. "Every split-off portion of libido [by which word Jung means psychic energy in general, not as Freud uses it, specifically sexual energy], every complex, has or is a (fragmentary) personality."[25] Fears struggle to retain our desires, desires for different kinds of fulfillment clash against each other, thoughts and feelings lock in endless debate. In an important way, myth is analytical even though it is not intellectual, for within a myth consciousness is analyzed, broken down into elements that exert themselves in recurrent patterns of tension. In the deeper levels of our minds, the "parts" are interfused. The sources of fear and desire, of strength and vulnerability, of controlled thought and spontaneous feeling are truly all aspects of one another. Yet they continue to play out the story which is the drama of life: of life facing death, of the person bound within society, of dignity resisting humiliation, of coherence restraining violence, of suffering under power, and of all such fundamental conflicts in which we must work out our own identities personally and together.

The principle of endopsychic identity explains with a flash of light why the characters of myth and folktale so often seem "unrealistic," artificially good or bad or naively single-minded and unchanging. They are single parts that merge into a whole. The myth itself is the realistic personality, characterized by tension, paradox, and the possibility of growth. Through the center of the tale moves the character of the hero, dramatizing the self. Whether or not we find him admirable or magnificent, he is "hero" simply because he is the unifying focus to whom the other parts belong. They embody his feelings and his consciousness. Whoever imagines the myth--hearing, reading, or enacting it--experiences

The Qualitative World: Its Operation

the whole as the expression of his or her self through the hero. The lovely and sublimely loving mother who dies in childbirth and the greedy, spiteful, and vicious stepmother who replaces her are extreme directions of the same mothering source of life.[26] Tree and bird are two aspects of consciousness itself as a living force. The one image is characterized qualitatively by its rootedness and stable sense of continuity, the other by its freedom and resilience and by the power of its vision.

Ambiguous Identity

In the characterization of myth, identity is often fluid. The epitome of this factor is the character-motif the "shapeshifter," like the Greek god Proteus, who assumes the form of anything he can think of in order to elude the grasp of the hero's will. His underlying identity does remain constant, since he is always Proteus, but as he takes on the body of now a serpent, of now a lion, of now the very wind, the hero must cope with what *they* are. In the motif of *metamorphosis*, much loved by the Greeks, a person turns into a flower, a bird, a river, losing his human reality entirely, a person whose experience is so extreme that it carries him back spontaneously into a primordial state of nature. In some instances, a hero achieves a transcendent immortality through such a change when he is transposed to the stars. When a person becomes trapped in a lower form of life, the quality of the change is partly a sense of paralysis. It is as though human consciousness comes suddenly up against its dependence on dumb flesh; or, unable to follow its slightest impulse, it is trapped into being *merely* conscious. At the same time, however, it has produced some feature of nature that is strangely wonderful simply for being itself.

Ovid, the great Roman poet of the *Metamorphoses*, is particularly dramatic when he captures the weird pathos of this moment. He seems to be repeatedly stricken by the strangeness of nature, the unfeasibility of our human place in it. After crossing a god or a goddess, his Callisto finds herself a bear, Arachne a spider, Arethusa a spring, Daphne a laurel tree, Io a young cow. A boy who insults Ceres in her grief becomes a newt. The maiden Echo, her love scorned by Narcissus, wastes away into a mere voice. (She has already been punished for chattering by being restricted to speak in only the last words of what other people say.)

> Yet he
> Ran from her, crying, "No, you must not touch--
> Go, take your hands away, may I be dead
> Before you throw your fearful chains around me."
> "O fearful chains around me," Echo said,
> And then no more. So she was turned away
> To hide her face, her lips, her guilt among the trees,
> Even their leaves, to haunt caves of the forest,
> To feed her love on melancholy sorrow
> Which, sleepless, turned her body to a shade,
> First pale and wrinkled, then a sheet of air,
> Then bones, which some say turned to thin worn rocks;

Identity

And last her voice remained. Vanished in forest,
Far from her usual walks on hills and valleys,
She's heard by all who call; her voice has life.[27]

In both African and American Indian myth, many primordial figures are at the same time animals and persons. In some contexts they have to be imagined as the one, in some as the other, but although we cannot "see" them as both at once, we have to understand that such they are. In them, the identity of animal and human is fully one: man is fused in nature, and nature's creatures are as full of consciousness as we. In his actual vision, Black Elk sees the Powers of the World both as horses and as old men, and he finds that they partake of his own identity.[28] The Winnebago Indians tell that all living things were at first neutral. They "could at will transform themselves into human beings or spirit-animals." At one time, they chose to become fixed in one state or the other.

> That accordingly happened and since then animals have remained animals and human beings human beings, except that there are a few human beings who still possess the power of transforming themselves, for short periods of time, into animals.[29]

This ambiguous animal-human status is particularly characteristic of the hero motif known as Trickster, often an animal, such as Coyote among the Navaho, Raven in the Northwest, Hare or Spider in Africa. He is in all cases a figure conspicuous for the nonlinear paradoxes of his character.

> Trickster is at one and the same time creator and destroyer, giver and negator, he who dupes others and who is always duped himself. He wills nothing consciously. At all times he is constrained to behave as he does from impulses over which he has no control. He knows neither good nor evil yet he is responsible for both. He possesses no values, moral or social, is at the mercy of his passions and appetites, yet through his actions all values come into being.[30]

In one Trickster tale, from the Tsimshian Indians, Raven appears as a young man "bright as a fire" in the place of a dead youth whose parents would not cease mourning. After a time, he becomes insatiably hungry (from eating scabs), so that his father has to send him away in order to preserve the tribe's provisions. He sends him forth specifically in the condition of a man-bird, with a "raven-blanket" to mark the transition:

> Before despatching him he addresses him saying, "My dear son, I am sending you away inland to the other side of the ocean." Then he gives him a small round stone, a raven-blanket and a dried sea-lion bladder filled with all kinds of

The Qualitative World: Its Operation

berries. Again he speaks to him, "my son, when you fly across the ocean (with this raven-blanket around you) and you feel weary, drop this stone and you shall find rest on it. When you reach the mainland scatter the various kinds of fruit all over the land; and also scatter the salmon roe in all the rivers and brooks, and also the trout roe; so that you may not lack food as long as you live in the world."[31]

The Raven is youth *and* bird. The thought of *which* he is cannot emerge from the thought *that* he is, and that he is both.

From palaeolithic times, we have thousands of figurines that seem to represent deity as a composite, or "hybrid," of a stylized human form with features of various animals, particularly birds and snakes. Some also show male and female aspects simultaneously. Thus a goddess who may appear to be carrying an egg inside her may have a headless neck that suggests both phallus and serpent.[32] Such ambiguities convey a sense that the god's true identity does reside in his-and-her qualities, qualities that are more fundamental than sexual differentiation, that necessarily embrace distinctions--like the sexual potency that must be male-female or the sinuosity of all life suggested by the different motions of both bird and snake. The style of such sculptures has been described as "rhythmographic," providing visual parallels to music and dance.[33] The mystery that the deity embodies are captured by the grace and intensity of form as a way of *seeing* qualitatively, in symmetry and grace, and in what Marija Gimbutas calls "the sanctity of protuberance."[34] It is not hard to see how narrative form can be as "rhythmographic" as sculpture.

The Identity of God

The ambiguous identity of deities is a topic that has serious theological implications for "primitive" religions as well as for some we are likely to consider more sophisticated. Paul Radin shows in three very different cultures a double-layered conception of deity in which an absolute godhead is conceived as existing also as distinct parallel divinities. The Oglala Dakota godhead, Wakan Tanka, has sixteen aspects that manifest themselves as distinct deities. He is the chief god, who is also the sun, the moon, the buffalo, and the spirit. He is the great spirit, who is the sky, the wind, the bear, and the ghost. He is the creator-god, who is in turn the earth, the feminine, the four winds, and the spirit-like. And he is the executive god, who is also the rock, the winged, the whirlwind, and the potency. Furthermore, he is also a number of other gods, benevolent and malevolent ones, who are themselves other beings as well.[35] Among the Bavili, in Africa, the conception is more clearly mystical, as Radin says. The godhead Nzambi is fourfold, consisting of

Nzambi, the abstract idea, the cause: *Nzambi Mpungu*, god almighty, the father god who dwells in the heavens and is the guardian of the fire; *Nzambi ci*, god the essence, god on earth, the great princess, the mother of all animals; and *kici*,

Identity

the mysterious inherent quality in things that causes the Bavili to fear and respect. [36]

The Batak, in Sumatra, pray to Asiasi, although they regard him as four individual gods combined.

This conception of deity composed of deities reminds us readily of the Christian Trinity. It is even more characteristic of Hinduism, most notably in its "triune deity." Brahma, Vishnu (who is himself worshiped usually as either Krishna or Rama, two of his mortal incarnations), and Shiva are all aspects of one another, while they also differentiate the ultimate godhead Ishvara, who himself personifies the absolute self of reality, which is Brahman. It should not be surprising, however, that the nature of God's identity may be elusive or ambiguous, mysterious or contradictory, or simply nonlinear. It is one of the important functions of myth, of course, to help our limited imagination grasp and elucidate what it experiences as the divine but cannot interpret in terms of ordinary consistencies. In this area, images that are not fixed into concrete shapes may be particularly evocative. American Indian conceptions of deity are sometimes described as vaguely conceived or ill-defined, a strange prejudice of myth study. How well-defined a character is Jehovah or the Holy Ghost? And what would be gained if they were more sharp in outline?

There is another kind of prejudice in the Western assumption that a religion is either polytheistic, pagan, and naively primitive; or monotheistic, spiritual, and exalted. "It is typical of traditional African religious systems," in fact, "that they include, on the one hand, ideas about a multiplicity of spirits, and on the other hand, ideas about a single supreme being. Though the spirits are thought of as independent beings, they are also considered as so many manifestations or dependents of the supreme being."[37] Aside from the fact that the pagan may be spiritual and the "primitive" exalted, a religion--such as the Oglalas', the Bavilis', the Bataks', the Hindus', and even the ancient Greeks'--may be polytheistic and monotheistic at the same time on different levels.[38] Then its mythology can freely complement a sense of ultimate being with views of its various facets. The relative abstractness of strict monotheism must sacrifice some of the creative freedom with which divinity is conceived. A leading scholar of Jewish mysticism observes that:

> once the fear of sullying God's sublimity with earthly images becomes a paramount concern, less and less can be said of God. The price of God's purity is the loss of his living reality.[39]

In Judaism, the many forms of Christianity, and Islam, however, God is rarely conceived without qualities of personality. Only in metaphysics and the most liberal religions does God become demythologized (and perhaps not even then).

Radin shows that a monotheistic sense of deity can be superimposed upon a system of subordinate gods without negating it. Much of

The Qualitative World: Its Operation

(above)**"Fiddle-shaped figurines."** *Early female shapes, often with phallic heads. From the Greek Cycladic Islands, 2800-2500 BC. Are these fetishes manipulated to ensure childbirth or are they representations of a Mother Goddess? Perhaps the distinct being or identity of deity remains dissolved in the ritual object, which embodies the qualitative forms of sexuality. (below) Terra cotta statuettes of stylized maternal figures, with bird or animal features or masks. Cyprus, about 1600-1200 BC.*

Identity

the Old Testament, it has been noted, seems to record a long struggle between monotheistic prophets and polytheistic masses. In these different conceptions, Radin sees evidence of two kinds of personal temperament at work, that of the ordinary active person who accepts a variety of gods for their different kinds of practical assistance, and that of the thinker, who is interested in ultimate truths. However, the essentially myth-sensitive mind is not simply practical or simply reflective but can appear on either level of sophistication. This is the kind of mind that can see both levels of truth at the same time. Since it sees reality in qualitative terms, it does not take in the discrepancies that disturb our logic. It cannot contradict itself. Looking at the Hebrews among the Canaanites from the prophets' point of view--The prophets wrote the books--we see superstition. It is also possible to see among the people a flexibility of mind for which the prophets were not themselves conspicuous.

Any conception of a distinct god already suggests a partially linear identity. One feels obliged to decide whether this particular god either does or does not exist. To the extent that he (or she) does, he is unique and clear in being who he is. A more distinctly nonlinear conception of supernatural reality, which defies any stable sense of identity, is the conception usually known by the Melanesian name of *mana* although it has been common among many cultures. *Mana* (or the *manitu* of the Algonquin Indians, the *orenda* of the Iroquois, the *wakanda* of the Sioux, or the *mulungu* in central Africa--or many less-known versions of the same theme) is not a deity or a spirit or a natural existent (like tree or moon) or a natural event (like thunderstorm). Nor is it a mental conception. It seems to be, rather, an element in the human experience of nature--the forceful and, therefore, the meaningful element.

> This is what works to effect everything which is beyond the power of the ordinary man, outside the common processes of nature; it is present in the atmosphere of life, attaches itself to persons and to things, and is manifested by results which can only be ascribed to its operation. . . . This *mana* is not fixed in anything, and can be conveyed in almost anything; but spirits, whether disembodied souls or supernatural beings, have it and can impart it; and it essentially belongs to personal beings to originate it, though it may act through the medium of water, or a stone, or a bone. [40]

The conception--or the experience--of *mana* and its correlates is usually described as an elementary or embryonic stage in the development of myth or religion. Jung calls it "a necessary or at least a very important precondition for the development of an idea of God."[41] While Cassirer argues that *mana* (and *taboo*, which goes along with it as its antithesis) cannot be seen as the "'foundation' of myth and religion,"[42] he still sees it as "perhaps" the "most fundamental form" of mythical thought.[43] Both *mana* and *taboo*

The Qualitative World: Its Operation

represent, as it were, primary interjections of the mythical consciousness. They still have no independent function of signification and representation but resemble cries of mythical emotion.[44]

Perhaps the mystery of *mana* is a secret that becomes obscured by the clearer evolution of civilization while still holding its charm, so that, instead of surpassing it, myth continues to point back to it and keep a kind of faith with its essence. This would mean that there is a quality of myth that is necessarily elusive, emerging in the heart of its revelation. When we think of myths simply as primitive or archaic beliefs, therefore, as conceptual stabs in the primeval darkness, we lose this sense of how they function *as myths*. The way they operate must be as nonlinear as the "far-fetched" shapes of their features in time and space, and it must reflect the elusive manner in which, as myths, they *are*.

Sharing Identity

After quoting Jean-Jacques Rousseau's doctrine that language originated in metaphor and that "the first speech was all in poetry," Lévi-Strauss describes the earliest modes of symbolization as "All-enveloping terms, which confounded objects of perception and the emotions they aroused in a kind of surreality . . . ."[45] Myth is the natural and even inevitable medium for such a sense of identity, for its continual theme is the involvement of "I" in "Thou," of consciousness in nature, and of nature in the "supernatural" order of living forces.

The hero of myth is often a king, or a prince about to become a king, and the sociological reason for this is obvious: traditional narratives come from traditional cultures, which simply *were* led by chiefs or monarchs. But because of his power and freedom and his central importance, the king makes a strong symbol for the self. In our fantasies, we imagine what we could be *if only* we had such power, untrammeled by others, capable of working out our will and following our fantasies to their climax or conclusion.[46]

Within traditional cultures, kingship possessed a kind of mystique that, as Frazer demonstrated, had more to do with the king's symbolic nature than with his political power. As a symbol and not merely a man or statesman, he embodied his land and his people. There was a flow of identity from man to king to land to people, with important magical significance. Shakespeare's plays clearly show this factor still at work in the Renaissance, and it remains vestigially not only in England's treatment of its royal family nowadays but also in the dangerous glamour with which Americans treat their leaders, who often seem to be elected so that they can be torn apart before too long. Among at least many early people, in fact (Frazer's generalizations are now so modified), kings were at first not rulers but honored victims of sacrifice, and we have seen the importance that, in a sacrifice, identity be shared between the offering and the people for whom it is offered.[47] He was sacrificed because he was also, in

Identity

fact, "the Dying God." In Egypt, for example, the Pharoah was always Osiris, whose body had been cut in pieces and scattered (sown) along the Nile Valley. It is customary to say that the earliest kings embodied the fertility of their realm, but fertility can here mean creative welfare of all kinds, on all levels of life. A major mythic motif is that of the "wasteland" imagery: a sterile land and nation must be redeemed through the king's own suffering.[48] At the start of Sophocles' *Oedipus the King*, the people of Thebes appear before their heroic ruler with the lament that their crops do not grow, their livestock perish, and their babies are delivered dead. The king's own tragedy will free them from this burden, so that life may proceed and prosper according to its natural course.

Like nonlinear time, space, and causality, an unstabilized sense of identity is natural to mythic consciousness. The poet Yeats writes:

> Men who lived in a world where anything might flow and change, and become any other thing; and among great gods whose passions were in the flaming sunset, and in the thunder and the thunder shower, had not our thoughts of weight and measure.[49]

In a typically suggestive phrase, he adds, "They had imaginative passions": passions that *would* express themselves in imagination. Reversing Yeats' thought, we can see how "imaginative passions" thrive upon such a fluid sense of identity and even need it for their own *accurate* self-expression. Passion (or sensation or perception) does not work by linear distinctions. Its nature is direct experience, emanating from the flow and the swarm of conscious energy, rather than from the multifarious world of separate things that the mind distinguishes around us. "Shared identity" responds to a sense that being is essentially qualitative and individuality just happens to manifest it.

THE LINEAR ELEMENT

If myth spoke entirely in nonlinear terms, it would be completely surreal, more dreamlike than dreams usually are. Any myth contains linear elements which make it more intelligible in obvious ways--so we can follow the story line, for example. The mythmakers themselves did not always spin their tales in trance--although sometimes, probably, they did--and they and their people may very well have come up with linear explanations of what they were doing. The conscious mind, asking linear questions, will seek out linear answers, and it will find them. But we can easily get drawn into fallacies of linear interpretation when we are taken up by appearances of the objective world.

The Trickster hero is particularly frustrating to the intellect because, as we have seen, he conspicuously eludes moral classification. He seems to represent a basic resistance to society's laws and niceties, a resistance that belongs to what we can see as the animal level of our nature.

The Qualitative World: Its Operation

It is a need for natural anarchy, because, being *of nature*, it precedes the restrictions of civilization.

> Disorder belongs to the totality of life, and the spirit of this disorder is the trickster. His function . . . is to add disorder to order and so make a whole, to render possible, within the fixed bounds of what is permitted, an experience of what is not permitted.[50]

When Indians were asked to explain their version of the motif, however, they had to decide for themselves whether he was a deity or a clown.

> In all these tribes we find the same break between Trickster conceived of as a divine being and as a buffoon. Nor is it only the outsider who feels this. Many Indians themselves felt it, and tried to explain it in various ways. Swanton found individuals among the Haida who insisted that the deity Nankilstlas, with whom Raven is identified, put on the skin of a raven when he wanted to act like a buffoon. An educated Tlingit told Boas that the buffoon-like incidents were added to offset the serious parts of the myth. Many other examples of the same kind of reaction could be found.[51]

Inevitably, linear elements will seem at times to direct the mythmaking process itself.

The most explicitly linear motif in myth is the *etiological*, or explanatory, factor--a story's claim that it tells why we have two legs or why the heron stands on one or why the earth is shaped like a pyramid. This explanatory function may tell us why a particular beast or bird exists, but not why the myth about it exists. As a motif it is not necessarily intrinsic to the tale. In fact, as Boas points out, a single basic story can be used to explain or justify any number of facts.

> The story of the woman who became the mother of a litter of dogs is a typical example. Among the Eskimo it explains the origin of the Europeans; in southern Alaska that of the Milky Way, the rainbow and of the thunderstorms; on Vancouver Island that of a number of reefs, and among still others the origin of the tribe. In the interior of British Columbia it accounts for the origin of a taboo; farther north for the origin of Orion and for the characteristics of several kinds of animals; among the Blackfoot the origin of the dog society, and among the Arapahoe why the dog is the friend of man.[52]

In *The Pickwick Papers*, Charles Dickens parodies one form of etiology, the myth of a city or a nation's origin. Here he explains how the English city of Bath had its beginning, a city that used to be a fashionable resort famous for its mineral waters. Bladud, a tragic price, loses his heart's love and wanders forlorn over the earth. "So heedless was he

The Linear Element

of time or object that, being bound for Athens, he wandered as far out of his way as Bath."

"Oh!" said the unhappy Bladud, clasping his hands, and mournfully raising his eyes towards the sky, "would that my wanderings might end here! Would that these grateful tears with which I now mourn hope misplaced, and love despised, might flow in peace for ever!"

The wish was heard. It was in the time of the heathen deities, who used occasionally to take people at their words, with a promptness, in some cases, extremely awkward. The ground opened beneath the Prince's feet; he sunk into the chasm; and instantaneously it closed upon his head for ever, save where his hot tears welled up through the earth, and where they have continued to gush forth ever since.

It is observable that, to this day, large numbers of elderly ladies and gentlemen who have been disappointed in procuring partners, and almost as many young ones who are anxious to obtain them, repair, annually, to Bath to drink the waters, from which they derive much strength and comfort. This is most complimentary to the virtue of Prince Bladud's tears, and strongly corroborative of the veracity of the legend.[53]

The wandering lover falls into a wish trap in the form of a spontaneous crevice. Being patently nonrational, myth is not very difficult to parody. There actually is a traditional legend of Prince Bladud and the founding of Bath that is no less extravagant than Dickens' lark. The "real" Bladud was banished from his father's court because he suffered from leprosy. Laboring as a swineherd, he transmitted his illness to his charges, who accidentally fell into the foul-smelling waters and were cured. Hence the discovery of the water's power.

In traditional etiological tales, the reader can feel often that the explanatory tag coming at the end is as whimsical, and therefore as non-linear, as the rest of the story, perhaps a late addition to it meant to add "meaning." It may be a mere pretense at explanation; since it must be deliberately invented, it cannot be very seriously believed. The "cause" is not an event similar to its "result," bound to it in a sequence of events, but a translation of the "result" into imagery. The "cause" story dramatizes its subject on a different level and, therefore, is simultaneous to it, not prior in time as a true linear cause would have to be. In philosophical language, the causation is an analysis of its "ground of being" in the subject.

In a Winnebago Indian tale, Trickster goes to sleep while he is roasting some ducks, instructing his anus, however to guard the fire and the meat. Some foxes come along and help themselves, undeterred by the anus' loyal acts of expelling gas: "Pooh! Pooh!" When he wakes, Trickster punishes his anus with a burning stick. Then, walking unconsciously in a circle, he picks up some delicious pieces of meat and eats them.

The Qualitative World: Its Operation

> After burning his anus, his intestines had contracted and fallen off, piece by piece, and these pieces were the things he was picking up. "My, my! Correctly, indeed, am I named Foolish One, Trickster! By their calling me thus, they have at last actually turned me into a Foolish One, a Trickster!" Then he tied his intestines together. A large part, however, had been lost. In tying it, he pulled it together so that wrinkles and ridges were formed. That is the reason why the anus of human beings has its present shape.[54]

This is about as far as traditional lore can go in the game of etiology, but the playful tendency is a common one. It reminds us that all myth is a play of the imagination, however serious, essentially free from the weight of objective relevance and the measure of practical results.

Two important exceptions to this qualified generalization--that etiology is pretense--are myths of the founding of "our" race (not, as in the *Aeneid*, of our *nation*, or political entity) and myths of the origin of major rituals--both of which are deep expressions of the culture's traditional identity. They are to be acknowledged devoutly, but like any mythic beliefs, their basis lies still in their qualitative or dreamlike idealism. A myth may be very serious in its import even though it culminates in a highly fanciful "explanation." Thus the origin of maize, as explained among the Abanaki Indians, tells of a particularly lonely member of the first generation, who tired of his spare primeval diet, and lay forlorn in dreams. He was visited by a beautiful woman "with long *light* hair," who somehow eluded his continued approaches. Finally, she offered to stay with him forever if he promised to do as she would say.

> She led him to where there was some very dry grass, told him to get two very dry sticks, rub them together quickly, holding them in the grass. Soon a spark flew out; the grass caught it and quick as an arrow the ground was burned over. Then she said, "When the sun sets, take me by the hair and drag me over the burned ground." He did not like to do this, but she told him that wherever he dragged her something like grass would spring up, and he would see her hair coming from between the leaves; then the seeds would be ready for his use. He did as she said, and to this day, when they see the silk (hair) on the cornstalk, the Indians know that she has not forgotten them.[55]

More than giving a mere explanation, this myth grasps feelingfully both the living beauty and the functional service of the crop and also the Indian people's attachment to it. The imagination seizes upon the reality of the maize through these attributes and lets it belong to the human mind. This is the manner of all creation myths, in fact, to show "how" things came to be in such a way that we are especially impressed *that* they came to be, the images endowing the world with ceremonial freshness and dignity.

THE MERCATOR PRINCIPLE

Linear processes have an important place in the mythic imagination insofar as myth *must* use the appearances of linear time, space, cause, and identity in order to dramatize its world. As I put it earlier, myth (and dream and poetry) makes reality look like what it feels like. It presents, that is, a subjective world corresponding to our feelings and asks us to take it as real. If I dislike you, I dream you to look as ugly of face as I *feel* you to be of heart. Causal logic and the rest of it go along with this premise, giving a subjective face to the universe. But at the same time, in many ways, myth takes a world which is subjective and transposes it into linear terms.

The familiar map system invented by Gerardus Mercator, which we use in our atlases and most of our wall maps, projects the globe of the world onto a flat rectangle, so that we can handle or carry it conveniently but also so that we can trace in a single survey the relationship of place to place over the whole. Of course, in the process distortion takes place. Greenland comes out bigger than North America. But the distortion is systematic and regular. The lines of longitude and of latitude are closer in the center and further apart toward the edges, steadily widening in proportion to the degree of change, so that we can read back in imagination (or in algebraic transposition) from the flat to the round.

In myth, what we can call the Mercator principle transposes the immediate sense of life, which is qualitative and nonlinear, into "flat terms." As far as we experience life, from within it, in any direction of space or any direction of thought, it is ongoing, vanishing into the horizon. Myth gives it a beginning and an end, or as for the Hindus, an endlessly revolving sequence of beginnings and ends. Life is made of forces and processes, energies and experiences of energy. Myth portrays all these as the efforts of separate personalities and dramatizes their impact on one another in story. The world of our feelings is always now and here. Myth lays it out in a universe that can be traversed by a wandering hero, though an extraordinary universe it is. Thus, in its spatial projections, myth imitates geography. It imitates history in several ways: by treating its processes as specific events, by tracing these events in sequence, by regarding them as fact, and by relegating them to the past. The conscious self is symbolized in the pseudo-biography of the hero, who is represented time and again, under one name or another, as being conceived and born, then growing up, then meeting his ordeals, marrying, ruling, and dying, or joining the gods aloft.

Whenever we get the impression of linear causation in the mythic processes, it serves a qualitative purpose, for the linear is subsumed into the qualities of the whole form. The typical hero is separated from his parents in childhood because of a linear sequence of events that spell danger--such as civil disorder, as in the case of Arthur. But according to the principle of the foregone conclusion, the hero must leave so that he can come back later. Then he will appear as a nonlinear visitation, like

The Qualitative World: Its Operation

Oedipus or Moses or King Arthur, at once our natural leader and a miraculous savior.

When an idea is turned into a song, it is no longer the idea as such but the experience of the idea that we are interested in, and an esthetic experience of it at that. We shift gears from a "discursive" to a "presentational" form of symbolism,[56] although our minds thinking may well be lagging behind our quicker faculty of imagination. It is through the Mercator principle, by stretching the round out flat, that myth can be said to *analyze* consciousness. Lévi-Strauss describes the process in Structuralist terms: "it is as if a diachronic succession of events was simultaneously projected on the screen of the present in order to reconstitute piece by piece a synchronic order which exists" in reality.[57] What is always true at once is presented to the imagination sequentially, so that it can grasp the nature of life by laying out its qualities and tracing their relationships. The result is a kaleidoscopic definition of life given not in abstract terms, which are hardly life-like, but in the felt languages of image and dramatic action.

PART TWO

MEETING

All real living is meeting.   --Buber

Diana and Actaeon, *by Titian*

CHAPTER SIX

THE VIEW FROM THE PSYCHE

> *To those who no longer need to kill, the man who indulges in murder is a sleep walker. He is a man trying to kill himself in his dreams. He is a man who comes face to face with himself only in the dream. . . . Always fear and wish, fear and wish. Never the pure fountain of desire. And so we have and we have not, we are and we are not.*
>
> --Henry Miller

THE PSYCHIC ORGAN

Myth is a way of experiencing the world that expresses the nature of the mind experiencing it. When I hear music, the experience of listening gives me information about the music but tells me just as much about the nature of hearing. The pleasure of my response has as much to do with the one as with the other: it depends upon what hearing is and how my auditory equipment works just as much as it depends upon what Bach or Beethoven has put together. Similarly, of course, my experience of looking at a book--or at anything else--tells me as much about eyesight as about what I see. I see the book differently with or without my glasses on. Smelling a flower is a different kind of experience from touching one. So to understand the *smelt flower* or the *heard music*, I must have some notion of what smelling is all about or what it is to hear. Each sense can give us only a certain kind of knowledge of the world. I need not understand it all anatomically. I need only pay attention to the experience itself and take in what I can, intuitively, about what goes on.

We can think of the psyche as our total organ of perception. It is the way we experience the world, and our experience depends, obviously, on what the psyche is like. It includes the senses but is itself more basic --a receptiveness, an acknowledging, and a response. Myth is a way of seeing the world *psychically*--not as the eye beholdeth or the ear heareth, nor yet as the reason thinketh, but as our psychic energy responds to it directly in its own terms. Understanding myth, therefore, requires some understanding of the psyche as an organ. We cannot say it is the *purpose* of myth, yet myth inevitably illuminates mind simply by going about its business "mything," elaborating images of the world, reconstituting time and space, and spinning out its myriad variations on motifs. Conversely, a sense of the psyche cannot help but clarify how myth does work to develop its particular kind of impact.

SELF AND OTHER

There are two aspects of psychic experience that have profound effect on mythic form. First, consciousness constitutes selfhood; it establishes the self that is conscious, and by doing so it separates two realms of being. *I* see *you* together with *it*. There is *self*, the subject, on one hand, the "internal" world, experiencing and knowing. And on the other hand, there is the *other*, the object, the "external" world, experienced and known. The two realms are certainly interchangeable to an extent. *You* can experience *me*, although *it* (unless it is an animal) cannot. Yet these realms are radically different in nature. There are two kinds of people: me and everybody else; me, that is, and you. We are not just in different worlds; we are in different kinds of world.

I--*as an I*--am full of consciousness, sensitivities, feelings, and proper values. You--*as a you*--are part of my world. You affect me and serve a use for me. You attract me, annoy me, get in my way, and lead me on, frustrate, or gratify me. You are enviable or despicable. You are of a simpler nature than I am, for though I *feel* myself to be full of contradictions and ambiguities, I can *see*, I can *tell*, that you are simply too selfish or too generous, a strong person or a weak one. I act a certain way because I cannot help myself; my behavior flows spontaneously out of the endless stream of my feelings. You, on the other hand, act deliberately and ought not to have done it.

The external world includes far more, however, than just other people. It includes everything else, every thing, the universe as opposed to the subjectivity through which I experience it. But as *my* universe, it follows the rules of subjective space and time that we have already observed: it is thicker and more vivid near my presence than it is in the distance and fades off into thought over the horizon, while its center moves with me. Yet it is endless and unconquerable, and absolute in its own kind of completeness. It is a field of obstacles and opportunities, of wonders and dangers. Continually I use it and continually I come up against it. Its totality stands against me, requiring that I face it and deal with it. The world, as such, is wholly *other*, yet I--strange to say--must work out my life, and make sense of my life, in relation to it.

The relation of self to "other" enters into mythic form through the endopsychic sense of character images.[1] The hero, as self, lives in a world that consists of others--*his* enemy, *his* parents, *his* bride, *his* helpers and advisors, and so forth. They are usually of minor interest in themselves and may seem to have no independent existence. They simply establish the reality that the hero has to deal with and elucidate the "magical" or "inspired" nonlinear resources of heroic nature. However, otherness, as we shall see, defines the hero's lot in a manner still more basic, as the whole field of being in which he confirms his consciousness.

CONSCIOUS AND UNCONSCIOUS

Consciousness, then, creates a split away from the world outside, or rather it puts the world *outside*, with the self *in*. However, con-

Conscious and Unconscious

sciousness produces another kind of division internally. If there is consciousness, there will be unconsciousness. There are three main reasons why this is so.[2] First, selective focus: we can be conscious of only a limited, a minute, range of our experience at a time. Every second I am thinking of something different, as my mind (in a linear image) keeps moving along. Everything else that I know, I know unconsciously. What I thought of a minute ago, I store in the unconscious, not to mention what happened to me ten, fifteen, twenty years ago. In a slightly different way, what I am going to think ten minutes from now may be present already in my unconscious, if it is an implication of what I am now thinking, contained *implicitly* in what I know.

The second reason is the consolidation of ego. As my sense of being a self separates me from the rest of the world, so too it separates itself from the rest of my psyche. What is left is the unconscious. The awareness of being a distinct and unique entity, this *ego*, comes to seem the entire self. But as I identify myself with my ego, I feel myself to be cut off from the stream of life. Hence the predicament called alienation, the sense of being alien, strange, in one's own nature.

Psychologists and mystics alike speak sometimes of the unconscious as being *oceanic*, infinitely vast in its range, intensity, and intricacy. That is not because it adds on an infinite quantity of experience, but because the conscious mind withdraws from the state of simply being, establishing quarters for itself right *here* in the midst of all space. In order to function as consciousness, it must become finite and specific, linear and self-limiting. The mystic is the person who experiences his base of reality, his real home, as the infinite--*un*finite, not *yet* finite. He is eminently conscious of the unconscious. Myth moves, at least implicitly, in the direction of mysticism, because it is a way in which the psyche keeps the two levels of the mind in contact, to lead the conscious mind back to its source in the vast subjective seas.

The third reason for this division in the psyche is the one we usually think of first from a psychological point of view: the avoidance of pain. The unconscious, as Freud taught us, is the repository perforce of all the experiences, feelings, and thoughts that we will not tolerate. In the technical language of psychoanalysis--now a common enough idea-- we *repress* the memories and the impulses that earn us too much shame or guilt. The traumas of childhood, which shocked our personalities into shape, the thoughts we consider wicked, the desires that are too dangerous to reveal, the traits we are ashamed of--all constitute a dark underside to the self, and we try to live as best we can as though it were not there.

What we wish to reject, however, we cannot get rid of.[3] We hate it because it is so powerful; it is so powerful that it will stick. We cannot forget what we fear. We can only make it more important by concentrating our energy on fending it off. What repels us fascinates. It magnetizes, tantalizes, tyrannizes. But we do not yield readily to its lure, for the repulsion increases with the fascination. To our prolonged frustration, repressed energy actually strengthens the conscious effort that keeps it repressed. In Jung's words:

97

The View from the Psyche

it is a peculiarity of psychic functioning that when the unconscious counteraction is suppressed it loses its regulating influence. It then begins to have an accelerating and intensifying effect on the conscious process. . . . For instance, when someone makes a rather bold assertion and suppresses the counteraction, namely a well-placed doubt, he will insist on it all the more, to his own detriment.[4]

Unconsciousness is, therefore, a self-perpetuating trap, one, in fact, that tends to make itself tighter and tighter. This drive of the conscious mind impelled by unconscious energy is what is known as "hubris." It allows the hero like Oedipus, Agamemnon, Lear, or Macbeth to assert himself in a way that is magnificent even while it destroys him and a good part of the world he lives in. Hubris is not a vice as it is commonly said to be, but a predicament that is tragic for the very reason that it cannot be deliberately avoided or controlled. Avoiding it produces it.

If we think of the relation between the conscious mind and the unconscious as constituting the *structure of the psyche*, the most important principle defining that structure is the dynamic of resistance. Inasmuch as myth expresses the nature of consciousness, this becomes the main principle in the structure of myth. The conscious mind bolsters itself against the unconscious, fearing to be swallowed up in a chaos, whether the chaos of inarticulateness (because of the first reason for the split), the chaos of the loss of identity (second reason), or the promise of endless pain (third reason). Ego becomes more *egoistic*: I feel I *must* be the specific worthy person whose virtues I have worked so hard all my life to cultivate. I am attached to my ego to the extent that I resist my unconscious. And the harder I resist, the more dangerous the unconscious becomes. The more I invest in my defenses, of course, the more I have to lose. The more I am determined not to lose it, the thicker and higher I will build the walls.

The unconscious is essentially nonlinear, following the course of nature. The conscious mind, however, is hardly limited to linear activity. We are quite capable of being conscious of our emotions and appreciating poetry. The various forms of symbolism can be arranged in such a simplified scheme as this:[5]

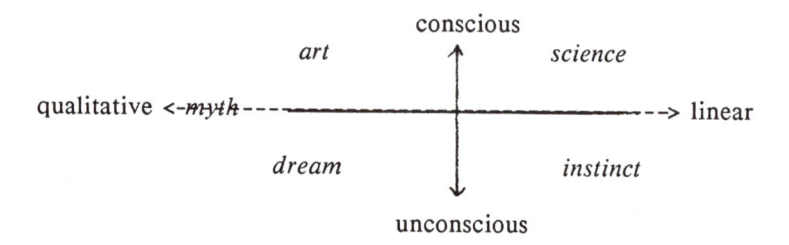

```
                          conscious
                 art         ↑        science
qualitative  <--myth---------|---------->  linear
                 dream       ↓        instinct
                          ↓
                        unconscious
```

98

Conscious and Unconscious

But as the history of Western civilization makes plain, the conscious mind, left to itself, tends to become more and more itself, more self-contained and linear. It is practical and works through control--utilizing the environment and restricting the emotions, legislating conduct and establishing standards. The more of the world we have come to control, the more we rely on our powers of control and on the world we have put in order.

Although the conscious mind directs itself in linear ways, the relation between the conscious mind and the unconscious is itself nonlinear, as we have been seeing. Leaving the unconscious behind us, we stumble upon it at every turn. The pattern of myth reflects this paradox in the hero's ultimate need to meet the monster that plagues this world: it will not be reasoned with or confined. The Minotaur is hidden within the Labyrinth of Crete, but it will have each year its diet of young men and maidens until Theseus, the hero, intervenes, without being called upon, to face up to it and take its murderous power upon himself.

A MYTH OF RESISTANCE

William Blake, the great English poet and artist, also produced an extraordinary body of original mythology, in which he analyzed the structure of consciousness with shrewd psychological insight, dramatizing traditional motifs in a way that continually reveals their nonlinear implications. His figure Urizen (apparently from "you[r] reason," "horizon," or "you are risen"--or all three at once) enacts the separation of consciousness from the infinite self.

> Times on times he divided & measur'd
> Space by Space in his ninefold darkness,
> Unseen, unknown . . .[6]

> Dark, revolving in silent activity:
> Unseen in tormenting passions:
> An activity unknown and horrible,
> A self-contemplating shadow,
> In enormous labours occupied.[7]

Forgetting that the other "immortals" are all aspects of himself, Urizen stands apart before them, dramatizing himself as their heroic savior.

> "First I fought with the fire, consum'd
> "Inwards into a deep world within:
> "A void immense, wild, dark & deep,
> "Where nothing was: Nature's wide womb;
> "And self-balanc'd stretch'd o'er the void,
> "I alone, even I! the winds merciless
> "Bound; but condensing in torrents
> "They fall & fall; strong I repell'd
> "The vast waves, & arose on the waters
> "A wide world of solid obstruction.[8]

The View from the Psyche

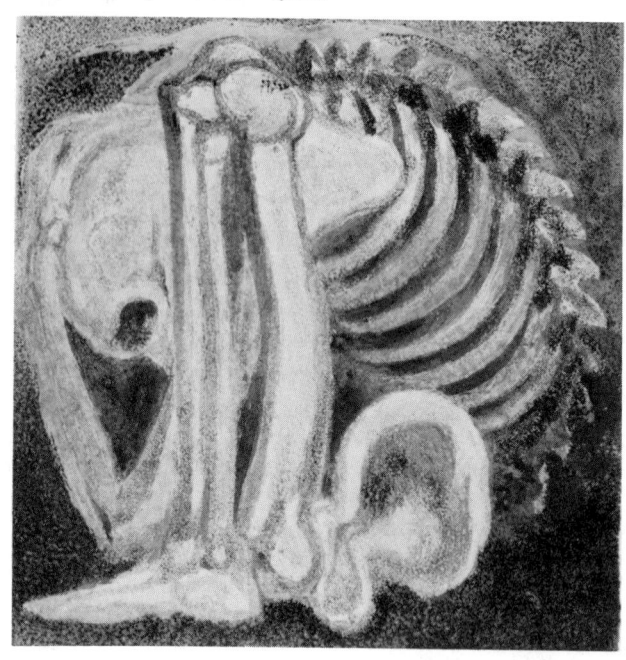

(left)
"The Changes of Urizen"--
"Los smitten in astonishment Frightened at the hurtling bones"

Four of Blake's illustrations to
THE BOOK OF URIZEN

(right) **Urizen in Fetters:** *the gratification of anguish*

100

A Myth of Resistance

(left)
"Los howld in a dismal stupor"

(right) *Los consumed by flames*

The View from the Psyche

Urizen has tried to establish a principle of control over the elemental forces of life, but almost immediately he finds that he is overwhelmed by his own creation. The harder he struggles to restrain life, the more solid and resistant it becomes.

Urizen's defection from eternity leaves the rest of the human self (properly eternal) now anxious and frightened, for its members have lost their integrated sense of reason.

> . . . Rage siez'd the strong,
> Rage, fury, intense indignation,
> In cataracts of fire, blood, & gall,
> In whirlwinds of sulphurous smoke,
> And enormous forms of energy . . .
> Sund'ring, dark'ning, thund'ring,
> Rent away with a terrible crash,
> Eternity roll'd wide apart . . .[9]

The imagination, dramatized as Los, fights back against the fallen Reason to bind *him* down to a finite existence in a solid form.

> Restless turn'd the Immortal inchain'd,
> Heavenly dolorous, anguish'd
>   unbearable;
> Till a roof, shaggy wild, inclos'd
> In an orb his fountain of thought.
>   In a horrible, dreamful slumber,
> Like the linked infernal chain,
> A vast Spine writh'd in torment
> Upon the winds, shooting pain'd
> Ribs, like a bending Cavern;
> And bones of solidness Froze
> Over all his nerves of joy.
> And a first Age passed over,
> And a state of dismal woe.[10]

His eyes turn into solid balls hidden within "caves," his ears twist into spirals, from the "Hungry Cavern" within his ribs a narrowly "channel'd Throat" rises, and strangest of all, his nostrils point downward to the ground. The human body has formed. His intellect limits him to a physical existence, in a world at once very meager and very dangerous. As an independent self who would master a world *outside* of him, he finds himself in a world that he himself cannot bear. The only solution he can imagine is to make the problem worse, to confront resistance with more intense restraint. Thus his new "order" is merely repressive and tyrannical, disrupting radically the organic order that has always existed. It is therefore "Disorganiz'd rent from Eternity."[10]

Urizen goes forth to explore his new world with the help of his inventions--weight and measure.

A Myth of Resistance

> He form'd a line & a plummet
> To divide the Abyss beneath;
> He form'd a dividing rule;
>   He formed scales to weigh,
> He formed massy weights;
> He formed a brazen quadrant;
> He formed golden compasses,
> And began to explore the Abyss...[11]

What he sees strikes him with horror. In a word Blake likes to use to similar effect elsewhere, it "appals" him.

> And his world teem'd vast enormities,
> Fright'ning, faithless, fawning
> Portions of life, similitudes
> Of a foot, or a hand, or a head,
> Or a heart, or an eye; they swam
>   mischievous,
> Dread terrors, delighting in blood.
>   Most Urizen sicken'd to see
> His eternal creations appear,
> Sons & daughters of sorrow on mountains
> Weeping, wailing.[12]

By isolating the conscious mind, he has created unconsciousness, and that is naturally a nightmare. Speaking with the authority of the visionary (the seer, who *sees* by means of unified consciousness), Blake portrays the irony of our predicament with compassion and wry humor but with the prophet's harsh clarity as well. This is the absolute severity of a nonlinear logic as sure in its way as the simplest addition of arithmetic.

The complement of the principle of resistance is the equally nonlinear law of integration: what is feared, will be appeased only if it is faced. The conscious mind becomes stronger in truth not by bolstering its defenses, which make it only more rigid and isolated, but by yielding to what it has feared, abandoning its defensiveness altogether. We are most in trouble when we must depend on being strong, or noble, or wise, when like Oedipus, we raise ourselves above the possibility of guilt, or rage against the terrible truth that stares us in the face.

We grow psychically not by intensifying consciousness but by expanding it, by becoming more conscious of what has been hitherto unconscious. This we do by softening the boundary that sets the conscious mind apart. We allow it more of the nonlinear resources that the unconscious has harbored. (We encourage intercourse between the hemispheres of the brain.) We learn to think not only by consistently working out the implications of ideas or tracing cause and effect, but also by observing the patterns of immediate experience or the effects of consciousness--and by being realistic about them. For Blake, integration

The View from the Psyche

comes through the Christian principle of the forgiveness of sins, which for him means dissolving the illusion that there is such a thing as sin. Among Urizen's unfortunate creations are the linear Ten Commandments together with the seven deadly sins (on the assumption that you cannot have guilt without righteousness, and vice versa) and the "nets" of moralistic institutionalized religion. Through forgiveness, Urizen's fall is ultimately reversed and he rises again, to take up his rightful position as the eternal wisdom of consciousness, joined with imagination in the propagation of meaningful "visions" or myths.

JUNG: THE OBJECTIVE VIEW

To develop a sensitive modern understanding of the psyche's role in myth formation, a look at the work of C.G. Jung is indispensible. Two aspects of his formulations, which are actually interdependent, are particularly famous, and he is usually celebrated or damned because of them: his conception of a "collective unconscious" and his identification of specific "archetypes" as universal patterns behind the most important mythic motifs. Myth follows certain identifiable tendencies, first of all, and takes form in familiar shapes because humanity as we know it, in all times and places, has shared a common unconscious fund of experience. It is more basic to the life of each of us than the personal unconscious that we store up from experiences in our own lives, and it has been transmitted throughout the ages, from nation to nation, generation to generation, so that the fundamental experiences of early man remain recorded in our psyches today.

The main characteristic of the collective unconscious is its archetypal patterning. The collective unconscious *consists of* the archetypes, which are not symbols, properly understood, but aspects of the psyche that express themselves in particular classes of symbol. Each is "a functional disposition to produce the same, or very similar, ideas."[13] Yet the archetypes are, for the most part, named and described mythically as though they were figures, albeit general ones. Particularly complex are the *anima* and *animus* (called as a pair the *syzygy*, a "joining together"), embodiments of sexual character traits, which we know as our own opposites. Within every man there is a woman trying to get out, and that is his anima, or repressed femininity; conversely, within every woman there is a "man," the animus, demanding self-expression. Psychic wholeness comes, in good measure, from one's ability to acknowledge, experience, and integrate his anima or her animus. Without such integration, we pursue in life persons, images, or romantic ideals that embody the anima or animus and supply us with an impression of fulfillment. The feminine qualities are primarily nonlinear ones: feeling and intuition, a sense of the whole, spontaneity, the natural rhythms of the body; while the masculine are essentially linear: rationality and purposefulness, action in time, individuality and self-assertion. For this reason, the anima also dramatizes the unconscious itself and is hence more

Jung: The Objective View

conspicuous in myth than the animus. The hero, as self, must work out his destiny primarily in relation to her various reflections.[14]

The anima occurs in myth either as a young woman or a mature one, either in a positive light or a negative one.[15]

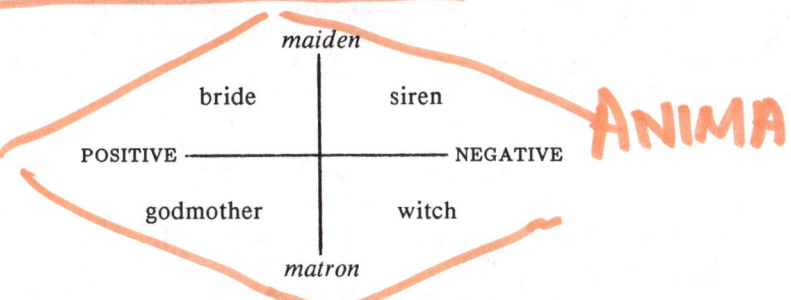

```
                    maiden
            bride  |  siren
      POSITIVE ----+---- NEGATIVE
         godmother |  witch
                   matron
```

ANIMA

The positive maiden usually denotes the hero's self-fulfillment by uniting with him at the end of a tale, or the intuitive impulse that leads him to success (Ariadne with her thread, whom Theseus abandons not out of callousness, perhaps, but a need to live with her power for himself[16]). The negative young woman is a trap--a temptress like Odysseus' Circe or the sirens--to draw the hero into self-indulgence and away from his quest for growth. The maternal anima suggests a general source of life from which each person has emerged as an individual. The positive mother, of course, is nurturing and carries life through its recurrent cycles of death and rebirth--like Isis mourning for her slain brother-husband Osiris and recovering the fragments of his body[17] or Demeter seeking out her daughter Persephone, who was abducted by Death. The negative mother-- Perseus' Gorgon, Oedipus' Sphinx, all the wicked stepmothers and witches--is the same source of life experienced as a threat to individuality, the mother who will not yield one up to an active independent life but would frighten one into repression and continual infancy.

The next most important archetype is the *shadow*, the side of one's own broader personality that one disowns under the conviction that it is evil. The shadow is evident in demonic or diabolic figures[18] but occurs also in lurking strangers, as disreputable brothers, as savage counterparts (Enkidu the uncivilized competitor of Gilgamesh who becomes his friend), or as a mysterious challenger who summons the hero to danger (Sir Gawain's Green Knight). Two other important archetypes are the *wise old man* and the *child*. The first is symbolized in seers and magicians, like the Greek Teiresias and the Arthurian Merlin, but often in passing strangers, usually (in the European tradition) hermits, who appear with magic help or nonlinear advice at the time of most critical need. "He" embodies the deepest intuitive knowledge that will henceforth be the center of the hero's sense of self.[19] The child as archetype expresses the self in its potentiality for fulfillment. It is the psyche's silent awareness of its own organic nature (its "innocence"), on a level that has not been touched by society's needs for linear adaptation and repression by the ego.[20]

The View from the Psyche

JUNG: THE SUBJECTIVE VIEW

Jung is usually evaluated on the basis of his concepts, but it seems to me that his greatest contribution lies in the *quality* of his insights and his appreciation for the qualitative nature of consciousness. It is a matter of how he speaks, not just what he says. The notion of an *inherited* unconscious seems to me (and to Jung's many much harsher critics) superfluous. As far as I can see, the universal factors of myth are accounted for quite adequately by the crucial ways in which the human situation remains necessarily constant:[21] especially by the very existence of the conscious mind as a self-reflector of the psyche. In his specific analyses of myths (and dreams), Jung and some of his adherents seem to me at times to become so involved in the analytic process that formulations and distinctions threaten to become a reality of their own.[22] Yet Jung was well aware of the ambiguity of the archetypes as conditions of the psyche and of the distortion of their nature that results just from naming them.

> Clear-cut distinctions and strict formulations are quite impossible in this field, seeing that a kind of fluid interpenetration belongs to the very nature of all archetypes. They can only be roughly circumscribed at best. Their living meaning comes out more from the presentation as a whole than from a single formulation. Every attempt to focus them more sharply is immediately punished by the intangible core of meaning losing its luminosity. No archetype can be reduced to a simple formula. It is a vessel which we can never empty, and never fill. It has a potential existence only, and when it takes shape in matter it is no longer what it was.[23]

Furthermore, there remains in most of Jung's work (that I have read)--as in this passage--an exemplary spirit, which gets closer to the import of myth than his actual formulations.

What seems to me most valuable in Jung's approach are these specifically nonlinear aspects of it:

1. He writes out of a sense of a common predicament that mankind shares, and he approaches this situation with humility, good-humor, urgency, and compassion, appreciating the difficulty of our position while realizing that our hope of dignity and our hope not only of growth but of survival lie in our ability to see it honestly.

> . . . anyone who has to do with the phenomena of the unconscious knows with what hair-raising irrationalism and with what shocking tactlessness and ruthlessness the unconscious "mind" dismisses our logical concepts and moral values.[24]

> . . . the unconscious is nature, which never deceives; only we deceive ourselves.[25]

Jung: The Subjective View

> The God who created such monstrosities, at the thought of which we poor mortals stiffen with fear [He is speaking of the Behemoth and Leviathan, in the Old Testament], must certainly harbour within himself qualities which give one pause. This God dwells in the heart, in the unconscious. That is the source of our fear of the unspeakably terrible, and of the strength to withstand the terror.[26]

Jung's "collective unconscious" is not, therefore, just a store-house of images. The conscious mind and the unconscious together *are* our experience of life, with all of life's incredible difficulties and all of its richness. Although he likes to regard himself as a scientist, he does not deal with the psyche or its symbols as phenomena outside himself to be merely observed, categorized, mastered, and disposed of. Rather he writes within the tradition of mythmakers and visionaries, in the spirit that has created myth, with the visionary's sense of creative purpose.

2. As a result, Jung writes of symbolism as experience, which makes its revelation subjectively about subjectivity. Symbols express, for him, not just the contents of the psyche but its nature. His conception of *libido*, as the flow of psychic energy, provides a dynamic sense of life that is rich with ambiguity, complexity, and continuity--not good or bad, right or wrong, liberal or conservative--and appreciating that it simply *is* cultivates an attitude of neutrality which releases energy in oneself.

3. Since, as energy, the psyche cannot be weighed or confined, and since we find ourselves in the midst of it, and since it carries us along through scrapes and struggles, leaving the rational mind panting behind, it is naturally mysterious to us, in the highest sense, and evokes the appropriate response of wonder. The unconscious, for Jung, transcends our efforts to understand it, although, being the source of consciousness, it is the source of all meaning. It reveals our images of the infinite, the eternal, the divine.

> The great advantage of scientific abstraction is that it gives us a key to the mysterious processes enacted behind the scenes . . . [Some] writers cheerfully talk of the "subconscious," without apparently realizing what an arrogant prejudice they are presuming to express. How do they know, forsooth, that the unconscious is "lower" and not "higher" than the conscious? The only certain thing about this terminology is that consciousness deems itself higher--higher than the gods themselves.[27]

Having such a profound respect for wonder, for the childlike, for the miraculous, Jung can write about myth with genuine response to the genius that inspires it and with sympathetic participation in its imaginative world.

4. The attitudes toward life with which Jung approaches myth, and which he sees myth foster, is one of basic receptivity. The

from the Psyche

> ...is a realm of what is, not what should or should not be, and
> ...mes in embracing the truth without prejudice, even without
> ... in the name of virtue. Thus the shadow, one's *own* evil or
> ...., must be "owned." Whatever we fear or despise must be seen in
the scheme of life.

> As a power which transcends consciousness the libido is by
> nature daemonic [not demonic]: it is both God and devil. If
> evil were to be utterly destroyed, everything daemonic, in-
> cluding God himself, would suffer a grievous loss; it would
> be like performing an amputation on the body of the deity.[28]

Thus integration, the taking responsibility for the full range of one's own experience, is the natural course of growth. Integration is the way of integrity.

5. Accordingly, Jung is deeply sensitive to the nonlinear values of myth that I have summarized in Chapter 3, particularly the theme of the integration of opposites.

> The conflict between the two dimensions of consciousness is
> simply an expression of the polaristic structure of the psyche,
> which like any other energic system is dependent on the
> tension of opposites.[29]

Myth works continually with such a play of energy, revealing the unified intuitive understanding that the unconscious harbors.

> The cross, or whatever other heavy burden the hero carries, is
> *himself*, or rather *the* self, his wholeness, which is both God
> and animal--not merely the empirical man, but the totality of
> his being, which is rooted in his animal nature and reaches
> out beyond the merely human towards the divine. His
> wholeness implies a tremendous tension of opposites para-
> doxically at one with themselves, as in the cross, their most
> perfect symbol.[30]

The crux of Claude Lévi-Strauss' Structuralist system of interpretation is a similar theme. He sees all myths as structures that juxtapose the terms of polarities in order to propose a solution to the conflict, most commonly the conflict between *culture* and *nature*, or, as he puts it in the title of one of his books, "the raw and the cooked": "mythical thought always progresses from the awareness of opposites toward their resolution."[31] But for Lévi-Strauss, the resolution of opposites is an ideal proposed by the mythic mind to ease the tension. The conflict is a fact of life; the solution exists only within the myth. The structure of polarities is taken for granted by Jung, but for him, the reconciliation is genuine, the paradox an insight into the nature of reality. Because the unconscious precedes consciousness, its balance is a true and reliable resource.

7. Another kind of paradox crucial to myth in Jung's interpretation is the paradox of rebirth, which is very familiar to us through Christianity. Rebirth is the symbol of integration. Death is, psychically, the yielding up of the ego to the unconscious forces that had been so powerfully resisted; rebirth, the new vitality in the natural flow of energy that is then joined. Death no longer feared is death undone. Violence owned is no longer destructive. Desire without guilt or shame is no longer obsessive. Hence sacrifice is the natural means of affirming life, whether in ritual practice or in the mythic hero's exposure of himself to danger.

8. Finally, as a healer, Jung sees myth as a therapeutic force. In its original community, it helps most people maintain a psychic equilibrium within the pressures of cultural life, while it provides a further challenge of self-integration for those who may hear the call. Myth is a positive and humane force in life, not (as for Freud) a symptom of mass neurosis; but more than that, it is a channel that culture itself has provided to correct its own tendency to unbalance the natural course of living things. We understand myths--and psychic "symptoms" in general --not *pathologically* by looking backward for their causes but *teleologically*, by appreciating their creative energy to move us onward. Thus the sense of wholeness, in the integration of opposites, in the recovery of childlike wonder, in the acceptance of "evil," leads to the quality of personal fulfillment which Jung calls "individuation." Myth is a process towards the clarification and enrichment of life, therefore, in an honest and an exuberant way.

THE IMPACT OF CONSCIOUSNESS

To read the nonlinear sense of the story, we may suggest that Cain strikes down Abel because society as we know it is born in the rivalry between brothers--and civilization in the separation between those who tend the beasts, with Abel, and those, with Cain, who tend the soil. With farming came a settled abode and a world of change. The first "crime," therefore, is civilization itself, the birth of consciousness as a way of life, for with that comes the peculiar separation of selves isolated together, and bonded also with shame as well as desire, violence along with art, theologies as well as myths, rules as well as revelations, the sense of history, and the tragic spirit which pursues fulfillment in its own despair. After the death of Abel, we are no longer exiles from Eden, a homeland to the West, but dwellers in another world entirely, native to humanity rather than nature.

The human animal is, of course, a creature of nature, living and dying according to the organic process of growth and decay, and, accordingly, both blessed and cursed with feelings, needs, limits, powers, vulnerabilities. However, it is at the same time an independent, responsible being, capable of knowing its nature while being unnaturally detached from it, all because of the consciousness with which it regards itself.

The View from the Psyche

To the birds flight, to the lions brute bulk and power, to the snakes elusive swiftness. The human strategy for survival--which has (so far) capped (and perhaps dead-ended) the evolution of the primates--is the conscious mind. Humanity has fallen out of the Eden of instinctive life into the time-bound world of conscious mortality. Our sense of linear time must serve our need to summon a past in order to plan a future--to organize a hunt, notably, and then to observe the changing seasons that we may plant *on time*. (Though the seasons revolve, they come and go in order.) Consciousness means also the capacity to summon other selves to work along with us and to summon the forces of life that seem to sustain us. It means, therefore, the evolution of man as Cassirer's *"animal symbolicum."*

> No longer in a merely physical universe, man lives in a symbolic universe. Language, myth, art, and religion are parts of this universe. They are the varied threads which weave the symbolic net, the tangled web of human experience. All human progress in thought and experience refines upon and strengthens this net.[32]

Animals other than man do some sort of thinking and certainly have experience that can be called consciousness. Study of the mind has advanced dramatically in the successful efforts to teach chimpanzees sign language. But we need only think of babies and of the deaf to realize that neither consciousness nor thought *depends on* an ability to speak.[33] We can catch our own direct qualitative realizations weaving in and out of our zigzagging streams of language. Yet what we generally experience as a conscious mind bound in tension to a dim unconscious--thinking of time, abstractions, lost alternatives, itself, and death (perhaps we should call it hyperconsciousness)--is at least *bound up*, intimately, with symbols and signs, especially on the basic level of language.

We must realize that things exist in themselves if we name them. When we put our own experience in words, we are immediately aware of ourselves at a distance from it. Selecting elements out of the transient feelings of experience, we create a stable *picture* of reality that we can contemplate, analyze, and act upon. Together with language came other forms of symbolic expression--the beautiful drawings in paleolithic cave sanctuaries, the carvings of fetish-figurines, the patterns of ritual, and, of course, the images of deity proliferated through myth. The poet-naturalist Loren Eiseley has captured the process of this extraordinary evolution in his own vision:

> [Man] was becoming something the world had never seen before--a dream animal--living at least partially within a secret universe of his own creation and sharing that secret universe with other similar heads. Symbolic communication had begun. Man had escaped out of the eternal present of the animal world into a knowledge of past and future. The

The Impact of Consciousness

unseen gods, the powers behind the world of phenomenal appearance, began to stalk through his dreams.[34]

As the conscious and symbolic mind came to prevail in man, mere survival was no longer the only goal. The means started to become as important as the end, for there is a charm to symbols. As experience expresses itself, it becomes concrete. Not only a new world but a world of worlds emerges, which must be reckoned with on its own terms.

The evolution of symbolic consciousness is thus also the evolution of human alienation. The symbolic web becomes a surrogate world more manageable than the given swarm of reality, but once we give names to transient feelings we get stuck with them. "Instead of dealing with the things themselves," Cassirer says, "man is in a sense constantly conversing with himself."[35] Jung describes this paradoxical development of *human* nature in somewhat more technical terms.

> . . . the absolute and apparently reliable guidance furnished by the instincts is displaced by an abnormal learning capacity which we also find in the anthropoid apes. Instead of instinctive certainty there is uncertainty and consequently the need for a discerning, evaluating, selecting, discriminating consciousness. . . . There then arises the . . . danger of consciousness being separated from its instinctual foundations and of setting up the conscious will in the place of natural impulse.[36]

Since focused thinking impedes spontaneous responsiveness, human consciousness is also self-consciousness, the sense of that radical split between the self perceiving and the *other*ness outside. With time-awareness comes the *I-now* as opposed to the *I-then*, the *I-am* as opposed to the *I-was* and the *I-shall-be*--and ultimately the philosophic self, *I-may-be*.

One thing I shall be is dead, and that awareness in itself opens, of course, the most intense conscious activity and the vast elaboration of symbolic expression in ritual and in myth. With this differentiated sense of self comes the grief of loss remembered, and an especially stark kind of loneliness, just as, with the sense of a future comes the special outlook of anticipation, with its ready undercurrent of anxiety. In the words of a psychiatrist writing about myth, "suffering assumed an entirely new, disagreeable connotation with the development of consciousness."[37] For on top of pain and loss came the will to prevent them and the strain of resistance. And inevitably, the corollary to the alienation of the self is violence toward others as frustrations explode. The naturalist Louis Leakey, who found in Africa human fossils 1.75 million years old, has suggested, in fact, that language is the source of our peculiarly human quality of aggression, for it enabled us to "invent words for things like hatred and malice and war--things that have never been in our consciousness" and it gave us "names for our enemies. . . . the biggest enemy [being] the name, and not the person."[38] If this is not completely true, if language didn't create hatred, it must have at least helped it to fix itself and flourish. It

The View from the Psyche

must have helped men know their hate, to sustain it, and aim it steadily toward the future of revenge.

Eiseley's dream animal abandons Eden in a pensive mood.

> For it was truly man who, walking memoryless through bars of sunlight and shade in the morning of the world, sat down and passed a wondering hand across his heavy forehead. Time and darkness, knowledge of good and evil, have walked with him ever since. It is the destiny struck by the clock in the body in that brief space between the beginning of the first ice and that of the second. In just that interval a new world of terror and loneliness appears to have been created in the soul of man.[39]

This alienation from nature, from the garden of innocence and spontaneity, leads to the starkly tragic quality of much of the greatest mythmaking. It leads also to the joy of vitality regained, of nature regenerated in human consciousness. For the natural source of our being lies still within the unconscious mind, stored in the images of paradise and its residents sublimely at home in deathlessness.

But if consciousness is the problem, it also makes possible the solution. Tempered by the habits of language and the need for pragmatic choices, the conscious mind does cultivate, thrive upon, and hobble itself with linear thought. The unconscious, in contrast, seems a shimmering, slime-ridden, bejewelled sea. To the extent that it *is* unconscious, it may seem nothing at all: a black sea, under a grey sky, revealing no hint of depth. Either way, however, it is only the conscious mind that can think so, that can be aware that the unconscious is unconscious, or that itself is conscious. It is the conscious mind that is tempted and struck with beauty and power--or that has the good sense to be bored with nothingness.

The conscious mind, so used to choosing between this belief and that, one arbitrary half-truth or another, is astounded by the fullness, the stubbornness, the perversity of the unconscious and has the opportunity to come upon it as a revelation. When the conscious mind acknowledges the infinity that both underlies and surrounds it, it enriches itself by becoming natural, by joining the universe. Its mortality becomes a source of strength, because it is able to function as what it really is, wielding its own muscle, supported by its own bone.

Without a conscious mind, there is no mystery and no wonder, for there is nothing to wonder, nothing to do the confronting, nothing to sense the *wonder*-ful gulf between. To appreciate magic is as wonderful as to perform it. To study the quest is itself a quest, and the cultured mind that feels myth's charm comes alive with its own infinite power. Without a conscious mind, there is also no facing of truths, no integration, and no responsibility. The mythic hero, at the center of consciousness, takes in the ugliness of Medusa, the beauty of Diana, the horrid appetite of the Sphinx, the fertile power of Zeus, and leads us, in myth upon myth, to know their manifold truth as the source of our lives.

CHAPTER SEVEN

THE DEFINITION OF MORTALITY

a voluntary death with a slight chance of redemption. —Lindsay's Apuleius

MYTH AS CONFRONTATION

The essence of Jung's conception of myth, in my reading, is that myth expresses the relation between the conscious mind and the unconscious.[1] These two levels of the psyche are constituted the way they are because of one another. The unconscious is unconscious only because the conscious is conscious. The contents of our unconscious are continually being altered by the attitude we take to them more consciously. Anima, shadow, and the other archetypes are reminders of what we neglect in ourselves. Exposed to the unconscious, the creative conscious mind continually evaluates itself. The conscious mind exists by forging itself out of the great mass of experience, against the pressures of unconscious forces. The unconscious, in the meantime, survives by concentrating and conserving its energies along the contours of the archetypes. The two levels are bound to one another by the perpetual flow of energy, or experience, back and forth. This bond is made all the tighter by the magnetic grip of resistance. . . . All of this is reflected in the structure of mythic reality, especially in the pattern of death and rebirth that underlies the ordeal of the hero.

But the psyche, we observed, is characterized by another kind of major split as well: between the sense of self and the sense of otherness.[2] We can reach an especially broad and deep and simple picture of mythic form by overlaying these two polarities upon one another. For *I*, being unconscious, experience my unconscious self as *other*. That is why different aspects of it appear to me as anima, shadow, wise old man-- until I achieve their integration, as the course of myth will show me doing.

A myth, then, is a symbol, in the form of a story, expressing (or producing) a confrontation between the limited perspective of the self and the unlimited context in which it exists.

This is my "working definition" of myth. I am not certain how thoroughly it covers all that everyone else considers myth to be, but it highlights what seems to me the most striking features of traditional mythology and the reflections of it in literature and in other aspects of culture. Myths are archetypal, I maintain, to the extent that they do express this one primordial and inevitable picture of consciousness and work out some of its powerful implications. The single fundamental

The Definition of Mortality

archetype (or *originating form*) is the structure of consciousness itself. It is thus the structure of consciousness, and not its specific contents, that myth is all about.

All mythic images--including the specific Jungian archetypes--seem to me reflexes of this basic play of psychic energy in relation to its living situation. Joseph Campbell demonstrates as much by systematically placing the major motifs in relation to the hero's circular journey of departure, initiation, and return, and treating myths of creation, fertility, culture-teaching, deluge, and world-annihilation all as dimensions of the basic circle.[3] The circle is the essential point, the minimal representation of the tension between consciousness and unconscious, self and universe, confront and yield. It expresses the essence of nonlinearity itself, as an order and a rhythm, and a principle of integration.[4]

My definition is a dynamic rather than an objective one, since it looks for the nature of myth in what it does and how it works rather than in what it looks like ("stories about gods and heroes"). It sees myth as a process that takes place, as an experience that one has, as a very natural human phenomenon, and as the reflection of a clear kind of knowledge. It looks for the meaning of myth in its reflection of psychic energy (as Jung does), in its experience of the absolute (as Buber does), in its special reality (as Cassirer does), in its structure (as Lévi-Strauss does), and in the relation of man to nature (as other anthropologists do)--but it sees all these features of myth as aspects of one another.

A look at the parts of the definition should help explain why myth takes the form it does:

1. The myth is, of course, a *symbol* (or, more strictly, a symbolic form). It is an organized experience known through the imagination, a kind of experience that suggests significance and establishes its own kind of existence, neither actual nor abstract. As *expression*, the mythic symbol, is literally, a *pressing out* or extending of direct experience, putting forth its qualities on a new level of reality, in a new kind of entity, as *mythic being*. It remains continuous, however, with the reality of life that it expresses and it needs to be understood in relation to it.

2. This symbol takes the form of a *story*. Within the myth itself appear gods and demons who are not, properly speaking, myths themselves but mythic images. The symbolic stuff of myth is shaped into narrative to express its proper kind of meaning. A story is dramatic; it is made up, that is, of tension and process. Forces conflict and then work out their impact on each other in a sequence of modified relationships. The narrative happens, it takes place, it unfolds. Mimicking the course of life, it runs through linear time, from before to after, demonstrating change. In all these ways and more, myths express the nature of life through its narrative form.

3. *Confrontation* is the central experience of myth. The dramatic process sets two dimensions of life face-to-face. There is a coming up against, a collision that is also a realization. There is impact: a force that makes a difference. The mode of knowledge is definitely "presentational," not thought about but *had*. Thus it cannot be denied or

Myth as Confrontation

reasoned with; it must be reckoned with, or integrated. There is no room for compromise.

This is the way in which "I" face "Thou."[5] This is the way "mystery" is known as mystery. It is the way anything is realized for what it is--through consciousness and not analysis. Thus does the hero *confront* his monster, the image of all that seems alien to him (or rather, the essence of what makes *anything* seem alien and makes anything, therefore, *need* confronting). Thus do the living ever confront death, thus do I confront the disruptive force of my own feelings or my reflection in another person's eyes. The religious parallels are revelation and epiphany--knowledge not through the intellect but through direct realization, where the event experienced is its own meaning, and its meaning is embodied in living fact.

The enormity of mythic imagery is an indirect reflection of confrontation. The weirdness of it all--the bizarre snake-hair that turns beholders into stone, the realization one is turning into a tree or a deer, the copulation with a god turned bull or swan or shower of gold, the three- or four-headed Indian deities smiling ecstatically with necklaces of skulls upon their breasts--all this conveys a sense of reality that is out there, strange, and *other*. The feelings that come toward us are like ours, but in a shape radically different. Also, the simplification of absolutes-- the perfect beauty of the beauties, the extraordinary strength of the strongmen, the wisdom and charity of the innocent children, and on and on--everything is truly what it is, standing forth definitively in full glory to be confronted and known, existing *utterly*. But most of all, the suddenness of mythic occurrence, shorn of linear cause, everything spontaneously manifested as though it were always there and also just occurring for the first time--this miraculous breakthrough strikes home the continually fresh truth of life waiting to be looked at.

4. The profundity of the confrontation is due, of course, to the nature of the two parties. It is because consciousness is confrontive in its nature--and because the context it confronts is everything beyond itself-- that the archetypal form is absolute in its impact and in its significance. Every kind of tale that has been called myth may not be archetypal--but every archetypal tale strikes us as mythic.

First, myth expresses the point of view of the limited, or finite, self: I behind my eyes, within my skin, the knower. Myth is a very human phenomenon, showing how *man* experiences god experiencing man. In one sense "I" seem endless, my power to wish or to imagine is ever-increasing; and also everything I see belongs to me, being my experience. But what I realize in confrontation is my helpless smallness, my specific factuality, *my* dependence on the world which envelopes me. The essence of ego-consciousness, says Jung, "is limitation, though it reaches the farthest nebulae among the stars."[6]

Most kinds of myth dramatize the confrontation as conflict between a human realm and a supernatural. The pattern is particularly clear in stories of a hero who stands up against a monster or the lord of death, usually guided by the inspiration of gods. In some cases animals represent either the human or the supernatural, since animal qualities can

The Definition of Mortality

suggest either inferiority in consciousness or superiority of a natural, unconscious kind. In some cases, as in the Prometheus myth, an immortal is associated with humanity and can stand in for us, or one generation of gods seems "relatively mortal" compared to another. However, many myths take place on the supernatural level alone. That is why I add the qualification that myth may "produce" the confrontation rather than "express" it. Then the confrontation is left for us to experience, as members of the human community imagining the world *in those days* of utter power and absolute being.

5. I can understand on many levels that endless context, or field, in which I experience myself through myth. It appears through gods and demons, monsters and fairies, underworlds and overworlds, in short through all the techniques of nonlinear space, time, causation, and identity. This "context" confronts me with my own limitation as it strikes me with its own totality. Psychologically, it is the unconscious, with its vast reservoir of pain and bliss. Existentially, it is nonexistence, which reduces my mere being to a speck in the dark. It is the world of nature, which includes me but goes on all around me, so vast, intricate, and indifferent that I feel (accurately) infinitesimal and negligible as I perceive its "eternal recurrence."[7] It is even the world of other people. They can be counted and they are all separate individuals, but together they present one of the ultimate factors in my life, limiting the way I see myself and the course my life will take.

The psychologist will interpret the mythic energy on one level, the anthropologist another, the philosopher another. The theologian will see the divine in the vast beyond. What myth dramatizes, typically and archetypically, is the sense of the confrontation itself, a pattern that *applies* on different levels but carries the common denominator of them all.

True archetypal myth is characterized, in its spirit, by the sense of an utter disparity between the self and its world. It is the *absolute* nature of what stands against the self that makes it *super*natural. The self seems so relative and so dependent upon it. The reality of the "beyond" is always extraordinary when seen from the perspective of limitation. When the linear confronts the nonlinear, the effect is doubly nonlinear, for the linear mind has no familiar way of dealing with what lies before it. It cannot solve the mystery as though it were a problem. The intellect rebels. This motif is fully developed in tragic drama, where the hero rages in fear, horror, and loathing. It is outrageous that he should live in a situation he cannot handle rationally, by planning his course and controlling his means! But while he recoils, he is also being drawn into the abyss that seems to be opening at his feet. What he resists so powerfully magnetizes him until he must yield to its terrible charm.

The mythic narrative moves our imagination typically, however, toward a transcendence of the confrontation. By confronting what holds me back and limits me, I experience my place in the scheme of things. The context in which I live is, simply, life--which is not *other* than me at all. I am not my ego, but a self that includes the unconscious. The knowledge of death gives life its mortal meaning. In other words, the

Myth as Confrontation

linear requires the nonlinear to unify its parts. When I have confronted my own reverse image, I attain a sense of life that is realistic because it is complex, ambiguous, and paradoxical.

THE QUOTIENT OF MORTALITY

$$\frac{\text{life}}{\text{death}} = \frac{\text{conscious mind}}{\text{the unconscious}} = \frac{\text{existence}}{\text{non-existence}} = \frac{\text{self}}{\text{universe}} = \frac{\text{control}}{\text{energy}} = \frac{\text{time}}{\text{eternity}}$$

As life is to death, as the conscious mind is to unconscious . . . as the linear is to the nonlinear.[8] Myth is a dramatic definition of the human condition. In these different ways, on these various levels, myth reflects the delicate balance: to be human is to be mortal; to be mortal is to exist by grace of dying. "What eats dies," as my little boy said.[9] Nonexistence does not only surround us with its still eternity, it infuses our being, like all the emptiness within the atoms of our body. Unconsciousness permeates every thought. Blake's Urizen discovers that we cannot fix ourselves into existence, but must flow with the changing tide, which never lets us *be*. The confrontation, as a ratio, is the measure of our nature. And it is a rhythm. The relation of top to bottom is death and rebirth. The linear dies into the nonlinear and finds its vitality there.

The ratio is always true. Through the "Mercator principle," the narrative lays out an interpretation of this constant fact in linear form, with its progression from before (*in those days*) to (*ever*) after. The essence of the myth, however, is the recurrent rhythm.

resistance: integration, *or*
control: spontaneity, *or*
defense: exposure, *or*
stress: composure, *or*
frustration: fulfillment, *or*
attachment: surrender, *or*
anxiety: wonder, *or*
compulsion: will, *or*
guilt: responsibility, *or*
education: revelation, *or*
civilization: nature, *or*
self-hate: love, *or*
fact: myth . . .

The rhythm is not simply a rise and fall, but a kind of opening and closing. The terms of the rhythm are not opposites. They are NO and YES. In the *no*, there is denial but there is potentiality. *Yes* is the fulfillment of *no*, the dissolving of its restraint; it is the solution of the problem, the unfolding of what is concealed, not a change but a simple clarification of what has always been true.[10]

The "ratio" can be seen clearly in different forms of myth.

The Definition of Mortality

Creation

In myths of creation, we confront the absolute universe confronting us.

$$deity \longleftrightarrow man\ created$$
$$\searrow mythic\ imagination$$

The manner in which we are created interprets our situation as human beings. "In general," writes Peter Koestenbaum, "the arguments for the existence of god . . . may profitably be reinterpreted as intellectual devices that call attention to the miracle and the mystery that things are.[11] The imagery of a creation scene highlights the nature of what is-- and even more important, the extraordinary fact *that* it is--by throwing it up against the state of "chaos," which is not simply confusion but the condition of potentiality. It is something that exists, for we cannot imagine nonexistence, but it exists without definition or form. It is energy wanting to be acknowledged.

Looking backwards towards creation, we call a stop to linear time, confronting the timelessness that always is. The nonlinear, the infinite, the other, is seen as the all. Then it itself makes the transition "forward." It allows the finite to exist. Of course, the "causal" line between the absolute and the linear is miracle, the nonlinear event *par excellence*. In this way, the natural world becomes its extraordinary self. And thus, the mythmaking mind, as Koestenbaum suggests, confronts the most essential fact about itself, its very existence, its utter discontinuity (to stress the point as the myths do) from the state of nonexistence. As deity creates man, furthermore, man creates wonder. The image of miraculous action evokes the meaningfulness of life through its imaginative energy.

If we consider "creation" to be a process that defines life as we know it, we can see in the Book of Genesis a series of steps that focus upon different "terms of mortality." Here they occur in a relatively coherent collection, but all of them are themes of creation myth that appear worldwide separately or in different combinations.

--The confrontations with reality. The actual creation, in which existence is contrasted with an absolute alternative and a transition is effected through divine thought or action.

--Alienation. The Biblical Expulsion from Eden, more broadly, the separation of man from deity, of the conscious mind from the unconscious, of the human from the natural, and so forth. Our self-consciousness creates a sense of rootlessness in the universe. Nature is dispersed.

--Mortality. Confronting the fact of our finitude. Death is introduced so that it can be acknowledged, but also other limiting factors, including work, loss, suffering; the mortal state is often experienced as a punishment.

--Fallibility. Human curiosity, the need to err, to break taboos, to assert independence, to disobey. Basically creative and poignant, it is seen by linear moralism as perverse and wicked.

The Quotient of Mortality

--Violence. The birth of evil in a primeval crime, the disruptiveness of life coming from within people themselves. The energy of life is turned against life; distorted energy is destructive energy. It often occurs as lust, especially incestuous lust, as well as murder (here intensified as the murder of one's brother, one's other self--or one's self as *other*).

--Family organization. The relation of the sexes is authorized as we know it.

--Historical reality. Our race proliferates and develops ancestral background against which we live in "modern" times. Hence the Biblical "begats."

--Disunity. In order to operate, energy splits into opposites or factions. The evil between Cain and Abel as the split between two lifestyles, agriculture and herding, and all that is represented in that split.

--Civilization. Humanity is split into peoples, far-flung and set against each other, separate in language (failing to communicate and therefore hostile), building cities, creating thereby a deliberate, conscious order of life in the midst of nature.

--The final separation from primeval times. The Flood sets a boundary between *those days* of mythic time and the linear time "succeeding." God regrets his severity and permits a fresh start. A more familiar reality follows.

--The codification of culture. The law and often the arts are given to man, sometimes fire, which is both the divine energy and the possibility of culture. Usually a unique primeval leader or demigod called the "culture hero," makes the gift, sometimes, like Prometheus, through self-sacrifice.

--The confirmation of ritual. People are taught how to worship. A bond is established and confirmed between man and deity. Sometimes deity founds his or her own shrines.

A stunning little tale from Madagascar dramatizes the origin of death in a way that makes an especially acute analysis of mortality.

> One day God asked the first human couple who then lived in heaven what kind of death they wanted, that of the moon or that of the banana. Because the couple wondered in dismay about the implications of the two modes of death, God explained to them: the banana puts forth shoots which take its place and the moon itself comes back to life. The couple considered for a long time before they made their choice. If they elected to be childless they would avoid death, but they would also be very lonely, would themselves be forced to carry out all the work, and would not have anybody to work and strive for. Therefore they prayed to God for children, well aware of the consequences of their choice. And their prayer was granted. Since that time man's sojourn is short on this earth.[12]

God proposes two ways of mediating between his condition, which is absolute existence, and man's condition, relative existence: the moon--

The Definition of Mortality

brilliant but soft, remote but placeless, always growing, diminishing, disappearing, and recurring, always singular; and the banana--familiar, plentiful and clustered, quickly consumed, quickly rotten. Of course, man chooses what is already and necessarily true. The special power of this myth lies in the fact that mortality *is* chosen, with a clear and poignant sense of its implications. Death comes not as a punishment or as a blunder or a sign of pathetic weakness (all common possibilities in African myth and elsewhere). Death comes along with the positive aspects of mortality: children, the satisfaction in one's achievements, and companionship. The confrontation with the absolute mirrors to us our nature and delineates the terms of our existence. It remains for us to take responsibility for the revelation by integrating it into consciousness. This myth is particularly sensitive to the meaning and feeling of such responsibility.

Cosmology and Sacrifice

Among the pagan heresies that the Church had trouble rooting out of the popular imagination in England was the celebration of festivities connected with Robin Hood, springtime rituals re-enacting a drama of death and resurrection apparently derived from the sacrifice of an ancient woodland deity dedicated to a primeval Maid Marian. In the sixteenth century, the illustrious bishop Hugh Latimer was distressed to find no one home at a village church where he expected to preach. It was May Day and the parishioners were making merry in Robin's honor. Recording this, Lewis Spence muses upon a pathetic irony:

> It is an extraordinary reflection that the pagan feeling of which the hapless bishop so roundly complained was to reveal itself at his own burning in 1554, some of the onlookers at the scene of his martyrdom being overheard to remark that had it taken place earlier in the season it might have saved the crops![13]

The Robin Hood ritual tradition is still part of the popular English practice of Morris dancing. It is performed at village fairs by men's clubs dedicated to the practice, and in modern time by some women's clubs as well. A strict traditionalist has denounced this innovation as follows:

> Morris is something from antiquity. It was always known to be a ritual fertility dance. As such it was a man's dance from which women were excluded. It was a man's love affair with mother earth; the young men shook and stamped the earth to waken fertility.[14]

Such ritual traditions preserve the heart of the ancient "fertility myths." To cite another British example, an old Scots ballad treats the spirit of whiskey to a sacrificial martyrdom. In an adaptation by Robert

The Quotient of Mortality

Burns, three kings "into the east" kill John Barleycorn with their ploughs but he returns to life in the spring. He is attacked again in the autumn when his summer's strength has started to fail. Then he is tied to a cart, beaten, hanged, and cast into a watery pit.

> They wasted, o'er a scorching flame,
> The marrow of his bones;
> But a miller us'd him worst of all,
> For he crush'd him between two stones.

Finally, there is a mystical apotheosis out of a savage communion. As men drink his blood, they joyfully experience his courage rising in their own hearts.

> And they hae taen his very heart's blood,
> And drank it round and round;
> And still the more and more they drank,
> Their joy did more abound.
> John Barleycorn was a hero bold,
> Of noble enterprise,
> For if you do but taste his blood,
> 'Twill make your courage rise.[15]

This song pretends playfully that there is a personage who instills in the grain its power to ferment and then to intoxicate. Only personal genius seems capable of such a transformation, and in the "communitas" of drink, an unseen hero of such caliber makes an inspired companion. But, in spite of the light-hearted quality that the tradition here takes on, it is essentially an agonizing murder and a miraculous rebirth that the imagination summons to make such "strong spirits" intelligible. The mythic pattern is still that of a "dying god" like the Egyptians' Osiris, whose body was cut in pieces by a vengeful brother; of the ancient kings sacrificed to ensure their lands' fertility; and even more clearly, of the wine-god Dionysos, who was said to have been torn apart as an infant and then boiled whole again in a cauldron, and whose rites and myths often involved death by dismemberment.

In all these agricultural rituals, human society confronts the forces of nature, tamed in part but ultimately well beyond control, and joins in their energies. The rhythm of sacrifice becomes more real than the existence of any individual--king, bishop, or drunkard--enlivening and impersonal at once. The act of love is the scattering of seed, and so is the dismemberment of the body, dispersing life directly into the soil. And dismemberment is the ordeal of coming to mortal consciousness. This is reflected also in the motifs of crucifixion (in the broad sense that makes it a motif) and the descent to the underworld, both of which confront the limits of life in the mortification of flesh and the humiliation of spirit.

In cosmological myth, which dramatizes the nature of nature, usually only deities perform. No human heroes confront them, but the

The Definition of Mortality

gods and goddesses themselves suffer the agonies of mortality, finding out the pattern of sacrifice as the course of life. There is, in the typical configuration, physical pain, isolation, extinction, or disgrace (or all these), matched by enormous grief which shakes the world. In the best known classical version, Persephone is carried off by Hades as his unwilling bride, while her mother Demeter wanders the earth in mourning, desperate to recover her. Yes, it is winter while Demeter weeps and Persephone remains below the earth--all the world is Waste Land then--but the story does not stand allegorically for the changing seasons. *Mythically*, the seasons manifest the force contained within these divine persons as they struggle among themselves. Desire and violence, seizing at beauty; sensitive youth that is violated only to grow in solemn power (for Persephone becomes queen of the dead); protective love that must learn its own limits even though its grief is limitless--these are forces of life of which the seasons are merely shadows.[16] (The death of Christ requires the grief of Mary just as it requires the various kinds of cruelty in the greed of Judas, the ferocity of the mob, the hesitation of Peter, and the compliance of Pilate.)

Another Mother Goddess, Inanna (or Ishtar) of the Sumerians, ventures below to the realm of her deadly sister Ereshkigal. There she hopes to rescue her lover Tammuz, the young "dying god," who prefigures the vulnerability of life in the midst of its ripeness. Through seven gates of descent (a maternal number), Inanna must strip herself of her accoutrements of power, dignity, and privacy, until she faces her hateful opposite and shrivels in humiliation. She herself is life, and death is her own shadow. Venturing into the underworld, she becomes *mortal* life. Imagining her story, we confront what we already are. The process is grotesque but the horror of it is only the natural feeling of mortal sensitivities at the full realization of their danger.

In a parallel Japanese story, the all-father Izanagi confronts the rotting corpse of his sister-wife Izanami now that she has become the queen of death. He responds heroically, however, hurling against her the marvelously nonlinear weapons of life: a headdress that turns into grapes, a comb that becomes bamboo shoots, and peaches that appall death's emissaries, so that he is able to confirm life's ascendancy over the vengefulness of death:

> he drew up a rock which it would take a thousand men to lift, and with it blocked up the pass. And with the rock between them, they stood opposite to one another and exchanged leave-takings. Izanami said: "My lovely elder brother, Thine Augustness! If thou dost behave like this, henceforth I shall cause to die every day one thousand of thy people in thy realm." Izanagi answered: "My lovely younger sister, Thine Augustness! If thou dost so, then I will cause every day one thousand and five hundred women to give birth."[17]

The Quotient of Mortality

Separated from one another sadly, but in necessary self-preservation, these two sides of life continue to revolve the turning circle of our days.

Myth of the Sexes

The hero is conceived typically by a union of the human and the divine. His conception is in some symbolic way spontaneous, breaking through the linear chain of history to reveal the constant pattern. This very widespread motif simply asserts the confrontation and the relationship:

$$\frac{\text{girl}}{\text{god}} = \frac{\text{linear}}{\text{nonlinear}} = \frac{\text{the conscious mind, etc.}}{\text{the unconscious, etc.}}$$

And the hero (or savior) born from this union is the integration of the two sides, imaging forth the paradox of life, which blends the two sides into one. He is the solution to the equation. "Eternity," says Blake, "is in love with the productions of time." Because our existence is simultaneously linear and nonlinear, we live out, we are, the continual result of their flowing together. Hence it is the proper business of deity to have intercourse with mortals.

Some of the most familiar images from Greek myth portray the rape of a mortal--or "relatively mortal"--virgin by a deity, often with a dominant sense of the literal meaning of the word "rape," carrying off. There is Zeus' abduction of Europa or of Leda, Hades' of Persephone, Apollo's hot pursuit of Daphne, and so forth. Such stories are familiar in good part because of the passionate and fleshly subjects they provided Renaissance artists, who saw in the moment of confrontation epitomes of life's dangerous richness, where the strange and the natural, the feared and the desired, the estranging and the uniting are all felt as part of one another.

More basically, these stories simply dramatize the will of consciousness, portrayed with male power, imposed upon poignant natural frailty. Thus Zeus unites with quite a few maidens in divine passion, usually adopting a strange bodily form in which to beguile the girl--a bull, a swan, a shower of gold. But mythically these forms emphasize the nonlinear nature of their union: the weirdness principle is at work. As myth, Zeus is not the literary figure of a callous philanderer, an Olympian Don Juan, as he may seem to be when his amours are collected in sequence, with his jealous wife always on the trail. In nonlinear terms, the "rapes" are not separate events at all but repetitions of the same non-event. They take place in time that does not move, simultaneous and absolute. They are all the same event, just as the heroes are in an ultimate sense always one, Campbell's "hero with a thousand faces."

The Definition of Mortality

Yashoda nursing her son Krishna, *copper sculpture, India, about 14th century.*

MOTHER AND CHILD:
Self and Other as a special whole.

The "Bear Mother" Princess Rhpisunt, *human wife of the bear chief, nursing her cub in pain. Haida Indian slate carving. For European parallels, see Gimbutas, pp. 190-95, 200.*

The Quotient of Mortality

Virgin and Child.
*German statuette
in painted wood,
15th century,
Rhenish School.*

**Buddhist demon queen
Hariti,** *with a few of
her 500 offspring.
India, 2nd or 3rd
century*

The Definition of Mortality

It is interesting to compare this general pattern with two others, from the Near East and from India. In the Near Eastern myth of the Mother Goddess, the mature feminine spirit of nature (and of the unconscious) loves and loses a young consort, sometimes a son or brother, who is dependent upon her: such as the story adopted by the Greeks, of Aphrodite and Adonis. In this pattern, humanity exists within the context of nature, which is mother and mistress in one. Nature is eternal nurturing, and human individuality (portrayed as male) knows his identity within her arms. He must meet death but he does not have to face it in solitude and anxiety. Therefore, he is not reflective or self-aware; he is pathetic rather than tragic. The poignancy of the myth belongs to nature, as the Goddess mourns for dead youth, the tenuous brevity of mortal existence. Thus the myth is conceived from the divine point of view. Humanity is the *other* who is confronted. Since the myth itself is, of course, an act of human imagination, what this means is that we adopt the view of the absolute and see ourselves in its terms, with appreciation but also with detachment, comforting ourselves with divine stability.

The Greek virgin is usually mother to a hero, yet she is the passive instrument of god's desire. At least in the versions that have come down to us, humanity must simply endure the force of the universe. The same mode of experience is represented in Greek tragedy, where the consciousness of individual selfhood evolves through the male ego of the hero, who must confront his mortality--his existence in nature--as something alien to his own mind. The relation between the cosmological myth of the Mother and the myth of the tragically independent Man is illustrated by the Gilgamesh Epic of Mesopotamia. In one episode the Goddess Ishtar is portrayed as an aggressive and malicious temptress, who would unman the hero by possessing him (In Jungian terms, she has become the negative anima). She desires Gilgamesh, but he spurns her with a masculine revised version of her known loves. In other words, the conscious mind has become paranoid about its source in the unconscious, projecting monstrosity upon the feminine:

> For Tammuz, the lover of thy youth,
> Thou hast ordained wailing year after year.
> Having loved the dappled shepherd-bird,
> Thou smotest him, breaking his wing.
> In the groves he sits, crying "My wing!"
> Then thou lovedst a lion, perfect in strength;
> Seven pits and seven thou didst dig for him.
> Then a stallion thou lovedst, famed in battle;
> The whip, the spur, and the lash thou ordainedst for him.
> . . . . .
> If thou shouldst love me, thou wouldst [treat me] like
>   them.[18]

In rage, Ishtar sends a Bull of Heaven to destroy Gilgamesh. He confronts it, however, by killing it, flinging its thigh in her face. The imagination forging the story denigrates the Great Mother so that the hero can reject her, but now he must go it on his own to deal with life in human terms, killing the "monster" to assert his own consciousness. The more familiar story of Gilgamesh's quest for immortality comes to us on separate tablets, but its psychology is of a piece with this episode. When his alter ego (or shadow) Enkidu dies, he realizes the full impact of his own mortality. Having alienated himself from Nature (and having withdrawn Enkidu out of Nature), he finds death impossible to accept. After an arduous quest, exhausting all hopes of escaping death, he must resign himself to the tragic state that his free mind has led to. Not only must he die, he must cope with the consciousness of death.[19]

In Greek culture, the development of consciousness led in two directions that were significantly interdependent--towards rationality and towards tragedy.[20] "The dream of reason," as Goya proclaimed--and demonstrated, "breeds monsters,"[21] and it is no strange paradox that the Greeks notably produced both. As consciousness attempted to free itself from the organic Mother, from the womb of the unconscious, and stand forth against nature to comprehend *it* objectively, it obliged itself also to face the void that resulted, the gulf of its own alienation. Henceforth, in Western culture, the acceptance of mortality would sound convincing only in anguish, in the authenticity of the solitary self.

In Hindu mythology, sexuality is characteristically a matter of seduction rather than rape or mothering. It is sometimes, as in the delightful amours of Krishna, mutual desire, drawing the infinite spirit of godhead and human individuality together for the fulfillment of each in the other's beauty and charm.

> From the time our eyes first met
> our longing grew.
> He was not only the desirer, I not only the desired:
> passion ground our hearts together in its mortar.[22]

Or, as in the stories of Shiva and his reincarnated goddess Parvati or Sati, a wooing of the austere divinity by the sensuous maiden's achievement in herself of a strength that can match his own. The contrast with the Greek theme of sexual violence is dramatic (although the violence of Greek myth is by no means specifically sexual). The tone of the Indian myths is ecstatic celebration. Sexuality is love as well as desire. Experienced with the vulnerability, the spontaneity, and the eagerness that the symbol of young femininity here conveys--human life renews itself through the divine. Sexuality, the drive of life, is playful, transcendental, personal, and profound. Although death is a part of life, even in its grotesque and arbitrary nature, it is such an integral part that the spirit of renewal easily dominates it. There is not much place here for the individual facing death alone, challenging the indifferent universe in the experience of unique selfhood. But there is a dignity in the play and flow of things, as the awesome confrontation yields to a continual sense of personal cosmic unity.

The Definition of Mortality

SEXUAL UNION AS CONFRONTATION. *Uma-Mahesvara. The Hindu god Shiva united with his consort, whose name in this form means "light." Central India, 11th century.*

The Quotient of Mortality

The sexual union of Geb, *the earth, and his sister Nut, the sky, interrupted by Shu, the air, to form the habitable world.* Egyptian sarcophagus painting, detail, 11th or 10th Century BC.

Hero and Monster

    Civilization on the verge of nature; the conscious mind on the brink of the unconscious: through will power and organized thoughts, humanity builds its own place according to its own laws, walled off from the threatening chaos with armed guards to watch the darkness. From Gilgamesh in Uruk--"the man to whom all things were known"--to Hamlet in Elsinore--"the courtier's, soldier's, scholar's eye, tongue, sword"--the Hero masters his world and, finding it wanting, feels compelled to seek out the nonlinear mysteries. Though he speaks only the language of his human world, he risks the apparent chaos of the wilderness, the darkness, and hell itself in order to know the elusive but more substantial truth over which his small human world is founded.
    The hero, then, embodies the human self accustomed to linear forms but larger than they are, fulfilling his society's standards of excellence but discovering also their sheer irrelevance before the prime facts of life and death. If the hero is usually masculine, that is because "he" is imagined through the active genius of civilization, driven by the ego to the full intensity of personal powers. At the same time he is driven into the radically different realm of universal and natural forces that is the ultimate source of all power. This intuitive, instinctual, recre-

The Definition of Mortality

ative and timeless level of the self is figured typically in the Mother or the Bride--the Jungian *anima*--the origin of his life, his inspiration, his fulfillment.

Built as a refuge from the wilderness and from eternal night (both literally and figuratively speaking), the hero's world defends itself against an enemy whose ways are radically unlike its own. The enemy has a form which unmans all those who see only with ordinary eyesight. It has powers beyond those of men, serving a heart which mocks all human vulnerabilities. This is, of course, the monster, who personifies whatever culture (or whatever the conscious mind) abhors and fears. In Jungian terms, it is the *shadow*, looming vestige of the rejected self.

What we fear becomes more monstrous when our fear of it grows. so the monster's power to appall and mangle, humiliate and annihilate enlarges our fears to an absolute degree, to the essence of what is utterly threatening. As we defend ourselves against the world of nature, nature must become monstrous. As we identify with our defenses, as we glory in our power to control our lives, we create the monsters that justify all the efforts we exert against them. Pride fears shame, intelligence fears obscure riddles, strength fears still greater strength, virtue fears the base desires which are not impressed with lofty sentiments, and fear fears those who do not fear. All our hopes are haunted by the fear of their failure. Our ideals are haunted by the spectre of meaninglessness.

The monster, in other words, is a reflex of the hero's world, confronting humanity with a mirror image of its achievements. He (or she) embodies those energies which civilization has distorted or simplified in order to build its strictly human, mainly linear realm within nature. By mastering this force and integrating it back into his culture's symbolism, the hero shows how a person may still be a full self within his limited world. He acts for the culture and exalts the culture, but he goes forth as a self, unique, complete, and splendidly able to prevail. For meaning in life comes only to the self. The community may recognize an idea, but only the individual can comprehend its force and live it out.

The great Anglo-Saxon epic *Beowulf* demonstrates this relation between hero and monster in three distinct episodes. Grendel, accursed descendant of Cain (in the Christianized text that has come down to us), plagues the fragile civilization that King Hrothgar has established on the edge of the sea around his timber meadhall Heorot. It is a realm of stern fighters all too aware of the tenuous hold they have attained in the world, of the brief space in which they may flourish. They bond themselves together with oaths of loyalty (all too easily broken) and boast of feats accomplished and feats purposed (left to burn in one another's hearts). And they are fiercely proud of that edifice, their hall, though it is so vulnerable (we are reminded) to the flames of plunderers.

Of course, the darkness of nature lurks close upon Heorot, ready to devour sleeping fighters in the night. The monster Grendel shadows their pride with his rankling envy as he watches their revels and hears their religious exaltation--spying on humanity as Satan later does in *Paradise Lost* and the monster, still later, in *Frankenstein*.

> Then the fierce spirit painfully endured hardship for a time, he who dwelt in the darkness, for every day he heard loud mirth in the hall; there was the sound of the harp, the clear song of the scop.[23]

Beowulf, the hero, comes to Heorot from abroad, with a solid sense of decency (and the strength of thirty ordinary men). He meets Grendel barehanded to face him out in his own manner, and he rips from the monster's shoulder the plundering arm. First, however, he confronts the human reality of envy in the person of Unferth, one of Hrothgar's thanes:

> to him was Beowulf's undertaking, the brave seafarer, a great vexation, for he would not allow that any other man of middle-earth should ever achieve more glory under the heavens than himself . . .[24]

Thus Grendel merely writes large the gruesome reality that the Danes' glory is built upon: when some lord it, others grovel, and deep within the proud heart something may be cringing too.

Having killed Grendel, Beowulf must deal with an extraordinary sequel, for the monster has a loving mother, who proceeds to carry on his tradition in Heorot. We are aware of her first of all as an image of the wild savagery of revenge. As such, she has special significance for Hrothgar's world. This specific society is held together partly by the Germanic rule of blood-vengeance, a very uneasy principle that bases order upon passion and the course of history upon private satisfactions, as various interpolated stories remind the assembled thanes. The violence which Grendel's Mother visits upon Heorot--wild hatred born of love--is a parody of the Danes' own legality, especially disturbing because it is not mere show of duty but the outburst of an apparently shattered--albeit monstrous--heart.

Grendel's Mother is the "Terrible Mother" of Jungian archetypology--the Great Mother (both of Nature at-large and of the individual psyche) as she is seen by the intimidated ego. As such, she is a malignant reflex of this grimly male world of warriors, in which women serve the beer, get shipped abroad as marriage pawns, and wait for doom. Accordingly, Grendel's Mother is not simply another monster, intensifying the effect of the first. She is a nightmare of violated mother-love tormenting the warrior's hall.

If, therefore, we take Beowulf's fight with Grendel and his fight with Grendel's mother together in the pair they naturally form, we have a further striking image in the composite. The relation between mother and child suggests a psychological theme along with the social implications that each figure presents in itself. Beowulf has established a masculine bond with Hrothgar, choosing him as a father by serving him. In other words, he claims his own identity and his own place in the world-society actively and consciously. Then by demonstrating his capacity to bring renewal to his second homeland, he earns the old man's symbolic paternity. However, to consolidate his position as a mature man, he must confront the Mother and his own bond with her as child.

The Definition of Mortality

THE HERO AND THE MONSTER. Krishna *as The child-god conquering the serpent Kaliya, who is shown in partly human form. South Indian bronze, 15th century.*

The Quotient of Mortality

(above) **Herakles and the Nemean Lion,** *Attic red-figured vase by the Kliaphrades Painter, 5th century BC.* (below) **Theseus and the Minotaur,** *Attic black-figured vase, 6th century BC.*

The Definition of Mortality

He encounters, in fact, an image of the grieving Madonna, which recurs in the Mother Goddess religions as well as in the Christian Pietà, as a tragic variant of the still more common figure of the divine mother nursing her supernatural child. The Mother is herself, as Jungians show, an ambivalent image, nurturing but also entrapping. She emerges in the imagination as basically good or bad according to the state of consciousness that is opening itself to the confrontation.[25]

In the Beowulf story, the Mother is to a degree pathetic but distinctly grotesque and very dangerous because the hero is making his claim for social maturity. The infantile self, who clings to the Mother, *is* threatened by the maturing ego and is itself dangerous to it. Beowulf chooses to take responsibility for his *culture* and that means he must sacrifice his dependence upon *nature*, which includes (and is portrayed by) his own child-like dependence upon the Mother. Already, in the shadow-figure of Grendel, he has sacrificed the monstrous child in himself and his fellows--greedy, envious, and violently heedless of the reality of others. Then, to everyone's surprise, he must face and destroy the grief and the rage for his own loss, the pain, essentially, of growing up, of becoming more fully committed to consciousness. But this depth of feeling remains implicit within his character, in the sensitivity, the steadiness of bearing, and the capacity for serious allegiance with which the poet imagines him.[26]

After he has been king of his own people for fifty years, Beowulf himself dies as, with a younger man's help, he kills a treasure-hoarding dragon. This monster is of a more conventional species, but he too reflects the culture's unconscious substructure. Gold is precious stuff of the earth civilized and *humanized* into beautiful and useful objects, transformed with the craft and art of the culture into goblets, hilts, crowns--or given value in relations between people. In early Germanic society, it provides a special bond, for the king is the "ring-giver," who rewards his earls with treasure, exalting himself with generosity and binding them to him with gratitude. The dragon's treasure once belonged to a people now extinct. Their artifacts, frozen remnants of their lives, return to the earth marked by the human memories implanted on them. They have lost their use and meaning now; they are anomalous valuables without *value*.

Just as the pride of Heorot reveals its nasty underside in Grendel's envy, and the blood-ties its inverse reflection in his mother's vengeance, the joy in treasure exposes its inglorious psychological roots in greed and sheer possessiveness, the security of mindless *having*, which medieval dragons seem generally to represent. The culture must, of course, fear such exposure of its ideals. Yet the hero's fortitude, his frank sacrifice and decent bearing justify them--in his actions and in their songs. Having mastered the more personal feelings of envy and revenge, it is no wonder that Beowulf finally succumbs as in old age he meets this final challenge echoing with the lost history of a bygone race, his own nation left to dwindle away without him.

The significance of the hero's enemy is not always as striking as it is in the case of Beowulf's three opponents. Among his famous Twelve

The Quotient of Mortality

Labors, Herakles must kill the Nemean Lion and bring Cerberus from his post at the gate of Hades. In other tasks, he confronts the wonderful: Diana's stags, the golden apples of the Hesperides. But the background of the story shows that Herakles is no mere paper Superman, but an anguished self coming to terms with his human nature. He has killed his wife and children in a fit of madness. His marvelous strength, in other words, has proved to be as much of a disaster as a wonder--terribly dangerous to himself as well as others. For punishment, he is obliged to serve King Eurystheus, his own timid cousin, but Eurystheus sends him on the hopefully impossible (that is, nonlinear) errands in order to be rid of him. It is Eurystheus who is Herakles' proper shadow.[27] The strongman, who has gloried thoughtlessly in his power, is humiliated by submission to his ego's underside: the image of craven weakness that a brash strongman very likely fears unconsciously. Herakles' main labor, therefore, is the wrestling with himself, using his colossal strength to subdue his colossal pride in it.

The enemy whom the Greco-Roman heroine Psyche must meet is Beauty herself, the goddess Venus, hardly a monster in the usual sense but in this story a Terrible Mother nevertheless. She appears as a wicked mother-in-law, rather than the familiar stepmother of fairy tales, whose position, structurally, she occupies. Like the vicious stepmother (and like Grendel and like jealous deities in general), she is that reflex of envy against the pride of our self-assertion, the unconscious will that we remain unconscious. However, a mother-in-law cannot be disposed of as easily as a stepmother! Venus must be transformed into a genial Mother, so that Psyche can become the wife of her son and the mother of her grandchild, Psyche thus fulfilling her own female destiny--or her own nature as the human spirit, depending on whether one regards her as a character or as the symbol her name suggests.[28]

Psyche must appease Venus by a sequence of absurd challenges that is familiar in fairy tales, tasks in which she receives the unexpected aid of magical helpers. As she herself matures by passing her tests, she transforms her Mother archetype. First she must sort a mess of grains into piles. Then she must deliver three separate prizes: wool from golden rams; water from Cocytus, one of the rivers of Hades; and a box of Proserpine's beauty, which she opens, with human weakness, in violation of a taboo.

Elaborate interpretations have been suggested for the individual symbols of this sequence, but it is worth observing what it is that Psyche actually does in each of her tasks. We need not interpret the symbolism by translating images into abstractions; instead, we can think how the hero(ine) deals with the symbols and the qualities that they elicit in her. We can then see her ordeals clearly as stages in *the psyche's* evolution of consciousness.

In sorting the grains into heaps, she must pay *attention*: observe assiduously so that she can clarify relationships. This complete self-application is enacted for her by an army of ants. To acquire the golden wool from the powerfully unruly rams who burn with the rays of the sun, she must demonstrate discretion, the capacity to act indirectly, by

The Definition of Mortality

cunning--for she is to take the wool not from the beasts but from the trees that they have brushed against. She is counselled to do this by a "green growing reed (foster nurse of flowing music) divinely inspired."[29] When she needs to fill a jar with the chill waters of the underworld, the eagle of Jupiter (Zeus) comes to her aid, showing her the power of forthright spontaneous action, the courage to face death itself. Finally, when Psyche needs to fetch a sample of the beauty of Proserpine (Persephone), who is Queen of Hades, she must pass over the waters of death with the steadfast discipline and determined self-control (as a talking tower, an erect and stable image, tells her) that lets her bypass the pitiful cries of the dead and the needy. Thus she acquires the mystical beauty of death for the Mother, which she appropriates appropriately enough for herself. Finally, through attention, discretion, boldness, and the visionary knowledge of mortality, the "psyche" who emerges from the testing ordeal is able to consciously integrate her lover Love (Cupid or Eros, the son of Venus), is reconciled with her archetypal Mother, and is welcomed to Olympian ever-after by Jupiter the Father, ruler of consciousness.[30]

<u>Tragic Myth</u>

The fully painful realization of the nature of mortality is *tragic knowledge*. The understanding that Gilgamesh attains by "failing" to achieve immortality and that the man and woman attain when they realize they prefer the death of the banana is in both cases tragic because it is endowed with a feeling of the price we must pay to live--the price being life itself.

In myths that center upon a "trap of commitment,"[31] tragic necessity is symbolized in the structure of the motif itself. The usual form of taboo trap leads to a liberating sense of personal responsibility but also the awareness, with it, of a lost paradise. The result of a taboo may be more painful than that and still be very positive. When Orpheus turns back from Hades with the wife he has rescued, he breaks the taboo against looking at her. He is not simply failing in his quest, however. On the tragic level, he succeeds, in fact, just as Gilgamesh does, by his apparent (linear) failure. If he had brought Eurydice, all the way back to earth, he would have deserved her less. His *love* causes him to break the taboo, and he is more human because he loves. The mortality that sends him on the quest in the first place, that makes the death of his beloved feel totally unacceptable to him, also requires that he lose her forever. Although Old Testament theology has obscured the mythological point known to the serpent of Eden, it is human to break the taboo. If we cannot say for sure that life is the better for it, we can at least say that true life, life as we know it, is thereby seen and confirmed.

When young Phaethon claims evidence of his identity from his father the Sun, he is told he may have whatever he wishes. The nonlinear source of life responds with an opportunity that is also a mirror, one in which our own naive consciousness discovers its real nature unexpectedly. Our identity is our mortality. Phaethon chooses honestly his real mortal desire, therefore, which is absolute fulfillment, the role of

The Quotient of Mortality

god himself: he will drive the sun-chariot through the sky. And of course, the natural aspiration of consciousness leads to death via disaster. The father's offer, the wish-promise itself, is the trap of love. Perceiving this, Ovid dwells upon Apollo's predicament and his stunned grief:

> Do you need further proof that you are mine?
> The true sign is my fear: look in my face;
> And if you could, look in my heart, see there
> A father's anxious look and passion.
> If you could understand, O son![32]

He has offered what the loving father and what life itself will in fact offer, the danger of free choice, the risk of personal existence. Our life --and our death--is the god's sacrifice. What establishes the trap, then, is the contrast, inherent in life, between the linear nature of conscious desire and the nonlinear nature of life-supporting love, or, in mythological terms, the contrast between the human and personal perspective on the one hand and, on the other, the divine. In an American Indian parallel, the sun is the hero's mother-in-law. She does not catch herself in the wish trap formally but simply follows the course of her affection, as she yields to the hero's pleas for the gift of her light, with which he uncontrollably destroys his entire people.[33]

The punishment of Actaeon is appalling and undeserved. For chancing upon a bathing goddess, he is turned into a deer and his well-trained dogs tear away at him. Yet our life is like that too. The naked goddesses of nature are as monstrous as they are beautiful, and they easily survive our judgments. Mortality is Actaeon's total vulnerability in the midst of his own chase, his own hunt for prey. Like Narcissus, like Oedipus and all other tragic figures, he is caught in a paradoxical structure, a double-bind which is the human condition. The hunter always, ultimately, seeks himself, for the lucid power of consciousness requires us to see, lucidly, our own terrible limitations.[34]

King Oedipus seeks the traitor who has slain his predecessor, the murderer of royal dignity. Proud of his wisdom--and not without cause, for he has undone the Sphinx with his cunning--he curses the enemy and comforts his people. Apollo, motionless and unseen, confronts him with his truth, as he has done over and again through his oracles: the ultimate enemy is oneself, *I* turn life inside-out, my curse against the criminal is the ultimate crime. The king of consciousness will not make life into what he will. He must try to do so, that is only human. But the more he tries, the more, that is, he insists on making sense of things, the more certainly he will have to face his tragic truth. The worst that he fears *can* happen, it is part of life. Oedipus is destroyed because he is mortal, and mortal is vulnerable. Apollo is Truth: he simply shows us what is. It is a hard lot all right, but can we take seriously for ourselves any other?

The Definition of Mortality
<u>Fairy Tale</u>

Adventure tales are likely to be either *tragic* or *transcendental*. The hero's confrontation with the other world leads either to the final acknowledgement of death or to the imagery of rebirth, *apotheosis*. Both patterns symbolize the nature of mortality, however, one by yielding to it, the other by embracing it. In one the emphasis is on the limits and the sorrows that make us mortal; in the other it is on the (literally) unmeasurable joys that come with those limits. Transcendental myths are found at the heart of great religions and in fairy tales.[35]

The fairy tale is often described as "secularized myth," since it retains mythic form and method while discarding myth's religious function and its overt seriousness. Fairy tales do not usually--at least in modern forms like Grimm's tales--picture deities; they reduce mother goddesses to godmothers, demonesses to witches, tutelary gods to wizards, and so forth. What is more important, however, fairy tales do not have myths' sense of venerable authority, which might suggest response through ritual or belief. They do not purport to be historical, they do not authorize society's institutions or arts. They engage us rather in the emotions of heroes and heroines, who are *personal* even though they are not particularly individualized or realistic. We get a definite sense of Hansel and Gretel or Cinderella as having personal problems, vulnerable feelings, and presence, a consciousness of the world they are in. Such characters are strictly typical, and they are limited in their range of experience, but they are *there* for us, with a natural sense of humanity that is emphasized by the fact that they are children (or in other tales, child-like adults).

Even when the fairy tale does confront the hero with gods and goddesses, as the Greco-Roman tale of Psyche and Eros does, the emphasis is on the emotional process that the central figure goes through and hence the emotional process that we go through as we respond to the story. In the Psyche tale, Venus and Zeus, Olympus and the heroine's apotheosis are not theological facts but elements in a human ordeal. The gods themselves are personal rather than sacred. Although the tale continually reminds us of familiar motifs--and does so in a way that is more emphatically a positive part of the narrative technique than in myth proper--we are focused upon the actual process of story-telling and the reality we are creating together *now* rather than referring to mythic truth that we wish to commemorate out of the racial past. *Once upon a time* is *ever-never* rather than *in those days*.[36]

Of course, there are obvious patterns of confrontation in fairy tales as in myths. In Grimm's tales, we move back and forth between two opposite ways of comparing simplicity and cunning. In one type of story, the heroes or heroines, often loving siblings like Hansel and Gretel, or else the youngest child of three, are sublimely simple. They are naive because they are natural, intuitively open to the life processes that make them vulnerable in the first place but guide them to fruition in what follows (They are, of course, expressions of Jung's child archetype). Their nonlinear genius is opposed by the restrictive cunning of the

The Quotient of Mortality

egoists--the stepmother and her daughter, the tyrant king, or the proud princess who sets impossible tasks. Then we see how the flow of nature sustains life by keeping it vulnerable and encompasses pain by dispelling greed and fear.

The impact of such stories is clearest when we perceive the endopsychic form that their surreal style suggests. As we partake of a story such as "The Juniper Tree" or "Hansel and Gretel," yielding to its charm, our sympathies and anxieties sort out the aspects of our personality that are defined by their relation to this norm of natural simpleness. What moves us particularly here is that the child is the savior of an ineffectual and perplexed maturity. A little boy functions usually as the active potentiality of a neglected but not quite lost innocence. As such, he must bear the suffering that comes from being exposed to consciousness, growth, time, and conflict with others. The sister evokes a more passive side of innocence, sharing his sacrifice through a trust in simple emotions.

The children have been brought into the world (or at least the boy has) by the mother whose creative power is, by the logic of mortality, her own death. Her yearning for a child, the birth, and her death all together manifest the full truth of love: *to be* is *to give* is *to acknowledge suffering*. Since what she gives in her love is real life, it exposes the child, alone, to danger and, therefore, to the possibility of growth. The danger is manifested in the other side of the Mother archetype, the stepmother or witch, who is as close and guarded as the true mother is open and vulnerable. Proud, greedy, and jealous, frightened especially of the child's simplicity, she expresses the anxiety of ego, of the self that is all too conscious of its limitations but totally unable to accept them. Her reality is, therefore, desperately linear. She must have *more* gold, *more* power, and a future of total freedom for her own child. Her response to life is painful resistance and violence, but her efforts to protect herself inevitably destroy her, because they are inherently dehumanizing.

The stepmother's replacement of the natural mother was a Fall from grace to which she (like our mother Eve) has bound the children's father. He, finally, is the self exposed to the depredation of consciousness, confused by all the conflicts of living. Well-meaning but in himself helpless, trapped in his own mortal limits, he must be redeemed by the spontaneous innocence of the child (often assisted by animal helpers or a crone of timeless wisdom, either of which reflects the child-hero's own integrity). Then the family union is rebuilt on a new basis--shared love and joy instead of anxiety.

In the other kind of story, the hero--Tom Thumb is a familiar example--is himself a cunning fellow who outwits a simple-minded populace.[37] The values of this pattern may seem to contradict the values of the other, but the impression is misleading. This hero's sharpness of wit is as nonlinear a faculty as the other's naivete, because it too seems to be a natural quality of genius that rises spontaneously and inspired. It enhances life with creative energy and pleasure in its own powers. Such a hero's opponents, on the other hand, are bound to thoughtless conventional assumptions through their own unconsciousness. With no

The Definition of Mortality

sense of self and no gusto or creative force, they restrict life to workaday social dimensions.[38]

In some stories, it is hard to tell the difference between cunning and naivete, as we are poised between the two. The Little Farmer, in Grimm, is a poor man with only a calf made of wood. He entrusts it to a cowherd, who lets it stay behind stubbornly at the end of its first day out to pasture. We cannot tell if the Little Farmer is stupid, naive, or clever to pass off the calf as a living creature, but the cowherd is certainly a fool to believe him. When the two men go together to bring in the lost creature, they cannot find it, so the mayor orders the cowherd to give the Little Farmer a full-grown cow, which is, of course, real, and the hero's fortune begins. He continues to increase his wealth at the expense of others but through their foolishness. Finally, all of the villagers jump into a lake where he tells them he has acquired a herd of sheep--an oblique truth--and when we see them all quietly perish, we must think they get what they deserve for their greed and their credulity (and a willingness they had shown earlier to drown our hero for deceiving them). The Little Farmer simply accepts what life brings him. He has outwitted everyone without exactly meaning to, in a goodnatured and imaginative way that the others could not believe in or comprehend.

As myth becomes more personal in fairy tales, it is also internalized. The customary mythic hero confronts the world of wonders and causes us to wonder *at it*. He beholds the awe-ful, recoils from it and strives with it, clearly expressing the impact of the universe upon mortality. The universe of a fairy tale like "The Juniper Tree" or "Hansel and Gretel," however, is entirely *in wonder*.[39] The children's forlorn home is as wonderful in its way as the mystic woods and the house of cake. The perfectly innocent child, his shrill stepmother, and the all-too-human father belong naturally to a world in which the monstrous and the marvelous are to be expected, because they themselves are expressions of its extraordinary nature. To live, in these tales, is to be wonder-ful. As we hear, tell, or read them, wonder becomes the breath of our own minds. More clearly and emphatically than myths, it is the function of the tales to cultivate wonder, and wonder is their heart and meaning.[40] Perhaps, to revise our earlier suggestions, we should contrast the wonder of fairy tales with the *awe* of myth. The very fact that we insist on calling them fairy tales, in spite of the scarcity of fairies on their landscape, reflects our awareness that wonder is their essence, for the thought of fairies conveys a sense of life that is ecstatically innocent. In the image of fairies, human feelings transcend human limitations, as all desire becomes complete and spontaneous, all energy free and happy.

Because wonder is thus internalized, the ratio of mortality folds in upon itself. The soul and the universe are fully integrated. It is mortality itself that is wonderful, mortality as personal existence, vulnerable yet perfect, existence felt and also flowing. Because there is no theology, there are no presuppositions about values and goals. Feelings are felt for their own sake as they work themselves out according to their inherent archetypal form. In the full intensity of basic emotions--love and grief, longing and bitterness--wonder arises simply as the love of life. It is for this reason that fairy tales remain the best material we have for educating the young in sensitivity and for re-educating ourselves as we do so. They teach the richness of the self, the possibilities of fulfillment through others, and an appropriately tender regard for our mortal condition.[41]

PART THREE

BEING

This between is measured out for the dwelling of man. --Heidegger

Chamunda, *a version of the Mother Goddess integrating the horrific or grotesque. A bronze figure from Nepal, 14th century.*

CHAPTER EIGHT

THE MYTHIC TRUTH

Before Creation, God looked into the Torah and made the world accordingly. --Hasidic saying

HOW MYTH IS

Dreams, myths, and works of art--and theories or histories too, for that matter--are not entities, separate *things* that exist in themselves. Nor are they counters or coins that have specific values, amounts for which they stand. They cannot be used as substitutes for anything else. As symbolic forms, they are all *utterances* and acts of conscious and unconscious energy. Like the direct verbal utterances of ordinary speech, they must be understood in the terms of their particular language, for dream is a different dialect, at least, from myth, while myth is a totally different language from chemistry or even history. On the other hand, all such symbols need to be understood as part of the living context from which they arise--the dreamer's life awake, the artist's culture and society--because our background provides the "vocabulary" of images that are at our disposal. However, on a third level, as I have stressed, myth can be known for what it is only through an appreciation of the psyche, or self, and *its* way of doing business.

From this triple matrix--the medium, the cultural context, and most importantly self--symbols stand forth to do their job of "utterance." Yet they continue to remain elements of their source and are constituted according to its nature. Although symbols have a public capacity and can be exposed to open view, still they have something of the evanescence of consciousness itself. Like web filaments from a spider, they are direct substance of their maker, although not themselves living matter. They have an equivocal existence: they are *and* they are not (as one of Shakespeare's characters says of our selves), and this paradox has a good deal to do with their flexibility and also with the fascination that they can exert, as well, we may suspect, with the linear mind's prejudice against them.

In linear terms there is existence and also there is the proposition of non-existence. I was going to say, there is existence and there is non-existence, but non-existence is what isn't, so I cannot properly say that it *is*. However, loosely and fairly, and linearly, we assume something either is or is not. My car is, my private airplane isn't. My sisters are, my brothers, since I never had any, aren't. The three-headed live-bearing duck-billed trolley-car is not. Chicago is, the land of Oz is not. (In Chapter 10 we will consider the sense in which Chicago is not.) Yet from

The Mythic Truth

books and film we have a strong image of Oz and remember it fondly from "times" we were "there," and the brothers I don't have may have been as important in forming my personality as the sisters I do. In the subjective symbolic world, as Lady Macbeth discovered about the blood that would not be washed from her hands, there are many powerful ways of being.

We assume that all things that *are*--living or inanimate--are equally existent, for objects have their identity as well as people. All propositions, similarly, must be true or false, all answers right or wrong. Nevertheless, although we like to know where we stand, we find ourselves hearing and saying things that are *sort of true*. We have to vote, if we vote, one way or the other, yet we know in our hearts that the politicians, at best, only *tend to* be right, and we may even feel sometimes that they all tend to be right (and surely *wrong*) in different ways. The languages of many tribal peoples do not actually have a verb that means "to be" in our sense.

In the mythic world, as in life, things often *tend to be so*, and once we have stated *how they are*, we often feel we have oversimplified by being too specific. Our prose language is weak in ambiguity. When we say something, our assertion seems too easily complete and definitive. But myth, like poetry, plays continually upon what Philip Wheelwright calls "assertorial weight."

> In expressive language . . . statements vary with respect to the manner and degree to which they are susceptible to affirmation and denial, ranging all the way from *heavy* assertorial tone, which characterizes the literal statement, the proposition, to *light* assertorial tone, which consists in an association or semi-affirmed tension between two or more images or other expressive units.[1]

The slang commands "drop dead" and "go to hell" are forceful to be sure, but as assertion they are "light." They are mythical--meant but not literally meant. "I don't like you" may be less convincing, but as assertion, it is a good deal heavier, and "I feel the tension of fear in my stomach when I see you" is heavier still, being more literally and less ambiguously true--yet it is not as likely to deter my enemies. Of course, all these statements, like mythic tales, *are* assertions. They are meaningful and communicate something. When they are essentially dramatic, they communicate indirectly from an intellectual point of view but very directly in emotional terms.

Since a mythic hero does not have the continuous existence of an identity in time, as we do, he is made up of facts that are not *true* but seem to hover in an elusive presence, an *almost*, or *virtual*, being.[2] This is one reason we cannot talk about causes of events or motives of character in the usual manner. "It must be emphasized," emphasizes the *Reader's Companion to World Literature*, "that a myth is not a specific literary work, but a floating tale."[3] A myth is like a scenario--a mere sequence of events, and a tentative sequence at that--and as such it is not

How Myth Is

yet fully alive. Its images suggest to the imagination intriguing possibilities, but they call for the concrete body of form that they realize in ritual or in one of the arts, particularly poetry or drama.

But though the myth must exist in some form, any form pins down the myth to a concrete reality that falsifies it simply by being concrete. As soon as we say the hero said something or did anything, as soon as we put any statement about him in the past tense--"Oedipus asked, 'Who are my parents?'" or "Oedipus struck out his eyes"--we must be lying. There are no specific words or concrete actions back there for us to record. There is something somewhere, but it is not factual. In order to discuss the tales, one easily falls into the linear fallacy of treating heroes as people. There is no need to avoid the fallacy, but we can understand better what we are doing if we are aware of it.

A realistic novelist can play with the limits of mythic reality by stretching them like a rubberband and letting them snap back again. The Greek hero Perseus killed the Gorgon Medusa, whose serpent-hair turned all who saw her into stone. John Barth's modern version of Perseus has received among his fan mail a flood of puzzling questions "from some dotty girl in Chemmis, Egypt."

> They were billets-doux, I admit it--but along with the hero-worship was a bright intelligence, a lively style, and a great many detailed questions, almost as if she were doing a dissertation. How many had been the Stygian Nymphs? Had Medusa always been a Gorgon? Was it really her reflection in Athene's shield that saved me from petrifying or the fact that Medusa had her eyes closed; and if the latter, why'd I need the shield? How was it I'd used the helmet of invisibility only to flee the other Gorgons and not to approach them in the first place? Did everything that saw Medusa turn to stone, or everything Medusa saw? If the former, how explain the sightless seaweed? If the latter, how came it to work when she'd been beheaded?[4]

And on and on. Although the myth itself expresses consciousness, the mythic hero really has no consciousness himself--unless a writer dramatizes his mind in words. Like a figure in a dream, he only acts for us, while *we* are conscious of his acts. Barth's joke, and his suggestive probe of the symbols, comes from imagining his hero's natural mind. When his girl-friend in the stars accuses him of getting his own mother's name wrong, Barth's Bellerophon replies:

> "As to Mom's name: some accounts give it as Eurymede, some Eurynome; that's a not-uncommon discrepancy in the case of accessory characters in a myth . . . So, I just call her *Mom*."[5]

The Mythic Truth

The myth itself as myth has some kind of existence, or we could not think of it at all, but its existence is not apparent. We have only *versions* of the myth. Even the scenario is not definitive.

> Two incompatible accounts of Oedipus's end survive. According to Homer, he died gloriously in battle. According to Apollodorus and Hyginus, he was banished by Iocaste's brother, a member of the Cadmean royal house, and wandered as a blind beggar through the cities of Greece until he came to Colonus in Attica, where the Furies hounded him to death.[6]

In the version we know best today, Sophocles suggests that the earth at Colonus opened up and received Oedipus to the company of the gods. We cannot say that older versions are "truer" than later ones, for a new writer can bring out deeper implications of the symbols by reshaping them. He can add or he can remove intrusions of linear logic. The real myth lives among its versions, defying form, rich only with possibilities.[7]

A myth, therefore, is not the work of art that portrays it. The myth of Oedipus lives only once again, reconceived, in Sophocles' tragedies. Even so, the imaginative nature of myth suggests comparisons with the arts. A myth is imagery that does not live simply through the senses. It is story but is not the telling. It is a poem that is not rooted into words. It is a picture but it is not visual. It is a rhythm but it makes no sound. It is a moving picture, but it is not depend upon a screening. Yet like a story it must be known as a process of incidents rather than a static picture. Like the metaphors of poetry, its images suggest what they cannot say. As a picture might, or a series of pictures, it strikes our memories with isolated visions of strange configurations. Like music, it leads us along a pattern of flow--through repetitions, climax, variation, and harmonic relationships--making us feel that its form is more dynamic than its references to the ordinary appearance of life. Like film, it organizes its life-stuff in a series of images that are linked by felt resemblance and shifting innuendo. Like music and film and story, it does unfold to work out its pattern into a time-flown process, but it is importantly timeless at the same transcendent "time." It is bud and blossom, seed and seedling, fruit and withering stalk, in sequence, in reverse, simultaneously, in part only, and not at all.

Myth's mode of existence--its ontology--may seem like an incidental point to discuss in paradoxical detail and at length. Yet in this way, by existing *as* it does, myth reveals more to us about our lives than it does through the data of its tales. The kind of tales and the kind of characters are controlled by the myth's manner of being. But even more fundamentally, by imagining the myth as what it is in itself, by experiencing it *as* myth, we become clearer about the nature of consciousness, and that means we become clearer about the way in which we experience our lives. Our image of who and what we are, our assumptions about the world, our personal and our public values sit more clearly, lit with the kind of reality that they too possess.

How Myth Is

The psyche is an organ (to speak mythically) and myth a tissue of that organ. Seeing it as it is, naturally we reach a truer appreciation of the organism and of organic being, or life. Myth responds to social needs and it is knowingly cultivated, but it is essentially spontaneous, in the way that life is, flowing forth into manifestation. Consciousness is energy bubbling to the surface of our minds and myth exists, as bubbles do, to release the air that has been contained in fluid. Thus, like the life whose nature it manifests, myth is more vital than the linear categories into which we would like to sort it. It seems elusive and vague until we confront it in itself. Then we can start to distinguish what we bring to it from what it brings to us.

How myth *is*, then, expresses the way that mind is. But the point is more basic yet: it expresses how life is, even, we may say, how anything is. Myth is a measure of ontology itself. No thing is really stable, fixed, utterly existent. The term "being" itself is too positive to convey its own nature. We have the concept so that we can know it in contrast to nonbeing. But existence is a slight exaggeration. Being is tenuous, tentative, liminal, transitional. Whether we are thinking in terms of molecular energies, time, perception, processes, or representation, what *is* is always almost just virtually so but then a little more than that. To speak figuratively, being is gaseous, vaporous, present in its own dispersion, not vague yet swarming. It is always "soft."

As for life, it is more clearly approximate in its continual coming and going at the same time, its unconscious consciousness, its liminal as-it-were-ness, its hovering among our perspectives (of them but not in them), its perpetual escape from words, theories, beliefs. It is fundamentally as uncertain and indeterminate as the positions of the atomic particles that manifest it in nature--at the same time that it is as clear, recognizable, and softly firm as the living bodies that those atoms manifest to our senses. As the archetypal patterns of myth remind us, life has form and its paradoxical indeterminacy is part of that form. Always dissolving and coming forth, life carries its rhythm along at once in and out of time, space, cause, and identity. The levels of truth, the dimensions of being, face each other in absolute contradiction but ultimate oneness as hero faces demon, as men face the gods, as the mind faces the weird and grotesque and beautiful images which register the more subtle world it dwells in--which cannot be anything but the world of being in itself.

Myth exists with a kind of truth that baffles the intellect. Myths are all lies, yet they are meaningful lies. They are obviously absurd, yet they are true *in a sense*. So we deal with them meaningfully when we perceive--imaginatively, qualitatively--what that sense is. Their truth is not like scientific truth and it is not like moral truth. It is not theory and it is not belief. Hovering between knowledge and fantasy, between assertion and design, this is the truth of just being, of saying "yes, I am" and "this is life" and "so do our energies work and play and trap us and release us again." Thus the existence of myth implies a conception of truth that is profoundly realistic with utter simplicity. It brings our minds close to the level of life's forces that we need to contemplate if we are to think meaningfully, honestly, and creatively.[8]

The Mythic Truth

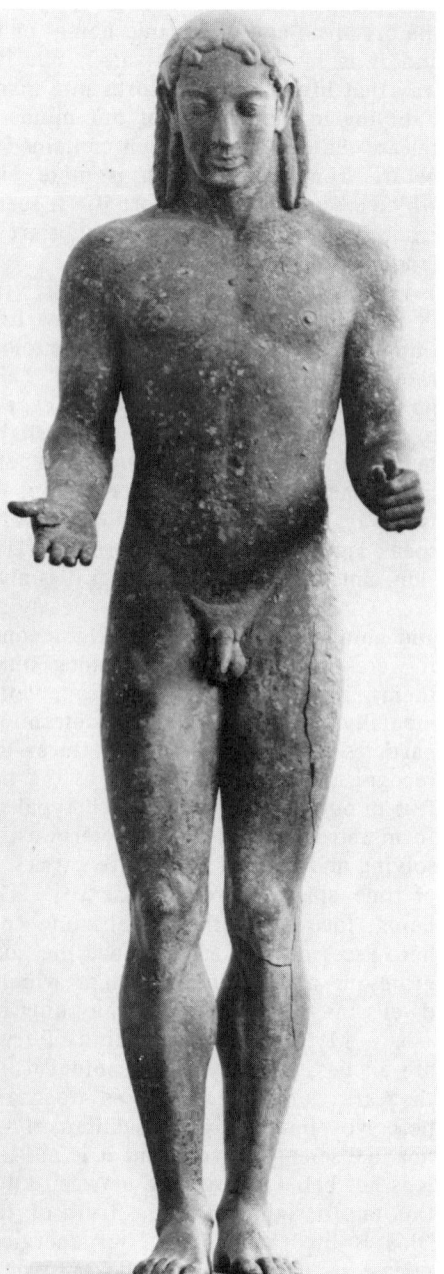

How Myth Is

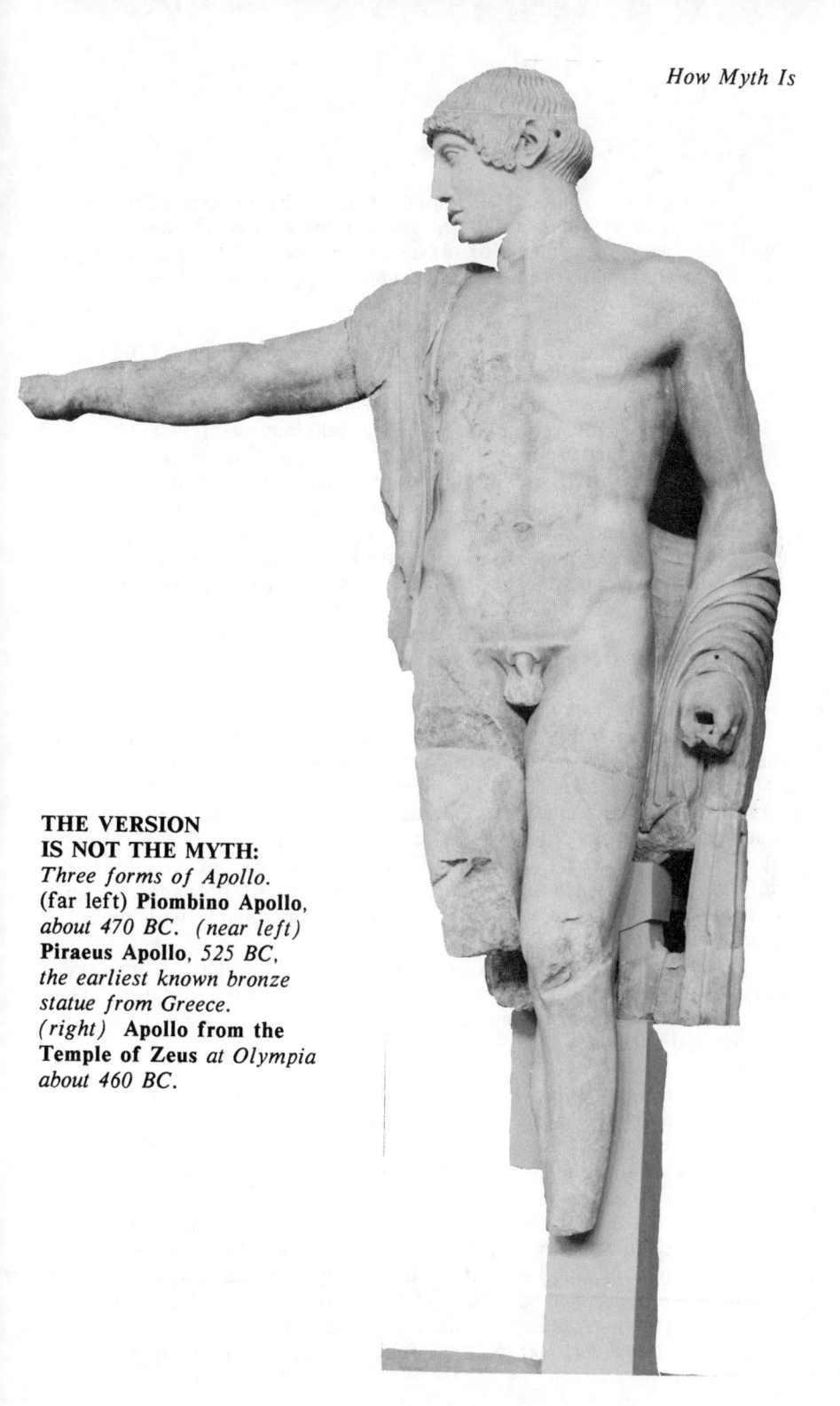

**THE VERSION
IS NOT THE MYTH:**
*Three forms of Apollo.
(far left)* **Piombino Apollo**, *about 470 BC. (near left)*
Piraeus Apollo, *525 BC, the earliest known bronze statue from Greece.
(right)* **Apollo from the Temple of Zeus** *at Olympia about 460 BC.*

The Mythic Truth

FUNCTIONAL THEORIES

In order to avoid the assumption that myths correspond to linear "meanings," it is of some use to speak of them as having *functions*, as though they were instruments or organs of the body. The anthropologist Bronislaw Malinowski formulated a version of myth's social function that has been very influential.

> Studied alive, myth . . . is . . . a direct expression of its subject matter; it is not an explanation in satisfaction of a scientific interest, but a narrative resurrection of a primeval reality, told in satisfaction of deep religious wants, moral cravings, social submissions, assertions, even practical requirements. Myth fulfills in primitive culture an indispensable function: it expresses, enhances, and codifies belief; it safeguards and enforces morality; it vouches for the efficiency of ritual and contains practical rules for the guidance of man. Myth is thus a vital ingredient of human civilization; it is not an idle tale, but a hard-worked active force; it is not an intellectual explanation or an artistic imagery, but a pragmatic charter of primitive faith and moral wisdom.[9]

Malinowski summarizes myth's effectiveness in three areas: belief, morality, and ritual. Literally, the myths may explain *why* beliefs are held and behavior followed, but his conception of them as *charters*, like the charter of a city or a club, turns attention, in a less linear way, to what they accomplish by their explanations. A charter permits us to do what we have already decided to do anyway. Its instructions, therefore, are not linear cause; their influence is indirect. They authenticate our activities, in fact, giving us the sense of a solid basis. We do as we do under the authority of law, or the aura of divinity. We act not merely with purpose but with meaning.

The principle of the mythic charter extends beyond Malinowski's three categories to the practical economic activities of daily life. The Northern Aranda of Australia remind themselves that their ways go back to primordial ancestors.

> The *gurra* ancestors hunts, kills, and eats bandicoots; and his sons are always engaged upon the same quest. The witchetty grub men of Lukara spend every day of their lives in digging up grubs from the roots of acacia trees. . . . The *ragia* (wild plum tree) ancestor lives on the *ragia* berries which he is continually collecting into a large wooden vessel. The crayfish ancestor is always building fresh weirs across the course of the moving flood of water which he is pursuing; and he is for ever engaged in spearing fish . . . if the myths gathered in the Northern Aranda area are treated collectively, a full and very detailed account will be found of all the occupations

Functional Theories

which are still practiced in Central Australia. In his myths we see the native at his daily task of hunting, fishing, gathering vegetable food, cooking, and fashioning his implements. All occupations originated with the totemic ancestors . . . .[10]

All of life may be lived under such supernatural sponsorship. In making their tepees circular, the Oglala Sioux Indians may have followed a fashion that was practical, convenient, simple, and appropriate for their materials. But they also felt the need to explain this shape as a divine mandate.

> The Oglala believe the circle to be sacred because the great spirit caused everything in nature to be round except stone. Stone is the implement of destruction. The sun and the sky, the earth and the moon are round like a shield, though the sky is deep like a bowl. Everything that breathes is round like the stem of a plant. Since the great spirit has caused everything to be round mankind should look upon the circle as sacred, for it is the symbol of all things in nature except stone. It is also the symbol of the circle that makes the edge of the world and therefore of the four winds that travel there. Consequently it is also the symbol of the year. The day, the night, and the moon go in a circle above the sky. Therefore the circle is a symbol of these divisions of time and hence the symbol of all times.
>
> For these reasons the Oglala make their *tipis* circular, their camp-circle circular, and sit in a circle at all ceremonies. The circle is also the symbol of the *tipi* and of shelter. If one makes a circle for an ornament and it is not divided in any way, it should be understood as the symbol of the world and of time.[11]

Although such an explanation may mythologize after the fact, it makes good nonlinear sense. The simple and natural way to raise the tent *would* be the divinely inspired way. The supernatural, mythologically, *is* the essence of what is natural. Thus the tent turns out to be round not *because* everything else is round--but for the same reason. The smaller world of home in which the Sioux encloses his family simply partakes of the large world's order, as his tent shares its form with the heavenly bodies and the turning of time. They all reflect one another as full bodies of unity, so that the private life within the tent and the greater life outside are naturally interrelated. Through the mythic idea, their relationship is affirmed and "celebrated."

Thomas Mann, whose notion of myth as celebration I am recalling,[12] provides in the same discussion a subtle version of the charter principle, one that goes well beyond the social needs of primitive tribesmen: "The myth is the legitimization of life: only through and in it does life find self-awareness, sanction, consecration."[13] Life becomes "legi-

The Mythic Truth

timate" as it joins in the organic rhythms of myth and in its miraculous sensibility.

Seeing myths in an operative way, however, as instruments with functions, can imply misleadingly that they are external objects to be utilized and put aside. But on the other hand, it could also assume that they are functional parts of the organism and, therefore somehow integral to the minds and lives of persons. Any social factor will also have psychological function, since we are individual selves in society and not just counters on a game board. Participation in any social pattern is obviously in itself a response to personal drives. It is Jung, of course, who emphasizes the personal value of myth. He would say of myth, as he says of ritual, that it "has, in fact, the functional value of a paradigm, and its purpose is to show us how we should act when the libido gets blocked."[14] One does not regard the paradigm, or model, I think, as reflectively as Jung's formulation here might seem to suggest. Nevertheless, we have seen that myth charts the logic of emotions (or as "paradigm" implies, their "grammar"), so that we can follow their movement in imagination.

Stressing the reality of myths more directly, Jung writes: "Not merely do they represent, they *are* the psychic life of the primitive tribe, which immediately falls to pieces and decays when it loses its mythological heritage, like a man who has lost his soul."[15] Jung speaks of his "archetypes" as though they were like bodily organs. If we ignore our archetypes, he argues, our health is endangered as much as if we ignored our livers or our hearts. Thus, in the words of Joseph Campbell, whose work on myth is predominantly Jungian, "Living myths . . . are not to be judged as true or false but as effective or ineffective, maturative or pathogenic."[16] When myth "works," it helps integrate experience by clarifying feelings; what makes us ill sustains the frustrations and turmoil, fostering self-deception.

In their personal function of clarifying the individual psyche, myths also have a profound public effect. It may not seem as practical as Malinowski's functions but it is at least as valuable, cultivating among the community a state of mind that is usually affirmative as well as cohesive.[17] As Victor Turner's work emphasizes, a creative relation to nature and to others is sustained in people's feelings.[18] When imagination is encouraged, the experience of life is nurtured and given that much room in which to flourish.

A clearly nonlinear logic operates on a different level when Benjamin Whorf speaks of the Hopi ritual dances as "preparing rain and crops" rather than causing them.[19] Of course, if you only prepare for the rain, you have not failed if it does not come. But the function of the ritual is seen here properly as one of orientation, sustaining the community's relation to the revolving world of nature, not simply as a fact but as a process of experience. Ritual is not simply magic used to control nature. "When the natives want crops they don't just chant: they chant *and they plant* seeds; they chant and they cast their fishing-nets; they pray and they go out and hunt."[20] In Jung's words, "it is indeed an objective fact that success attends the sure rather than the unsure."[21] While the words of a chant may say, "Let the clouds water us, let the herds foregather," *the*

Functional Theories

process of uttering the words says, "Let us together be ready for life." Thus the process operates through a nonlinear direction, reaching nature by action inwards. The energy which the chant or the dance, the fast or the sacrifice will summon in the participants is, first of all, a purpose of its own. Then the energy can deal with the world beyond, in hunting, planting, marrying, or dying. Richmond Hathorn makes a similar point about ritual in quite poignant terms:

> Not practicality, but *participation* is the motivating principle of religious ceremony. A scapegoat must be found at the turn of the year not primarily because the tribe hopes that a good season is made certain by that means--surely the tribesmen could remember many a year when the ceremony had no such effect--but mainly because man cannot bear for the year to turn without his having joined in the turning.[22]

What is true of ritual in this sense is likely to be true of myth, for in the activity of ritual, the mythic world is evoked, encountered, and negotiated.

To ask the purpose of the ritual or the myth, actually, can only perpetuate an endless line of questions. Why do the Indians perform their dance? To insure the rain, of course. (A more subtle answer, note, than to *produce* it.) But why do they do a *dance* to insure the rain? Because their myths and elders tell them to. Why do their myths and elders tell them to *dance* for the rain? Because dance is one of their culture's forms of self-expression. And so forth. . . . If, however, instead of why, we ask *what*, we might get somewhere. What *is* the event itself? What is it like as an event, what is the experience of it like, what does it do for the participants? Then we get a sense of living function, expressing itself naturally and fruitfully.

MAKING BELIEF

Traditional archetypal storytelling may develop in a spirit of religious revelation, perhaps as part of a ritual practice. Or it may develop in a spirit of significant entertainment--perhaps of *esthetic* revelation--as in legends or folktales, including much of what we first think of as Greek myth: stories like Phaethon or Icarus, the rape of Helen and the Trojan Horse, the wanderings of Odysseus, or the voyage of the Argonauts-- which have no connotations we can easily recognize as religious and no clear suggestion of ritual origin.[23] The kind of traditional myth that develops as part of a culture's religious system exists only in a state of belief. It is cultivated because it is considered "true."[24] All that an outsider can study is the fossils of such myth. Once it is treated as "poetry," it tends to become fantasy, or metaphor, or allegory, instead of myth. However, traditional esthetic myths--even folktales--carry a sense of authority about them that is something like belief. The temptation of Circe and the ordeal of Hansel and Gretel imply no dogma, but they seem *somehow* factual. They are a sort of phenomenon existing in themselves,

The Mythic Truth

like the hills. They seem "as old as the hills," in fact, and as likely to be *there* forever. Aside from traditional lore of both kinds, of course, we can create literary myths in works like *Moby Dick, King Lear*, or *The Tempest, As I Lay Dying*, or (with reservations for a degree of cuteness) *The Lord of the Rings*, but that is another (though related) matter. The author may be following archetypal form, we can say meaningfully that his work becomes mythic, but he *is* an author, trying through traditional patterns to make something new, a consciously crafted work structured in words, and he generally speaks to his (limited) audience in his own voice or in a stylized presentation of himself as narrator.

True religious myth exists ordinarily only in a state of belief and thrives under limited consciousness.[25] It may cultivate consciousness of the experience which it embodies, its feelings and its orientation in life, but it stops short of a consciousness that it *is* mythic and that there is, accordingly, something arbitrary about its formulations, for in order to formulate anything significant, it must express the archetypal confrontations through the individual culture's influence, in concrete shapes.

Although religious myth exists only in a state of belief, therefore, we can know it as myth only without belief. Reflecting upon the stories without any commitment to them, we appreciate their qualitative value and we can see truth in them all. It often seems that we can understand myth only *because* we cannot create it spontaneously or live within it naturally.

This striking paradox about myth and belief is more understandable, however, if we look closer at the concept we call belief. What we mean by belief depends upon what we mean by truth. As the Dutch scholar Johan Huizinga writes, "we always judge archaic man's belief in the myths he creates by our own standards of science, philosophy or religious conviction."[26] Within a truly mythic culture, people do not have convictions, however, because they do not have to be convinced. They have made no decision. Belief as we know it exists only where there is choice, and choice exists, of course, only where one is aware of alternatives. The member of a mythic culture has assumptions that permit him a knowledge of the coherence of experience.

Our usual concept of belief is based upon the cool assumption that we speculate upon reality and then affirm likely conclusions. Or else we subscribe to ideas that we prefer to hold about reality even though we know that they are not absolute. We don't consider ourselves to have beliefs until we are aware of the beliefs of others. Before we reach this stage, of course, others are simply heretics or fools. Thus a rational scholar describes a shaman's trances as a kind of manipulation of the group through self-deception:

> In states of this kind, the human being experiences the feeling of being independent of the limitations of space, time and his own bodily existence . . . The human being imbued with this euphoria feels himself superhuman, possessing divine power-- even a god. Inasmuch as he believes these ecstatic experiences to be real, the possessed man becomes convinced that he

Making Belief

is capable of extra-ordinary achievements (and his fellow men are likewise so convinced).[27]

During this event the shaman and his community, it would seem, fall under an illusion that they would otherwise want to see through.

In dealing with mythical truth, then, perhaps it is best to speak about belief as little as possible. In many contexts, it is more accurate to speak of *how* myth-oriented peoples have *experienced reality* than it is to speak of what they have believed or thought *is* true.[28] Myth and experience are incontrovertible; belief is not. The shaman does not experience just a "feeling of being independent," he experiences actual independence. When he is not in a trance, he experiences the universe as a place where such an event can transpire. The Yoruba experience the boxes they carry about with them as being their head or souls.[29] The Nuer experience the cucumber as an ox (although they do not *think* it is one), the Desana experience the earth as a giant cobweb, the Elgonyi experience the rising sun as a revelation of deity.[30] The Egyptians experienced the Pharoah as the god Osiris. The followers of Dionysus experienced his presence in wine and ecstatic dance, those of Demeter experienced hers in the grain. The early Greeks in general experienced the universe as being presided over and inspired by the Olympian pantheon. And so forth. Myth and ritual are not vehicles for philosophy nor are they simply metaphoric *expressions* of experience. They are ways to experience the nonlinear aspect of experience itself.

The German anthropologist Leo Frobenius pleasantly circumvented the question of belief by proposing that "archaic man *plays* the order of nature as imprinted on his consciousness.[31] He emphasizes thereby the exuberance of myth and ritual, their necessarily impractical and irrational nature, and also their freedom from the categories of truth and falsehood. Of course, myth is not *only* play. It is profound play, playing "the order of nature," and confronting it thereby as Thou. Huizinga, who quotes this statement by Frobenius, develops the theme extensively in his *Homo Ludens*, "Playing Man" or "Man the Player." "In all the wild imaginings of mythology," he asserts, "a fanciful spirit is playing on the border-line between jest and earnest," but he precedes this sentence with a more "serious" consideration: "In myth, primitive man seeks to account for the world of phenomena by grounding it in the divine." He goes on to his broader thesis:

> In myth and ritual the great instinctive forces of civilized life have their origin: law and order, commerce and profit, craft and art, poetry, wisdom and science.[32]

Civilization itself, in other words, has extended itself out from the mythic sense of play.

A problem with the play formulation is that it suggest a linear alternative which is seriously *not* play--work or instruction or spirituality perhaps--whereas what does make myth like play is itself the lack of awareness of such contrasts and their lack of relevance. Still, once we

The Mythic Truth

have called myth a form of play, we can look more directly at the qualities that have come to mind and notice in the meantime what has happened to the idea of truth. Myth cannot be true, simply because it is not a form of assertion. Sharing some of the nature of ritual, it too is a kind of activity, an exercise in experience. As in play, myth and ritual are activities performed with intent pleasure and excitement, cultivated primarily for the luxuriance in *being* which they provide. The sense of life enjoying its own processes is itself the all. There is no real linear goal beyond, only the flow of living form, conscious of its own nature. Unfolding in this way, however, myth and ritual do make contact with the deeper recesses of consciousness and the more solemn problems that characterize our existence.

INTRINSIC IMAGES

If we assume that mythic images are functions of consciousness, or of psychic energy, then we see that they exist not as pictures on the wall but as elements in a process. This need not mean they are "only in the mind" as long as we remember that it is the experienced universe--the world as mind encounters it--which we have been talking about all along. Kenneth Burke goes so far as to assert that "there are sheerly technical reasons, intrinsic to the nature of language, for belief in God and the Devil."[33] A prayer requires a prayee, so to speak; a curse (as we have seen) wants a demon. Both of these uses of language express states of mind--states of helplessness in both instances--and it is perhaps arbitrary to separate the language act from the state of mind it expresses. But either way, we can make a case that the specific image addressed resides in the experience, that it is in Burke's word *intrinsic*.

It is not simply in language but in the intensity of ritual--such as prayer--that the myth thrives. Gratitude calls upon a benefactor, conscious energy upon a source. Truly ecstatic celebration calls for a universe that can join in one's dance, as the joy in living flows out upon a vital world. Philip Wheelwright makes the subtle point that the image of the god in a petitionary prayer, begging a favor, will differ appropriately from that in a penitential prayer, in which one confesses one's sins. To relieve the anguish of guilt, one is likely to project deity as a wise and forgiving father rather than as "a cosmic trust fund banker."[34] An important school of thought used to argue that myth always derived from ritual. In Robert Grave's words,

> True myth may be defined as the reduction to narrative shorthand of ritual mime performed on public festivals, and in many cases recorded pictorially on temple walls, vases, seals, bowls, mirrors, chests, shields, tapestries and the like.[35]

It is reasonable to assume, however, that myth often developed free of rites and must have influenced them as well. Hathorn suggests it is a question of the-chicken-or-the-egg. Still, it is easy to see how ritual is likely to precede myth--as gesture is more spontaneous than words, as the sweep of the arms, the bow, or the cry is more immediate, closer to experience itself, than the ideas we must formulate to interpret them. As image, myth stands halfway between ritual (gesture) and theology (interpretation). It is a qualitative utterance or putting forth, but it is one that can be shared among minds. Although it invites interpreters, it leaves the party before they arrive.

The importance of this equivocation becomes clearer if we return to the sense of mythic identity. The ritual of sacrifice, we have seen, serves to unite the worshipper and his god through the intermediary victim or offering.[36] "It is no mere play that the dancer in a mythical drama is enacting," writes Cassirer; "the dancer *is* the god, he *becomes* the god."[37] Dionysos, patron of ecstatic rituals, himself must have arisen to embody or to focus the experience of his worship. His band of revelling followers, "the *thiasos*," writes Jane Harrison, "is before the god."[38] The Great Spirit with whom a youth communes in his initiation ritual "had his origin in those rites which it was his function to represent."[39]

PROJECTION

To see the mythic image intrinsically is to locate its existence in the process of projection. "Projection," however, has two relevant meanings, the technical meaning of psychoanalysis and a more basic one. In Freudian terms, projection is the way we extend outside ourselves the qualities of our own minds. Thus "primitive man," Freud observes, "transposed the structural conditions of his own mind into the external world"[40] --although the founder of modern psychology cannot help but apply a scientific skepticism to the process, finding it "in our eyes an *over*-valuation--to psychical acts."[41] Jung writes that "mythological man perceived the unconscious in all the adversities and contrarieties of external nature without ever suspecting that he was gazing at the paradoxical background of his own consciousness."[42]

In personal experience of projection, we may discover through other people those feelings that we repress into our own unconscious. "Projections change the world into the replica of one's own unknown face."[43] The qualities we will not acknowledge in ourselves we attribute readily to enemies, and we fight out with them actively the struggles that divide us within. We live out the emotional conflicts we cannot resolve, reenacting them in all our personal relations, our ambitions, competitions, and fantasies, in the entire course of our lives. "The psychological rule says that when an inner situation is not made conscious, it happens outside, as fate."[44] Thus the mythic hero himself follows the call of haunting voices to venture into unknown realms which cannot be known, in fact, except through the evolution of experience. His struggles with forces of darkness and his quests for symbols of immortality image forth the fears and the fulfillment that await us all amid our own rather more mixed emotions.

The Mythic Truth

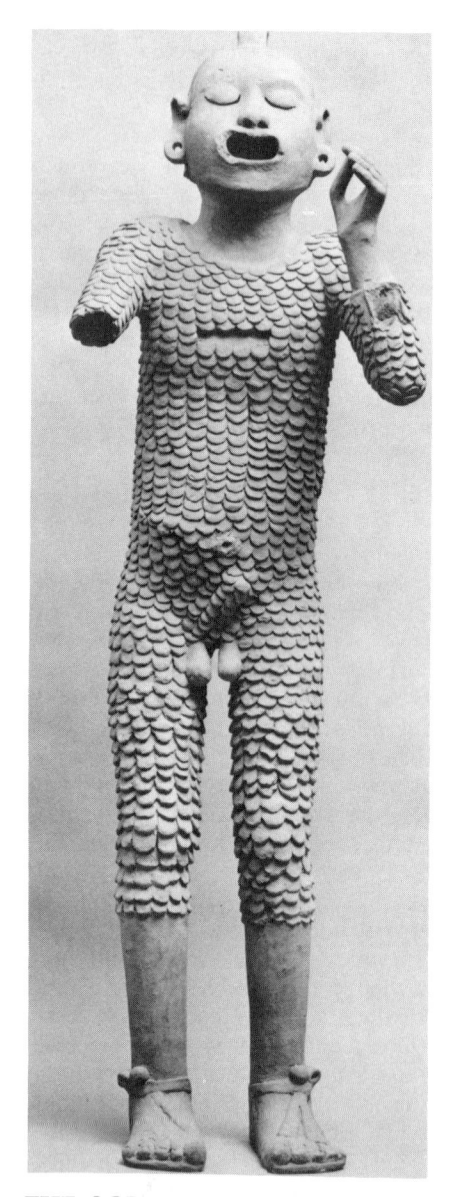

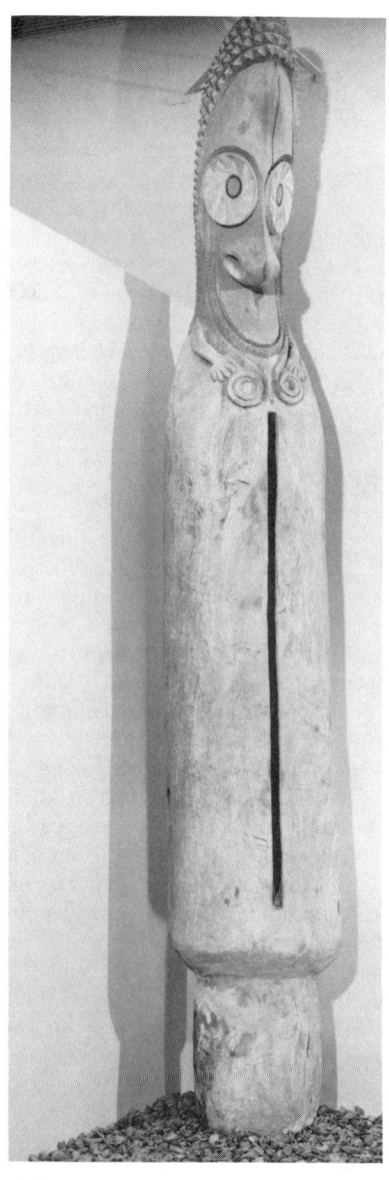

THE GOD IN THE RITUAL. (left) **Xipe Totec**, *Aztec god of spring fertility, wearing flayed skin of sacrificed victim. Ceramic figure.* (right) **Wooden slit gong**, *a monumental musical instrument called "The Mother," sounded in rituals of sacrifice and initiation to invoke ancestral voices. A modern carving, 168 inches high, from New Hebrides.*

Projection

(left) **Bull Kachina.** *Hopi Indian. The doll represents the masked dancer, who embodies the spirit of the animal.* (right) **African Nail Fetish.** *Ba-Kongo figure, (Lower Congo). These are used to judge and punish offenders. Driving a nail into the body releases the spirit residing in charms within the belly.*

The Mythic Truth

In the second sense of the word, underlying the problem of mythic ontology as its broadest basis, projection is the way any kind of symbol, symbolic form, or symbol system comes into its mental existence. The mind simply projects, or casts forth, images that it can encounter and share, much as a movie projector throws its pictures on a screen. The specific images of art and the general systems of science, the doctrines of religion and the interpretive records of history are all projected from the events of life through human consciousness. In myth, the projections may be cast freely onto the horizons of imagination itself, in which case they approach the condition of the fairy tale, or they may be cast upon a grid of doctrines, so that they commit the mind to belief in them. Often myth has been a process projected upon historical events or living persons, a language in which to memorialize them by grasping the essence of their specialness.[45] On a minor level, close to home, the value--and not just the factuality--of a George Washington or an Abe Lincoln is caught in familiar tales of childhood prowess or integrity.

More importantly, the founders of religion, the meaning of whose lives fully transcends logical historicity, are at once remembered and celebrated in mythic terms. The mythic nature of their teaching merges with their identities. The Iroquois League (to take now a less familiar example), a strong confederacy that is said to have inspired the American Constitution, was organized by a Mohawk, Hiawatha, who was himself said to be carrying out the teachings of a more mysterious prophet.

> It seems that around 1570 a saintly prophet named Dekanawidah, born of a virgin mother, put an end to warfare among the five tribes and established "The Great Peace." Dekanawidah was supposedly inspired by a dream in which he saw a huge evergreen tree reaching up through the sky to the land of the Master of Life. This was the tree of the sisterhood (not brotherhood, for the Iroquois were a matrilineal society), and its supporting roots were the five Iroquois tribes.[46]

Many a prophet has received the call to his mission in a vision or a dream. A real Dekanawidah may have had such an experience, or such an archetypal incident may have been attributed to a real person, or a prophet-hero may have been projected beyond the authority of Hiawatha complete with the natural and appropriate vision motif. The great tree joining the land and the heavens, and the virgin birth are, of course, primary motifs. If we say that they were influenced by Christianity (or any other sources), we still want to know why these particular motifs caught on, and we are back to archetypal logic.[47]

There are times (fortunately) when it seems too easy to distinguish clearly between history and myth. Events in the life of Jesus alone may suggest that mythic forms can emerge spontaneously in at least some dimensions of the objective realm. If myth expresses the forms of life, it might well arise in living form. Though some may insist it does so only once, the fact that so many different groups have made the claim

Projection

throughout historic time reminds us that myth is natural, simply projecting, or extending, the rhythms of life onto a symbolic level.

PROJECTING THE UNIVERSE

A Kato Indian text about the world's creation shows the primeval world *in those days* arising dramatically in the very process of mythic projection. The world as we know it came to us after a great deluge.

> Water went they say. Land was not they say. Water only then, mountains were not, they say. Stones were not they say. Fish were not they say. Deer were not they say. Grizzlies were not they say. Panthers were not they say. Wolves were not they say. People were washed away they say. Grizzlies were washed away they say. Panthers were washed away they say. Deer were washed away they say. Coyotes were not then they say. Ravens were not they say. Herons were not they say. Woodpeckers were not they say. Then wrens were not they say. Then jack-rabbits, grey squirrels were not they say. Then long-eared mice were not they say. Then wind was not they say. Then snow was not they say. Then trees were not when it didn't thunder they say. It didn't lighten they say. Then clouds were not they say. Fog was not they say. It didn't appear they say. Stars were not they say. It was very dark.[48]

The chant-like repetitive form annihilates linear time and linear cause together, surrounding our minds with the stillness before time. Water, land, fish, deer, and grizzly bears, all the elements and members of the natural world, or so many that it seems like all, are evoked in order that they can be canceled. We are reminded of everything we know in order to imagine not knowing it. The chant is hypnotic; repetition is a nonlinear argument of cause: what seems so so often must be so. When the conclusion comes, "It was very dark," it is a climax and a fact, for the darkness has been spreading without our direct awareness, while we have been watching the things that are not there. (Reality before creation is conceived in more emphatically nonlinear terms in the Hindu *Rig-Veda*: "Then was not non-existent nor existent: there was no realm of air, no sky beyond it."[49])

One more consideration should be particularly illuminating. We know all this is true because point by point "they say" it is. The maneuver that negates each concrete image is carried on the authority of the "Fathers," but who are "they" and what kind of identity do they have? They are not simply our linear forebears, our great-great-*x*-great grandparents, who were as ignorant of such matters, and as dependent upon mythic authorities as we are. "They"--like the "they" who say it is bad luck to walk under a ladder and good luck to throw salt over your shoulder, who say that virtue is its own reward and that, if we do not at first succeed, we must try, try again--"they" are nonlinear beings who are pro-

The Mythic Truth

jected in the very process which commemorates them. At the same time, however, as we perform the recitation, it is literally *we* (through the taleteller or priest) who say so. But the process we are performing is a "they-saying." We are projecting a nonlinear time in nonlinear space in which nonlinear cause is about to operate in the great acts of primal creation. We do so naturally by evoking the identity of an authority who is the nonlinear image of our own mythmaking powers. "They" are voices of the imagination, the unconscious archetypal knowledge. As in the projection of the Greeks' muses, however, the mythmaking power sees itself mythically, as itself a "Thou," alive with presence or personal being.

The nonlinear "they" make all proverbs proverbial and all superstitions hauntingly convincing. "They" also make all myths truly mythic, even when, as is usual, "they" are not explicitly invoked. The reality of myth is defined by an aura of self-sustained truth, which is its mandate, the privileged status of its charter. No matter whether some talented individual himself brought forth the tale or whether it passed through countless lips before it took the form we know, its sources seem to fade off into the great beyond back to *source* itself, a transcendent origin. The myth seems therefore definitive, authoritative, to be accepted in its own terms without reference to practical tests or the criterion of reason. Modern literature often adopts the traditional patterns of mythic narrative or, like John Barth's "Perseid" and "Bellerophoniad," plays with familiar images out of old myths; but as the work of conscious artists deliberately being mythic, it will not really summon this authority. True myths seem to live free of their texts, to be recorded rather than composed, to come from those far voices which, as far back as we can imagine going, will still have come out of the past, from the realm of inspiration itself and the timeless knowledge of intuition.

We need to remember, as we think about myths, that myth developed in cultures without writing. The early projections were not frozen for all time in print but were made and made again in the processes of story-telling and ritual. It is hard for the modern reader to appreciate the significance of this, for in his act of reading, he looks almost invariably for knowledge rather than experience.[50] Myth calls for a special willingness on a reader's part *to imagine*, since he comes to the text alone and in silence. But both ritual and story-telling--like preaching, for that matter, and spiritual training--are dramatic programs that happen, and they are transactions among individuals whose lives are allowed to touch. The vital heart of myth, its nonlinear being, depends upon "the *viva vox*, transmission by living fellowship and the inspiration of personal contact."[51] As the group merges, as the listeners blend into the story-teller's mind, their individualized rationality dissolves and consciousness rises in qualitative forms. The flow of feeling and the sensuous pleasures of imagination create a spell in which the images can thrive and establish their own conviction.

If myth served originally (as in Robert Graves' definition) to record the pattern of ritual, to give its content, that is, a form in consciousness, or if it served to provide a charter (as Malinowski says) to sanction the rite, still myth must have come soon enough to hold the

Projection

imagination with its own charm or spell, and ritual, similarly, must have come to the point where it would seem to dramatize the myth by fleshing out its skeleton of events with emotional intensity, so that it could become fully subjective and alive.

In literate times, since at least the Greek tragic playwrights (or earlier, the Babylonian author of the *Gilgamesh Epic*), literature has often served something of this function of ritual in relation in myth. Especially in the suggestive and highly charged language of poetry--with the spell of its rhythms and its habitual defiance, in metaphor, of linear distinctions--literature can recreate the *effect* of myth. It may lose (except to some degree in drama) the sense of communal transaction, it may lose that aura of a transcendent source and authority, and it may lose the sense of solidity that comes with actual adherence to myth. But perhaps it gains a freedom to see the myths *as* myths, to appreciate their essentially qualitative significance, and their special status in reality. "The mythogenetic zone today," writes Joseph Campbell, the place in the world from where myths grow, "is the individual in contact with his own interior life, communicating through his art with those 'out there.'"[52] Despite its communal nature and its archetypal form, myth has always been about the predicament of being a self. Perhaps it has required modern times and Western culture to fulfill this side of its nature.

MODES OF PROJECTION AND MODES OF BELIEF

I see my image in a mirror. I see my image in a snapshot. I see my image in a fantasy. Each image is a very good "likeness." If I see my image in a painting, it may be quite realistic or quite clearly stylized by the artist's systematic distortions or the effect of his medium. In each of the four cases, however, I relate to the image on a totally different basis; I have a different sort of experience of it. I project it in my imagination, with or without a physical medium, in a different way. Although all four are essentially the same image, they all exist in different ways, and what is more, they all have not only a different significance but a different *kind* of significance for me.

While the photograph is stable, caught in the past, factual but gone, the reflection is flitting with me through the elusive present (as soon as I say it is now, it is past), moving back and forth and out of the frame; and the fantasy is a mere potentiality or less, a shadow of what I wish. The images confront me differently: the photo with my history, perhaps nostalgically; the reflection with my conscious sense of being; the fantasy with a sense of my arbitrary limitations, my dependence on the circumstances I live in. Each kind of image--and the form of projection that holds it--tells me something about the nature of pastness, presentness, futurity, which are themselves not only three aspects but three *kinds* of reality. Each is elusive in its own way, but each is *there* (or *here*) for me in its own way. The painter's image is different from the others, however, largely because it is interpretive, his own statement about me,

The Mythic Truth

and because it is enmeshed with a concern for paint, pattern, and proportions.

There are undoubtedly many ways that mythic images project, and though they all *as myth* have common mythic qualities, they can differ from each other in their existence even while they differ from the reality of history or social statistics. Without too much difficulty, we can pick out at least three ways of projecting deity in myth--leaving aside strictly metaphysical or theological possibilities that do not take on "character," and expecting the likelihood of combinations. Deity can be realized as Agent, as Essence, or as Potentiality. As Agent (in the sense of *actor* or *doer*), deity is the ultimate power of existence and the force behind it. This is god as creator (Plato calls it the demiurge) and, having the total power of creation, god as protector.

As Essence, deity can be broadly the truth of What Is (Jehovah as "I Am," the Hindu goddess Sati as "She Who Is"), or more specifically the embodiment of a certain aspect of life (what can be called the allegorical-function god, like the late development of Athene as goddess of wisdom; Ares or Mars as god of war), or the spirit of a natural force (Thor as thunder, Poseidon as sea). What the Greeks called the *daemon* is, I think we can say, deity as the essence of process (life is What Happens). Dionysos is projected on this mold and the Mother goddesses as the creative but passive sources from which life flows, to which it continually returns.

As Potentiality, deity projects fulfillment of the human state. In psychological terms, this is the unconscious become conscious, a model of the integrated self. The hero who has faced death and overcome it, in some symbolic form, is in this way to be regarded as a god. Some myths make explicit his apotheosis, or promotion to immortality. A transition point between nature and the supernatural, or between mortal and immortal, is often his sacrificial death, which registers the impact of mortality and transcends it. The sacrificed becomes the savior, as Christianity makes clear, although it certainly did not invent the pattern. Overlaying our three types of projection, however, it is tempting to see in the Christian Trinity a tendency to fulfill them all at once, in Father, Holy Ghost, and Son (with Mary, as Jung would suggest, a subsidiary Great Mother.)

Now, it is not important whether these three modes of projection represent all possibilities or even whether they do fall out into three nice types. The breakdown does suggest, however, that there *are* some quite distinct ways of projecting deity and, what is more, that the images that come forth will have different kinds of reality. Furthermore, since we cannot completely avoid the question of belief in discussing the reality of divine images, we can see that the kinds of adherence that may be called for will differ from type to type. This is not exactly a matter of *whether* or not one believes, but of what such adherence itself might consist of.

The kind of "belief" depends upon the kind of projection. The kind of existence depends, more obviously, on the kind of "belief." If Mars *is* war, if Thor *is* thunder, they simply exist in a different sense than an image of man as god and, again, in a very different sense than an

Modes of Projection and Modes of Belief

image of a creator who may be able to help us in our need. Since they are identical with their essence, they are not exactly metaphors. Exactly *what* way each can exist must be left up to the reader's imagination, to his capacity for projection, but it will depend also upon a range of projection suggested by an individual myth or by an individual version of a myth. Is the mythic process an intellectual or an emotional one as it is dramatized in the story? Is "Thou" actually confronted or is it only acknowledged? Is the image experienced along the continuum of one's own consciousness or as a separate entity? As we find in reading ancient texts or anthropological field work, projections of a deity can vary distinctly among believers within one culture. We can tell as much from talking with our friends.

CHAPTER NINE

MYTH IN NATURE

the individual can never stay within a unit which he does not at the same time stay outside of . . . he is not incorporated into any order without also confronting it . . . to be one with God is conditioned in its very significance by being other than God.
  --Simmel

PARTICIPATING MEMBERS

When we call anything beautiful or ugly, interesting or boring, valuable or useless, we know that living involves us in the world, so that we feel properly diminished if someone says that such judgments are only subjective, as though they had nothing to do with the world itself. Not only do myth and the arts depend upon our assumptions that qualities are in the world and not just in our minds, but so does loving and choosing sides, so does working, by and large, and playing and sightseeing. How many people would pursue "valuable" goals or even analyze "interesting" topics if they really thought that the appeal lay only in their own minds? Living *is* being in the world, *being* is being implicated, life is never self-contained.[1]

It is one of the main functions of myth, as of ritual, to dissolve particularity, the separateness of being. "The myths have taught . . . that the form of individuals is only an accident."[2] That is from Lucien Lévy-Bruhl, the French philosopher of ethnology who contributed the standard term for the sense of fusion that myth fosters--or rather its tendency to elude differentiation: *participation mystique*, mystical participation. This includes the sense that one exists in the excrescence, or effect, or "appurtenance," of one's body--such as hair, nails, clothing or footprints;[3] that one is an element of one's society with "an almost organic solidarity;"[4] that the self can be identical with specific animals and other natural beings; that the human world is interpenetrated with spirits; and that the living are involved in the existence of the dead. It is "the *power to be otherwise*, for which things and beings have a double reality, one visible and one invisible."[5] Accordingly, it is a faculty impervious to *either-or* logic and the law of self-contradiction.[6] Most importantly, it does not make our usual assumption that experience is *inside us* and is personally one's own. Rather, it regards experience itself as being as much outside--in nature, alive and aware, *from* the world and involved in the world--as it is in us.[7]

Many anthropologists have challenged the usefulness of Lévy-Bruhl's term as he presented it, but even though it may not typify the thinking of nonliterate people overall, as he originally argued, still it applies well to mythical thought, whether it occurs in the forests, in the classics, or even in modern culture.[8] A Siberian shaman ascends to heaven by beating a drum, because the drum is made from the world-tree. The drumming becomes a process of climbing, the hypnotic rhythm of the drumbeat being *identical in essence* with the timeless and spaceless action of ascending the umbilical tree.[9] After the Flood, to take a classical example, Deucalion and Pyrrha are dismayed to hear that they must scatter their mother's bones behind them to renew the human race. Then they realize the mythical significance of their task: the earth is Mother, and rocks are her bones:

> They left the temple
> With floating robes and veiled heads, then furtively
> Dropped pebbles in their trail and as they ran
> (Some find this fable more than fabulous,
> But we must keep faith with our ancient legends)
> Pebbles grew into rocks, rocks into statues
> That look like men . . .
> And veins began to stir with human blood--
> Such were the inclinations of heaven's will.[10]

To start the world again, they must involve the earth Mother as the source of all procreation, so that life may flow from Life. They are not caught in a quibble, but the surprises of a nonlinear realization, through the kind of irony that riddles and oracles typically convey. The rocks participate in the Mother and therefore they *are* potential men and women, children of the living universe.

Participation, Lévy-Bruhl suggests, "might be something essential to the human mind."[11] If it is an aspect of primitive mentality, then "primitive mentality is an aspect . . . of human mentality in general."[12] On the broadest level, in daily life, the world of self rises through our consciousness and spreads around us. As we project our values, we extend our own being with them, so that it often seems impossible and meaningless to say where we stop and where this world of ours begins. Things that we "identify with"--house, cars, clothing, also people and even ideas--become in a real way part of our selves. We transfer feelings about our personalities to our bodies. So much more do obvious symbols such as money, uniforms, and flags help carry for us our sense of who we are. Anything we *own* is *our own*. The arbitrary syllables of our "own" names are infused with our sense of self and our most personal feelings. One type of magic, we know, is based upon the manipulation of people through their names. But "even today," writes Cassirer, "we often feel this peculiar awe of the proper names--this feeling that it is not outwardly appended to a man, but is in some way part of him," and he quotes Goethe saying:

> A man's name is not like a cloak that merely hangs around him, that may be loosened and tightened at will; it is a perfectly fitting garment. It grows over him like his very skin;

Myth in Nature

one cannot scrape and scratch at it without injuring the man himself.[13]

In fact, Cassirer considers it "one of the fundamental assumptions of the mythmaking consciousness itself . . . that the potency of the real thing is contained in the name."[14] Mythmaking takes the names of *things* as seriously as we take the names of persons. Having a name makes something a self. Being a self, it has relationships. With relationships, it has a story.

SAVING THE ENVIRONMENT

The rational mind, by its nature, breaks down experience into falsely separate elements. In particular, it cuts off the self observing, the subject, from the object, the world observed, leaving us all tourists in a foreign country from which we cannot easily return. One reason, then, that myth establishes its emphatically nonlinear universe is that it reflects the reality in which that split has not occurred. Alan Watts and Gregory Bateson, among others, have propounded the idea that mind must be understood in an ecological relation to nature. Although our own culture has isolated, or *abstracted*, mind from nature and overvalued the abstractness that results, consciousness is still properly at home in its concrete experience of the world-at-large.[15] Just as animals and vegetation evolve together in a continuous "ecosystem," just as bees and flowers depend utterly on each other's dependence on themselves, so does human consciousness and its environment evolve through their mutual dependence. "This earth is honey for all beings," say the Upanishads, "and all beings are honey for this earth."[16]

It has become increasingly obvious in our time what the principle of ecology implies about the literal survival of our species and our planet. Our biological crisis is serious enough, but it can be understood in relation to the problem of mental ecology, which is at least as important. This involves three kinds of environment that are not strictly separable, and they are all subject equally to the depredation of neglect: the world of our experience of nature; the world of other people, society; and the world of mind in which we know ourselves. And this third, strictly human world is twofold. There is the world of more-or-less direct experience through the spontaneous spreading of our being around us, including our participation in the world; and overlapping upon it there is the world made up of all our representations of this experience, the world of culture. Each new idea grows from the seeds of other ideas, crosspollinated with experience. Each image of our symbol systems must be able to flourish in a complex environment that itself, on each level, depends upon all of our individual creations, decisions, interpretations, and ambitions.

Along with the theme of mental ecology, Watts proposes a field concept, which also makes the point that myth and poetry are ways of dealing with life *in relationship*: "for there is no thing, no event save in what science calls a field."[17] Much of our material so far, particularly

Buber's formulation "I and Thou," Lévy-Bruhl's "participation," and the discussion of mythic confrontation, has pointed in the same direction. As in physics, the conception of a field dissolves the picture of separate identities, helping us to see a universe of energy in which we participate, so that "meaning" does not depend upon ourselves alone but upon the way we are enmeshed in the world. "In the beginning," writes Buber, "is the relation," and myth restores that primeval state.[18]

In our discussion of nonlinear identity, we noted the special reality that the primitive experience of *mana* suggests.[19] We can see it now as a function of the field. "The true significance of the concept of *mana*," Cassirer claims, "lies . . . in its characteristic 'fluidity,' in its merging of properties which to our way of thinking are clearly distinguished." It appears "where there is no clear dividing line between physical and psychic, spiritual-personal and impersonal reality."[20] In its elusive simplicity, it expresses the quality of the sacred, which itself "designates a specific ideal relation rather than a specific objective property."[21] The quality of myth that *mana* suggests is just this sense of relationship. It is as though the factor of relationship were itself given identity and confronted out in the beyond.

PLAYING THE FIELD

Myth establishes an imaginative field in the mind. It also extends this field to include the world around, so that the three levels of reality--the mythmaking mind, the community, and the realm of nature--blend into a single assertion of life. First, the mythmaker, the inspired vessel of creative energy--priest, prophet, bard, or village storyteller--who speaks forth from his home in nonlinear reality to affirm its truth, its vital importance to all. All members of the society may participate in transmitting the tales and different persons may be at the center of the process at different times, but such specialists (Eliade calls them "technicians of the sacred") sustain their traditions with all the necessary intensity. The ultimate figure of mythmaker is the shaman--popularly called the "medicine man" or "witch doctor"--a key personage in his societies, with a special facility for moving back and forth between his people and the world of spirits. Some have theorized that he was the origin of all myths among prehistoric men, the source of all heroes and gods.[22] He usually heals the ill by his own self-transcendence, but also he brings to the tribe its ritual songs and dances. Most importantly, he is living evidence of the vitalizing force of the unconscious (or the supernatural) and the channel to its powers.[23]

In the process of mythic projection, the mythmaking mind and the community at large blend together as all enter the spell of imagination. Anthropologists and psychologists may quarrel whether a social or personal function can explain myth better, but in the field they are inseparable. Myth unites the personal and the public selves into a communion, a coming together of individuals. Its archetypal form focuses each member of the community on the level of his nature that he shares with the oth-

Myth in Nature

ers. It elicits, so to speak, their psychic common denominator, symbolizing it through the culture's common language of images, assumptions, and principles. Behind these symbols resides the self which characterizes the group as a unit but goes deeper still, holding the group's members together in *communitas*, on their *human* basis.[24]

Of course, the culture's myths bind the community with its own distinctive style of values and manners, but what gives the myth its real sticking power, making it really work as social glue and extending its appeal still to us beyond the culture, is its responsiveness on this deeper level to the most basic ways of consciousness. Much of the material of myth deals with the frustrating experiences of people living together. But though the manner of social behavior varies from one culture to the next, the human situation remains basic: we are all selves among others, each at the center of a universe. Myth, in fact, frequently deals directly with conflict between deep personal feelings and the claims of our society. As with an Oedipus, an Antigone, a Herakles, or a Job, a real sense of this relation may very well have to come through tragic agony, yet the result is an orientation between the two worlds that gives each its human meaning.[25]

The third element of the field also combines the psychological and the anthropological perspectives. Myth blends the human world with the world of nature. Although his broad view of myth is close to Jung's, Watts criticizes Jung for neglecting nature in his concentration on "inner" forces.[26] Myth confirms the unity of human and natural rhythms--or the *natural*ness of human nature--and it does so by continually involving the experience of nature in its view. The cycle of the seasons (with the spring growth of vegetation), the "heavenly" bodies (as we still occasionally call them), the swarming enormity of ocean, the living stability of trees, the tremendous bulk of mountains, the dramatic contrast (away from the lights of civilization) between night and day--all the presences and processes of nature conjure the mythic mind to its fantasies, fascinate it with their endless forms of power and animation, and provide a mirror for it to see its own features in. The vivid, continual reality of one's place in nature as it is experienced by mythmaking peoples is almost beyond our comprehension, not only for the quality it gives to their daily and nightly, monthly and yearly way of life, but for every need of their survival.

In their main ceremonies, the Huichol Indians of Mexico experience the identity of life that flows in them and in their staple crop of maize. They reach this understanding as a condition of consciousness through their ritual use of peyote. In an annual pilgrimage, they "hunt" the peyote exactly as if it were living deer, and the blood of a sacrificed

Playing the Field

Master of Animals *(or mistress). Horned deity of forest and hunt, shown controlling lions and goats. Bronze cheekpiece from a horse bit. Luristan (in Iran), about 1000-650 BC.*

deer (or, more recently, of a bull substituted for it) feeds the growing maize. The Huichol's highest wisdom, accordingly, is the coalescence of the apparently distinct orders of existence in one flow. "Now I will tell you of the maize and the peyote and the deer," speaks one of their shamans. "These things are one. They are a unity. They are our life. They are ourselves."[27] The human self conscious of nature, the vegetation whose cycle of growth sustains life, the sacrificed animal that dramatizes mortality, and the vision-yielding cactus reveal the essence of life in their oneness--not in their similarity or their interdependence but in their actual identity. The vision of consciousness *is* the cycle of mortal growth. In ancient Greece, initiates into the Eleusinian mystery religion probably had a similar realization of the divinity of Demeter in the grain, while initiates into Orphic mysteries experienced their sacred oneness with Dionysos in the grape.

An extreme sense of the interrelation between human society and nature is dramatized through a remarkably coherent system of myth (or theology) and ritual by the Desana Indians of Colombia. In their vision, life depends upon a closed "circuit of energy" that revolves between themselves, the animals, and the plants. The Desana rigorously maintain this flow, which is quite clearly substantial for them, being limited, in fact, in quantity. Spirits of their own dead replace the hunters' prey, and

Myth in Nature

their sexual abstinence allows the beasts increased fertility. They hunt their prey as though they were making love. Their shaman, the *payé*, having partaken of a hallucinogenic powder, enters the hill which is the animals' house, where he negotiates with the Master of the Animals.[28]

> When a payé arrives at one of these places, *Vaí-mahsë* receives him and shows him his animals hanging from the rafters of the maloca "in bunches." After having agreed on the price in souls, the payé chooses the game animals that the hunters have asked him for. Walking through the maloca he shakes the rafters and beams to wake up the animals that then go out into the jungle. The price is charged "per shake" and sometimes more are awakened than had been agreed upon and the payé must reopen negotiations.[29]

The mythological ecosystem of the Desana has continual practical function in the economy of the rain forest. It has the distinct disadvantage that it induces considerable anxiety and sexual repression. Still, it allows also a profoundly alive consciousness of belonging to nature with an intense sense of responsibility for it.

In myth, then, the inspired self, the community, and the world of nature, coalesce. We should add a fourth element to the list, however. It is a world that is sensed through the self but beyond it. We can call it, loosely, the supernatural, including within its reach all aspects of experience that do not correspond to objective data.

The supernatural, in this sense, is the realm of experience that floats free of nature. There my feelings have no concrete object or no other, separate person that can account for their impact upon me. It is my own consciousness, which I experience as the *subject* of my perception, but it is also consciousness as an environment in which I exist, and which I can confront. Furthermore, if consciousness is energy and nature is energy too, my experience participates in something that reaches beyond itself. In dreams, fantasies, and the arts, this flow of experience finds out forms that must be free of linear and "realistic" connections. In myth, it overflows into the realm of beings, places, and times that we more properly call the supernatural: the gods and demons, the heavens and hells, which resist our linear order of things and celebrate in our minds their own independence.

THE LIMITS OF SUBJECTIVITY

Some traditions of the East, such as Buddhism and Hinduism, can be completely explicit about the subjective nature of mythic imagery. An extremely impressive example is *The Tibetan Book of the Dead*, the *Bardo Thödol* (literally, "Liberation by Hearing on the After-Death Plane").[30] This is a series of discourses read to a person who has just died, in order to guide him out of the cycle of rebirth to final liberation in the state of Buddhahood. As he is being led along, challenged and terrified by deities and demons for as long as forty-nine days, he must come to recognize,

The Limits of Subjectivity

with his guide's assistance, that the visions he sees are all reflexes of his own mind, resulting from his attachment to life in his body and to his deeds in the world. He is exhorted to keep these words in his mind:

'Alas! when the Uncertain Experiencing of Reality is dawning
    upon me here,
With every thought of fear or terror or awe for all
    [apparitional appearances] set aside,
May I recognize whatever [visions] appear, as the reflections
    of mine own consciousness;
May I know them to be of the nature of apparitions in the
    Bardo;
When at this all-important moment [of opportunity] of
    achieving a great end,
May I not fear the bands of Peaceful and Wrathful [Deities],
    mine own thought-forms.'[31]

The dead subject is met first by divine lights of wisdom, which will frighten him with their brilliance if he is not yet ready for liberation, and by a dazzling array of deities, who embody various aspects of his world. He is reminded:

These forty-two perfectly endowed deities, issuing from within thy heart, being the product of thine own pure love, will come to shine. Know them.
O nobly-born, these realms are not come from somewhere outside [thyself]. They come from within the four divisions of thy heart, which, including its center, make the five directions. They issue from within there, and shine upon thee. The deities, too, are not come from somewhere else: they exist from eternity within the faculties of thine own intellect. Know them to be of that nature.[32]

If he is not yet able to loosen his grip on his bodily life, and merge with the Peaceful Deities, he meets the Wrathful Deities. They are the implications of his misdeeds and his improper living, his avoidance in life of the path of the Buddha. More terribly now, he must recall this further urging of his living guide:

O nobly-born, when such thought-forms emanate, be thou not afraid, nor terrified; the body which now thou possessest being a mental-body of [karmic] propensities, though slain and chopped [to bits], cannot die. Because thy body is, in reality, one of voidness, thou needest not fear. The [bodies of the] Lord of Death, too, are emanations from the radiances of thine own intellect; they are not constituted of matter; voidness cannot injure voidness. Beyond the emanations of thine own intellectual faculties, externally, the Peaceful and the Wrathful Ones, the Blood-Drinking Ones, the Various-Headed

Myth in Nature

Ones, the rainbow lights, the terrifying forms of the Lord of Death, exist not in reality; of this, there is no doubt. Thus, knowing this, all the fear and terror is self-dissipated; and, merging in the state of at-one-ment, Buddhahood is obtained.[33]

If the subject accepts the vision as the work of his mind, the symbolic playing out of his life, he realizes that his temporary life in the world was a passing illusion. Then he is ready to embrace the ultimate and eternal reality awaiting him. He takes responsibility for his myths, in other words, in order to attain a full sense of his true self. The projections (or "thought-forms")[34] are withdrawn, the terrors faced, and his consciousness is free. An awareness of the nature of myth, therefore, is here a definite means toward a higher, or clearer, state of consciousness both in life and afterwards.

The principle of projection implies that all mythic images are symbols of psychic forces. But after we have observed the process of projection and realized its implications, we may feel a need to recognize a contrary kind of truth, or at least to qualify our generalizations. Thus one major vulnerability of Jung's approach, as his critics have often pointed out, is its complete internalization of the mythic forces.[35] If myth operates in a field, it is interfused with a world that is not myth, and it merges consciousness with what is not human. It confronts, of course, an *other* in the vast "Thou" of mystery. Defining wonder, in fact, as "the sense of otherness," Mary Midgley, an English philosopher, writes:

> We need the vast world, and it must be a world that does not need us; a world constantly capable of surprising us, a world we did not program, since only such a world is the proper object of wonder.[36]

We have frequently seen that myth is a way of *getting at* that world. It is the world we experience ourselves *in*, as well as the world we *are*.

Somehow, paradoxically, the projection is also an encounter. Athene and Apollo, Odin and Thor, Brahma and Krishna, should strike us properly as serious absolutes in themselves. They are not merely metaphors or other figures of speech. They are not substitutes for ideas or for experiences. They do not exist *as if* or *as it were*. They are the terminal points of the experiences that know them. They are, and they are as they are. Athene is not just a dramatic way of saying "wisdom," or Apollo "truth." There is something alive and personal, dramatic and mysterious, in wisdom and truth, in warfare and in love, in thunder and in flood, that the gods speak from to manifest its nature. At some point, one may sense that the gods *are* this quality of life. The myths are their means of revelation.[37] This is the point, perhaps, where religion takes over from mythology.

The Greeks' god Dionysos actually embodies this problem. The puzzle of his reality is central to his myths. He is the vine and he is wine: vegetation and intoxication. He is the irrational organic surge of

The Limits of Subjectivity

life, especially as it invades the linear mind in madness or ecstasy. Thus he is the unconscious as energy at once dangerous and creative, violent and beautiful. His primary symbol, the grape (or is he the symbol of the grape?) is, of course, one of the most suggestive images in religion, poetry, and popular idiom. It makes clearer, probably, than any other mythic image how the qualitative nature of the symbol not only *is* its meaning and *is* its reality but transcends its reality to *be of* the universe. Lush and pungent, rich with juice suggesting blood, growing in clusters "communally," trodden-down and fermented into a higher potency, the corrupted fruit of life which "becomes" an exalted state of mind as one participates in it--the grape is at once the fruit of nature, both flesh and blood, sustenance and spirit. No wonder (and yet more wonder . . .) that it is taken as man and god at once, the presence of the mystery! Known to all the senses and to the quality of consciousness itself, it is the perfect image of life's wholeness, the place of reality which has not yet been reduced to contrasts. It summons the whole range of ambiguous experience: potency-violence, delicacy-coarseness, exhilaration-desperation, lethargy-ecstasy, the present time and timelessness. It is a subjectivity shared, *communitas*; it is substance and sensation; it is escape and it is confrontation; it is the self and it is the all.

For as a force of nature, Dionysos is also much more than the unconscious, something that the unconscious only participates in. Myth after myth, Dionysos is met with the rational resistance of those who would prefer not to believe what is happening to them. They *will* not believe, because this strange god (who comes to them from the East) makes no sense and is unseemly, but their resistance destroys them. This god cannot be believed in; he demands instead to be confronted. However, one cannot choose to confront him. The confrontation happens, therefore, only through resistance, and through the destruction of the rational mind that follows when the resistance becomes so intense that it explodes.[38]

In a forceful book on Dionysos, Walter F. Otto discusses the need to understand this god's independent existence. All myths, Otto argues, arise from a sense of something beyond the human. As a model of what he means, he cites the imagery of the muses: "the human mind cannot become creative by itself, . . . it needs to be touched and inspired by a wonderful otherness . . ."[39] For Otto also, myth is a form of confrontation, but one in which the ultimate realities face *us*:

> That which confronts mankind in epiphanies is not a reality which is completely unrecognizable and imperceptible, affecting only the soul which turns its back on the world, but the world itself in a divine form, as a plenitude of divine configurations.[40]

Dionysos, for Otto, is "the god who is mad," because he yokes the most extreme opposites and reveals their oneness in a way that the rational mind cannot cope with sensibly.

Myth in Nature

> We know him as the wild spirit of antithesis and paradox, of immediate presence and complete remoteness, of bliss and horror, of infinite vitality and the cruelest destruction. The element of bliss in his nature, the creative, enraptured, and blessed elements all share, too, in his wildness and his madness. . . . The love which races toward the miracle of procreation is touched by madness. So is the mind when it is staggered by the impulse to create.[41]

Dionysos represents all this, and yet to speak of him as "representing" it is to reduce him to a metaphor and to refuse to believe in him. It is to miss the point of his mystery and court destruction, therefore, along with his other victims.

Is the god a projection or is he a reality? We can hedge around the issue by saying that the myth is a projection *as image* but an encounter *as experience*. We seem to have two necessary perspectives on the truth. We can clarify the psychic nature of myth when we consider it as projection. Confrontation, however, is a function of archetypal imagery and is built into the system. Together, the two perspectives remind us that our experience overlaps upon the physical universe, that music is as much "about" the ear as it is about the orchestra. If myth reflects our play in the field of nature, we must see that its images are not *merely* projection. Because the energy within us is part of the energy without, what we project is really there. The stuff we project is the stuff of the universe, which also does face us from beyond.

THE PHYSICAL UNIVERSE REVISITED

When we think of the exotic realms of myth, we may expect to contrast them to the more familiar and clear-cut world-picture of science. In our century, however, science has become at least as notoriously problematic and paradoxical as myth has always been. Out of their objective motivations--to analyze nature as it is in itself and chart a consistent and coherent pattern of all its parts and the parts of its parts, physicists, mathematicians, and astronomers have developed a view of reality that is in many ways strikingly nonlinear. In order to continue analyzing nature, the linear intellect has had to turn itself inside out. Modern science does not personalize the world with heroes, gods, and monsters, but no Gorgon, Sphinx, or centaur is more startling to common sense than quanta or quarks. Neither Hell nor Hades sounds more fantastic to most of us than black holes. In speaking about the "field" of myth, we have already anticipated the point. We have had to borrow a clear nonlinear metaphor from physics. Perhaps we do the same when we speak of "energy."

In *The Tao of Physics*, Fritjof Capra, a physicist, explores the intriguing parallels between post-Einsteinian science and the age-old teachings of the Far East, particularly Hinduism, Buddhism (including Zen), and Taoism (the "*tao*" is *the* "way").[42] For our purposes, we can substitute myth for his "mysticism." The vision of reality will be essen-

The Physical Universe Revisited

tially the same, as we shall see by summarizing some of the points that he emphasizes.

In "traditional" science (the opposite of "traditional myth"), we can see the universe in terms of three distinctive factors, time, space, and matter. Space contains matter in the form of objects. Time elapses in space. Matter changes during time. Matter can be broken down into separate particles which hold to each other in bodies. Portions of matter act and react upon one another with forces of energy. Each element has its own coherent kind of identity which makes it distinct from the others. Each remains what it is. Each extends itself in a way that can be measured. We can orient ourselves in this world with confidence that we know where we are and what we need to do to get somewhere else. It is a world, therefore, that we also exist *in*. It contains us, we observe it, and we act upon it.

Our practical reasoning and our intuitive responses are clearly attuned to functioning in such a world. So are our Western languages. In this shape and form, we recognize everything we see and touch. It suits our senses. Our conception of human history is based upon such a sense of reality: people have lived in certain places through the succession of time, working towards certain ends, altering the world about them. We work ahead--as individuals, hour by hour; as a culture, through the generations--on the same assumptions.

But this sphere of ordinary experience, thought, and action is only a "zone of middle dimensions."[43] As the "new science" has come to ask more and more fundamental questions about *how this world exists*, it has focused upon a dimension enormously greater and a dimension enormously smaller. It has looked for ultimate reality on the super-microscopic scale within the atom and the cosmic scale of galaxies, in proportions that we cannot know by experience or comprehend by common sense. The differences in scope are not just relative difference of size however. They present a world-picture that is discontinuous from our usual sense of things.

In the real universe, according to contemporary science, time, space, matter, and energy are all aspects of each other. One cannot be thought of *in* another, and they cannot be thought of properly as interacting. There is curved spacetime, the famous four-dimensional continuum. What is more, "Space is curved to different degrees and time flows at different rates in different parts of the universe."[44] Rather than being a grand receptacle, space is itself dynamic, intimately involved, in its nature, with matter and gravity. There is the field, "a condition in space which has the potential of producing a force,"[45] and which condenses into "matter." What appears to us as particles of such matter are also waves of force. The particles that comprise the atom, as well as light and electricity, are understood as quanta, or "packets" of energy.

> The fact that the mass of a particle is equivalent to a certain amount of energy means that the particle can no longer by seen as a static object, but has to be conceived as a dynamic

Myth in Nature

pattern, a process involving the energy which manifests itself as the particle's mass.[46]

Thus the dynamic of energy patterning itself *is* reality.

The word "physical" has usually implied the hard and solid. The physical universe is really, however, a world of events and relationships, rather than ultimate units of stuff. Its substance is closer than we had thought to the "substantiality of experience!" The universe is seen as a thoroughly unified flow.

> One is led to a new notion of unbroken wholeness which denies the classic analyzability of the world into separately and independently existing parts . . . Rather, we say that inseparable quantum interconnectedness of the whole universe is the fundamental reality, and that relatively independently behaving parts are merely particular and contingent forms within the whole.[47]

In this flow, the oppositions that appear to our coarser understanding are not to be distinguished.

> Examples of the unification of opposite concepts in modern physics can be found at the subatomic level, where particles are both destructible and indestructible; where matter is both continuous and discontinuous, and force and matter are but different aspects of the same phenomenon.[48]

According to the "bootstrap hypothesis" of Geoffrey Chew, everything in the universe is dependent for its nature upon everything else, so that there is no reality more basic than any other, in terms of which the others can be understood.

> All natural phenomena are ultimately interconnected, and in order to explain any one them we need to understand all the others, which is obviously impossible.[49]

The "objective world" must be understood, therefore, in relation to its observer. Consciousness enters the picture.[50] Following Einstein's revolutionary theory, measurements of space-time are relative to human perception. According to Werner Heisenberg's "Uncertainty Principle," we cannot know a particle's momentum and its position accurately at the same time. Most of the particles that make up our supposedly solid world are in the process of disintegrating. When they do disintegrate, their location and the time they will be at any particular place can be known only as probabilities. Particles are described as *tending* to exist at certain times and in certain places. These probabilities are seen as waves which account for the non-existence of the particles as well as their existence.

The Physical Universe Revisited

> The introduction of probability waves, in a sense, resolves the paradox of particles being waves by putting it in a totally new context; but at the same time it leads to another pair of opposite concepts which is even more fundamental, that of existence and non-existence. This pair of opposites, too, is transcended by the atomic reality. We can never say that an atomic particle exists at a certain place, nor can we say that it does not exist. Being a probability pattern, the particle has tendencies to exist in various places and thus manifests a strange kind of physical reality between existence and nonexistence.[51]

The reason that myth only tends to exist is that everything else in the world does also! Existence *is* a tendency. It is always mortal.

Recently, the psychologist Karl Pribram in California and the physicist David Bohm, in England have been developing the emphatically nonlinear conception that both consciousness and physical matter are aspects of a common ground of being. Bohm sees the primary level of reality as an "enfolded" or "implicate" order, in which all parts contain or *imply* the whole and all other parts. Out of this level of fact the "explicate" order *unfolds*, giving us time, space, and objects as we perceive them and relate to them from our own unfolding consciousness. Everything we know with a specific identity--person, place, event, or object--is in its way exactly like a moment of consciousness emerging from the unconscious seas of endless experience. It is there only provisionally, manifested out of a universe of space that is also packed with unseen energy.

Pribram and Bohm both use as an image of their sense of universal order the hologram, a photograph that produces a three-dimensional image in space when it is properly illuminated. Virtually the same complete image can be produced from any part of the hologram, with some change in the angle of view, just as you could see virtually the same scene outside if your window were smaller than it is, or higher or lower. Every part of the hologram, therefore, contains information about all the other parts and about the unified whole. We have seen that this is true of myth as well. The archetype, we can say, is a hologram, and so is every myth. The hero's miraculous conception implies the conquest of his monster or his divine message. Enfolded in the creation of the race is the flood; and of the person, the fall. The dismemberment of each young god scatters the seeds of universal rejuvenation. Nothing perpetuates itself but mortality. That is implied in every arc of the archetypal circle, no matter how long or short, for any arc is alike $360°$, and so is the circle.

The "explicate order," or the "zone of middle dimensions" between the microscopic and the astronomic--like mythology's "middle earth" between heaven and the underworld--seems the real one to us because of our daily preoccupation with the business of living. Yet is is minute in comparison with galactic space and exceedingly gross in relation to the electrons and neutrons, protons, pions, kaons, muons, and on and on.

Myth in Nature

(Not to mention the matterless energy that David Bohm attributes to "empty" space.[52]) We realize as much when our eyes become adjusted to the unaccustomed sunlight or moonless dark outside our moderately lighted homes. It should be no surprise, therefore, that aside from the middle range of consciousness there spreads a vast range of personal experience as different and strange, at first, as curved space is different from a Mercator map. On one hand, an unconscious, as fundamental to our lives as the inner galaxies of atoms, and on the other hand, the sense of a living cosmos beyond, throbbing with deities and demons, together make one world, like the atoms and the stars a natural continuum. We may well suspect, furthermore, that the "worlds" of physics and the mind, thus mirroring each other, unite in one flow as well, a flow of energy being and conscious of being, acting and reflecting.

It would be comforting to see in the parallels between traditional myth and nontraditional science a resurrection of the mythic spirit in a way that could work appropriately for the modern world. We should be able to see, in this coming together, in this rediscovery of ancient vision through modern eyes, a validly unifying sense of life that might actually revitalize our culture by lightening the weight of its hard materialism. Perhaps this will come, but it is premature to celebrate a marriage of science and mysticism. For one thing, contemporary science is at least as esoteric and remote to most of us as any mythic or mystic lore, while our culture continues to evolve according to strictly practical values, the separation of specialists from each other and from everybody else, the divisiveness of politics, and the superficial collectivism that results from mass communications. The most extraordinary theories soon become common hardware. If we cannot simply reverse all this or transcend it *en masse*, it is all the more important, it seems to me, to keep adding, consciously, what the drift of the culture misses--and to keep bringing back into focus, *in terms relevant to our culture*, the sense of reality that complements, fills out, our own.

Of course, that is why we need to study myth and to take it seriously, to find out its own kind of truth: precisely because it is so different from the way we have gone. If myth reflects in its deep old waters the latest flights of intellect, that is all the more reason to keep exploring its depths. For we do not need only to confirm the scientists or have them confirm the mythmakers. We need to keep the nonlinear intellect in touch with the intense qualitative imagination, the right brain with left. We need to keep thought related to feeling, in *their* natural field, and the universe related to each self in the flow of all life's energy, which is continually personal.

CHAPTER TEN

THE PSYCHO-MYTHOLOGY OF EVERYDAY LIFE

We know only in so far as we create.
--Novalis

COMMON MYTH

In describing the mythic universe, I have suggested some ways in which mythic reality applies beyond the range of traditional imagery to the ordinary subjectivity of our lives--in our felt sense of time, in the personal meaning we give to certain places, in fantasies and memories, in our identification with our homes, clothing, and names. The main reason I have done so has been to make the nonrationality of it all seem less remote. The felt world of myth should be fairly intelligible to us because it is really quite natural. But if we have seen now that traditional myth creates a subjective order of reality, we might turn the telescope around to see what happens if we consider any subjective presentation of reality a myth.

Let us extend the concept just a little further: myth is any version of reality. We can never represent reality exactly--any kind of reality: real feelings or thoughts, real trees or water, real energy or heat. Any means by which we represent it will be limited just by being the particular means that it is. English cannot do what French (or Hopi) can. Poetry will not say or see what prose will, let alone what algebra will. Physiology will see a different kind of body than anatomy. Every time you describe a single event, the result will become another event. The original will sound different but, also, you will have introduced a whole new element, the event of your own description, which depends upon a circumstance between you and your listener.

We are used to calling *falsehoods* "myths"--superstitions, outworn theories, the prejudices of mass hysteria. With just a little more sophistication, we use the word for fictions perpetrated on us by the popular press, movies, and television--by advertising especially--glossy ideals of life that lull us into complacency or into the supermarket. James Baldwin has said that the myth of America can be seen in the pages of *Life* Magazine. We vote for the politicians, it often seems, who will authenticate the myths we feel we need. The structuralist Roland Barthes has analyzed in depth such topics as "striptease," "ornamental cookery," "the new Citroen," and "wine and milk"--he is a Frenchman--in a collection called *Mythologies*.[1] Social progress often takes the form of exposing "myths" of our culture--white supremacy, male supremacy, machismo, the sanctity of

The Psycho-Mythology of Everyday Life

the nuclear family, America's military partnership with the Lord, and so forth. All such myths capture ideals that are highly charged with feeling and allow us to judge or act without having to look at evidence or consider our assumptions. We can call them *practical myths* because they invade the proper province of practical logic, inciting us to act without calling for any understanding, in ways that can be simply convenient but that also, of course, may be very destructive. They are "pseudo-myths," because they foster unconsciousness and block self-fulfillment. They cultivate sensation rather than emotion, or, at best, they settle for *ideas about* emotions--gratifying ideas about love in the pop songs, for instance --rather than exploring feelings along their natural lines of development. On a usually meretricious basis, they foster artificial identification with trivialities, like all the mental garbage of advertising: *participation plastique.*

However, there is also a myth of the debunker of myths, who may go so far as to convice us that any point of view is arbitrary and any idea is, therefore, ultimately meaningless: *just* a point of view, saying more about the speaker than the bespoken. Then we are left with a sterile kind of relativism, which insists that no communication has anything to do with reality. A more interesting argument asserts that communication is always a dramatic interchange between speakers rather than a statement about reality beyond them. This may a revealing point of view about *the reality of communication*, if not about the reality of a world beyond. Like archetypal myths, this web of "common myths" establishes a field in which the distinction between inside and out appears to evaporate. But can we also see in these common myths a valid kind of special truth? Can we apply to them something of what we have learned about the ontology of archetypal myth?

The point of view from which we see a landscape is not a fabrication. We may see a mountain from the eastern exposure or from the western. We may see it from five miles away or half-way up. Our position will be arbitrary for certain, but it can still be meaningful *as a point of view*. A point of view does not tell us what the reality is, but neither is it isolated from reality. The famous ancient parable of the five blind men and the elephant (one "sees" the tail as a rope, one "sees" the sides as a wall, one "sees" a leg as a tree trunk, and so forth) is the perfect myth to illustrate the limitations of our vision both physically and otherwise. But, as images, the rope and the wall and the trunk of a tree do make strong myths to evoke aspects of elephantness. The five "seers" are not mistaken in their conclusions, only in the kind of truth that they give to them, for they fail to discount their blindness and allow for its limit to their perception. They make theology out of their myths and fall to quarreling. One glance would have revealed to them the need to integrate all their points of view. One glance, however, would have kept them from handling and feeling the strange creature for themselves, from the vivid experience that issues into their boldly imaginative visions of its truth. Because of their blindness, they achieve the power of myth and myth's own kind of accuracy.

Common Myth

Any version of reality, in other words, will still have some relation to reality. It will represent a motivation; it will express a range of experience; it will play out part of the drama of life continually unfolding, never unfolded or finally laid out. Any myth, in this sense of the word, may be valid and make its contribution to an understanding of life, as long as we understand it for what it is, a myth asserting mythic truth. To the (considerable) extent that we are limited and linear creatures caught between birth and death, always here and never there, needing to speak in one language or another, explaining ourselves step by step, we can hardly help but express (or know) ourselves mythically.

FORMS OF COMMON MYTH

Our minds, then, live in versions of reality. We live not by illusion but by half-truths. In many ways, on many levels, the same ambiguity balances consciousness. At the risk of repetitiveness, we should consider some of the familiar ways this principle does manifest itself in ordinary life.

--<u>any belief</u>. We all *believe* in our opinions. We argue them and act on them, allowing ourselves to accept them as fact, although we generally know--and may even acknowledge if we are pressed to it--that there is something arbitrary or at least something provisional about them. They are tenable to us, the evidence that our train of thought has picked out seems to fit them, they have a certain consistency with our other assumptions, and even if we do recognize that there may be logical arguments on the other side, they *feel* right. We squint a bit and plunge ahead. Sometimes we may suspect that virtually all of our opinions are expressions of our personalities.

To see opinions or beliefs as myths means that they can be valuable and valid *up to a point*, without having to be objective versions of *the* truth. They represent particular ways of looking at things. They are more-or-less intellectual formulas that project our feelings. We would hardly be willing to fight for them if they were not.

--<u>any system of beliefs</u>. Although we proclaim any one belief as though we judged it on its own merits, each of our beliefs is implicated in other beliefs, ultimately in all our other beliefs. Furthermore, a system of beliefs--political, metaphysical, or what have you--is more than a set of related opinions. It takes on a mystique, an aura that transcends its logical weight--whether the near-sanctity of our own high principles or the demonic spell of the dogmas and ideologies that perversely oppose us. Any system is, by definition, self-limiting, and it determines in advance what range of experience it will encompass, as well as what attitude it will strike when considering new evidence. It is also self-perpetuating, therefore, as each further stage of thought merely spells out newly appreciated or newly applied implications of what has come before. The fundamental insight may well be penetrating and evocative, but as a rule we can hardly help but over-generalize it. As we continue to identify with it, we cannot help but insist upon its absolute value.

The Psycho-Mythology of Everyday Life

Yet each doctrine is bound to represent a single attitude among many possibilities, which are all complementary. The drama (or the game) of life requires that we play some parts and that we take them seriously. Life proceeds creatively through the intense interplay of energy that then takes place and all our myths bloom and flourish until they wither and die or else find themselves new bodies in which to germinate anew. In their continual combat, they may help to refine one another, and as they do so, consciousness can sharpen itself, concentrate its focus, and elaborate upon its own flexible powers of penetration.

Few, if any, systems of belief--or specific beliefs for that matter --record a direct realization of living truth. They arise, as a rule, in opposition to other beliefs. Each intellectual generation, each new movement, must find its life-forms by revolution, re-inventing truth with its own slant so that it can speak with conviction. We can hardly think at all without clarifying what we disagree with, so inevitably we reject one limited truth for another. We think by what must *not* be true, in order to create "on the other hand." As the kaleidoscope turns, new patterns emerge among the stones, new myths out of the old living experience. (The metaphor, or myth, of the kaleidoscope ignores the possibility that new intellectual "stones" may join the figure and old ones drop aside.)

--one's world view. One's entire "address to life," or "mind set" in a less lovely phrase, is composed of all sorts of doctrines, assumptions, and predispositions, all mingled with facts and feelings, containing most likely much contradiction and at least a little muddle. All aspects of one's culture contribute to it, and as much as one knows of other cultures. It includes all the possible ways of thinking one is aware of but rejects. It has its scientific elements, and it encompasses all one's practical wisdom, or all that one has cared to learn from. One lives it out more certainly than one lives according to one's doctrines. Yet it too is a narrowing of focus, a complex but partial version of life, one set of human possibilities, selected according to the circumstances of one's life with a certain amount of hit-or-miss leading the way.

--personality. Behind one's doctrines--at least behind another fellow's--we can usually detect some personal disposition fumbling to disguise itself as intellect. It is remarkable how, sometimes, the opposite opinions can suit the same person. But personality itself is mythical. My configuration of habitual feelings represents, again, one version of human possibilities, a selection--whether made by nature or by social pressures or by some esoteric quality of will--from the full range of emotions, tastes, ambitions, and the like, with my particular emphasis, combination, and forms of symbolic expression. Through the language of my whole life, I continue to characterize myself, articulating my variations on the theme, my myth.

However, we generally characterize people in a more clearly mythological way. The German social philosopher Georg Simmel observed:

We conceive of each man--and this is a fact which has a specific effect upon our practical behavior toward him--as being the human type which is suggested by his individuality.[2]

We save ourselves a lot of difficulty, that is, by labeling our best friends, not to mention almost all passing strangers, as "lazy," "ambitious," "arrogant," and so forth. But we also present ourselves to others and even think of ourselves privately, in typical aspects--according to roles we like to play or attitudes we like to adopt. As a simple test, think of three adjectives that describe the kind of person you are. Then think of three opposites to them, and, after a pause, see where you really fit it. Thinking of oneself or someone else as lazy, strong, stupid, or sensible invariably fixes one into an unnatural pattern. As children, we hear such descriptions of ourselves and unwittingly identify with them for the rest of our lives.

--self and other. In the process of confrontation--as in all forms of polarization--we make our characterizations especially concrete. We tend to give the self and the other more clear-cut identity than we might if we were being reflective. We are especially eager to pin down the other. To a large degree, we may experience the self as a field of uncertainty, or indeterminacy, shifting among scattered motivations and webs of feelings, but in facing an other--whether friend or enemy, a person or a group, a prospect or a project, a particular mountain in the midst of a range--we want to see "it" as fixed and regular, at the center of its own world but focused for us. And this goes for self in the plural as well. "Every society," as Friedrich Nietzsche said, "has the tendency to reduce its opponents to caricatures . . ."

I ignore your indeterminacy to fit you into my picture. As I do so, of course, I limit myself as well to the role of the moment. We are in the same script. To some extent, therefore, we regard ourselves as entities because of the way we perceive and interpret others. I expect a consistency and specificity of experience in myself based on the unity of character that I think I see in you. Thus I mythologize an "objective self," a fairly specific personality that I polish and protect as though I were the servant instead of the master or a ghost inconveniently pretending to exist.

But otherness itself is myth. *Other* is like *there*; it is a function of the self, *here*. Basically, we are a world of beings all of whom are selves to the extent that they are capable of experiencing anything *for themselves*. *I* perceive you, him, or it as you, him, or it, of course, only in relation to myself perceiving. And, obviously, *how* I perceive my other depends upon how I experience my self and what I am *in myself*. The thought "woman," for example, is very different in quality for a man, a woman, a little girl, for a homosexual or a heterosexual, all depending upon the otherness (or identification) involved. Others are made by selves. So what I can confront is myth to begin with. As soon as it is there for me to confront, I have laid claim to it as part of my world.

--time. It is obvious how clock and calendar mythologize time, by apportioning it, naming it, classifying it. But what, if anything, is

The Psycho-Mythology of Everyday Life

time itself? We like to think of it as an ongoing linear process that has always existed whether or not anything is happening--as a continuous show we have walked into in the middle; as a conveyor belt we have jumped onto and need to hold our balance on so we won't fall off; as two-dimensional space, a line on which now is a moving dot. Yet the idea of time depends upon existence. It cannot matter without things to come and go, configurations to change, being to endure, and, arguably, minds to think of it, feel its "work," and take its measure. And we think of time as being made up of past, present, and future, which are after all only points of view, only perhaps acts of faith.

--the future. My vision of what I would like to see happen, of what I fear will happen, of what I think might happen, but also my sense that *something will* happen: the future is my sense that there *is* a future, my expectation. Or, the future is potentiality, a dimension of the present. Or, the future is what *in the future* will have become the past. The future is what has not existed and does not exist. Yet it exists to me, *my* future, as an aspect of life perpetually with me and I cannot imagine going on (where would I go?) without it.

The French sociologist Georges Sorel argued that we act politically according to myths of the future which may never materialize literally but which motivate us nonetheless into productive action.[3] Actually, we construct an entire future on the basis of such practical overstatements. It is a future no more in real time than *tempus illud* or ever-after, but flows continually with us as a stream of images mythologizing our ideals and hopes.

--the present. Where did it go? Is/was there really any "it" at all? If I say "now" it already refers to "then." I can say "now" only *then*. In order to think about "the present" I must extend it into the past and future, setting up a rough extent of contemporaneity. Is the present "a time"? Does it have boundaries? When did it start being now and when will it stop? Why do I speak of it in questions if not to grasp at something which I cannot say is there--or here?

--the past. The past too is what cannot be, because it was. I must understand it *to have been* and remember what I trust is true, which other people may or may not confirm. (Then I am moving from the past as time to the past as events.) Obviously, my memory of what occurred to me is my version of just my past, and it may even change from day to day as I think back differently on things. And your version of an event we both experienced will be your myth. Reading a newspaper's "authoritative" account of the same event, we may realize still more acutely the hopelessness of being ultimately factual. Perhaps, we may suspect, there was no "real" event at all, just as there is no real myth except in its variations. But, unlike the myth, the event did take place. Only there is no real version of its truth.

The newspaper mythologizes all events by transmuting them into news--or reviews or editorials, which are specializations of the same journalistic process. As the sculptor transmutes a face into lifeless but lifelike stone, so *any* medium creates necessarily a version of life dictated by its own conditions. ("The medium," in McLuhan's mythic phrase, "is

Forms of Common Myth

the message.") The news, of course, exists in order to deny this factor, in order, that is, to tell the truth, but we can easily see how its style and its selectivity, its motivations and the kind of rapport it seeks to establish with readers or television viewers cannot help but make life over.

--history. On a more sophisticated level, scholarly history continually renovates the past. Or else there would never be two books on the same subject. Each selects and emphasizes different aspects of events, organizing the flood of life into a story, and each such shift of organization alters the picture of what "was." Implicitly, in such selection, and explicitly, in commentaries, the historian re-interprets history. The more sophisticated the scholar is, in fact, the more we are interested in *his* version of the "truth." Each new age and each cultural movement fosters its own versions of the past and makes a new mythology obligatory.[4]

--the arts. If history mythologizes, how much more obviously do the arts--poetry, drama, novel, painting, music, film--each projecting its own kind of world on the basis of its peculiar medium. Within the stylistic variations of cultural movements and the artists' temperaments, in the concrete form of each particular work, a new mode of existence is envisioned. Art thrives on the rich play of subjectivity that it cultivates. Unlike the news, art's distortion is deliberate, a kind of creative distortion that communicates through its permutations. If any subjective representation is a myth, then art's communication must be consistently and emphatically mythic.

--self-expression. We extend our sense of being into many media through all sorts of symbolic forms--art works certainly, since they are stylized in one's own unique manner, but even in clever phrases and ideas. What we make becomes surrogate Self, to show us at our best and be evaluated for us. Clothing, hair styles, make-up and other aspects of our personal appearance (such as girth and posture) permit us some control over the most immediate symbol for our selves, the body. A curious extension of this process is the current fad of "expressing" oneself in pre-packaged form through printed slogans on shirts and car bumpers (mottomyth) or through trade-marks (designer myths). Of course, we tend to identify with anything we own because we choose it or just because we have and use it--a car or house in particular. But isn't everything we do the creation of life-stuff and the extension of self, the mythologizing of being?

--assertions. In all the forms and formulas of culture, we try to grasp the nature of life. But any kind of form must miss the essential quality of life's continual flow, simply because of its limitations *as* form. Life, of course, will always resist the languages of culture, outpace them, and stand out against them.

> The achievement of every structure is at once a signal to seek
> out another one, in which the play . . . is repeated. As life it
> needs form; as life, it needs more than form.[5]

The point applies not only to ideologies and cultural artifacts, but quite fundamentally to any act of language. Any formulation at all, literal or

The Psycho-Mythology of Everyday Life

figurative, mythologizes. Everything in the world is just what it is. When I use other words to describe it, if I say A is B plus C, I am subtly distorting: only B plus C is exactly B plus C. The verb "to be" purports to express identity--what simply *is*--while it transforms its subject into a different mode.[6]

The historians will always have enough work to do not only because the past keeps growing or because new evidence comes to light. Language itself continually alters the perception of events by the very fact that it must distinguish what is (or was) from what is (or was) not. If I say "London is the capital of England," I refer, first of all, to a convention, not a fact, an agreement to regard London as a political seat. I refer to two geographical areas that have been given arbitrary boundaries and I refer to political entities that have no literal existence. "Londoners" and "Englishmen" do not exist, only individuals who mythologize themselves into groups. The business of government is enacted in London, but not all of it, and government is only an aspect of what the people involved are doing when they are doing it. If I try to picture London directly, and I can see only a minute portion or a hazy broad view, I realize readily that the capital of England is not what this huge and multifarious city *is*. By designating London a capital, we give it mythic status in more ways than one--it not just *is*, but it is meaningful. It is not only the site of government buildings, it is the site of power, of magnitude. Everything that is must seem ambiguous to language, which can only sort out ways of seeing it. In a much-quoted phrase of Alfred Korzybski, the founder of semantics, "the map is not the territory." The mythic world that words create readily distracts us from actual experience. Reducing the complexities of life to more manageable proportions, it enmeshes us in what Robert Graves calls "the cool web of language":

> Children are dumb to say how hot the day is,
> How hot the scent is of the summer rose,
> How dreadful the black wastes of evening sky,
> How dreadful the tall soldiers drumming by.
>
> But we have speech, that cools the hottest sun,
> And speech that dulls the hottest rose's scent.
> We spell away the overhanging night,
> We spell away the soldiers and the fright.[7]

Graves' poem emphasizes the way in which our self-encapsulation in language cuts us off from the world of even our own feelings. Yet his use of language is able to give us that very insight and, what is more, it conveys poignantly familiar feelings about the predicament it speaks of. Such a predicament is best overcome, we see, by the kind of deliberate mythologizing that takes place in poetry, when language overcomes its ordinary limits by the nonlinear means of imagery, connotations, and a heightened sense of language as a medium.[8]

--<u>description</u>. I may say confidently enough that the sea is blue, when it verges on grey and green and brown without being any of these.

Forms of Common Myth

Even if I call it grey-green-brown, I cannot verbalize how much of each and with what shifting motion. We perform a similar process, we have seen, in our conscious versions of our own personalities and in characterizing other people. Whenever we characterize a person or event with a vivid phrase, we fix upon him, her, or it a mythic interpretation that is readily believed, because it gives us some orientation, some expectations, a sense of how to go ahead.

Certain of the qualities we attribute to people, things, or events depend upon the fact that we do experience them as we do. I think something interesting because I am interested in it, beautiful because I find it so--projecting the attributes I "find" or desiring them to be *there*. But it is not just that. Truly I cannot distinguish between the object and my response to it. *Its* true beautifulness is a mythic truth about the space between us, about the nature of *my* experiencing *it*, about the field, as we saw, in which we are involved together. Just as the god may exist by virtue of the prayer, the beauty can be *there* by virtue of appreciation.

--the sciences. The most factual or assertive representations of reality, in the spare languages of mathematics and the sciences, are still representations, and as such they cannot be exactly true. Each is limited to its own perspective, from which it makes its mythic contribution. Modern science, in fact, has moved toward this position. Some of its practitioners recognize the need to qualify their pictures of reality in such a way in order to make them realistic.

> Physicists have come to see that all their theories of natural phenomena, including the "laws" they describe, are creations of the human mind; properties of our conceptual map of reality, rather than of reality itself. This conceptual scheme is necessarily limited and approximate, as are all the scientific theories and "laws of nature" it contains. All natural phenomena are ultimately interconnected, and in order to explain any one of them we need to understand all the others, which is obviously impossible. What makes science so successful is the discovery that approximations are possible.[9]

The sciences, in this sense, are not simply direct accounts of the world. They are contraptions in which to catch the world's reflections. The images that they show are determined by the material that mirrors them: is it water or glass or polished brass? Each branch of a science, in other words, gives us a self-contained world to the extent that it is consistent within itself. The consistency that makes it effective, of course, also limits the accuracy--or at least the breadth--of its view. But conversely, as in all myth, what limits it also allows it to be effective.

In *The Structure of Scientific Revolutions*, Thomas S. Kuhn has shown how scientific thinking can be regarded as mythic in this sense.[10] Scientists are guided in their research, he argues, not by abstract laws or theories but by dominant *paradigms*, or exemplars, which are concrete and specific acts of scientific work. They indicate workable procedures and appropriate problems, while they commit the community of practi-

The Psycho-Mythology of Everyday Life

tioners to a tradition such as "'Ptolemaic astronomy' (or 'Copernican'), 'Aristotelian dynamics' (or 'Newtonian'), 'corpuscular optics' (or 'wave optics'), and so on."[11] Being concrete (thus in our terms *mythic*), the paradigm allows one to work with the kind of tacit understanding that makes possible subtle and creative engagement with a subject.[12] The paradigm implies assumptions about nature and definitions of terms; yet the scientists who work under its aegis may interpret them in quite different ways, so they have plenty of room for debate, hypothesis, and experimentation.[13]

The paradigm determines how the practitioners perceive nature and therefore, in a significant way, it is constitutive, determining the world in which they operate. When a new tradition, such as Copernican astronomy, dislodges the old, it introduces a radically new way of seeing, a new way of using its terms, and consequently a new world to be experienced, dealt with, and explained. Any paradigm, however, can represent nature only partially. Although newer forms of science may have an improved capacity to solve problems, therefore, they do not necessarily "fit" nature better than the old ones.[14] In fact, advantages of old paradigms are lost to view when new ones make the old systems seem totally fallacious.

--explanation. The transmutation of experience by assertion is especially telling when we explain why something happened. We pin down events to the myth of a single cause lifted out of the natural condition of "multiple determination," in which events flow out of events on many levels at once through a play of ambiguities. The courts of law exist in order to reach "verdicts" (from French, *true-sayings*), but, of course, they must content us often with probabilities that may not be true at all. The important point is that they content us. A verdict is clear-cut and simple, so that it can be plausible. Did the kidnapped newspaper heiress rob the bank willingly or was she forced to do it? Perhaps she can no longer tell the truth once she has made up her mind how to plead. Once we do decide how things were--or must have been, once we reach a judgment or evaluation, we dispose of reality itself and enter further into the realm of myth.

--generalization. Anything I say about people in general, about the French or the Americans, about the Middle Ages or the Twentieth Century is going to be as mythic as the Man in the Street. Generalizations lead us into all sorts of presumptions and prejudices and away from the specific nature of reality, so that some semanticists have urged us to avoid them altogether. Whatever I say about two people is that much less likely to be literally true than what I say about one. Yet we can hardly think very far or very efficiently without generalizations. We need to grant them a hypothetical value while keeping a cautious eye out, so that they can be of service without trapping us. As we have been seeing all along, mythical truth is like that.

Generalizations are a form of abstraction, and we can extend the point to all those isolated qualities of experience like happiness, fortitude, beauty, evil, and love, which we all love to generalize about. Being *abstracted*, or "drawn away" from reality, they can't be real in themselves.

Forms of Common Myth

Philosophy is in itself a mythical activity, struggling for ultimate truths about fictions. Not only are our beliefs myths, but so are *what our beliefs are about*. When abstractions are as relative to each other as wealth, poverty, and the tax burden, they mean something only in relation to each other, to a specific setting, and to the hidden desires of the speaker. Being mythic, abstractions have a proper place in traditional myth, which does treat them as real in its special sense, projecting Truth, Wisdom, Fate, Death, or War as deities. In ordinary use, without capitals, we are all too likely to take them for objects, which we should be able to pursue and possess.[15]

--negation. Another special case of assertion is saying what is not. As the French philosopher Henri Bergson argued, negation is always created by the human mind.[16] Creatures without language can be aware only of what is. Thinking of "nothing" is a positive action that produces some kind of image no matter how vague, how black or bleak it is. To say something is not, in fact, we must first think of its being. We require consciousness to think of anything not being and we need language to posit it:

> The negative is a function peculiar to symbol systems, quite as the square root of minus-one is an implication of a certain mathematical symbol system.[17]

Un-truth is always, therefore, necessarily mythical. "That which is denied," writes Sartre, "must be imagined"[18]--and the reality of nothingness, as a human experience, is a central theme in his Existential philosophy.

Nothing obviously, by definition, has no kind of reality in itself. Everything is, nothing is not. Logically, it is not possible for something to become nothing, because possibility and becoming can only refer to being. Yet consciousness tends to materialize nothing, to treat it as though it existed, so that it haunts us in our ordinary anxieties as well as in the monsters of traditional mythology, the sphinxes, Grendels, and dragons, which can be seen as the embodiment of nothing in our being. "I cannot get rid of the idea that the full is an embroidery on the canvas of the void," as Bergson puts it.[19] "Bestriding the positive solid reality to which it is attached, this phantom objectifies itself."[20] Nonexistence is *something* that we think of and think in terms of habitually, both carelessly and deliberately, even philosophically, so that it becomes a presence in our lives, coloring (shading) our existence as it interweaves our thoughts.

The strangest and most dramatic way we imagine nothing is in our concern with death, which is not an idea or an image, but a myth, like all abstractions, a reality which is not. There is dying and there are dead bodies, and our being may extend beyond our physical life-time, but there can be no state in which we are not. Nevertheless, the prospect of not being is as terrifying for many people as the prospect of eternal punishment is for many others.

--photographic reality. A photo makes an assertion visually: this is what such and such looks like. In the hands of a photographic artist,

The Psycho-Mythology of Everyday Life

the effect of conscious stylization is obvious, but a news photo or a snapshot illustrates an interesting effect of common myth--in its static removal of situation from time, in its flattening of space, and in its limitations (even in color photography) of color and tone. As photographs age, they convey a strange vision of a past that still has presentness lingering about it.

> Hence the charm of family albums. Those grey or sepia shadows, phantomlike and almost undecipherable, are no longer traditional family portraits but rather the disturbing presence of lives halted at a set moment in their duration, freed from their destiny; not, however, by the prestige of art but by the power of an impassive mechanical process: for photography does not create eternity, as art does, it embalms time, rescuing it simply from its proper corruption.[21]

When we finally see in the flesh a famous personage we have known before only through pictures, and see that he or she is shorter than we had thought and moves about like anybody else, we sense that, even on just a visual level, we have stored them on a special plane of pseudo-physical existence. If we also see the star or President or queen scratch a nose or laugh nervously, we may realize that a sense of their importance or their public capacity has endowed them reality beyond mortal terms. Whether we adore or despise them, they live to us in an aura out of linear time and space, in a symbolic dimension.

In television, this transformation of reality takes on special importance, for we are daily given quasi-experience of current history, in such a way that we may feel part of it without being touched by it until it seems that all the world's a screen and all the wars and famines merely pictures. If television helped to end the war in Vietnam or relieve the famine in Ethiopia, it may be as much because we were repelled and embarrassed to see such things in such a slick, convenient form--between the myths of underwear and car-lust, before the sports and weather--as we were shocked by the distant realities we could see and *not* see in the comfort of our homes.

--<u>any perception</u>. Photographic reality is a particularly clear variety of *representational reality* in general. The way we represent anything--even in our thoughts--makes it radically different from the thing in itself and gives us an essentially different kind of experience. Our senses themselves and our focusing minds pick out portions of the world and arrange them into patterns that are coherent to us: specific areas of space, moments of time, clusters of objects, classes of people. Our senses show us (fortunately) the myths of solid bodies or continuous fluids instead of swarming molecules. Our minds tell us habitually what we must be seeing. One of the main concerns of modern European philosophy--especially from Kant to Schopenhauer and Nietzsche--has been the extent to which we see the world as we do because of the way in which the mind itself is constituted. E.H. Gombrich traces this notion to the ancients:

The distinction between what we really see and what we infer through the intellect is as old as human thought on perception. Pliny had succinctly summed up the position in classical antiquity when he wrote that "the mind is the real instrument of sight and observation, the eyes act as a sort of vessel receiving and transmitting the visible portion of the consciousness." Ptolemy devotes much thought in his *Optics* (c. A.D. 150) to the role of judgment in the process of vision. The greatest Arab student of the subject, Alhazen (d. A.D. 1038), taught the medieval West the distinction between sense, knowledge, and inference, all of which come into play in perception. "Nothing visible is understood by the sense of sight alone," he says "save light and colors."[22]

Since any perception comes from a point of view, it is always in itself a relative knowledge. The bee's blossom is not the bird's--or the child's. When I say "the sky is up," its upness is my point of view, unless I define the sky as whatever *is* up. When I say "the sky is blue," however, my senses are still mythologizing for me: no matter how far up I go, I will not reach the blue or find whatever it is that is colored blue. And if I did come up against an azure curtain, still its color would result from the light playing off it onto my retina. Ultimately, the sky itself: I say "it is," while there *is* no *it* to *be*. The sky itself is a point of view, a myth.[23]

The myth that the sky exists as a thing in itself derives, according to Whorf, from the particular kind of language that we use. Similarly,

"Hill" and "swamp" persuade us to regard local variations in altitude or soil composition of the ground as distinct THINGS almost like tables and chairs. Each language performs this artificial chopping up of the continuous spread and flow of existence in a different way.[24]

Aside from what language does by *being* language, individual languages perceive for us in differing ways. As we saw in the comparison of (relatively) linear and nonlinear languages, each language is a continual processor of a mythic world, the linearly inclined no less than the others. Language selects, organizes, and interprets the world for us as, in Whorf's phrase, it "builds the house of [every person's] consciousness."[25]

--<u>figures of speech</u>. In our casual everyday language, we continually communicate by "misrepresenting" reality in more obvious ways, and we understand others by not taking their word. Our talk is full of prosaic poetry. We need to tell each other about *the truth we feel*-- whether you are "a no-good dirty rat" or "the nicest person in the world." Both overstatement and understatement rely upon the mythic force of dislocation between their own "truth" and objective fact. Any strong statement, such as a proverb or aphorism ("the course of true love never did run smooth") lays itself open to linear objections, yet we discreetly allow it its special degree of general relevance. "The aphorism," it has

The Psycho-Mythology of Everyday Life

been said, "never covers itself with truth, it is either half-true, or one-and-a-half times true."[26] Clichés are usually said to be "dead metaphors" (a dead metaphor if ever we saw one) and all such unnatural combinations of the world's pieces, whether fresh or stale--such as "the heart of darkness" or "the heart of the matter"--constitute their own new order. We say casually that "the sun is trying to come out," conjuring a little mythic drama though hardly noticing it. When things go wrong for me, I proclaim it is "just my luck"--and behind that expression there is a fierce world controlled by the projection of my feelings. The inherently metaphoric nature of language has often been observed. It means that we can "get at" reality only indirectly, perhaps, but it also means that we can get at it more sensuously, more dramatically, and therefore--in a way that is true to the natural drama of life--more accurately. How much it adds, even in a supposedly dead metaphor, to be on the *threshold* of a discovery, or to realize the tangibility of a supposedly abstract relation in an influence *flowing in from a source*, the implication *unfolding* its strands. We can object to this only if we expect language to be a code of static signifiers, whereas it is a mythical process that acts, engages, creates, and recreates with continual dramatic presence.

--<u>prophetic truth</u>. This kind of myth communicates somewhat as an epigram does, through the sweep of dramatic generalization, but with it we move from common myth back to the sense of archetypal vision. It reflects a deep insight into life that speaks necessarily in broad and powerful terms, which also like an epigram, are open to literal reservations, exceptions, and qualifications. Yet there is an integrity, as well as an urgency, in such "prophetic" voices, and an oracular spell. They speak directly from the logic of consciousness and the rhythms of emotion. R.D. Laing, for example, writes of experience itself:

> As adults, we have forgotten most of our childhood, not only its contents but its flavor; as men of the world, we hardly know of the existence of the inner world: we barely remember bodies, we retain just sufficient proprioceptive sensations to coordinate our movements and to ensure the minimal requirements for biosocial survival--to register fatigue, signals for food, sex, defecation, sleep; beyond that, little or nothing. Our capacity to think, except in the service of what we are dangerously deluded in supposing is our self-interest, and in conformity with common sense, is pitifully limited; our capacity even to see, hear, touch, taste and smell is so shrouded in veils of mystification that an intensive discipline of un-learning is necessary for *anyone* before one can begin to experience the world afresh, with innocence, truth and love.[27]

It is pointless to measure how far this is literally true. The colossal scope of such terms is beyond either equivocation or examination. They reflect a truth that *must* be meaningful in general terms, no matter what else can be said on the subject as well. In this way, myth is doubly "mythical."

Forms of Common Myth

Its truth always expresses the broad contours. Psychological theory often comes in this "mythical form"--perhaps why there are almost as many theories as psychologists (a mythical proposition, untrue but possibly suggestive). Theories of myth are likewise themselves mythical, and all our talk about consciousness takes place on such a level.

--<u>system and chaos</u>. We create common myth as we organize our thoughts, focus our attention, see the world in a certain way, state our truth. Almost immediately, when the conscious mind activates itself, it picks out, extrapolates, projects, imagines *system*--and it produces, as a result, chaos.

Real chaos, then, is not a lack of order. Consistent disorder, if that is possible, would be an order of its own. Chaos is inconsistency, systems that are not coherent, that stop and start again, that drift off into other systems, that change their sense of direction over and over or redefine their origins. Chaos is the way in which systems don't work, like capitalism or communism left to themselves. It is the plentitude of contradictory truths.

Every system presupposes and creates its own chaos; chaos is, so to speak, the unconscious of system. Without systems, chaos cannot exist, for no system can be adequate to deal with reality. All systems need to be complemented by other systems, which still cry out for more and more corrections, more systems. That is cultural history. Chaos is violent, because systems do violence to life, and they are violent to the degree that a system is restrictive or unconscious. But thank God for chaos, which saves us from the system and restores to us what eludes it. Not that we can pursue chaos for its own sake: we cannot choose it, since it exists by virtue of order.

Each system, in other words, is a myth, a version of reality (and all myths are systems). Chaos, as the condition outside the system that will be resolved by it, is therefore also a myth: the antimyth, we may say. The creation myths of traditional mythology demonstrate this process when they project back prior to the system an aboriginal "chaos" as the given condition which our world will bring to order--but then show the world itself falling into confusion, or history, the kind of chaos that is familiar to us. The myth which states that chaos continually threatens us says we must create new systems or believe more passionately in the old. But as history shows us all too well, we readily identify everybody else's systems as chaos against which we proceed to save the world with our own. The extreme of system is obsession: in the blindness of panic it produces the world of chaos which justifies its own defensive intensity.

Biologists describe all living things as systems, and they (we) are designed to *not* work--that is, to die--as well as to work and, after a sort, flourish. They work by being able to not work. We live by dying, though we can say so only by the expedient separation of terms. Commonly we experience death as chaos and, in archetypal myth, we project our death as monstrosity so that we can confront it. But that is possible only because this chaos is utterly inherent in the nature of our systems. It is only *because* death is completely natural to us that we find it so utterly appalling and want to separate ourselves from it. As in a nightmare,

The Psycho-Mythology of Everyday Life

we see ourselves besieged by our own fears, then wake to reassure ourselves it was all illusion and we are safe, living in a world that is really there outside. The monster is the chaos that we cannot get out of our system.

--<u>the fine world and the gross</u>. If we return to the idea that we function in a "zone of middle dimensions,"[28] a world of illusorily solid objects to which our senses are attuned, then the world of atoms and the world of galaxies seem as mythical as gods in their nonlinear transcendence of our experience. They constitute a "fine" world of ultimates, while we go on bumping into things under the impression that they are "there."

Language also has both fine and gross kinds of truth. Looked at literally, expressions like "it is raining" or "the sky is blue" are imaginative projections. There is no "it" to be raining (grammarians beg the question by calling the word an expletive when it is used this way), there is no sky, no blue. If we think carefully about *how* we say what we mean, we become aware of all the ways in which words are arbitrary, indirect, ambiguous, and figurative. Yet we understand such language immediately in the gross sense, without any spiritual revelation taking place. We grasp a *gestalt* of sense, a unifying whole which transcends its parts, and we communicate with one another surprisingly well.

The same difference holds true in perception and in logic. Phenomena that are impossible when we analyze them happen just the same --like the paradox of the hare which can never catch up with the tortoise because it covers half the space, then half that space, and so on to infinity--and perhaps like life itself, or like the "fact" that we can't know anything because we can't understand the knowing mind in any terms but its own.

But which is mythical, the fine world or the gross? The fine seems mythic because it constitutes a seemingly ultimate reality remote from our ordinary experience and our ordinary understanding yet pictured by the mind as a model that *must* serve. (In some instances we may not be sure whether the mind is knowing indirectly or projecting its own nature, yet we seem to know that we are encountering here something strange that determines our nature.) But seen the other way around, it is the gross which is mythical--a world that is not there literally, the illusion of solidity, which we find adequate to function in and understand by that particularly mythic faculty called common sense. We may say we do not believe in it, yet we engage in it with total confidence.

--<u>the linear world</u>. If myth is the creation of a special reality, then in the last analysis it is the linear mode of expression that is distinctly mythic. The nonlinear may violate common sense, but it does so the better to approximate real experience. On the other hand, the positing of an actual realm of spreading space, distinct from a solid progression of time, the abstracting of ideas out of reality, the plotting of specific causes for individual results, the images of coherent personalities that represent who we are, and all the other clear and simple figments of thinking give us a world that seems manageable at the expense of a world that is real. What could be more mythical than the concept of objectivity, the peculiar assumption that we can get absolute and direct knowledge of the world *through* the human mind or through any instruments that the mind conceives--that we can see, in other words, with the eyes of a god?

Thus our "linear" notions are just one sort of nonlinear form, as nonsensical as that may sound. In other words, the distinction between linear and nonlinear is itself a trick of myth and mind. By starting out with it, as the basis of our whole discussion, we simply worked out assumptions built into our civilization and followed them to the point where they dissolved. Now we are left with the immediate sense of our own mythmaking minds and their awesome power to create and ensnare, to interpret and confront, to escape and to leave us exposed. In other words: 1) All thinking is, naturally, artificial; 2) How could it be realistic otherwise? Because it is imaginative, it can be about life. If we remember the roots of thought in the human organism, as well as its fruits in a world we can confront, thinking has its best chance of being reasonably coherent.

The linear world belongs to what Hindu culture calls *maya*--the illusion which we are all born into, the universe as a play of dazzling but insubstantial images. Even our impression that it is manageable is an illusion, for it is a world of continual contradictions, confusions, and shortsightedness, with myth laid upon myth, but with no ultimate meaning that is clear to more than a few people at a time. As soon as we look beyond our immediate myths of the moment, we can see that the whole world of common myth is continually bursting at the seams and breaking down. This is the world between the atoms and the stars: incredibly rich to all the senses, yet fragile and tentative. Although we take it utterly for granted and tramp about it roughshod, it needs a certain delicacy of handling, a certain tact. We cannot be quite sure in what way it is really there.

After looking even so briefly at some of the ways we construct our pictures of reality, the conclusion is clear: the texture of our minds is entirely mythic. By saying so, we risk a danger of misunderstanding. "Mythic" so often means fallacious that it will seem as though we are devaluing mind and all its works together. I would not expect our altered sense of the word to become clear for general use. But are there any real advantages to the word even for the space of our present consideration, or are we merely adopting a new term, perhaps one that seems clever because it goes against the grain of ordinary assumptions? Does this use of the word have enough to do with traditional mythology to justify harping upon it at such great length?

THE ORDINARY AND THE ARCHETYPAL

There are five real advantages, I think, to taking a distinctively mythic view of culture and the rest of our mental life, and we can appreciate them only now, after we have seen the nature of traditional myth.

The Psycho-Mythology of Everyday Life

1. their substantiality. Beliefs are not simply abstractions like algebraic ratios. They are expressions of life, they are dramatic processes, they are ways of seeing. Most importantly, they are themselves forms of experience, actual portions of being and organizations of consciousness, sharing the qualities of life and, as a result, reflecting life's nature. We speak mythically to say so, but it is important to note that they have their density and weight, that they establish an environment and take on form both around us and within. They take on their proper meaning, in fact, only when they are seen from within and experienced in the process of living.

If intellectual history cannot treat beliefs in such a way--and it rarely can, it studies only their corpses. If there is a danger in taking *ideas* abstractly, there is a more serious one in reducing the arts to abstract analysis. And danger lurks still closer to home when psychology sees personality in terms of physical forces or in terms of computer programs. Even a sophisticated term like one's "self-concept" abstracts an organization of consciousness into a mere idea, implying it can be taken up or abandoned arbitrarily.

2. their truth. Since all these forms of common myth have a kind of reality similar to that of traditional myth, they assert a like kind of ambiguous truth. To our great expense, we force them too into linear molds and argue endlessly over their absolute worth or worthlessness. Seeing them as myths, however, allowing them to float free--poised between truth and falsehood, revelation and deception, consciousness and unconsciousness, we can see richer value in them. As versions of reality, they can be true without having to be *the* truth, and they can be "true" to varying degrees, in varying ways. They can function, like all myths, as vehicles for our energy and channels of experience. They can confront the world, revealing something of its nature and something of our own in a flow of involvement.

Thus we can answer the common charge that a theory which challenges the truthfulness of thought and language is self-invalidating: if language cannot state truth, how can you say so? Is a theory that truth is myth also a myth? Of course it is, but not "merely a myth." We could say that we are using what is sometimes called "meta-language," a language about language, and show that as such, because of its self-consciousness, it is transcendental, transcending its limits by observing them. But we can also argue a law of estimates. It is accurate to approximate an estimate. I can say it is exactly 5:33 or I can say it is *about* 5:30. I would not say, however, that it is about 5:33 and 17 seconds. For an ambiguous reality, we have, naturally, an ambiguous language. Perhaps an elusive reality requires a fallible language. We need to gauge our myths to be as sensitive to reality as they can. If they become too precise, however, they become rigid with error. In a world of experience, which is composed from perspectives, in which the human situation must (happily) be particularized as your version and mine, in which we will always have second thoughts, third, and fourth, only partial truths can be true, only creative portraits can capture the original truly.

The Ordinary and the Archetypal

Throughout our lives and throughout the history of civilization, we can see human energy reorganizing itself and continually recreating the motifs of thought. In addressing another person or another society, we can validate the truth that meets us while we flourish in our own. And, perhaps, we can see emerging, in the space between ourselves and others (I and Thou), a more meaningful truth than either of us can assert alone. In the pattern of a growing dialogue, in the meshing of our words, a further truth, unspoken, awaits our tacit notice.

3. their symbolic nature. Like traditional myths, common myths constitute a symbolic reality. They take on their own kind of being because they exist in symbolic projection. This means, first of all, that they are expressions or representations of reality: representing it, that is, by expressing its nature.[29] According to my own definition, "symbol is an expression of reality that takes on a reality of its own" and myth is, in one sense, the reality that it does take on.[30] And that means, secondly symbols can work because they are different from reality. They are creative, or constitutive, a human contribution to the world. They can be *about* reality because they are *not* it. They achieve a distance from which to see. At this distance, they constitute their own world, in which they exert their power and their "charm." But, of course, when we look for reality in them (even if, as usual, it is the reality of experience), we find "the truth" distorted, or at least transformed. "All symbolism," writes Cassirer, "harbors the curse of mediacy; it is bound to obscure what it seeks to reveal."[31] Symbolism represents reality by misrepresenting it. If we look to symbols for "meaning"--and we must, we should acknowledge that they speak with forked tongue. They are oracular by nature and tempt us to misunderstand. If their function were only to express a literal factuality, symbols would be inevitably self-defeating. Factuality must be known without expression, in its *im*mediacy. What we get in the symbol is something familiar *and* new. It expresses but it brings forth its own truth, and this curious contradictory way of being that it has, its mythic ontology, itself expresses the freshness and the familiarity, the perpetual creativity and the blind destructiveness that we most need in order to know about our existence.

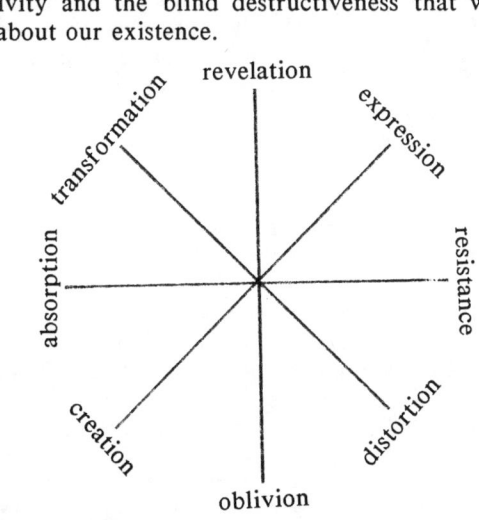

```
                    revelation
        transformation    expression
absorption  ─────────┼─────────  resistance
         creation         distortion
                     oblivion
```

The Psycho-Mythology of Everyday Life

Archetypal myths like the Oedipus or Actaeon stories are symbols that we hold loosely in our minds as images of character, of dramatic confrontations, and of events unfolding. They become embodied in symbolic forms when they are portrayed in a play by Sophocles, a poem by Ovid, or a painting by Titian. Some common myths, such as versions of history or the news on television also are clearly enough set in symbolic forms. Others, however, like past and future, affirmation and negation, are more tenuous. We can say only that they are symbolic thoughts or predispositions to think in a symbolic way. Yet they become something like images when we think *about* them, and they are certainly conceptions through which we see reality and represent it to ourselves. They present versions of reality to us and underlie what we can call the "versionary" quality of life.

It is through their symbolic nature that common myths have their strongest link to traditional myth, but not simply because the two forms happen to share symbolic existence. The archetypal form is the structure of symbolism itself. The archetype confronts consciousness with the unconscious, thought with nature, etc., and the same confrontation takes place in every symbol. When the hero descends into the hell of chaos or of death, he records the impact of the symbol's form upon the untouchable, irreducible world outside its range, and he joins the consciousness which lives creatively through symbols to his immediate world. The archetype marks the boundaries, therefore, between culture and life at-large. Since culture is composed of myths, the archetype defines the stuff that common myth is made of and interprets their being.

4. <u>the power of their unconsciousness</u>. Generally speaking, traditional myth grew and thrived without an awareness of itself as myth. Free of self-consciousness, it drew spontaneously on the creative resources of the unconscious, which inspired it with power, with true sensitivity to feelings, and with the charm that still compels attention and assent. Deep in the soil of life, its roots have fed on all the mingled elements of our being, finding its richest nutriments typically where we would not think of looking for them. Common myths draw likewise on the mind's resources spontaneously and dynamically because we take them too for granted, thinking of them simply as being true or inevitable and working them out without being able to be aware of all their implications. Unlike fictions, which we concoct on purpose, our common myths are responses to our direct involvement in living--to our participation in society and culture, to the play of our needs and desires. Our myths come along with our work and our passions. For that reason, they have some half a chance to express life's shifting and ambiguous nature. They thrive, in other words, on their own unconsciousness, on *our* unconsciousness.

But like traditional myth, common myth can be destructive for the same reasons that it is creative. Its power may be self-defeating. Its unconsciousness may easily outweigh its revelation. Our myths may very well conflict with their practical purposes, frustrating our basic desire to live in fulfillment.[32] Our myths are so common that we are often content with them when they do not work, even when they make life harder and

The Ordinary and the Archetypal

more dangerous. Their "charm" produces a world for us to live in so thick with its own atmosphere that we can no longer see through it. Their force blinds us to the need for correction that contrary myths provide. They demand allegiance that drains our energies and, needless to say, easily blinds us to the humanity of other people, dehumanizing us ourselves as it does so. . . . This negative side of things proves how desperately we need to recognize our myths as myths, in spite of the loss of fervor that may result; we need to see their creative force, however, to understand those we oppose or discard, as well as those that we embrace.

    5.   <u>their relation to the archetypal structure of consciousness</u>. These ordinary myths do not usually represent, as traditional myths do, the archetypal confrontation of conscious mind and unconscious. Traditional myths are definitive, with a sense of ultimate realizations at the limits of human experience, but common myths seem partial, tentative, and provisional. If all forms of knowledge are at least somewhat arbitrary, are they not all relative to the circumstances from which they emerge? And if that is so, are they not all ultimately meaningless? Yet even our common myths reveal their full meaning in a way that they reflect back upon the structure of consciousness itself and the pattern of traditional myth. It is not only shallow, I think, but dangerous to consider these common myths merely as impostures or fictions, simply because they are all vehicles for human energy (even if it is in some instances very destructive energy) and versions of the basic psychic possibilities. They often corrupt true mythic insight--out of experience perhaps, anxiety, or myopia--water it down, drop its sting, dissolve its paradoxes into sentimentality or pervert them radically into justifications of violence, yet they are tangents off the true mythic circle, oblique, skewed, or fragmentary readings of the mythic field, and have their life force in relation to it.

    As organizations of consciousness, all myths--traditional and common--need to be understood in terms of the consciousness that they organize. It is bound to be superficial to look only at the surface, the *image* of the myth (even if, in an idea, the image is an intellectual proposition) to argue about the consistencies and inconsistencies of the images among themselves, without conceiving the images as shapes of life. All myths are efforts of life to survive and flourish, to give its living force form so that it can be. The conscious mind and the unconscious working together--striving against each other while striving together forward--issue images. They are all blends of consciousness and unconsciousness. They are all approximations, therefore, no matter how remote, of the basic confrontation.

    Just as my personality is one complex variation on the theme of human nature, so all myths are variations on the archetypal structure or rhythm. The relationship of variation-on-theme is one definition of mythic reality, showing how points of view can be valid without being conclusive. In this way, they can exist among one another, without canceling each other out. They can, in fact, be complementary, each realizing different potentialities of the energy that is their source, each filling out deficiencies of all the others.

The Psycho-Mythology of Everyday Life

But though all myths have their validity, can we justly conclude that they are all equally valuable? Critics of a mythic approach raise frequently a sensitive challenge: mythic analysis tends to avoid the whole question of values. There are several answers to the challenge, and they provide, I believe, a strong position. Generally, we can acknowledge any myth as a statement in its own terms, no matter how limited its range. But we can value most those myths that channel the broadest scope of human experience, with the most sensitivity to its nonlinear nature. These will be the myths most conducive to consciousness, that are most creative. Others, like the myths of one's own superiority, will be based upon an avoidance of consciousness. They will induce further unconsciousness and prove eminently destructive. Beyond this, the value of myths depends upon the way in which they are used--whether we distort them with linear misapplications, whether we attach ourselves to them in ways that block our own further experience and deny the experience of others.

From the point of view of authentic mythic vision, common myths mimic archetypal form without being able to endorse its integrity. They are compromises that allow us to function reasonably well, with the co-operation (or the conspiracy) of others, without asking too many difficult questions, without our all having to be "heroes." William Blake sees in the world of time and space a "Divine Analogy," which inverts or parodies the inspired images of true life:

> The priest . . . is an analogy of the prophet, and both king and priest are symbols of fatherhood, hence parodies of the city of God which is eternal brotherhood and has no fathers. The state or nation, the church, or an exclusive and partial body of men with a defensive shell around it, is an analogy of the community, which is no respecter of persons. . . . The nobility is an analogy of the free and privileged life in an unfallen world, freedom and privilege being interpreted in the Selfhood terms of idleness and domination.[33]

A view of the archetypal structure behind the whole array of common myths, or analogies, provides the context, the field, in which they take on their full significance. As soon as it takes on *any* form, even in a traditional culture or in the mind of a visionary like Blake, the absolute terms of the archetype must have specific, and therefore limiting, form. The culture, with its ideological myths, its traditional style, and its familiar images, will effect--and perhaps compromise--the vision quite naturally. But as visionary seers have always taught, the way to a higher consciousness is the realization of our present state. Just as the archetypal structure illuminates our daily myths, an awareness of ordinary myths *as myths* leads us back to the basic rhythm of the psyche and the perception of an absolute form in our lives.

In fact, a further relation between common and archetypal myth can be seen in the way our culture has evolved, and presumably others as well. It has been, so to speak, an unfolding of the Word. Out of its

The Ordinary and the Archetypal

mythic inspiration in medieval Christianity, the common myths of each period trace a growth of self-consciousness that is also a gradual rejection of the myth, an advancement by regression: from the despotic coherence of the myth in the Middle Ages, to its explosion (brilliant violence) in consciousness during the Renaissance, to its hopeful neoclassical rigidification, to the romantic reaction caught between dream and nightmare, to the objective agony of our own smart times. This outline is undoubtedly rough, but it has the kind of truth, I think, appropriate to a myth--the play of an inherent tension as it casts itself forth in time and dramatizes itself in the forms of living. The tension between the two directions of consciousness works itself out through an evolution by paradox, for a law of compensation, or of economy, seems to hold, that within the terms of any culture every area of openness is balanced by an area of closure. Each advance is a retreat. Consciousness casts a shadow--in its unconsciousness, of course.

In other words, we have been descending the mythic circle itself, stage by stage into an underworld of mythic chaos. The old symbols have remained, but the relation between them and consciousness, between myth and mind, has been altering rather steadily and naturally. This means that the mode of projection has continually transformed itself and with it the kind of reality that symbols have, the way in which they exist. Ontology recapitulates mythology. The loss of myth is itself archetypal. Thus the meaning of the civilization is both its origin and its history; the history has interpreted the origin, an origin that is always present. As in the Old Testament, history has been our myth. Seeing it in the broad view, in its mythic sense, we can return to the archetypal pattern in our selves at least and renew its vision.[34]

* * * * *

Taken in its own terms, the mythic view of culture provides a perspective on human subjectivity that is itself subjective in one sense-- working through direct perception of experience, while it is in another way singularly objective--providing a perspective that is essentially detached and disinterested. It speaks for no party because it is a perspective on partisanship itself. Throughout this book, we have seen that even all theories of myth are useful myths in themselves. Aside from the insight it offers into religious and esthetic problems, simply on the level of ontology alone, this view suggests a theory of cultural history and a theory of social forms, a theory of knowledge and of education, a theory of the psychology of personality and, perhaps, therefore, a theory of psychotherapy. Because its vision illuminates the consciousness which sees, its implications reach out everywhere within the range of our experience, both in the ways we know ourselves and the ways we know the world.

If the conception of common myth is generally valid and useful in its relation to archetypal myth, then the two together suggest a view of truth and knowledge which contemporary culture badly needs, for it suggests a principle for relating a kind of relativism to a kind of absolutism. The archetypal confrontation with one's context simply is a basic feature

The Psycho-Mythology of Everyday Life

of the human presence and it has provided--in religion and in the arts--a magnetic field to which the human mind has been drawn in its perennial efforts to know its own nature. Common myth, in contrast, is naturally always relative, a *getting at* experience that is successful to very varying degrees, bound by motivations, circumstances, the questions to be answered, the previous myths to which it reacts and the continually shifting, conflicting, multi-layered, and ambiguous qualities of human consciousness as it is continually qualified by the resisting unconscious.

In other words, we have an overall picture of relative relativism. In fact, if relativism were *not* in itself relative, something would be wrong! It is successfully and meaningfully relative because it has something to be relative to. The modern belief in utter and definitive relativism has been just another self-canceling common myth. We have then the possibility of a real knowledge of a kind that has urgent importance for us, around which the mind plays in its continual reassessments of its lot, its continual projection of meaningful and misleading arbitrary truths.

CHAPTER ELEVEN

SYMBOLIC CONSCIOUSNESS

A myth that cannot be consumed becomes a specter . . .   --Yeats

INSIDE AND OUT

Human consciousness opens a dimension of intricate possibilities in its relation to symbolism. As the mind thinks in different kinds of symbol, it constitutes itself differently. Linear, discursive symbolism establishes an objective form of consciousness, in which self regards the world from a distance, aware of its own function as observer and commentator. The symbol is then a means towards the end of seeing the world, or nature; our symbols are *about* the world. Although each discursive symbol system remains limited by its own assumptions, its language, and its methodology, still, whether it is history, biology, or metaphysics, it is, in its own way, applying itself to the world.

In qualitative symbolism, on the other hand, consciousness becomes absorbed "subjectively" in its symbols. Mind enters within the symbol and experiences it as a world around one. The symbol is about the experience of the symbol. The love poem is not simply about love but about the love theme as it is played upon by language and imagery--and hence by consciousness. The apple painting does not reveal an apple more than it reveals the nature of color, shape, and texture. The sun myth, as we have seen, is about the experience of the sun and the experience of mythologizing about the sun. It is about imagination, which is to say that it is about the interplay of consciousness and the unconscious. Hence, we are interested in the qualitative symbol and its symbolic experience for their own sake. Such a symbol is opaque, holding our attention with its own rich qualities--or translucent, enriching the light that it lets through. In myth, subject and object--the self thinking and the world that is thought: mind and nature--are inseparable. Consciousness is turned back upon itself, dissolved in the field of projection.

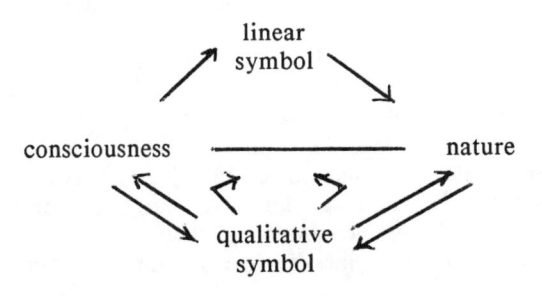

```
              linear
             symbol
           ↗        ↘
consciousness ——————— nature
           ↖  ↗    ↖  ↗
            qualitative
              symbol
```

Symbolic Consciousness

Knowing the world mythically and knowing ourselves mythically, we find ourselves in a world with vivid features, apparent form, and significance. This is true when we are engrossed in a play or a novel or a painting, each of which envelops us with a space made of image-stuff alive with implications. It is true when we really imagine a myth, and it is also true when, in our lives, we respond unconsciously to a mythic element of our culture as we make choices, pursue our values, and relate to others. In a traditional culture, one that is unified by the mythic ambiance of a religion, a value system, an idealized way of life, one does not simply know one's myth, one lives it, so that any aspect of life may be colored by its qualities.

Consciousness, therefore, constitutes itself differently under different cultural circumstances. A change in the culture or a change in one's own relation to society is a change in consciousness. In different types of civilization, there are different patterns of what experience is conscious and what is unconscious, but also there are, critically, different relationships to culture itself as symbolism.

Thus a traditionally mythic culture is not just one that has plenty of nonlinear symbols available for experience to be expressed in; it is itself a predisposition to absorb consciousness, to envelop or contain it in a state of *intra-symbolic consciousness*. In this state, to be aware is likely to be a matter of focusing through or within symbols. Practical reasoning may be necessarily linear, but one thinks about the nature of life, as a rule, mythically and acts in relation to mythic assumptions of value. Such a culture is one in which the mind's center of gravity (so to speak) is located in the nonlinear or right-brain process. Nonlinearity is the norm of reality. There is more easy traffic, as a result, between the conscious mind and the unconscious. Within such a world of experience, the myths are completely assumed, not merely believed in, and no alternatives to them may be conceivable. Consciousness may diverge from the mythic norm, but it does not ordinarily contravene its truth.

The norm in contemporary American culture, by contrast, is one of *extra-symbolic consciousness*. There is no longer, by and large, an inevitably inherited and assumed body of beliefs through which life is known. Reality is located ideally in direct sensation. Symbols of all sorts are suspect. Language itself, let alone the arts--as a college teacher of English is well aware--seems strange, unnatural, artificial. Such symbols (and symbolic forms and symbol systems) are regarded as objects that have to be imposed on us from without but that do not share our nature. They are tools, that are convenient and practical, *making* meaning, perhaps, but not *having* it. The condition is a kind of symbolic paranoia, a jealous fear of symbols' capacity to swallow up consciousness and the prerogatives of the self. Hence a profound crisis in education, which *is* the cultivation of symbols and should be also the cultivation of a meaningful, creative attitude *about* symbols.[1]

Of course, the claim that our culture is extra-symbolic requires at least one strong kind of qualification. As our practical values--moral, political, technological, or economic (perhaps the strongest of all)-- interpret reality for us, in more-or-less subliminal ways, they envelop consciousness in a sense of reality that is *virtually* mythic. (And religious beliefs as well still help determine many people's sense of reality, even though believers now must be aware that their system is a preference among other possibilities.) The McCarthy Era proved incontrovertibly how close "Americanism" can come to religious dogmatism. Communism, obviously, can control one's sense of reality in at least as rigid and all-inclusive a manner and has been described as a religion even more often than capitalism has (by capitalists, that is).

These belief systems of our cultures, West and East, are symbolic and "mythic" to the extent that they form a version of life that we may live by and through. Yet, for the most part, they are what we can call "pseudo-myths," provisional substitutes for real mythic coherence. They lack the archetypal form--the sense of confrontation with the absolute by the authentic self--of the real thing, together with the cogency and depth of experience that true myth conveys. In fact, the failure of such "myths" to substantiate life is evidence that our mentality *is* extra-symbolic, fundamentally pragmatic and rationalistic in its commitment. Some of the critical conflicts between the West and other parts of the world--notably Arab nations--have shown themselves to be fundamental differences between mythic and extramythic ways of being, rather than simply between ideas, economics, and national interests.

An intensely traditional culture, of course, pays heavy prices for the power of its symbol systems, in particular the tyranny of the group mind. The very positive side of our modern predicament is, eminently, the high value placed on direct personal experience and creative experiment; the negative side is frustration, violence, and incoherence that goes along with that freedom.

In the traditional cultures that still make up much of the world, where political revolution has not uprooted them, even in modern Europe, the old mythic bodies of symbol systems continue to effect the quality of life. The "center of gravity" has shifted, or is shifting, to the linear pragmatism of the conscious mind, but, to a significant extent, the culture's symbols still hold something of the natural relation to consciousness that may be possible only when symbols are inherited from the authoritative past. There is sophisticated awareness of alternative systems and a sense that one is born to one's particular world. There may be intense friction between ideologies, but there is a sense that symbols in themselves--the arts and the national language, and to quickly lessening degree religion and the political system--are natural to human consciousness. They are continuous with self.

These generalizations about cultural symbolism are drastically oversimplified, but they suggest the basic problem about the relation of symbolism to consciousness. They suggest something essential, I think, about the way in which symbolism and consciousness need to be understood in terms of each other. They suggest that different conditions of consciousness illuminate each other. Each possible relation to symbols implies a kind of limitation. Each sacrifices the advantages of the other.

To know what human consciousness is, we must see it backwards and forwards, through these three stages. Therefore, what I take to be,

Symbolic Consciousness

ultimately and ideally, the appropriate attitude toward symbols is one that acknowledges the full range of possibilities. Only in the overview, perceiving the different kinds of truth and their relation to each other, can we within our own culture achieve any honest perspective on the human mind and all its works, any sense of the value in whatever we have to teach and learn, or any fair meaning of our own drives to learn, teach, create, or simply think about our lives and make our daily choices.

IN THE END

It is obvious how modern culture has demythologized the world. We can even say that the reduction of myth has been its driving force: by way of the faith in facts, the assumption that only physical things are real, the obsession with consistent general principles, the insistence, ultimately, on living in terms that the conscious mind can comprehend and control. Fact has come to mean not the concrete experience so much as the abstraction drawn out of it. Our way of life has cultivated, therefore, not the image but the idea. The culture's heroism, of course, has been purely human integrity, but this has meant its distrust of any reality suggested by human feelings. "It is wholly modern experience," in the words of one writer, "to try to live without a story."[2] In America the main channel of consciousness has been, under the influence of economics and technology, a kind of general pragmatism, which leads to the conclusion that the best life is the easiest, the most manageable and comfortable. We try to gratify our sensual appetites and appease our anxieties, so that no ineluctable confusion or paradox or sense of void may strike us with uncouth feelings like terror, pain, despair, or helplessness, so that no ultimate "soul" may seem so stricken. Perhaps most of humanity has always lived in this way, but probably never before has such a standard of life been absorbed so blithely as the basis of a culture's values and never before has it been made to *work* so consistently. We may say, in fact, that progress, success, comfort are our gods; yet also, we know better. Gods they are not; the worship and ritual that they inspire convey small wonder.

Basically, our pragmatism has shifted the emphasis of consciousness from the self experiencing to the world being experienced. In other words, consciousness has attempted to expunge itself, to prove its own irrelevance. It promotes the illusion that it itself is insubstantial, transparent, provisional. The state of mind which results must be, naturally, a delicate balance of impossible resolution. A student of mine, David Gallagher, once wrote in a final exam: "This is the modern dilemma--an inaccessible object which promises secure foundations or an accessible subject which yields no foundation." We will never stand before the real physical world. In fact, post-Einsteinian physics has quite dissolved it. The ideal of progress, furthermore, will lead to no point of satisfaction, to no ultimates except, perhaps, the perfect power of destruction, which may finally resolve the world with complete efficiency. But on the other side, the subject, the self drifts in the freedom of chaos, aware nonetheless that chaos--the void--spells its own revelation.

With the charm of myth no longer readily available to guide us and to channel our energies, we are finding it more and more obvious, however, that we must cope with the phenomenon of consciousness itself. When consciousness withdraws from its myths, it is left with itself. The predicament can be a desperate one but it may also be one of the most fertile opportunities in the history of civilization. As Paul Ricoeur argues, it is a modern necessity that we know symbols by interpreting them. Interpretation, in a receptive spirit, is our way of still reaching the sense of life behind the myths, which produced them without self-consciousness or sense of purpose. For "it is by interpreting that we can *hear* again."[3] Although the mind has withdrawn from its myths, it need not deny them. A consciousness of symbols, in fact, should restore the vitality of consciousness itself.

An archetypal vision frees us from the constraints of belief. Any mythic system, no matter how radiant, limits the mind to its own values. Even if its dogma is minimal, still it excludes areas of experience that other ways of seeing may capture--as Christianity avoids the sensual and the violent features of divinity in which Hindu imagery luxuriates. To give the archetype form, a myth must also disguise it. But seeing the truth in many (if not all) mythic systems, we may see how they supply each other's deficiencies and how the features that they share touch our own reality most significantly. The myths dissolve and we are there, the archetype within us having been illuminated by the myth's light.

And yet, there is a limit to this view also. To accept everything, it may be, is to have nothing. The god who has no form may have no substance. Nor can we confront a reality that is not embodied. Anyone who upholds a traditional *way* of life will argue: it is the commitment, the being *within* the system that brings its life to fruition. Perhaps it is not understanding that we need so much as the dangerous vitality of immersion in the myth, the submission to its spell, and the sacrifice of more sensible considerations, which protect us with the security of detachment.

In trying to understand myth, one can argue, we are doing something patently opposed to the mythic spirit. In some cultures, notably the Hindu, myths have been deliberately shaped by spiritual teachers to convey a meaning that should be just beyond logical grasping. But by and large, myths are not made to be understood. Perhaps the unconscious forces that project them are protecting us from understanding too much. A functional interpretation would say that myths are made to work. They are made to engage our feelings as they traffic along the roads of consciousness, to glow in the light of the mind. In the words of Albert Camus, "myths are made for the imagination of breathe life into them."[4] Even where they are part of a teaching method, they are used for the effects they have as they are comprehended, more than for philosophic ideas than can be drawn out of them. A Jewish theologian observes that final conclusion which has since earliest times been drawn in the recognition of a sacred text, namely, that the effect upon the soul of such work is in the end not at all dependent upon its being understood.[5]

In the modern experience, it seems that we must appreciate by understanding, but is what we then have still myth? Or does the real myth evaporate when we think we know it?

So in the end is the question. It too is a mystery and perhaps can be lived by. Can it be, in the end, that questions are more revealing and more realistic than answers? It is the question that confronts, like a suppliant to the oracle, asking life its nature so that it can meet us. If the reality that we need to know is too ambiguous for statements to insist upon, this is not the failure of language but its measure: against the force of life which breaks into words, checks itself, counterdances, teases, erupts again, and recedes into babble, if not silence. And the question is a myth, to be known as an experience, for the realization that it brings.

Most people, of course, will take sides, or fall into them--action, participation, belief, creation; or reflection, detachment, consciousness: myth *or* mind. Yet, seeing the alternatives, it can be honest to *simply* see, to confront them, to realize the range of possibility and the flow of energy from one extreme to the other. If we think the alternatives exclude each other, we may fall into despair, but perhaps they depend on each other instead. Perhaps we do understand the situation better when we merely ask.

An extra-symbolic consciousness must, of course, be parasitic upon symbols. Because of this, we cannot possibly adopt an enlightened position as such. If we wish to be "healthy skeptics" or liberal-minded eclectics, we must have believers and literalists in our midst to keep their myths afloat for us--including all those kinds of common myth that one can easily be dogmatic about. This is one good reason, I should think, though there are undoubtedly more, why we will never have a wise society. In this way, the truth is dialectical and comes from the relation between positions, from the confrontation of living forces, as myth has always told us. Which makes things difficult for us when we wish to be right.

There is one way, therefore, of relating the paradox in more positive terms. That is the mythic way itself. What we are seeing, if we look closely, is an archetypal theme finally emerging once more: the attempt to avoid tragedy is the root of tragedy, Oedipus fleeing the oracle. Rebelling against the mythic universe as our culture has done, breaking the taboo of Eden, and insisting upon the independence of consciousness produces the myth, *is* the myth. We are back where we started, in the great nonlinear scheme of things, except that now we may see that the myth is not simply to be told but to be lived. All of culture, all of the cultures, comprise our story and mirror our own forms as we inevitably prolong their continuing reverberations. Our lives are myths unfolding, one by one and all together.

In the End

When a mythic hero kills his monster, the myth that it existed dissolves. Then, bringing new life with him, he may return to the ordinary world he rejected when he chose to follow the adventure of the unknown. The ultimate achievement of Arthur's Round Table is its dissolution as the quest for the Holy Grail begins. Mystics and esoterics treat lightly the myths that the congregation regards with dread, for to be myth is to fulfill it, to transcend it by finding the place of myth in mind, its ambiguous forms in our own life ongoing.

APPENDIX I

ABOUT CONSCIOUSNESS

thought is itself the thinker . . .
--William James

TRYING TO SAY WHAT IT IS

What makes me alive to myself is my consciousness, which makes the world my own, from my own body outward to the stars, from the room I see to other familiar places I recall. It also comprehends an endless universe of scenes I can imagine whether my own images of them have geographic counterparts or not. My consciousness is driven with feelings, churning with thoughts scattered and thoughts directed, visited with continually drifting images. It is the foundation of my living self. All that I contemplate and do and intend to do, all the importance of other people to me rests upon their place in my consciousness. Yet, so close that it *is* me, consciousness is so far that I can never reach it with my thoughts. I know it, but can I know what it is?

If I want to say what something is, certainly at least if I want to define it, I can describe its construction, its purpose and its manner of use; I can categorize it within a broader class, while indicating elements that fall within it; I can account for it as the opposite, alternative or negation of something else that can be understood alone. None of this can I do for consciousness. I am not even sure I can do it for anything that I have to know *as* conscious experience. I can say what a table is, but not *red* or *sour*. Much less can I grasp in concepts or convey in words the *quality* of consciousness itself, *its* "taste" or "odor."

What is most important to me, therefore, is most elusive. But perhaps that is just as well: it is also what is most private and most appropriately mysterious. It is a secret that everyone has and no one shares. It is the center of our lives and the outer bounds. It is the source of all creativity, all will and responsibility, of what does charm us most in others, of all the sorts of value that we find precious, all that makes humanity human.

We can all too easily ignore the fact of consciousness, no matter how pervasive it is. Once we start talking in a language that cannot account for it, we construct worlds of words that leave no place for its spell to work. In the very consciousness of our *objects* of attention, we lose the *subject*, "I" who am conscious.

We can describe consciousness loosely and even analyze it. We can point to it and suggest clues for focusing upon it. But it must become tangible by its own operation. We can know consciousness, not surprisingly, only by consciousness. Trying to define it is turning away from it, going through language to the world that language must either detect in the beyond or project there. It is by meditation that we know the quality of consciousness, reflecting upon it directly, when we cannot

About Consciousness

say what it is we are knowing in an awareness stripped of content to the direct sense of its own reality.

When we take the word literally, we realize that consciousness cannot be located or described as an entity or a state. It is a word like "hardness" or "lowness" merely a quality of an entity or state--how it is; and a quality perceived, furthermore, in contrast to an opposite--how it is *not*. In this sense, we speak properly of the consciousness of one's mind, the degree of consciousness, etc. . . . And yet we do also speak of consciousness as the state itself, something I *have*, which is also something I am doing (*being conscious*) or that is happening to (or *through*?) me, as *I am conscious of your approach*. This brings us to consciousness as experience: the experience I am having is my state of consciousness. . . . On this second level, are we merely abstracting an attribute and giving it being in itself?

In the following notes, I have experimented with some ways of describing and analyzing consciousness, putting aside for the time the problem of depth--the relation of the conscious mind to the unconscious--and looking mainly at the elusive qualities of the essential phenomenon.[1]

THE FUNDAMENTAL FLOW

We observe consciousness in important ways through its energy and through its functions.

<u>Its Energy:</u>

Although we cannot define it, we can *approach* definition in various ways, by saying, for example, that *consciousness is felt energy mobilized into attitudes*. Then we realize that "felt" here means "conscious" and has sneaked in as a substitute for it. Without such a word, however, the tangible quality is missing and therefore the essence of the matter. We could say "mental energy" to distinguish it from the physical, but then too "mental" would mean "conscious"--and also we cannot be sure, consciously, that the distinction is valid. Still, our near-definition dramatizes consciousness as a living force, in such a way as to suggest its constitution.

Energy: the non-stuff that makes up being, the universal flow, here manifest without apparent embodiment. Whatever else it is too, consciousness is a process or event that exerts itself. It is dynamic, it does, goes, happens, operates. I have it happening. I speak of it awakening, moving, focusing.

Correction: Consciousness is not energy; it is a field of energy. It is a context created by the play and interplay of energy, it *is* the interplay of energy, energy creating its own context.

Consciousness is minimal in one sense although it is total in another. It is *merely* so, as it stands by watching. It is in this way passive, soaking in the whole of what makes its world at any moment. But it is a paradoxically passive activity, going on, reaching out into the world, carrying on the manifold business of life. And waiting.

Appendix I

The duality of active and passive is a split that consciousness itself develops in order to get perspective, to "mobilize an attitude," to operate its energy. Perhaps we have to speak from opposite perspectives to get a conscious view of what consciousness is.

Is consciousness a river, an ocean, a lake, a pool, a storm, a leaky faucet, none of the above, or all? Obviously, the metaphors are limited, and we can use all of them. William James emphasizes continuity as one of the attributes of consciousness, and we readily assent to that. But can we experience the continuity of consciousness? Can the fish see the river? It is always totally now when we are here at home (collecting metaphors), though the present is adorned with memory and anticipation. Consciousness overwhelms its context from within. Continuity must be seen from outside.

<u>Creating a Universe</u>:

How does consciousness mobilize an attitude? Energy itself is motion, tendency, direction, *a directing* and hence *a way to go*.

More than one direction going along at the same time is *conflict*. All lines meet somewhere in the universe, even if we see them only when they are leaving each other.

Direction means both time and space to go through, here and there, now and then, a trail to cover and moments to elapse. To the mind focusing ahead, it suggests intention or purpose.

Also, energy is heat, and conflict is especially hot. Out of heat, sensation: comfort and pain.

Explosion: energy directed outward, lighting up the world, doing and seeing. Implosion: energy directed inward, the self illuminated, the self bedeviled.

The energy is also light. The mind does not only perceive light but gives it. The energy simmers: warms, scorches, and glows.

<u>The Functions</u>:

The energy of consciousness operates in direct awareness and also through all the "functions" of the mind or person: perception and sensation, conception and reasoning, emotion and intuition, appetite and will, imagination, symbolization. It penetrates and suffuses them, it surrounds and perceives them, it drives and responds to them. It specializes itself more concretely into its functions. It becomes more or less absorbed into the experience of them.

In regard to emotions, it is useful to distinguish between:

a) those which arise through interaction with the environment--feelings about people, food, work, scenery, and so forth.

b) those which arise through the operation of consciousness itself--feelings that arise directly from critical personal experiences, from philosophy, art, religion, meditation: existential and cosmic feelings. In contemplating death, for example (or in particular), consciousness cannot help but wrestle with its own substance and the question of its nature. Turned back upon itself, mind develops the anxiety that darkens all of life.

About Consciousness

THE SUBJECT: PARALLEL TERMS

These terms help to define one another. Some authorities, like Freud or Sartre, may use one or another in a special sense, to make specific distinctions. I take them to be, in general use, largely interchangeable, with some overlap.

terms	reference	that is, we might say:
consciousness	"substance"	I exist through my consciousness.
subjectivity	quality	My mind is characterized by its subjectivity.
awareness	state	I am aware, in a state of awareness; but also, I exercise my awareness, as an instrument.
attention	process	I focus attention or pay attention to. This is the process that sets limits to consciousness.
experience	event	I have experience, but it is something that takes place.
psyche	organism	The psyche experiences and responds, as a system.
self	person	I know myself; I know who I am.
mind	entity	I have a mind, I use my mind.
"I"	identity	I am.

Which is not to mention such terms as *soul* or *spirit*. What about *being*? Subjectivity is the condition of being a subject--a being who is be-ing, who is alive to being, who is one's own. . . . Having said that, we can condense: subjectivity is being.

DESCRIPTIONS OF CONSCIOUSNESS

Since we cannot define it, what more can we say about it? Here are some possibilities . . .

Appendix I

--It is both individual and in three ways universal:
  a) the cosmic sense--it fills the universe from each center. Each of us creates the whole world.
  b) the communal sense--it occurs simultaneously from all possible centers. We all create our worlds together.
  c) the archetypal sense---it is of one nature in its essence. We share the worlds we create, and they are one world in spite of ourselves.

--It is personal (experienced *as* the self) and private (*as* self, or limited communicability).

Although it is not continual--since we are continually lapsing out of it--it is continuous, an indivisibly ongoing event, and a sense of continuity (as William James emphasized). We can say so only if we have been aware of discontinuity, for the terms can be conceived only in contrast to each other. It polarizes all *conceivable* aspects of its experience, focusing through division. Against its own measure, it habitually conceives discontinuity.

--It selects and allows itself to be attracted. It limits and concentrates itself in focus.

--It organizes material within the field of its experience by outline, pattern or rhythm, and its own need or purpose to perpetuate its nature.

--It accumulates experience. It adds to itself, ingests.

--It recalls and imagines; and forgets.

--It develops and integrates its experience along rhythms of habit, as predisposition, preference, personality, working through polarized feelings.

--It confronts what is not itself, the *other*.

--It responds to the universe without, according to its own needs and habits.

--It is capable of doubling back on itself, either negatively in a constricting "self-consciousness" or positively in a liberating "self-awareness."

--Through language and other symbolic media, it defines and names (attributes identity and limits it). In this way, it finds expression that can be recalled, reflected upon, and communicated in place of direct experience, expression that deposits experience and also suggests experience.

BEING CONSCIOUS OF CONSCIOUSNESS

When we consider the problem of self-consciousness (become conscious that we are conscious that we are conscious), we seem to be caught at once in and out of a Chinese puzzle. If we are outside looking in, who is out, who is in, where is the Self? Thus self-consciousness has the connotation of self-defeating awkwardness. It would seem, therefore, to be impossible to think about consciousness at all. The consciousness that I am thinking of is no longer simply consciousness; it is self-consciousness, which is not simply more of the same but a transmutation of it, and it is the consciousness that I am thinking *with*. Logically, moreover, I must think *of* myself from a new level of self, so I can never experience what I am thinking about. To think about subjectivity, in other words, I must make it objective, which denies its very nature. Any consciousness I can think about is no longer the kind of consciousness I experience, which I experience *through*, from the "inside," in the present. And I can never think about the present, because it is past when I think about it. When I think about consciousness, I imagine it in memory-thoughts as a fact that can be seen from the outside. It becomes opaque, rather than transparent in the way that consciousness *is* when it is conscious of something. Thus the mind flickers back and forth, inside and out, from subject to object, from process to prospect.

But is this so clearly true? When we think of inside and out, we apply a spatial model that may misrepresent the situation. We can see red and we can be conscious of seeing red. We can be aware of what we are doing. We really can walk while we think of putting a right foot in front of a left. We can think conscious or unconscious of the fact that we are thinking. Consciousness can permeate (the rest of) experience to a lesser degree or a greater, with lesser or greater consistency, with more or less clarity. Is this also flickering, faster flickering? We *can* think about life while we are alive, about language while we are speaking, and about consciousness while we are conscious, for consciousness does not only watch, it permeates. Or, if "permeate" preserves a separation between the two substances in the same space, it emanates, it irradiates. It is the light of its own being, the light of its fire.

THE POLARIZATION OF ENERGY

The structure of consciousness provides an axis, or a set of axes, upon which attitudes mobilize, upon which ideas grow. Our ideas develop by energizing one another in pairs of opposites. We think of them as the offsprings of one another, each generation, each school of thought, but also each inspiration, begetting the next. "Ideas," however, flesh out in our conscious minds subterranean tendencies. These tendencies do not just arise from buried contents, such as lost dolls and early beatings. They are constant within human culture, and basic to the nature of consciousness itself. They belong to one aspect of what consciousness is, determining how experience constitutes itself. As the mind is, so it thinks. How else could it interpret the world but in its own image, seeking values that belong to mind itself? While coping with a world it half sees and half imagines, the mind--through its individual personality as you or me--justifies its own limitations. Because it needs to make choices, to grow one shape or another, go one way or the next, exist as Tom or as Harriet, it invests the conscious forms of our opinions with the maya-illusion that they refer to reality. Taking on conscious forms, energy develops momentum. As it multiplies itself, pulling us along by the bootstraps of our own conceptions, thought takes over and energy pretends to be its servant.

TERMS OF CONSCIOUSNESS

	value	CULTURAL		PSYCHOLOGICAL	value
1.	− restriction + coherence	↘ *structure*	← ORIENTATION →	*individuality* ↗	isolation freedom
2.	− oversimplification + efficiency	↘ *selection*	← FOCUS →	*integration* ↗	overgeneralization integrity
3.	− loss of self + selflessness	↘ *immersion*	← PROCEDURE →	*withdrawal* ↗	sterility self-awareness
4.	− dogmatism + meaning	↘ *belief*	← RESPONSE →	*scrutiny* ↗	cynicism discrimination
5.	− immobility + stability	↘ *stasis*	← MODE →	*change* ↗	dissipation growth
6.	− bigotry + fulfillment	↘ *satisfaction*	← DISPOSITION →	*curiosity* ↗	triviality learning
7.	− violence + vigor	↘ *intensity*	← QUALITY →	*diffuseness* ↗	vagueness complexity
8.	− reactionism + continuity	↘ *recollection*	← TIME SENSE →	*anticipation* ↗	anxiety preparation
9.	− ignorance + responsibility	↘ *action*	← ADDRESS →	*awareness* ↗	passivity comprehension
10.	− conventionalism + community	↘ *propriety*	← ETHIC →	*spontaneity* ↗	egoism self-fulfillment

About Consciousness

The mind chooses economically between two kinds of possibility. Perhaps it should be able to go all the points of the compass, with infinite divisions, but it finds out polarities--back or forth, up or down, left or right, conservative or liberal. Two ways are the minimum for motion, yet they are all we need in order to appear free. If I can choose, I can focus my attention in a particular way and set energy to work. But more fundamentally, as we look at the possibilities of *conscious* movement, the alternatives seem to arise from a deeper sense of form.

My chart of the "Terms of Consciousness" is skeletal, intended to suggest the form of the energy that becomes embodied in our life styles, philosophies, and cultural patterns. It schematizes a neutral--unintellectual and unjudging--view of the principle at work. The word choices are all tentative but they represent attempts to avoid judgmental assumptions. Primarily, they are meant to chart relationships across the line according to a very basic pattern and to suggest an elusive relationship among the "terms" themselves.

Each "term" (designated by the center column) suggests a flow of energy that can move in two directions. These directions seem to correspond on the one hand, to an involvement in the culture at large, and, alternatively to a fuller sense of self-realization. I suspect, however, that the "cultural" or "psychological" factor is not a cause of the difference but only one result or implication among others. Each of these polar tendencies itself tends, furthermore, toward either negative or positive expression (the outer columns). This can happen in two ways: We can regard a person's choice as good or as bad, and also one's own way, left or right, can be either beneficent or harmful.

In reality, any state of mind may be an ambiguous complex of these tendencies. The mind can multiply itself and go in several different directions at once. This can mean either a complicated harmony or a state of helpless conflict. But within any complex state of mind such tendencies seem to be working themselves out and interweaving, often blind, no doubt, to their discrepancies.

In the first "term," ORIENTATION, consciousness may recognize itself contributing to an outside structure and identify itself according to it. I know myself as a member of society, family, profession, or class, and I absorb meaning and value by occupying my own particular niche, which I alone fill. From my place, I relate directly to others who are placed separately but similarly. I restrain my subjectivity so that I can be aware that others exist in the same way that I do. We are all "other" people together, commonly human. Furthermore, I see myself in the scheme of nature or history, or I see an act of mine as it has been influenced by others, or an idea as part of a cultural movement.

In the other direction, I experience my self as the center of the universe. The world that matters to me is the world I am conscious of, with everybody else, everything, and every place important as I experience them. I am unique, because I am total, defining the universe in the process of filling it out. Nothing else I can experience is like my expe-

Appendix I

rience itself. Since nothing else has to me the same kind of reality, nothing really can limit my being. When I feel my emotions or am simply aware of anything at all, especially when I am so absorbed in an experience that I am not aware of myself experiencing it, then my life just *is*, in a world which my mind gives form. My consciousness is life. (If this is solipsistic, it is "parallel solipsism," for I can recognize that everyone else has the same form of experience.)

Neither direction, the need to clarify context or the need to affirm unique individuality, is in itself right or good, but of course we are quick to establish value about the choices we are led to by unconscious factors and which we cultivate with conscious ones. Moreover, there are advantages and disadvantages, of a psychic nature, in each way. The outer columns of the chart suggest versions of the negative and positive perspectives. Each direction of the term is, to our eternal frustration, "good" in one sense and "bad" in another. Although we see only the "right" side of our own way and the "wrong" of the other fellow's, the happy-unhappy truth is that the energy itself is ambivalent. Structure provides a meaningful sense of the world we relate to; yet it is restricting, imposing on our energy a framework it must yield to and preventing its full self-expression. Individuality, on the other hand, can be seen and can be experienced either as the source of one's freedom in the universe and of one's responsibility for it as well--or as the cause of sterile isolation and alienated despair. However, it is our own attitude toward experience itself that determines which value we emphasize in our own lives. The love of life--the acceptance of our feelings and all the experience of the self--assures both relationship and freedom. The rejection of consciousness that is one's own self-hate, energy turned violently against itself--no philosophy or opinion but a radical condition of the psyche--drastically isolates consciousness and restricts any flow, making any self-expression seem dubious in value.

The other "terms" I have suggested on the chart work out parallel but overlapping implications. In each view, we see that there is simply a range of energy operant and it focuses itself according to the limited possibilities inherent in the nature of that energy. In each way, however, we get a somewhat different emphasis, which develops a somewhat different aspect of human activity. To "look at" energy and sense its dynamic nature is to see that (1) it *will* orient itself in its universe both within and without, (2) it *will* focus by distinction or by connection, (3) it must proceed in a manner that relates self to environment, (4) it will respond with an organization of itself, (5) it will operate in a mode that retains its position or changes it, (6) it does take some form of interest in its world, (7) its quality of being will determine how it operates, (8) it will evoke time as a sequences of events, by anticipating and recalling the images and implications of its own experience, (9) it will address itself to life with a kind of operation, and (10) it will act either by some sense that guides action or by the impulse of its own energy.

Writers who speak of a "binary" structure or compare the mind to a computer in its dependence on a two-term "language" are correct in view of the surface form that is apparent here, but they are likely to miss

About Consciousness

the actual relationship between the paired elements. Seeing from within, we realize that there is no pair at all. Rather than two opposed units facing each other, we have a field of energy that probes back and forth seeking direction, with possibilities of movement split asunder. We have then not separate units but tendencies of a whole. Just as a computer cannot possibly be "intelligent" without consciousness (for intelligence is the awareness of knowledge and of its implications), so the mind is radically different from the most refined machine conceivable because of this dynamic sense of its own organic presence. No mechanical sets of terms make up this structure but the life of willful awareness feeling its powers and needing to find them expression.

PROBLEMS WITH THE WORD "CONSCIOUSNESS"

Strictly speaking, the word "consciousness" refers to an open state of perception, a knowing receptivity to experience or an acknowledgement of it. Here it is clearly contrasted to unconsciousness, which seems, in the contrast, simply the blackness of the void, the nonexistence of consciousness.

But I have followed the practice of speaking of consciousness as *conscious experience*, identifying it with the full range of thoughts, feelings, perceptions, etc. Can consciousness be both the container and the contained? Or is that a false, mechanical distinction? Does the "field" relationship solve the problem or is it too a misleading physical analogy based on a given separation? I have identified consciousness with energy, but if it is the container, it is essentially passive. Is receptivity energy: is there an energy to receive?

The unconscious, as well as the conscious mind, is a "body" of experience. In dream, the boundary between the two realms is a blurry one. It may be continually shifting and there is likely to be an amorphous range of semi-conscious experience (Freud speaks of the "preconscious") that we fade in and out of. When we are aware in a dream, or aware that we dream, we may be unconsciously conscious. Others have pointed out that the conception of an unconscious "realm" is itself mythical. The spatial image makes it seem distinct, with a uniform presence. We need to remember that it is, like ignorance, rather a kind of absence. Unlike ignorance however, it seems to contain (the container again) what it is ignorant of.

When we think of consciousness as experience, we may be more aware of the continuity between conscious and unconscious experience than we are of the distinction. It all seems to make up an organism operating coherently, while we are conscious only of part of it at a time. This is true even though the fact of unconsciousness profoundly affects the range of feelings that we have shut out (or in). We do not seem to have a good word for the full range of experience or psychic energy as an active force. Jung calls it the *libido*, too technical a term and very different in this meaning from Freud's more familiar usage. "Experience" is itself too loose and ambiguous; "psychic energy," as well as being clumsy and mechanical, is unclear about the nature of the energy. Consequently,

Appendix I

I often find myself thinking of consciousness as though it included the unconscious in order to describe the whole body of knowledge and feeling, or elements within it, when I am interested in them for their own sake rather than for their relation to my awareness.

We can, in perhaps a moral sense, identify consciousness with the full acknowledgement of experience, or the acceptance of responsibility for it. We are "unconscious" of feelings we know about but are not willing to own. Resistance is then the measure of unconsciousness. In confronting unconscious experience, integration may consist of three phases: our awareness of feelings, our actual experience of them, and, most critically our acceptance of them.

Consciousness, it follows, is the degree of responsibility with which one lives one's life. We can describe it from one angle and a bit perversely as one's consciousness of one's unconsciousness, which is not very different from saying, an awareness of one's limitations, or of one's mortality. From another angle, consciousness is a sense of how one's individual characteristics relate to one's qualities as a human being--or how one's personal myths relate to the archetypal form of consciousness itself.

APPENDIX II

MYTHS, FICTIONS, METAPHORS

MYTH OR FICTION?

The view that we think by means of literally false conceptions was developed most systematically by the German philosopher Hans Vaihinger in his "Philosophy of *As If.*"[1] A follower of Immanuel Kant (who changed Western philosophy with his rigorous argument that our perceptions of the world-especially in the fundamental "categories" of time and space--depend upon the nature of our own minds), Vaihinger started from the position that all we know truly of reality is the flow of sense impressions and impulses to action. We have some knowledge of reality directly but that is extremely limited. Our need in life is to act and we do so with the aid of thought, whose only goal is "facilitating the interrelation of sensations, i.e. . . . rendering action easy."[2] However, the "ways of thought cannot be those of reality."[3] We can think about the interrelation of sensations only indirectly, through fictions, which serve our needs even though they contradict reality and usually contradict themselves as well. Our psyche is a machine that manufactures these fictions for us, and it keeps producing more efficient models.[4]

According to Vaihinger's survey, fiction permeates our thinking unavoidably in mathematics and all the sciences, in law, ethics, and of course in religion and arts. It includes methods of classification, simplification, thinking by analogies, generalizations, averages, value judgments, imagining distinct entities behind our sensations and abstracting qualities from them,[5] referring to absolutes, asserting dualities, distinguishing between a whole and its parts, distinguishing things from what we think of as their opposites, and asserting that anything can be equal to anything else. *Matter* is a fiction[6] and so is *motion.*[7] Every *idea* is "a necessary evil."[8] "Truth is really merely the most expedient type of error."[9]

Fictions, Vaihinger argues, are perfectly necessary and appropriate errors, important because they are useful. Moreover, "all the nobler aspects of our life are based upon fictions,"[10] which does not detract at all from their nobility. We are capable of thinking only *as if* our fictions were true. However, if we think by errors, logic must also be able to correct our errors, which it does by realizing that they are fictions and also by counteracting them with further, "antithetic errors." Unfortunately, because of the "Law of the Preponderance of the Means over the End,"[11] these provisional and practical forms of thought tend to take on interest in themselves, leading to endless confusion. Throughout history men have deluded themselves and each other disastrously by (a) treating fictions as though they were hypotheses (which, unlike fictions, can be

Appendix II

proven true or false), and (b) holding on to them as dogma, being "content with the mere husks of things."[12] By realizing that fictions are simply "conceptual aids," we can have sufficient *knowledge* of the world, although, he says engagingly, "The wish to understand the world is not only unrealizable, but also it is a very stupid wish."[13]

Vaihinger derived his concept of the pervasive fictitiousness of thought primarily from his less systematic but far greater predecessor Friedrich Nietzsche, who strove vigorously and persistently to unthink the hidden assumptions that underlie our Western conception of reality and that betray its tenuousness. Nietzsche sometimes called his philosophy "perspectivism," arguing that since truth is always determined by the perspective from which it is seen, it is never really "true." Consciousness itself is such a perspective, obliging us to live under the illusions that it creates. "Delusion and error," he wrote, "are conditions of human knowledge and sensation."[14] Yet it is the point of wisdom, he held, to embrace our illusions and live them joyously, a condition that is typified in art.

Although he is most famous for denying truth value to moral and religious declarations, Nietzsche also anticipated Vaihinger's critique of the fundamental thought processes through which we interpret nature, as well as Vaihinger's argument that we cannot consider our thoughts true simply because they work.

> We have arranged for ourselves a world in which we can live --by positing bodies, lines, planes, causes and effects, motion and rest, form and content; without these articles of faith nobody now could endure life. But that does not prove them. Life is no argument. The conditions of life might include error.[15]

But unlike Vaihinger, Nietzsche exulted in the rich life of instinctive feelings which becomes falsified by consciousness and the languages that consciousness formulates--"Thoughts are the shadows of our feelings--always darker, emptier, and simpler"[16]--and he also dismissed the criterion of usefulness that Vaihinger regards as the justification for all our fictions:

> We simply lack any organ for knowledge, for "truth": we "know" (or believe or imagine) just as much as may be *useful* in the interests of the human herd, the species; and even what is here called "utility" is ultimately also a mere belief, something imaginary, and perhaps precisely that most calamitous stupidity of which we shall perish some day.[17]

On the whole Vaihinger's picture of the mind is bleakly mechanical, a machine manufacturing the practical, logical tools called fictions, which we need to use and to use up in order "to do the world's work." Our mental life is as insubstantial as the extremely shadowy world outside. "All our mental life is rooted in *sensation* and culminates in

Myths, Fictions, Metaphors

movement; what lies between are mere points of transit."[18] Vaihinger's "Critical Positivism" assumes that the sole function of thought is to deal with this "outside" world even while he should be raising his eyebrow at the mind's distinction between outside and in. Nicholas Humphrey, an English psychologist, has recently suggested the far more appealing idea that humanity developed consciousness in its early stages because we are a peculiar kind of social animal who need to be "natural psychologists," able to understand the feelings of other people through awareness of our own.[19] We can go even further than that, however. We can see that in the arts, which Vaihinger treats essentially on the same practical basis as scientific fictions--as well as in the esthetic elements of myth, ritual, and play--experience proliferates for its own sake. We luxuriate in the awareness of our emotions, our thoughts, and our fantasies just as we do in the sensuous feelings of our bodies. This is not at all gratuitous, nor is it essentially practical, even in Humphrey's terms. It is life happening. What is essential is what Nietzsche would emphasize: the joy and the power in it all.

Vaihinger calls the mind's works "fictions" because he is making a startling point in contradistinction to people's ordinary assumptions: What you think is true (he says) is really false. Nietzsche's iconoclasm is prone to the same excess of zeal, turning "truth" inside out to cleanse the stables thoroughly. He speaks regularly in the voice of "prophetic truth." Of course the words "fiction" and "myth" (and Nietzsche's "illusion") can be used interchangeably, but we have a good idea of what "fiction" means to Vaihinger and how he oversimplifies the problem with the concept that he means by the word and the assumption about truth that lies behind the concept. As we have been interpreting the nature of myth, however, this notion suggests a special quality of creative elusiveness that makes it more serviceable for the purpose. "Myth" provides a more flexible way of seeing things. It is a way which is more clearly true to the equivocal nature of the reality we want to talk about, of the mind with which we think and talk about it, and of the relation between reality and the mind, which are deeply, richly, and subtly involved in each other.

MYTHS AND METAPHORS

In a recent book called *Metaphors We Live By*, linguist George Lakoff and philosopher Mark Johnson analyze the inherently metaphoric nature of language, drawing from their findings a broad theory of knowledge. Lakoff and Johnson argue that we unconsciously interpret experience through certain basic metaphors that imply a system of assumptions and values. These metaphors, therefore, control how we might think within our language, within our culture. A few of the examples that they discuss in some detail, with many illustrations, are: "argument is war" (as in "He *attacked* every *weak point* that I *advanced*."), "ideas are commodities" ("It's important how you *package* your ideas if you want them to *sell*."), "love is a patient" ("Their relationship was *dying*; now it's *on the mend*."), "life is a container" ("There's *not much left* for him *in his*

Appendix II

life."), and "the mind is a machine" ("I'm a little *rusty* today.").[20] Lakoff and Johnson claim that the way our bodies orient us in space leads us to organize the world with "orientational metaphors" (such as, in our culture: "High status is up; low status is down"); and that, in "ontological metaphors," we tend to treat abstractions, experiences, and qualities as though they were concrete entities ("I went to *a lot of trouble* to *dig up* this information.").[21] Personification is a common form of the ontological metaphor; related to it is some forms of metonymy, identifying something by a related term ("He's got a *Picasso* in his den"; *"Nixon* bombed Hanoi").[22]

Lakoff and Johnson make three basic points about metaphors that definitely apply to common myths. Two of them I have emphasized in discussing archetypal myth and the third holds good also for both kinds of myth. First, it is an important part of their thesis that metaphors are experiential: not simply concepts but factors that qualify our experience of life as we experience *their* operation in our minds. In reference to the orientational metaphor "up": "verticality enters our experience in many different ways."[23] Secondly, metaphors are interactional, a matter of our involvement in the world. "The kind of conceptual system we have is a product of the kind of beings we are and the way we interact with our physical and cultural environments."[24] And thirdly, conceptual metaphors are, generally speaking, inconsistent with one another. Since they each apply to particular aspects of experience and since each interprets experience according to its own capacity, they are likely to contradict one another in some ways even though they may overlap and support each other in other ways. "To operate only in terms of a consistent set of metaphors," in fact, "is to hide many aspects of reality. Successful functioning in our daily lives seems to require a constant shifting of metaphors."[25] Myths of both types, I would say, are discontinuous and exclusive. Each is based upon a fresh act of projection. Each myth is vulnerable to the truth perceived by others and may be nonsense outside its own terms. It does not take into account what it does not observe and reveal. Thus you cannot move from one directly into another. Every princess is the most beautiful of all. Oedipus's riddle can't be addressed to Herakles. Plato's premises don't lead to Aristotle's conclusions.

But is there any advantage to speaking of myth where Lakoff and Johnson speak of metaphor? It does seem to me that by doing so we can emphasize certain points better and clarify some others. The way I have been speaking of myth, it is on one hand an aspect of all metaphors-- their qualitative substance; and on the other hand it is a broader phenomenon that includes metaphor as one type--the tendency of all cultural forms to produce their own truth. Lakoff and Johnson's metaphors are our myths simply because they exist through language, for what is true *in words* is true in a verbal way, in a verbal world. In moving from just one aspect of language to a theory of knowledge, Lakoff and Johnson arrive too fast at a generalized conclusion that we may be able to reach more securely because we *are* using a broader term.

It seems to me that Lakoff and Johnson weaken their argument by depending upon a rhetorical notion of what metaphor is, and this in par-

Myths, Fictions, Metaphors

ticular we can avoid if we consider the mythic aspects of their images. They keep returning to the conventional assumption that metaphor is a comparative formula showing the similarity between two distinct kinds of activity or object: in it we "understand one domain of experience in terms of another."[26] Metaphors, they say, give us "a handle on" concepts.[27] Thus, in their own metaphor, *ideas* remain *things*, for metaphors are tools, one thing which handles another thing, the concept, which presumably handles another thing, the reality. However, they are really interested in a view of understanding and truth that is subtler than rhetoric and more basic than language itself, as is especially clear toward the end of the book in their brief discussion of ritual.[28]

This subtler view is inherent in their emphasis on the experiential nature of the images, for in the experience a new reality appears, a new term *in* the interaction. They do stress that "the comparison theory most often goes hand in hand with an objectivist philosophy in which all similarities are . . . inherent in the entities themselves"; they themselves argue in contrast "that the only similarities relevant to metaphor are similarities as experienced by people."[29] Their rhetorical grounding, nevertheless, causes them to treat their metaphors as though they were uniformly coherent and specific. Giving the two sides of the metaphor so much weight--the direct experience and the image (or tenor and vehicle)--they don't fully appreciate the new reality of the space between them. And that, I would say, is the realm of the myth, which is not exactly image and not exactly meaning. It is a familiar elusiveness, at once a kind of experience, a kind of performance, and a kind of understanding.[30]

The images that Lakoff and Johnson cite are often what literary critics call "submerged metaphors," which lend the force of their associations in a subliminal way but are likely to be disruptive if they are realized too explicitly. They are not simply *there*, like objects waiting to be excavated. They may be suggestive, in fact, to varying degrees.[31] The concrete image is particularly hard to locate when Lakoff and Johnson speak of bodily orientation and the ontology of abstractions as metaphors.[32] In neither case is there a concrete vehicle that would really constitute a metaphor according to the conventional definition. These expressions may be good examples of personification, and personification can be thought of logically as a metaphor. *A disease is an opponent*: "cancer finally caught up with him." But personification is certainly one of the main features of myth, because it animates and humanizes, it experiences the world as alive with the world's *own* experience. And it does this through the special experience of the myth's new and extravagant reality, its subjective truthfulness.

Rather than handling a concept, then, myth *gets at* the *experience*--by the experience that the myth evokes. Rather than being simply a logical comparison, myth is an animation from within, producing its distinctive kind of reality, which relates to our direct experience by transforming it. In other words, it is a dramatization, and drama is the accurate way to express what is dramatic in life: its liveliness, fraught with energy, tension, and conflicting points of view. It is expressive *by* being creative. It is mimetic in the sense that it *mimes* or mimics its

Appendix II

theme, playing upon it with insightfully imaginative distortion. Metaphor is mythic because it is drama and, therefore, a form of play. Of course, a drama is *a play*: we and the actors play at literal truthfulness; and play is *making believe*, and making believe is creating conviction, or an experience of knowing.

Now, play, ritual, and myth are importantly discontinuous from the linear, objective kinds of action and experience we ordinarily call reality. They are liberating assertions because they are apart, while they are expressive still of the nature of existence, the nature of experience. Accordingly, one way in which metaphor is mythic is that we use a metaphor for its differences as well as for its similarities, for its negative, as well as its positive, value. It is right, partly but significantly, because it is not true. I can call love a rose only because we all know it is *not* a rose. The word is deliberately misapplied: now I'm gonna tell you a whopper; and like all good lies, it has its gratification in the bravado of deceit. It is playfully absurd. When we speak of an argument as though it were a war, in a battle of wits for example, we are serious--we do mean that it *is* a war, with true ferocity and maybe even desperation--yet we are also playing that it is a war. We know that we are not going to kill or get killed. Like boys building a "fort" to throw snowballs from, we bring an excitement to our quibbles by the pretense that they are as consequential as they can be. Or rather, we give to the excitement that is already there a ritual form in which to play itself out.

It is not only metaphor but language in general that is mythic, dramatic, playful. In metaphor it is just more obvious than usual. All language--all symbolism, in fact--has a power that comes from making believe, from overstating, understating, misstating, and equivocating, from a spirit of extravagance that is an important part of our linguistic experience. Language never *is*, of course, what it is about. It plays with chunks of sound; the chunks of sound *play the roles* of representing meaning, even as they constitute their own world, the *life of the play*. Or better, perhaps, they make up the roles that *we* play as we pretend to be fully accurate and authoritative. Putting *things* in *words* is itself a ritual, transforming things, as all rituals do, into a kind of stuff that is almost all form, while stabilizing things at their most equivocal to make them our own. And language is as likely to have originated out of that kind of motivation, I should think, as any other.

Whenever we talk, whether we are giving commands or descriptions, we take for granted that we are doing something *by* using language. We are not just stating facts or conveying our expectations; we are in some way confronting and also celebrating an event, by immersing ourselves in it and at the same time claiming it as *our* perception, *our* experience. Even if we are lying, we commit ourselves to the lie. As in all forms of symbolism, we are mythologizing the world as our world, so that we can know, and say and perhaps face up to what it means to us. For we hardly ever want to just communicate information; we want to evoke experience in the context of attitudes and interactions. For example, as Lakoff and Johnson point out, the figure of metonymy lets us understand something properly in its *relationship*, but our understanding of that rela-

Myths, Fictions, Metaphors

tionship interprets it for us and gives us a relationship to *it* as it does so. The drawing *by* Picasso claims our reverence because it *is* "a Picasso," even if it's not one of his best. The image takes note that the reality of the man is properly extended into his works. Nixon is responsible for the bombing, therefore he performed the acts even though he was not in the planes.[33] Both men are more than themselves. In observing this extra-physical relationship, and in appreciating it, insisting upon it, we establish our own relation to the event. In the first case, Picasso, our metonymy, in its mythic pose, its extravagant self-dramatization, celebrates the mystery of art; in the second, Nixon, it might very well be an execration (celebrating the act of execrating, like the high spirits of a lynching party).

The myths of language, like all myths, take part in our experience, themselves a way of experiencing: enriching and also confusing, certainly complicating, our experience in general. As they do so, they dramatize the concreteness of experience, its felt texture. To do this, they have to swerve to be accurate. It is probably in the swerve, actually, that we feel most strongly about what we have to say: Nixon *did* bomb Hanoi, this debate *is* war, language *is* play and drama and myth. We are most honest and most earnest where we can least expect, logically, to be believed. Making believe, we get at the truth of our experience. Dramatizing the situation, we convey the urgency of it all, the existential sense that it really is, it really happens, it really matters.

NOTES

PREFACE

1. Claude Lévi-Strauss, "The Structural Study of Myth" in *Structural Anthropology* (London, 1968), p. 206.
2. Heinrich Zimmer, *The King and the Corpse* (Princeton, 1956, 2nd ed.).
3. Three very important precursors, in the 18th and 19th centuries, are Vico, Blake, and Schelling. I have a brief account of Vico in note 24 to Chapter 2. Blake appears often in the book. Schelling is hard to come by in English, but an idea of his views can be had from one of my main sources, Ernst Cassirer, *The Philosophy of Symbolic Forms,* Vol. II: *Mythical Thought* (New Haven, 1954).
4. Clifford Geertz, "Thick Description: Toward an Interpretive Theory of Culture," reprinted in T*he Interpretation of Cultures* (N.Y., 1973), p. 14.
5. Ludwig Wittgenstein, *Philosophical Investigations*, translated by G.E.M. Anscombe (Oxford, 1953; 1968), p.32. Wittgenstein introduces the point in discussion of games, which have a family relationship to myths through the relation each has with rituals.
6. In Chapter Six, I give a brief account of Carl Jung's brilliant conception of archetypes, but go on to speak of archetypal structure in the broader sense that I have suggested here.

CHAPTER 1: The Image-ing Mind

1. Bachelard, *The Poetics of Reverie*, translated by Daniel Russell (1969; reprint, Boston, 1971), p. 81.
2. A tactful understatement, against which might be set the powerful language of R.D. Laing in *The Politics of Experience* and *The Bird of Paradise* (London, 1967), especially "Persons and Experience: Normal Alienation from Experience." I quote from this discussion below in Chapter 10.
3. See Franz Boas, *The Mind of Primitive Man*, revised ed. (N.Y., 1938), p. 212. The last two examples are his.
4. Alan Watts, *The Joyous Cosmology* (N.Y., 1962), pp. 31, 33.
5. Neihardt, *Black Elk Speaks* (N.Y. 1932; reprint 1972), p. 22. Radin includes a brief account of an Indian visionary's induction into the peyote cult as an appendix to *Primitive Man as Philosopher.*
6. Neihardt, p.25.
7. Neihardt, pp. 26-28.
8. Neihardt, p. 41.
9. *Blake: Complete Writings*, edited by Geoffrey Keynes (Oxford, 1957), pp. 804-6. In an account of his painting "A Vision of the Last Judgment," Blake wrote:

    > I assert for My Self that I do not behold the outward Creation & that to me it is hindrance & not Action; it is as the Dirt upon my feet, No part of Me. "What," it will be Question'd, "When the Sun

Notes to Pages: 15-16

rises, do you not see a round disk of fire somewhat "like a Guinea?" O no, no, I see an Innumerable company of the Heavenly host crying "Holy Holy Holy is the Lord God Almighty." I question not my Corporeal or Vegetative Eye any more than I would Question a Window concerning a Sight. I look thro' it & not with it. (Keynes ed., p. 617.)

CHAPTER 2: *Felt Logic*

1. At the same time, nonlinear form, we shall see, has its own kind or kinds of consistency, which we can call "rational" because it makes sense in its way. In the study of myth, it is easy to confuse expectations of an absolute, external rationality, which can be verified by other means, with the realization of relative, internal "rationality," which holds a system of thought together by its own premises. See Steven Lukes, "Some Problems about Rationality," in *Rationality*, edited by Bryan R. Wilson (Oxford, 1970), pp. 207f. Whether or not mythical statements are coherent in themselves, they need not be consistent with each other. They all may be unique individually, but they do not necessarily refer together to a total unique world.

2. For an account of the "split-brain" theory by one the leading researchers in the field, see Joseph Bogen, "The Other Side of the Brain: An Appositional Mind," *Bulletin of the Los Angeles Neurological Societies* (1969), reprinted in *The Nature of Human Consciousness: A Book of Readings*, edited by Robert E. Ornstein (San Francisco, 1973); Carl Sagan, *The Dragons of Eden: Speculations on the Evolution of Human Intelligence* (N.Y., 1978); or, in a more controversial vein, Julian Jaynes, *The Origin of Consciousness in the Breakdown of the Bicameral Mind* (Boston, 1976).

3. Benjamin Lee Whorf, "The Relation of Habitual Thought and Behavior to Language," in *Language, Thought and Reality* (Cambridge, Mass., 1956), p. 147. All cited essays by Whorf are in this selection from his work, edited by John B. Carroll. A powerful earlier account of the present problem can be found in the works of Friedrich Nietzsche, who argued that "There is a philosophical mythology concealed in *language* . . ." For a summary of his views on the subject, see Appendix C in R.J. Hollingdale's translation *of Twilight of the Idols* and *The Anti-Christ* (Harmondsworth and N.Y., 1968), which includes this quotation, drawn from *The Wanderer and his Shadow* (1880).

4. Whorf, "The Punctual and Segmentative Aspects of Verbs in Hopi," p. 55. Whorf's position requires some qualification, as his critics have charged. There is not a thorough correspondence between language and experience. Language transmutes the experience it represents; we understand language by transposing it back to a sense of the experience itself, with varying degrees of clarity. In the process, a good deal is lost but not everything. A culture's syntactical forms and vocabulary correspond, perhaps, to the experience that the language makes conscious, but they hold in unconscious solution an uncertain range of further knowledge that we can relate to as well. We know more than we say (thank God). At the same time, our language does make unconscious

assumptions for us about what is true, associations that effect the way we experience things by their influence upon our expectations--*and it is equally true that unconscious assumptions shape our language.*

5. Whorf, "Habitual Thought," p. 145. "Lasting" and "tending" may be abstract adjectives in use, but they retain the dim sense of an active consciousness. So does the verb "retain"--and "does"--when we speak of abstract or impersonal entities.

6. Whorf, "Habitual Thought," p. 146.
7. Whorf, "An American Indian Model of the Universe," p. 59.
8. Whorf, "American Indian Model," pp. 59f.
9. Whorf, "Habitual Thought," p. 144.
10. Whorf, "Thinking in Primitive Communities," p. 85.
11. Dorothy Lee, "Codifications of Reality: Lineal and Nonlineal," *Psychosomatic Medicine* (1950), reprinted in Ornstein, p. 132.
12. Lee, p. 133.
13. Lee, p. 138.
14. Lee, p. 141.
15. Lee, p. 133.
16. Lee, p. 134.
17. Jung, *Symbols of Transformation*, translated by R.F.C. Hull (N.Y., 1956; reprint Princeton, 1976) p. 18.
18. Langer, *Philosophy in a New Key* (N.Y., 1942), esp. 126f. These two kinds of expression sometimes appear together, as in philosophical or didactic poetry and documentary art. Discursive symbols may deal with a nonlinear sense of reality, as the *discourse* of this book is doing; presentational symbols have linear elements, as a novel may deal with social problems. However, the way in which discursive symbols relate to reality is itself linear: they stand aside and talk about what is true out there; and the way of presentational symbols is itself nonlinear: they engage themselves with reality so that their being and our experience of life merge into a special kind of existence. In the very valuable formulation by the poet Coleridge, symbol "partakes of the reality which it renders intelligible." As we think about mythic symbolism, we should keep in mind distinctions between:

symbolic forms--individual works, such as myths, rituals, poems, theorems, thought of as units shaped out of "symbolic stuff" or composed of individual symbols.

symbol systems--"languages" or media that interpret reality according to specialized intentions, methods, symbols, and principles of relationship--mythology, chemistry, Buddhism, Spanish, and so forth.

symbols--individual images with suggestive powers: in myth, a character, place, journey, accoutrement, structure, any motif or action. The term may be applied at times to a symbolic form when it is thought of as a single utterance: a myth or poem thought of as a symbol of eternal frustration, etc. Symbols, as expressive images, are often distinguished from *signs,* which stand for, or "refer to," specific referents without expressing their nature: flags, traffic signs, letters of the alphabet, etc.

19. Joseph Bogen provides two charts of alternative sets of terms, p. 111 and p. 120. Historians of ideas often make similar contrasts between the world views of the major seminal thinkers: the Aristotelian and the Platonic,

after the great Greek philosophers; the Euclidean and the Pythagorean, after the Greek mathematicians; the Newtonian and the Einsteinian, after the modern physicists.
20. Burke, *Counter-Statement*, 2nd ed. (Chicago, 1957), p. 124f.
21. Ernst Cassirer, *An Essay on Man* (New Haven, 1944), p. 79.
22. For a detailed account of some common mythic symbols, including *up* and *down, light, fire*, and *blood*, see Philip Wheelwrights's chapter "The Archetypal Symbol" in his book *Metaphor and Reality* (Bloomington, 1962).
23. Some writers describe myths and symbols as "polyvalent," "multivalent," or "multireferential," suggesting that they have many levels of meaning at the same time. This is more sophisticated than saying that each myth has a specific meaning, but it is only a more liberal kind of allegorizing, implying that certain meanings, with a prior existence, are collected into the symbol. I would say that a myth has a single meaning, which is its rich qualitative condition, the essence of its symbolism, which we cannot paraphrase completely, and that this qualitative form suggests unlimited specific aspects of life to which it can refer by implication. Myth is not metaphoric, both for this reason and because of the function it has to effect confrontation, which I shall discuss in Chapters 7 and 9. It is more accurate to say that myth is paradigmatic, except for the sense in which a paradigm is properly an example of what it represents; myth is a projection--a qualitative extension--of the condition of life that it embodies. When we say that myth is symbolic, what is symbolized is first of all that qualitative condition that it "gives off," and secondly the aspects of life which share that complex of qualities.
24. The idea that myth is based on "poetic logic" in a "language invented by the imagination" to express "poetic wisdom" was developed into a "New Science" by Giambattista Vico, an 18th-century Italian philosopher. Although he considered the sense of wonder that produced myth to be "the daughter of ignorance" ("The power of the imagination is proportionate to the weakness of the capacity to reason."), he concluded that that fact allowed early men to be sublime poets. *The New Science*, Third Edition, Book I, Section II, axioms XXXV-XXXVII, in *Vico: Selected Writings*, edited and translated by Leon Pompa (Cambridge, 1982), pp. 171f. Vico saw myths as allegories of early social history --but an "ideal eternal history" (p. 181)--and as "a metaphysics . . . sensed and imagined" (p. 209). He had, therefore, an archetypal theory. "Poetic characters" are "imaginative genera or universals." (Paragraph 209, p. 175.) There is "a mental language common to all nations, which uniformly signifies the substance of things practicable in human social life and expresses it with as many different modifications as there are different possible aspects of things." (Axiom XXII, p. 167.)
25. Sigmund Freud, *The Interpretation of Dreams*, in The Standard Edition of the Works of Sigmund Freud, Vol. IV (London, 1953), p. 313.
26. Freud, p. 320.
27. Freud, p. 314.
28. Freud, p. 314f.
29. Freud, p. 316.
30. Freud, p. 318.
31. Freud, p. 314.

Notes to Pages: 25-33

32. Alan Watts, *The Two Hands of God: The Myths of Polarity* (N.Y., 1963, reprinted 1969), p. 16. The image is imprecise only by linear standards, I would think. Benjamin Whorf writes on this theme: "covert categories are quite apt to be more rational ['closer to natural fact'] than overt ones." "Thinking in Primitive Communities," p. 80.

33. Philip Wheelwright, *The Burning Fountain: A Study in the Language of Symbolism* (Bloomington, Ind.), p. 18.

34. See Boas' chapter on "The Emotional Association of Primitives."

35. Claude Lévi-Strauss, *The Savage Mind* (London, 1966), p. 264. Lévi-Strauss takes the *conceptual* nature of "savage thought" quite seriously, and I do not.

36. Lévi-Strauss, pp.76, 78. His source is W.H.R. Rivers, "Island-Names in Melanesia," *The Geographical Journal* (London, May 1912).

37. Lévi-Strauss, p. 164f.

38. E.E. Evans-Pritchard, *Nuer Religion* (Oxford, 1956), quoted in Lévi-Strauss, p. 224. The statement that "the resemblance is conceptual, not perceptual" suits Lévi-Strauss's basic argument, that myth is an intellectual activity. It seems to me, however, that there is a third alternative (which, in Levi-Strauss's own terms, "mediates" between the two): *the symbolic relationship*, which is qualitative (like perception) and meaningful (like conception) without acquiring the full self-consciousness of intellection.

39. As narrated by Carl Kerenyi, *The Gods of the Greeks* (London and N.Y., 1951), pp. 89f.; reprinted in Joseph L. Henderson and Maude Oakes, *The Wisdom of the Serpent* (N.Y., 1963, pp. 116f.). The motif directly connecting bloodshed and birth is widespread. It emphasizes the qualities of fertility through the "logic" of sacrifice: Life proliferates at the price of death. When the Titan Cronus castrates his father Uranus (according to Hesiod), the drops of blood impregnate Mother Gaea, the earth, who gives birth consequently to the Giants and the retributive Erinyes. Aphrodite is born from the sea after the severed genitals are cast into it. She is said to be "sex-loving, because she appeared from the sexual organs." *Theogony*, translated by Norman O. Brown (Indianapolis and New York, 1953), p. 58.

40. If I ask you to draw a circle, the chances are you will draw the circumference of a circle. *Is* the circumference the circle? Is the circle *within* the circumference? Do you draw a space when you draw its outline? In *The Marriage of Heaven and Hell*, William Blake wrote, "Reason is the bound or outward circumference of Energy." We perceive the shape of the form through Reason, which allows us to know and understand, but the substance of the form, its Energy, is the stuff of life. (Blake precedes this statement with "Energy is the only life and is from the Body" and follows it with "Energy is Eternal Delight.") Just as the circle is the area extended to its circumference, so Reason and Energy, in Blake's terms, are two perspectives on the same reality, the substance which we comprehend in its form.

Notes to Pages: 36-40

CHAPTER 3: The Meaning of Wonder

1.   Gregory Bateson, "Ecology and Flexibility in Urban Civilization," in *Steps to an Ecology of the Mind* (N.Y., 1972). All cited essays by Bateson are reprinted in this volume.

2.   *Anatomy of Criticism*, p. 156. Frye goes on to say: "The student of comparative mythology occasionally turns up, in a primitive or ancient cult, a bit of uninhibited mythopoeia [or mythmaking] that makes him realize how completely all the higher religions have limited their apocalyptic visions to morally acceptable ones."

3.   G.S. Kirk, J.E. Raven, M. Schofield, *The Presocratic Philosophers*, 2nd edition (Cambridge, 1983), p. 190. The major Christian figure to emphasize this theme is the 15th-century German philosopher Nicholas of Cusa, for whom also "the coincidence of opposites" occurs in God.

4.   Rafael J. Gonzalez, quoted by Barbara G. Myerhoff, *Peyote Hunt: The Sacred Journey of the Huichol Indians* (Ithaca, N.Y., 1974), p. 247n. See her discussion of Huichol balance, 74f.

5.   Alan Watts' anthology *The Two Hands of God* collects and discusses a broad selection of "myths of polarity."

6.   William Butler Yeats, "Crazy Jane and the Bishop"; William Blake, *The Marriage of Heaven and Hell*"; *The Way of Life According to Lao Tzu*, translated by Witter Bynner (N.Y., 1944, 1962), p. 60; *The Song of God: Bhagavad Gita*, translated by Swami Prabhavananda and Christopher Isherwood (Mentor edition, N.Y., no date), p. 60.

7.   In the Chapter "A Christian Saint and a Pagan Hero."

8.   See "Sabbatianism and Mystical Heresy" in Gershom G. Scholem, *Major Trends in Jewish Mysticism* (Jerusalem, 1941; New York, 1946) and "Sabbatai Zevi" in *The Jewish Encyclopedia*.

9.   Mary Shelley, *Frankenstein; or, The Modern Prometheus* (New York, 1965), p. 50. In her preface, she justifies the book with a statement of mythic methodology: "however impossible as a physical fact, [it] affords a point of view to the imagination for the delineating of human passions more comprehensive and commanding than any which the ordinary relations of existing events can yield" (p. xiii). As Harold Bloom says in his "afterword" to this edition, the monster is a version of "the shadow or double of the self." He is a prime example of Jung's archetype of the Shadow, which I discuss briefly in Chapter 6.

10. Shelley, 125.
11. Shelley, 104.
12. Shelley, 126.

13. For an explanation of why this is so, see David Punter, *The Literature of Terror* (London and N.Y., 1980), pp. 121-128.

14. Popular imagination has, of course, transferred the doctor's name to his monster, sensing apparently that it is more important for a mythical being to have identity than it is for his maker. In this particular confusion, K.K. Ruthven has observed, "possibly we have a paradigm of the processes by which myths are made." *Myth* (London, 1976), p. 71.

Notes to Pages: 40- 46

15. Shelley, xii. At the end of an illuminating account of the work's conception. The phrase occurs in the author's conventionally modest-affectionate farewell to her book.

16. *Toward a Psychology of Being* (Princeton, 1962), p. 151. He also is that which he is afraid of being, as Dr. Frankenstein is his monster.

17. See Philip Wheelwright, *Metaphor and Reality,* pp. 134f.

18. "The Structure of the Psyche," in *The Structure and Dynamics of The Psyche,* translated by R.F.C. Hull (N.Y., 1960; Princeton, 1969), p. 154; also *Memories, Dreams, and Reflections* (London, 1961), p. 296. Cassirer quotes Herder for whom "the narrative of the creation is nothing other than the story of the birth of light. . . . This dawning is for mythical vision no mere process; it is a true and original creation. . . ." *Mythical Thought,* p. 97. Notice, in my last sentence, the linear assumption of the word "seemed," which "seems" to speak of an appearance that is not true.

19. *Language and Myth,* translated by Susanne K. Langer (N.Y. 1946; reprint 1953), p. 32.

20. In James Hillman's terms, "psychological faith, the faith arising from the psyche which shows as faith in the reality of the soul . . . begins in the *love of images,* and it flows mainly through the shapes of persons in reveries, fantasies, reflections, and imaginations." *Re-Visioning Psychology* (N.Y. 1975), p. 50. Hillman quotes Jung saying "Image *is* psyche," and adds: "The making of soulstuff calls for dreaming, fantasying, imagining. To live psychologically means to imagine things . . ."

21. This theme is developed from a somewhat different perspective by Kees Bolle, in *The Freedom of Man in Myth* (Nashville, Tenn., 1968).

22. Gerardo Reichel-Dolmatoff, *Amazonian Cosmos: The Sexual and Religious Symbolism of the Tukano Indians* (Chicago, 1971), p. 25.

23. Lévi-Strauss, p. 238f.

24. Richmond Y. Hathorn, *Tragedy, Myth and Mystery* (Bloomington, Ind., 1962), p. 25.

25. Gabriel Marcel, *Being and Having,* quoted by Hathorn, p. 16.

26. It may be argued that myth is strange only to us, not to the myth-makers. I have the impression, rather, that the sense of "strangeness" is itself more familiar to them than to us. "Strangeness," in this sense, is an effect of the nonlinear, part of the *making special* in ceremony or in the play of imagination. The most nonlinear culture must have its daily practical life in its very well-known surroundings. That what is familiar can be realized *also* as strange and extraordinary is one of the haunting qualities of myth. It is a realization, in fact, at the heart of the mysteries.

27. Martin Buber, *I and Thou,* R.G. Smith translation (N.Y , 1958), p. 4.

28. The same authority, at seven, reminds us that we should not discount in symbolism a certain arbitrary factor; this is an assertion of freedom engaging one's own participation: "I know why the American flag is red, white, and blue. Red is for devils, white is for angels, and blue is my favorite color."

29. Cassirer, *Mythical Thought,* p. 35.

30. This "ecological" aspect of mythical thought is developed further in Chapter 9, including a discussion of "participation."

31. Henri and Mrs. H.A. Frankfort, *Before Philosophy* (Harmondsworth, 1949), p. 14. "In the last analysis," writes Eliade, with similar intent, *"the World*

Notes to Pages: 46-51

reveals itself as language. It speaks to man through its structures and its rhythms." *Myth and Reality,* translated by W.R. Trask (N.Y. 1963; reprint 1968), p. 141, his italics. Eliade discusses the point further on p. 143. In *Primitive Man as Philosopher,* Paul Radin shows that such generalizations as the Frankfort quotation begins with are by no means valid for all tribal peoples. Yet they do describe the mythmaking temperament where and when it does appear.

32. Myerhoff, *Peyote Hunt.* Except for the third quotation, the speaker is a native religious leader, the *mara'akame* Ramón Medina Silva.

33. Myerhoff, p. 218. Carlos Castaneda demonstrates this theme very dramatically in his popular *Teachings of Don Juan* (Berkeley, 1968) and later books, which are still considerable feats of mythmaking, if as has been charged, they are not authentic anthropology.

34. Myerhoff, p. 217. *Híkuri* is the native name for peyote.

35. Cassirer discusses a conception of the "momentary or special god," drawn from H.K. Usener. Cassirer, *Mythical Thought,* pp. 169f. He discusses the point also in his earlier *Language and Myth,* translated by Susanne Langer (N.Y., 1946; reprint 1953), pp. 17f. "Whatever comes to us suddenly like a sending from heaven, whatever rejoices or grieves or oppresses us, seems to the religious consciousness like a divine being." This on p. 18.

36. Chapter 3, "Liminality and Communitas," in *The Ritual Process: Structure and Anti-Structure* (Chicago, 1969; Ithaca, N.Y., 1977). The term "liminal" derives from Arnold van Gennep's classic study *The Rites of Passage,* which has been translated by Monika B. Vizedom and Gabrielle L. Caffee (London and Chicago, 1960). See p. 11.

37. Turner, p. 137, quoting *Between Man and Man.*

CHAPTER 4: *The Qualitative World--Its Form*

1. *The Complete Grimm's Fairy Tales,* translated by Margaret Hunt and James Stern (N.Y., 1972), pp. 220f. There are some suggestive parallels and contrasts between this story and the birth of Attis, which I discussed in the second chapter. The Grimm brothers embellished their traditional material artistically and consciously, so it may not represent "folk material" as well as it generally has been believed to do. See John M. Ellis, *One Fairy Story Too Many: The Brothers Grimm and Their Tales* (Chicago, 1983). Nevertheless, their art is exquisitely sensitive to archetypal themes, forms, and implications.

2. *Grimm's,* p. 224.

3. Any detail, of course, that is not part of ordinary living.

4. For Jung, four denotes wholeness and stable organization, characteristic of the unified personality.

5. Albert B. Lord, *The Singer of Tales* (Cambridge, Mass., 1960; N.Y., 1965).

6. Copenhagen and Bloomington, Indiana, 1955-58, six volumes.

7. *Morphology of the Folktale* (Austin and London, 1968). Propp published his book in 1927, but it was not known in English until 1958, so its main influence is recent.

8. *Morphology of the Folktale,* Appendix I.

9. Chapter VI.

Notes to Pages: 51-68

10. My analysis of mythic reality follows Cassirer, in *Mythical Thought*, but very loosely.
11. *Mythical Thought*, p. 83.
12. *The Anatomy of Criticism*, p. 159. A good brief summary of Frye's account of the mythic picture can be found in Hazard Adams, *The Contexts of Poetry* (N.Y., 1963), which draws also on Cassirer and on Freud's analysis of dreams.
13. Frye, p. 158.
14. *The Hero with a Thousand Faces* (N.Y., 1949). Campbell is describing in myth the pattern that van Gennep had demonstrated in ritual. See Chapter 3, note 36.
15. See Victor and Edith Turner, *Image and Pilgrimage in Christian Culture* (N.Y., 1978) and Barbara Myerhoff's *Peyote Hunt*. The pilgrimage, unlike the hero's journey, is undertaken in a group. As the Turners emphasize, its function is to develop what they call the state of *communitas*. See above, at the end of Chapter 3.
16. *The Sacred and the Profane*, translated by W.R. Trask (N.Y., 1959), p. 20. Cassirer used the same terms earlier.
17. Neihardt, p. 36. I spoke of Black Elk in Chapter 1.
18. Neihardt, p. 24.
19. Eliade, p. 42, a section heading.
20. Eliade, p. 24. He regards this "example of crypto-religious behavior" a "sort of degradation and desacralization of religious values and forms of behavior"--a strangely prejudiced point of view, I think.
21. This theme is developed further in Chapter 10.
22. Jung, "The Phenomenology of the Spirit in Fairy Tales," *Spirit and Nature*, Vol. I, reprinted in *Psyche and Symbol*, edited by Violet S. de Laszlo (N.Y., 1958), p. 79.
23. Flach, quoted in Sartre, *The Psychology of Imagination* (London, 1972), p. 113.
24. Sartre, p. 115.
25. Above, in Chapter 2.
26. Jaynes, p. 60.
27. We can see the mythic hero as an extension of the "analog I" serving us all together. The image of oneself in a dream may be a clearer variation.
28. *Symbols of Transformation*, p. 155.
29. See the use of "redundant" in my quotation from the Frankforts, p. 56.

Notes 30-48 are on page 260.

CHAPTER 5: The Qualitative World--Its Operation

1. Frazer makes a well-known distinction between two kinds of "sympathetic magic": Homoeopathic Magic, based on the Law of Similarity, "that *like produces like*, effect resembling cause"; and Contagious Magic, based on the Law of Contact or Contagion, "that *things which have once been in contact continue ever afterwards to act on each other*." Sir James George Frazer, *The New Golden Bough*, edited by Theodore H. Gaster (Garden City, N.Y., 1961), p. 5.

Notes to Pages: 68-79

2. For Marcel, see Chapter 3 above.
3. *Essay on Man*, p. 92.
4. The reasons why characters say they do things often seem quite independent of their actions. Propp, p. 76.
5. In Susan Feldmann, editor, *African Myths and Tales* (N.Y., 1963), pp. 42f., reprinted from Paul Radin and J. Sweeney, *African Folktales and Sculpture*. My discussion of creation myths, in Chapter 7 below, develops further the point I am making here.
6. Emphasizing a logical function, Lévi-Strauss speaks of primitive thought operating through "explanatory cells." *Myth and Meaning* (London, 1978), p. 39.
7. Propp suggests limits and the range of possibilities, pp. 112f.
8. For the purposes of myth, the distinction between seduction and rape may be an academic--that is, a linear--one.
9. For an interesting parallel in scientific thinking, see Douglas R. Hofstadter on "retroactive causality," in *The Mind's I* (N.Y., 1981), "composed and arranged" by himself and Daniel C. Dennett, p. 197.
10. The Brome play, in a 15th-century manuscript. A.C. Cawley, ed., *Everyman and Medieval Miracle Plays* (N.Y., 1959), p. 54.
11. Conversely, "deceitful proposals [by the villain] are always accepted and fulfilled." Propp, p. 30.
12. *The Infernal Machine* is Jean Cocteau's play about Oedipus. The phrase refers to "fate."
13. *The Myth of Sisyphus and Other Essays*, translated by Justin O'Brien (N.Y., 1955), pp. 88f.
14. *The Mahabharata*, Vol. 1, translated by J.A.B. van Buitenen (Chicago and London, 1973), p. 357.
15. *The Mahabharata*, Vol. 1, p. 369.
16. Just as oral poets, "the singers of tales," developed their epics with the help of standardized verbal formulas. See Albert Lord, *The Singer of Tales*.
17. According to the Oxford English Dictionary at least. If this derivation is correct, and the words "mind" and "man" are cognate, I would suggest "mental" in the sense of "conscious" rather than "rational": *we being aware of ourselves*, the sense in which "mind" and "man" (=human) may be the same.
18. See R. D. Laing, "Phantasy and Experience," in *Self and Others* (London, 1961).
19. Northrop Frye has an important paragraph on this topic, showing the correspondence, in romance literature, of identity, integrity, and absolute existence. *The Secular Scripture: A Study of the Structure of Romance* (Cambridge, Mass., and London, 1976), p. 54.
20. *The Interpretation of Dreams*, p. 322.
21. *Symbols of Transformation*, p. 328.
22. *Symbols of Transformation*, p. 390.
23. *Anatomy of Criticism*, p. 136.
24. *Mythical Thought*, p. 51.
25. *Symbols of Transformation*, p. 255.

Notes to Pages: 80-86

26. The divergent symbolism of negative and positive motherhood is analyzed in great detail by the Jungian Erich Neumann in *The Great Mother* (N.Y., 1955).

27. *The Metamorphoses*, translated by Horace Gregory (N.Y., 1958), p. 97.

28. See the end of Chapter One above.

29. Radin, *Primitive Man as Philosopher*, p. 250.

30. Paul Radin, *The Trickster: A Study in American Indian Mythology*, with commentaries by Karl Kerenyi and C.G. Jung (N.Y., 1972), p. xxiii. The rest of the paragraph is also worth observing: "But not only he, so our myth tells us, possesses these traits. So, likewise, do the other figures of the plot connected with him: the animals, the various supernatural being and monsters, and man." The name of the Huichol Indians' trickster and cultural hero, Kauyumari, means something like "one who does not know himself" or "one who makes others crazy." Myerhoff, p. 85, suggests that the name may recall an actual shaman, but it is an extremely apt depiction of the Trickster archetype. Compare the account of Dionysos in Chapter 9 below.

31. *Trickster*, p. 163.

32. See Marija Gimbutas, *The Goddesses and Gods of Old Europe* (Berkeley, 1982).

33. Levko Chikalenko, quoted by Gimbutas, p. 135, who herself sees in this style a religious expression of divine qualities *in* nature. The motivation must be both ritualistic and esthetic; or, rather, it illustrates the esthetic dimension *of* ritual.

34. Gimbutas, p. 95.

35. *Primitive Man as Philosopher*, pp. 329-334.

36. *Primitive Man*, p. 335.

37. Robin Horton, "African Thought and Western Science," in *Rationality*, edited by Bryan R. Wilson (Oxford, 1970), p. 143.

38. Horton quotes E.E. Evans-Pritchard (1956) saying: "A theistic religion need be neither monotheistic nor polytheistic. It may be both. It is a question of the level, or situation, of thought, rather than of exclusive types of thought."

39. Gershom Scholem, *On the Kabbalah* p. 88. "To preserve the purity of the concept of God without the loss of His living reality--," Scholem goes on to say, "that is the never-ending task of theology."

40. R. H. Codrington, the first Western authority on the subject, in *The Melanesians*, quoted by Jung, "On Psychic Energy," *The Structure and Dynamics of the Psyche*, translated by R.F.C. Hull (N.Y. 1960, Princeton 1969), pp. 63f.

41. Jung, "On Psychic Energy," p. 65. Cassirer refers to an article by Robert R. Marett with the telling title "The Taboo-mana Formula as a Minimum Definition of Religion," *Mythical Thought*, p. 76n.

42. *Mythical Thought*, p. 78.

43. *Mythical Thought*, p. 76.

44. *Mythical Thought*, p. 78. Cassirer's footnote is worth repeating in part: Thus it is reported, particularly of the Algonquin manitou, that the term is used wherever the imagination is aroused by something new and unusual. If, e.g., a fisherman catches a new variety of fish, the term "manitou" is immediately applied to it.

45. *Totemism* (London, 1964), p. 102.

Notes to Pages: 86-103

46. Conversely, the organization of traditional societies is itself a symbolic reflection of such psychological tendencies on a political level.
47. See the third example under "Primitive Thought" in Chapter 2.
48. The name of the motif is drawn from the medieval Holy Grail myth. The theme is explored in Jessie Weston's controversial book *From Ritual to Romance* (reprint: Garden City, N.Y., 1957), made famous by T.S. Eliot's poem *The Waste Land*.
49. W.B. Yeats, "The Celtic Element in Literature," *Essays and Introductions* (London, 1961), p.178
50. Karl Kerenyi, in Radin, *The Trickster*, p. 185.
51. *The Trickster*, p. 162.
52. Boas, p. 245.
53. *The Pickwick Papers*, Chapter XXXVI.
54. *The Trickster*, p. 18. The African tale of God's withdrawal, quoted earlier in this chapter, is another good example of etiological whimsy.
55. Stith Thompson, *Tales of the North American Indians* (1929; Bloomington, and London, 1966), pp. 51f.
56. Susanne Langer's terms, explained in the second part of Chapter 2 above.
57. *Myth and Meaning*, p. 38.

CHAPTER 6: *The View from the Psyche*

1. Discussed in Chapter 5 as "The Self Dispersed."
2. Burke discusses eight in *Language as Symbolic Action*, pp. 63ff.
3. Zimmer provides a delightful discussion of this theme in his opening chapter, on the Arabian tale of "Abu Kasem's Slippers."
4. "The Transcendent Function," in *The Structure and Dynamics of the Psyche*, pp. 79f. "Since the psyche is a self-regulating system, just as the body is, the regulating counteraction will always develop in the unconscious." P. 79.
5. I insert instinct into a linear unconscious as a mere suggestion (although to do so may contradict my assumption that the unconscious is strictly nonlinear), because it is practical and goal-directed, but I do not know much about the subject. The place of myth on the chart should become clearer in the later sections of this chapter.
6. *The First Book of Urizen*, in *Blake: Complete Writings*, edited by Geoffrey Keynes (London, 1957), p. 222. Blake never wrote beyond the first book of this particular work, but developed the theme and symbolism much more elaborately and extensively in *Vala* (or *The Four Zoas*) and *Jerusalem*. A good guide to these difficult "prophetic books" is Harold Bloom, *Blake's Apocalypse* (Garden City, 1963).
7. Blake, p. 223.
8. Blake, p. 224.
9. Blake, pp. 224f.
10. Blake, p. 228.
11. Blake, pp. 233f.
12. Blake, p. 234.

Notes to Pages: 104-106

13. *Symbols of Transformation*, p. 102. A very accessible introduction to Jung's "analytical psychology," including its treatment of myth, is the profusely illustrated *Man and his Symbols* (London and Garden City, 1964), written by Jung together with several of his colleagues.

14. It seems to me that the anima might well belong to women also, projected in relation to their ego, which is experienced as masculine, just as the male hero expresses the discontented, assertive, seeking aspect of the personality for women as well as men.

15. Adapted, and greatly simplified, from material in Neumann, *The Great Mother*. For a brief discussion by Jung see "The Syzygy: Anima and Animus," from *Aion: Contributions to the Symbolism of the Self*, translated by R.F.C. Hull (N.Y. 1959; Princeton, 1979); essay reprinted in *Psyche and Symbol*.

16. Symbols of integration often look, to the linear eye, like evidence of unconsciousness. The hero kills the monster not to repress its monstrosity, as one might think, but to take its power upon himself. The principle being: what you can match in its own terms, you are. Magic and the psychology of warfare often follow this principle.

17. The doubling of roles is not linear incest but a full identification with masculine and feminine roles, integrating different forms of relationship and intensifying the bond.

18. "The Shadow," from *Aion*, is also reprinted in *Psyche and Symbol*. A diabolic male may also be, to a heroine, a negative animus, especially if he is the seducer or evil wizard who would keep her from the positive animus of her "Prince Charming." The shadow is of the hero's, or self's, own sex.

19. "The Phenomenology of the Spirit in Fairy Tales," in *Psyche and Symbol*.

20. "The Psychology of the Child Archetype" and "The Special Phenomology of the Child Archetype," both in *Psyche and Symbol*.

21. A notable essay on the universal conditions behind myth is Joseph Campbell's "Bios and Mythos," in *The Flight of the Wild Gander: Explorations in the Mythological Dimension* (South Bend, Indiana, 1951).

22. Also, Jungians sometimes adopt a clinical view of myths which seems to me at variance with Jung's emphasis on the universal pattern of myth and its endopsychic form. They see myths expressing specific stages in personal development or particular kinds of personal problem. See, for examples, Erich Neumann, *Origins and History of Consciousness*, and Edward Edinger, *Ego and Archetype* (N.Y., 1972; Baltimore, 1973)--both books that are nevertheless very rich in Jungian insight. Edinger speaks of a "Phaethon complex," in which a young man remains immaturely over-confident because of an indulgent father. He does have the flexibility, however, to assert that "all mythical images are ambiguous. We can never be certain in advance whether to interpret them positively or negatively." (P. 29.) I will argue (in Chapter 7) that such a myth is neither positive nor negative but *tragic*. Neumann has written a rewarding essay on the psychological development of women as a commentary on Apuleius' "Cupid and Psyche" tale, portraying Psyche as a typical girl growing into feminine individuation. (*Amor and Psyche: The Psychological Development of the Feminine*.) But Apuleius makes the archetypal symbolism transparent. His heroine is *psyche*, and he includes the myth in a sequence of tales that trace *a man's* spiritual regeneration. Endopsychically, "she" is part of every man as well as

Notes to Pages: 106-112

every woman. Another prominent Jungian, Marie-Louise von Franz, interprets the story in this manner in *A Psychological Interpretation of The Golden Ass of Apuleius* (Zurich, 1970), indicating that Jung approved of both views. . . . I can see no reason myself how the collective process of mythmaking could produce material referring only to individuals or even types of individual. Here the method appropriate to dreams does not fit myths. The application of mythic images to situations in life can be legitimate, dramatic, and enlightening, to be sure, but it is not the same as the interpretation of myth. Not being professional psychologists, Zimmer and Campbell avoid this problem, tacitly adopting the broader view.

23. "Special Phenomenology," *Psyche and Symbol*, p. 145.
24. *Symbols*, p. 368. An especially fine example of what I am stressing, too long to quote here, is a passage on pp. 356f.
25. *Symbols*, p. 62.
26. *Symbols*, p. 56.
27. *Symbols*, p. 430. Jung is criticizing the Freudian usage "subconscious."
28. *Symbols*, p. 112.
29. Jung, "On the Psychology of the Trickster Figure," in Radin, *The Trickster*, p. 209.
30. *Symbols*, p. 303.
31. Lévi-Strauss, "The Structural Study of Myth," *Structural Anthropology* (London, 1968), p. 224. Lévi-Strauss also emphasizes the *relation between* elements as the key to a myth's meaning and warns against studying individual symbols. Jung's archetypes are, in fact, principles of relationship in the psyche-- most obviously the anima, animus, and shadow, which have meaning only in terms of the ego. Turner's "structure and anti-structure" is another principle of integrating opposites, parallel to culture and nature. See above, the end of Chapter 3.
32. Cassirer, *An Essay on Man*, p. 43.
33. On the deaf, see Hans G. Furth, *Thinking Without Language* (N.Y. and London, 1966). For a good review of recent studies among the primates, leading to a helpful discussion of the dependence of human nature on animal nature, see Mary Midgely, *Beast and Man* (Brighton, 1979; Cambridge, 1980).
34. *The Immense Journey* (N.Y., 1946), p. 120.
35. Cassirer, *An Essay on Man*, p. 43.
36. *Symbols of Transformation*, p. 434.
37. Julius Heuscher, *A Psychiatric Study of Myths and Fairy Tales: Their Origin, Meaning, and Usefulness* (Springfield, Ill., 1974), p. 9n.
38. Louis S.B. Leakey and Robert Ardrey, "Man, the Killer," *Psychology Today* (September, 1972, pp. 73-85), p. 75. Language, Leakey conjectures, was the major by-product of fire, for at night early men were able to discuss the prolonged day's experience and plan for the next--speech being too disruptive during the hunt itself.
39. Eiseley, p. 125.

CHAPTER 7: The Definition of Mortality

1. Compare Bateson's description of art as "a message about the interface between conscious and unconscious." "Style, Grace, and Information in Primitive Art," p. 138.
2. For Jung, the "self" is the sense of "the total personality." It is largely unconscious and ranks as an archetype. I have been using the word more loosely, referring usually to the state of subjectivity. I am reflecting our ordinary assumption that this state is conscious. My self is what I am aware of when I am aware of being aware. The self is that which confronts the world.
3. In *The Hero with a Thousand Faces*.
4. Emerson explored this theme rhapsodically in his essay entitled "Circles."
5. See how "confrontation" figures naturally into the Frankforts' account of mythic experience, towards the end of Chapter 3 above.
6. In "The Meaning of Psychology for Modern Man," quoted by Campbell in *The Mythic Image* (Princeton, 1974), p. 7.
7. The important theme of a split between culture and nature, which Lévi-Strauss makes central to his interpretations, reduces to this confrontation, for myth always sees nature, naturally, from the perspective of culture. The mythmaking mind is an aspect of culture, the aspect that needs to seek out its relation to nature, to touch the source and realign itself with its origins.
8. The terms are not equivalent, of course, across the line.
9. See the end of "Qualitative Form in Myth," in Chapter 2.
10. The same formulation appears in John S. Dunne, *Time and Myth* (Notre Dame, 1975), p. 88.
11. Peter Koestenbaum, *The Vitality of Death: Essays in Existential Philosophy and Psychology* (Westport, Conn., 1971), pp. 97f.
12. Susan Feldmann, editor *African Myths and Tales*, pp. 114f., reprinted from H. Abrahamsson, *The Origin of Death*. There is an interesting contrast between this tale and a Tsimshian Indian myth that Radin reports in *The Trickster*, p. 159. Raven tries to make humans out of both a rock and a leaf. The rock method is too slow, so we rot like the leaf. Here the unconscious Trickster factor is responsible for our mortality, not conscious choice. Compare the less conscious African tale in my section "The Foregone Conclusion," Chapter 5. A Biblical parallel comes to mind in this passage from a Danish scholar, Benedikt Otzen: "According to the primitive cast of thought, the tribal ancestor lives on through his descendants; thus in Genesis Adam and Eve are seen as achieving yet another form of immortality, namely so to speak a collective immortality. In so doing, they have made themselves equal to god." In Otzen, Hans Gottlieb, and Knud Jeppesen, *Myths in the Old Testament*, translated by Frederick Cryer (London, 1980).
13. *The Outline of Mythology* (1944; N.Y., 1961), p. 52.
14. David Ward, "Stepping out of Line," *The Guardian* (London and Manchester, Dec. 22, 1978), p. 9.
15. "John Barleycorn: A Ballad," *The Poems and Songs of Robert Burns*, edited by James Kingsley (Oxford, 1968).

Notes to Pages: 122-134

16. On interpreting Demeter and Persephone, see Helen M. Luke, "Mother and Daughter Mysteries," *Woman: Earth and Spirit--The Feminine in Symbol and Myth* (N.Y., 1986).

17. From *Ko-ji-ki*, "Records of Ancient Matters," recounted by Campbell from an intermediary source, *The Hero with a Thousand Faces*, p. 206.

18. "The Epic of Gilgamesh," translated by E.A. Speiser, in *Ancient Near Eastern Texts Relating to the Old Testament* (Princeton, 1950), edited by James B. Pritchard, p. 84. Gilgamesh has also alienated himself from nature by fighting Humbaba (or Huwawa), demonic lord of the Cedar Forest.

19. A contrary pattern appears in the Cupid and Psyche tale--which may have been consciously crafted by the Roman-colonial Apuleius (an adherent of the Egyptian Mother Goddess Isis) in the 2nd century A.D., or it may have evolved as a deliberate teaching story within the spiritual tradition of the "mysteries" that he adopted--but in either case it clearly belongs to the same genre as the European "fairy tale" of later times. In this story, the male deity, who is Love himself, takes the virgin princess lovingly as she prepares to encounter a violent death, but then, after her taboo-breaking shatters their unstable paradise, she actively wins him back. The Mother Goddess, Cupid's mother Venus, is again hostile and vengeful but she also is finally won over. It is significant that she is converted by a younger *female* representation motivated by self-abandonment rather than self-perpetuation, by vulnerability, responsibility, and love.

20. See E.R. Dodds, *The Greeks and the Irrational* (Berkeley, 1951).

21. The epigraph to *The Caprichos*, noted by Neumann, p. 162.

22. *In Praise of Krishna: Songs from the Bengali*, translated by Edward C. Dimock, Jr., and Denise Levertov (Garden City, N.Y., 1967), p. 41.

23. *Beowulf: A New Prose Translation* by E. Talbot Donaldson (N.Y., 1966), p. 3. The *scop*, or "shaper," is the bard.

24. *Beowulf*, pp. 9f.

25. See Neumann, "The Negative Elementary Character," *The Great Mother*. The poet Robert Bly includes a lively brief analysis of the Mother archetype, summarizing her various permutations, in his book *Sleepers Joining Hands* (N.Y., 1973).

26. The story of Gilgamesh, which we looked at in the previous section, projects a negative image of the Mother Goddess in order to express the hero's instability, his resistance to mortality. Ishtar appears to him ironically as a seductress whom he scorns. The Beowulf story makes a more serious defense of its culture, yet we can correlate the subservience of women in the Germanic warrior-society and the tragic tone of the poem with the grotesque portrayal of the Mother. Tragedy ordinarily involves a suppression of the feminine principle, the anima. We see the same phenomenon in Shakespeare, where Othello kills Desdemona in the spirit of a sacrificial murder, Lear renounces Cordelia (which puts him at the mercy of the negative anima in her sisters), and Hamlet abandons Ophelia when he denounces the mother who has come to repel him--the treatment of Cordelia and Ophelia being essentially murder. In a significant gesture, Brutus rebuffs Portia. Lady Macbeth suppresses her own maternal femininity; the witches parody the Mother Goddess as the Fates. In other words, tragedy is about the pain and the violence of consciousness as it emerges out of the unconscious field of life, the civilized self as it experiences itself *vis-à-vis* nature--

Notes to Pages: 134-141

vulnerable, incomplete, yet isolated in its own kind of reality, caught in the combination of power and sorrow with which it finds itself momentarily present amidst eternal darkness. For more on tragedy in this vein, see my *Tragedy and Innocence* and essays on Shakespeare. For a specifically Jungian reading of Shakespeare's plays, see Alex Aronson, *Psyche and Symbol in Shakespeare* (Bloomington, Ind., 1973).

27. In contrast, Hrothgar, whom Beowulf serves, is essentially like the father in such fairy tales as "Hansel and Gretel" or "The Juniper Tree": the well meaning but helpless aspect of self living in society's manner with as much vision as one can expect from an ordinary person but needing redemption from a more inspired source.

28. See notes 22 in Chapter Six and 19 in the present chapter.

29. Lucius Apuleius, *The Golden Ass*, translated by Jack Lindsay (Bloomington & London, 1962). p. 135.

30. For what may be a more complete version of the test-sequence motif, see the Grimms' "White Snake," where the hero first endears himself by acts of kindness (sacrificial gestures) to the creatures who show up one by one to save him in his need. Their rescue of him is, therefore, an expression of his own *caritas*.

31. These were discussed in Chapter 5.

32. Ovid, p. 59.

33. Reprinted in Dell Hymes, "Folklore's Nature and the Sun's Myth," *Journal of American Folklore*, Vol. 88 (1975), pp. 345-369. The myth was recorded by Franz Boas as it was told to him by Charles Cultee, a Chinook Indian.

34. See Northrop Frye's account of Actaeon, "the victim of his own pursuit," *The Secular Scripture*, p. 105.

35. In literature, this is the difference between tragedy and comedy. See Northrop Frye, "The Argument of Comedy," *English Institute Essays, 1948* (N.Y., 1949), pp. 58-73, and Joseph Campbell, "Tragedy and Comedy," in *The Hero with a Thousand Faces*, pp. 25-30.

36. The same *literary* qualities appear in tragic myths also, of course, when they are developed as drama and epic.

37. Trickster stories are close to this pattern but more ambiguous. Both lie behind the tradition of picaresque fiction.

38. "The wisest thing--so the fairy tale taught mankind in olden times, and teaches children to this day--is to meet the forces of the mythical world with cunning and with high spirits." Walter Benjamin, "The Storyteller," *Illuminations*, translated by Harry Zohn (New York and London, 1968), p. 102.

39. For the type of tale in which the hero is cunning, it would be more accurate to speak about delight rather than wonder, although it is an extraordinary delight, touched with the marvelous.

40. Thus Eliade speaks of a "rank-loss of the sacred" in fairy tales, as opposed to a full "desacralization." *Myth and Reality*, p. 200.

41. See the Introduction and first chapter in Bruno Bettleheim's Freudian commentary on Grimm, *The Uses of Enchantment* (N.Y., 1975). For a Jungian view, see Marie-Louise von Franz, *An Introduction to the Psychology of Fairy Tales* (Zurich, 1970). Heuscher's psychiatric interpretation combines Freudian, Jungian, and also phenomenological approaches. A useful treatment of the nar-

Notes to Pages: 146-153

rative surface of the tales is Max Lüthi's *Once Upon a Time: On the Nature of Fairy Tales*, translated by Lee Chadeayne and Paul Gottwald (1970; Bloomington and London, 1976.)

CHAPTER 8: The Mythic Truth

1. *The Burning Fountain*, p. 94.
2. Susanne Langer speaks at length of the "virtual" reality of art, with its setting in virtual time and virtual space. See *Problems of Art* (New York, 1957), pp. 5f, and *Feeling and Form* (New York, 1953), chapters "Semblance" and "Virtual Space."
3. *Reader's Companion to World Literature*, edited by Calvin Brown (N.Y., 1956), p. 309.
4. John Barth, *Chimera* (N.Y., 1972), pp. 79f.
5. Barth, p. 270.
6. Robert Graves, *The Greek Myths*, Vol. II, p. 14.
7. Hans-Georg Gadamer has written of "festival" (in order to clarify, through a parallel, the being of a work of art): "it is its own original essence always to be something different." *Truth and Method* (London, 1975), p. 110. It is in this context that Saussure's linguistic distinction between *langue* and *parole*, which the structuralists often cite, may be useful (for example, Roland Barthes, *Elements of Semiology*, pp. 13ff.). *Language* is available to us and we can "know" it (as we can know French or German), but it comes into existence and can be observed only through individual acts of *speech*. Archetype is the language which is "spoken" in image. Also, the floating myths-in-themselves constitute a language which is spoken in ritual performances or in the poets' texts. We can know the theme only through the variations played upon it.
8. Immanuel Kant introduced the idea, continued by the German Idealist philosophers and picked up by the Romantic poets, that the work of art reflects in its nature the constitution of reality. Thus F.W.J. von Schelling, who was also an important early theoretician of myth, wrote that "the real world proceeds wholly from the same original opposition as that from which the world of art must proceed," which he described as an opposition between the subjective, conscious activity that the artist contributes and the objective, unconscious element which enters into the creative act. *German Aesthetic and Literary Criticism*, edited by David Simpson (Cambridge, 1984), p. 128. . . . Philip Wheelwright ends his book *Metaphor and Reality* with a chapter called "The Sense of Reality," which is parallel to my discussion in this section and can be read profitably to supplement it. He summarizes his analysis in these words, introducing terms that he then proceeds to analyze: "The principal characteristics of living reality appear to be three: it is presential and tensive; it is coalescent and interpenetrative; and it is perspectival and hence latent, revealing itself only partially, ambiguously, and through symbolic indirections." p. 154.
9. *Magic, Science, and Religion and other Essays* (Garden City, N.Y., 1954), p. 101. To avoid confusion, I have omitted the statement that myth "is not symbolic." Malinowski seems to assume a linear meaning of "symbol."
10. T.G.H. Strehlow, *Aranda Traditions* (Melbourne, 1947), quoted by Lévi-Strauss in *The Savage Mind*, p. 235. Cuts within the quotation are by

Lévi-Strauss, but I have omitted a negative conclusion to the passage, which Lévi-Strauss discusses.

11. Radin, *Primitive Man as Philosopher*, p. 277, quoting the passage from James Walker. Radin includes this material in a chapter on "Speculation for its own Sake" as evidence of independent intellectual activity among so-called primitives. It seems to me that these thinkers, like most of our own, are working out implications inherent in the culture's motifs rather than developing new ideas. Most "thinking" in any culture, I imagine, consists of going over familiar territory, working out for oneself the thoughts that others have worked out before. Thus another Oglala says similarly, ". . . we know that all things which are round are related to each other," p. 286. Although his presentation of "primitive" thought is very valuable and duly appreciative, Radin does not include a conception of such *traditional thinking*. He does not distinguish speculation proper from what we may call *reflective projection* or from encounter with the numinous. For an example of what I mean, see his pp. 362f.

12. Cited in "The Experience of Infinity," Chapter 4, above.
13. Mann, "Freud and the Future," p. 373.
14. Jung, *Symbols of Transformation*, p. 170.
15. Jung, "The Psychology of the Child Archetype," *Psyche and Symbol*, p. 117.
16. Campbell, *The Flight of the Wild Gander*, p. 6.
17. The other side of the picture would require a complex discussion: myth's role in fostering violent distortions of life's energy, particlarly in warfare and human sacrifice but also just in the neurotic anxiety that characterizes some aspects of life in a myth-bound culture. Dislocated mythic images have often supported political oppression. It is not myth itself, however, that causes atrocities but a literal interpretation of them in theology (including political theology) and a literal enactment of them in ritual. Also, economic pressures can keep the archetypal form from developing fully or coherently or receptively.
18. See above, pp. 47f.
19. Whorf, "Habitual Thought," p. 149. Whorf has been showing how basic the orientation of preparation is in Hopi language, where it takes the place of our future tense.
20. I.C. Jarvie, "Explaining Cargo Cults," in Wilson.
21. Jung, "On Psychic Energy," p. 45.
22. Hathorn, p. 84. Hathorn argues, beautifully I think, that myth and ritual are ways of overcoming the separation from nature that the conscious mind effects. ". . . the savage's ceremony originates in an awareness that a man both is and is not akin to a leopard. The savage realizes that there is a breach of alienation between himself and the universe, but that this breach can be intermittently closed--not closed in actuality, but mimetically." P. 23. As we return toward the unconscious, we return toward nature, and the inevitable way back is the logic of nonlinear form.
23. A point emphasized by G.S. Kirk, *The Nature of Greek Myths* (Harmondsworth and Baltimore, 1974).
24. An equivocal exception is the use of myth as a teaching device, to convey a higher (more receptive) consciousness.
25. Lévi-Strauss puts what I think is the same point in broader terms: "it is only under conditions of under-communication that culture can produce."

Myth and Meaning, p. 20. This assumes our norm, however, of what communication should be.

26. *Homo Ludens: A Study of the Play Element in Culture* (1950; Boston, 1955), p. 143.

27. Ernst Topitsch, "World Interpretation and Self-Interpretation: Some Basic Patterns," in Murray's *Myth and Mythmaking*, p. 169. At the end, Topitsch indicates that his purpose is "to analyze the metaphysics of the cosmos and the soul in a scientific and truly objective manner."

28. Lucien Lévy-Bruhl makes a stronger statement: "the myth is a revelation (and a contact) like the dream: a revelation expected, foreseen, known in advance, but nevertheless a revelation. Here, neither 'belief' nor 'experience' are adequate expressions: revelation and contact are better." *The Notebooks*, p. 153. Lévy-Bruhl's extended discussion of reality, belief, and experience (147-161) is based on the realization that "there is a certain emotional tonality peculiar to . . . the representation of the myth, that constitutes . . . the content of that myth." P. 149.

29. Borrowing an example from Martin Hollis's discussion of the present problem, "Reason and Ritual," in Wilson's *Rationality*. They do not *always* have this kind of experience, I presume, but resort to it for significance.

30. Examples to which I referred in "Mythic Thought," Chapter 2, and "The Realization of Wonder," Chapter 3.

31. Quoted in Huizinga. p. 15.

32. Huizinga, p. 5.

33. Burke, *Language as Symbolic Action*, p. 20. Burke relates his point to Buber. He is not saying that language provides the only reason for such beliefs.

34. *Metaphor and Reality*, p. 150.

35. Graves, Vol. I, p. 10. The theory is associated with the "Cambridge School." See the quotation from Jane Harrison in the next paragraph.

36. See the third example in "Mythic Thought," Chapter 2..

37. Cassirer, "Mythical Thought," p. 39 or 40. Martin Heidegger writes in a similar vein that the sculpture of a god "is not a portrait whose purpose is to make it easier to realize how the god looks; rather it is a work that lets the god himself be present and thus *is* the god himself." And "it is in the dignity, in the splendor that the god is present." *Poetry, Language, Thought*, translated by Albert Hofstadter (New York, 1971), pp. 43f.

38. Jane Harrison, "Epilegomena to the Study of Greek Religion" (1921), in *Epilegomena . . . and Themis* (New Hyde Park, N.Y., 1962), p. xxxiv.

39. Harrison, p. xxxi.

40. Sigmund Freud, *Totem and Taboo*, translated by James Strachey (N.Y., 1950), p. 91.

41. *Totem and Taboo*, p. 89.

42. *Symbols of Transformation*, p. 260.

43. Jung, "The Shadow," *Aion*, p. 9.

44. Jung, "Christ, a Symbol of the Self," *Aion*, p. 71.

45. See Raglan, "Myth and the Historic Hero," in *The Hero*.

46. Peter Farb, *Man's Rise to Civilization*, p. 100. Hiawatha's name alone was adopted by the poet Longfellow.

Notes to Pages: 162-168

47. This simple argument remains the best response to diffusionists, who meticulously trace recurrent motifs back to original source myths that must have spread their influence, historically, over the world.

48. From Pliny Earle Goddard, ed., *Kato Texts* (Berkeley, 1909), as condensed and reprinted in *Technicians of the Sacred*, edited by Jerome Rothenberg (Garden City, N.Y., 1968). The original text runs on to 44 lines, listing many more animals, before proceeding to the arrival of the horned earth, who walks down through the waters from the North. In the original, "It was very dark" is also followed by "they say." Goddard's native authority, Bill Ray, tells all of his stories, including a number of animal trickster tales, with this "quotative" formula--except for one about his own supernatural experience. Quoting a similar Hawaiian text, which repeats the formula "It is said that . . .," Kees Bolle makes a point that seems to be opposite to mine, about what he calls "subjective reservedness." The expression, he argues, makes the speaker present in the narrative process. He puts himself in the process of telling the story, however, by distancing himself from the process of its taking place, keeping it out *there* in its own proper realm. Bolle, pp. 60f.

49. From Hymn 10, translated by Ralph T.H. Griffith, reprinted in *The Portable World Bible*, edited by Robert O. Ballou (N.Y., 1944), p. 32.

50. The nature of oral transmission and its effect upon mythic form is the subject of folklore study. For a concise statement of its scope, see Dell Hymes, "Folklore's Nature and Sun's Myth."

51. Rudolf Otto, p. 61, speaking, however, about the transmission of religious experience. Otto is best known for his concept of "the numinous," the sense of "holiness" in the world, which he writes, is "induced, incited, and aroused" by the symbols of religion (p. 60).

52. Joseph Campbell, *The Masks of God*, Vol. IV, *Creative Mythology* (N.Y. & London, 1968), p. 93.

CHAPTER 9: *Myth in Nature*

1. See Owen Barfield, "Language, Evolution of Consciousness, and the Recovery of Human Meaning," in the Columbia University *Teachers College Record* (Spring 1981). Barfield cites an observation by Logan Pearsall Smith of the appearance in the 18th Century of "a curious class of verbs and adjectives which describe not so much the objective qualities and activities of things, as the effects they produce on us, on our own feelings and sensations (p. 428)." The following essay, by Huston Smith, deals in part with the same theme. Both are drawn, as the entire issue is, from the 1980 Woodstock (Vermont) Symposium "Knowledge, Education, and Human Values: Toward the Recovery of Wholeness."

2. *The Notebooks on Primitive Mentality*, translated by Peter Rivière (Oxford and New York, 1975), p. 31. In these notebooks, compiled in 1938 and early 1939, Lévy-Bruhl reevaluated and reinterpreted his controversial views, which first appeared in 1910. "Accident" has here the philosophical meaning: an inessential attribute.

3. Lévy-Bruhl, pp. 69ff.
4. Lévy-Bruhl, pp. 75ff.
5. Lévy-Bruhl, p. 96.

Notes to Pages: 168-172

6. Lévy-Bruhl's examples of litigation in colonial courts (pp. 40f.) are particularly interesting in this respect.

7. See Owen Barfield's subtle analysis of participation (which I have here altered) and his provocative historical view of its place in Western culture, *Saving the Appearances: A Study in Idolatry* (New York and London, 1957).

8. For opposition to Lévy-Bruhl, see Radin's *Primitive Man as Philosopher* and Lévi-Strauss's *Savage Mind*, p. 268, both of which argue for the rationality of "primitive" man. Lévi-Strauss is himself close to Lévy-Bruhl in my quotation from him at the start of "Sharing Identity," in Chapter 5. Those who argue that the nonliterate cultures are as logical as ours, give us perhaps too much credit. See Boas.

9. Eliade, "The Yearning for Paradise in a Primitive Tradition," in *Myth and Mythmaking*, edited by Henry A. Murray (N.Y. 1960; Boston, 1968), p. 66.

10. Ovid, p. 42, who concludes with an allegorical reading:
Beyond, behind the years of loss and hardship
We trace a stony heritage of being.

11. Lévy-Bruhl, p. 99.
12. Lévy-Bruhl, p. 104.
13. *Mythical Thought*, p. 40.
14. *Language and Myth*, p.3. Cassirer further develops this point in the chapter "Word Magic," especially pp. 49-55.

15. See the essays grouped together as "Crisis in the Ecology of Mind" in *Steps to an Ecology of Mind*. Bateson has the phrase "ecology of ideas" from Sir Geoffrey Vickers.

16. "The Brihadaranyaka Upanishad," *The Upanishads: Breath of the Eternal*, translated by Swami Prabhavananda and Frederick Manchester (Hollywood, 1948; N.Y., 1957), p. 89.

17. *The Two Hands of God*, p. 5. We return to our theme from Watts in "The Visionary Image," Chapter One.

18. *I and Thou*, p. 18. Note his present tense.
19. In "The Identity of God," Chapter 5.
20. *Mythical Thought*, p. 77.
21. *Mythical Thought*, p. 74.
22. For an example, see the discussion of the Norse god Odin in H.R. Ellis Davidson, *Gods and Myths of Northern Europe* (Harmondsworth, 1964).

23. The brief account of Black Elk in Chapter One gives some sense of the shaman as a source of what could become mythic culture.

24. Folklorist Dell Hymes lists five functions of language, adding to the customary three--*to state, to ask, to direct*--two more that are especially relevant to traditional material: *to play* and *to relate*. Hymes p. 349. By *relate*, he means the "replaying" of experience, but we may suggest as a further function, this other use of the word, the cultivation of feeling among persons. It is evident in casual inquiries about one's health and apparent declarations about the weather, as well as in the whole traditional activity of story-telling. Still another function of language evident in myth (and in art) is *to respond*, as to wonder or to recoil. Myth, we may propose, is narrative as interjection.

25. Using Sophocles' *Antigone* as his main example, Hegel interpreted tragedy as the conflict between two such claims with equal power.

26. Watts, pp. 12f. Jung states that the conscious mind is continually interacting with the environment, while the collective unconscious is completely independent of it. (*The Structure and Dynamics of the Psyche*, p. 152.) But if the unconscious is colored by the restraints of the conscious mind, and if myth reflects, as I suggest, the interaction of the two, then it is this tension itself which we should see responding and corresponding to other rhythms in nature.

27. Myerhoff, p. 189; see p. 205 as well. The speaker is Ramón Medina Silva. The book is an anthropologist's first-hand account of the hunt.

28. Reichel-Dolmatoff, pp. 50, 66f., 220, and throughout. See "The Realization of Wonder," in Chapter 3 above.

29. Reichel-Dolmatoff, p. 82.

30. W.Y. Evans-Wentz, editor, *The Tibetan Book of the Dead; or, The After-Death Experiences on the Bardo Plane, according to Lama Kazi Dawa-Samdup's English Rendering* (1927; reprinted N.Y., 1973), p. 2. A more recent version by Francesca Fremantle and Chogyam Trungpa, presents a shorter version of the text in a modernized idiom with emphasis on its psychological significance (Boulder, 1975).

31. Evans-Wentz, pp. 103.

32. Evans-Wentz, pp. 121f. Emphasizing the relative nature of the images, the text says: "the size of all these deities is not large, not small, [but] proportionate."

33. Evans-Wentz, p. 148. *Karma* is the chain of interrelated events, or "consequences," that makes up one's situation in life.

34. The Tibetan word, "snang," means literally "light" or "appearance." The Fremantle-Chongpa translation uses "projection." In her introduction, Fremantle claims it is actually more appropriate (xvif.).

35. He sees God as psychic energy, "a real but subjective phenomenon"; "in God we honour the energy of the archetype." *Symbols of Transformation*, pp. 86,89. See also pp. 60f. One of his associates writes more ambiguously, in a fine gnomic statement: "The human psyche is the place where God can become conscious." Marie-Louise von Franz, *Fairy Tales*.

36. *Beast and Man*, p. 362.

37. See Lévy-Bruhl, as I quoted him above, Chapter 8, note 29.

38. The ideal text for this view of Dionysos is Euripides' tragedy *The Bacchae*. William Arrowsmith speaks of Dionysos' opponent and victim in the play, Pentheus, as "the self-ignorant man confronted with the humanized shape of his necessity." "Introduction" to *The Bacchae* in *The Complete Greek Tragedies* (Chicago, 1959). In the play, Cadmus and Teiresias parody the futility of belief.

39. Walter F. Otto, *Dionysus: Myth and Cult* (1933; reprinted Bloomington, Inc., 1965), p. 24f.

40. Walter Otto, p. 33.

41. Walter Otto, p. 136. This description intensifies some of the paradoxes that Paul Radin attributes to the Trickster, as quoted in "Ambiguous Identity," Chapter 5.

42. Berkeley, 1975. A similar point is made by Gary Zukav in his "Overview of the New Physics," *The Dancing Wu Li Masters* (N.Y., 1979). "Wu Li," the Chinese word for *physics*, has also these meanings, which Zukav uses for his section headings: *my way, nonsense, I clutch my ideas*, and *enlightenment*.

43. Capra, p. 77.

44. Capra, p. 178.
45. Capra, p. 59.
46. Capra, p. 77.
47. David Bohm, quoted by Capra, p. 138.
48. Capra, p. 149.
49. Capra, p. 287.
50. Capra quotes Chew: "Carried to its logical extreme, the bootstrap conjecture implies that the existence of consciousness, along with all other aspects of nature, is necessary for the self-consistency of the whole." Capra, p. 300.
51. Capra, pp. 153f. Capra quotes Robert Oppenheimer: "If we ask, for instance, whether the position of the electron remains the same, we must say 'no'; if we ask whether the electron's position changes with time, we must say 'no'; if we ask whether the electron is at rest, we must say 'no'; if we ask whether it is in motion, we must say 'no'." From *Science and the Common Understanding*, quoted by Capra, p. 154.
52. David Bohm, "The Enfolding-Unfolding Universe and Consciousness," in *Wholeness and the Implicate Order* (London, 1980).

CHAPTER 10: Psycho-Mythology of Everyday Life

1. Barthes, *Mythologies* (London, 1972).
2. Georg Simmel, *On Individuality and Social Forms: Selected Writings*, edited by Donald N. Levine (Chicago, 1971), p. 10.
3. Sorel, *Reflections on Violence*. A relevant extract is reprinted in Murray.
4. For a powerful statement of this theme, Franz Grillparzer, 19th-century Austrian dramatist: "What is history but the way in which the spirit of man apprehends *events impenetrable to him;* unites things when God alone knows whether they belong together; substitutes something comprehensible for what is incomprehensible; imposes his concept of purpose from without upon a whole which, if it possesses a purpose, does so only inherently; and assumes the operation of chance where a thousand little causes have been at work." Quoted by Nietzsche in his great essay "On the Uses and Disadvantages of History," *Untimely Meditations*, translated by R.J. Hollingdale (Cambridge, 1983), p. 91. See also Simmel, "How History is Possible," and Lévi-Strauss, *The Savage Mind*, p. 242 and the last chapter of the book, "History and Dialectic," especially p. 257.
5. Simmel, p. 370. See the essays "Social Forms and Inner Needs" and "The Transcendent Character of Life" throughout. Simmel's discussion of time is very suggestive in relation to our earlier considerations.
6. Linguists distinguish between the existential and the predicative use of the verb "to be," but I am not sure our minds observe the distinction. Predication mythologizes existence.
7. From "The Cool Web," *Collected Poems 1975* (London), p. 37.
8. Much has been written on the obliquity, the inherent inaccuracy, of language; for example, this from William James: "language works against our perception of the truth. We have our thoughts simply each after its thing, as if each knew its own thing and nothing else. What each really knows is clearly the thing

it is named for, with dimly perhaps a thousand other things. It ought to be named after all of them, but it never is." *The Principles of Psychology* (Cambridge, Mass., and London, 1981), p. 234. An important earlier exponent of this view was the German philosopher Wilhelm von Humboldt, who wrote: "Man thinks, feels, and lives only within language . . . At the same time he senses and knows that language is only a medium, that there is an invisible realm beyond it, in which he hopes to come to be at home, but only through it. Common experience and profoundest thought both bewail the inadequacy of language, and conceive of that region as a distant land, towards which only language leads, and it never quite." Quoted by Irving Massey, *The Uncreating Word: Romanticism and the Object*. (Bloomington and London, 1970), p. 113. Nietzsche argued that language and consciousness together are bound to be superficial because they need to be shared. *The Gay Science*, translated by Walter Kaufmann (N.Y., 1974), p. 299. See also Cassirer, *Language and Myth*, p. 7.

9. Capra, p. 287. In the words of Werner Heisenberg, one of the chief theorists of modern physics, "What we observe is not nature itself, but nature exposed to our method of questioning." Quoted by Capra, p. 140.

10. First published Chicago, 1962; revised with a Postscript, dated 1969, reconsidering some aspects of the original discussion in response to critics.

11. Kuhn, p. 10.

12. Kuhn draws on Michael Polanyi's valuable conception of "tacit knowledge," which is also very suggestive of the way myth in general resides in the mind and influences one's life without conscious cognition. Kuhn, p. 44. For Polanyi in brief, see *The Tacit Dimension* (London, 1966).

13. Kuhn, p. 44. Just as one traditional myth may mean different things to various members of the culture or religion that it inspires, and the point can be extended to various kinds of common myth as well. Kuhn here invokes Wittgenstein's notion of "family resemblances," which I referred to in my preface and which, for him, unites the divergent ways of understanding the paradigm.

14. The point is argued most clearly in the Postcript, p. 206.

15. James Hillman argues for the psychological value of personifying abstractions in a polytheistic manner and experiencing them in oneself as living forces. *Re-Visioning Psychology*, p. 42.

16. In the first part of Chapter IV, *Creative Evolution*, translated by Arthur Mitchell (London 1911, 1960), pp. 287-314. Although the meaning of his extant fragments has been debated, Parmenides, in the 6th Century B.C., based his philosophy on a similar insistence that negation be avoided.

17. Kenneth Burke, *Language as Symbolic Action*, p. 9, picking up the theme from Bergson.

18. Sartre, p. 218. His major philosophical work is, in fact, *Being and Nothingness*.

19. Bergson, p. 291.

20. Bergson, p. 312.

21. André Bazin, "The Ontology of the Photographic Image," *What is Cinema?* (Berkeley, 1967), p. 14.

22. E.H. Gombrich, *Art and Illusion: A Study in the Psychology of Pictorial Representation* (Princeton, 1960), p. 15. "All culture and all communication," writes Gombrich, "depend on the interplay between expectation and observation, the waves of fulfillment, disappointment, right guesses, and

Notes to Pages: 195-210

wrong moves that make up our daily lives." P. 60. He later quotes an unidentified source saying: "Perception may be regarded as primarily the modification of an anticipation" (p. 172).

23. Which is not to say that what I am talking about as "*the* sky" exists only in my mind. A meteorologist, incidentally, assures me that the sky is the atmosphere and is truly there as the sky. It still seems to me that when I say "sky" I mean the expanse itself which is *up* from my point of view on the earth.

24. "Language, Mind, and Reality," p. 253. There are similar discussions of "wave" and "flash" on p. 262.

25. Whorf, p. 252.

26. Karl Kraus, Austrian journalist and polemicist, quoted by Allan Janik and Stephen Toulmin, *Wittgenstein's Vienna* (New York, 1973), p. 200.

27. *The Politics of Experience* (New York, 1967), pp. 10f.

28. In "The Physical Universe Revisited," Chapter 9.

29. Compare the account of Hans Vaihinger's "fictions" in Appendix II. In his more mechanical terms, fictions can be effective because of their "centers of similarity," which make contact with the real world. Vaihinger is closer to the so-called science of semiology, which treats cultural forms as signs rather than symbols, ignoring their nature as myth (in the sense covered by these five points). The founder of semiology, Ferdinand de Saussure, clearly warned against treating symbols as signs (*Course in General Linguistics*, translated by Wade Baskin, 2nd edition, London 1974, pp. 68, 73), but the Structuralists, who have been his followers, have done just that. For a detailed history of symbolic theory, which makes a similar response to semiology, see Hazard Adams.

30. *Tragedy and Innocence*, pp. 103f.

31. *Language and Myth*, p. 7. An important statement of this theme is the chapter "Symbols" in Thomas Carlyle's *Sartor Resartus*. The idea can be found in the writings formerly attributed to St. Dionysius the Areopagite; see Theodore Bogdanos, *Pearl: Image of the Ineffable--A Study in Medieval Poetic Symbolism* (University Park & London, 1983), p. 6.

32. Contrary to Vaihinger's idea about "fictions," Appendix II.

33. As explicated by Northrop Frye, *Fearful Symmetry: A Study of William Blake* (Princeton, 1947), pp. 394f. The source in Blake in *Jerusalem*, plate 49, line 58; plate 85, line 7. In the *Complete Writings*, pp. 680, 730.

34. This process takes place, I suspect, in an historical culture, to the extent that it *is* historical. In a traditional culture, common myth is a rigidification of archetypal myth, in dogma and, more simply, in belief.

CHAPTER 11: Symbolic Consciousness

1. In an essay on Shakespeare, I suggest that the Renaissance can be studied fruitfully as the incursion of extra-symbolic consciousness in European culture. "Between the Mirror and the Face: Symbolic Reality in *Richard II*, in *Shakespeare and the Triple Play: From the Study to the Stage to the Classroom*, edited by Sidney Homan (Lewisburg, 1988).

2. Sam Keen, "The Art of Dreaming," *Psychology Today* (December 1977), p. 42.

Notes to Pages: 211-226

3. *The Symbolism of Evil*, translated by Emerson Buchanan (reprinted Boston, 1969), p. 350. At the start of the passage, Ricoeur writes that "demythologization is the irreversible gain of truthfulness, intellectual honesty, objectivity."

4. *The Myth of Sisyphus and other Essays*, translated by Justin O'Brien (N.Y., 1955), p. 89.

5. Gershom Scholem, "Introduction," *Zohar: The Book of Splendor* (N.Y., 1949), p. 9.

APPENDIX I: *About Consciousness*

1. There are good brief discussions of the problem of defining consciousness in Peter Koestenbaum's *The Vitality of Death* (Chapter 6, "the Sense of Subjectivity") and Julian Jaynes' *Origins of Consciousness* . . .

APPENDIX II: *Myths, Fictions, Metaphors*

1. *The Philosophy of "As If,"* translated by C.K. Ogden (London, 1924). The first part of the book was published in German in 1911.
2. Vaihinger, p. 70.
3. Vaihinger, p. 157. He quotes Salomon Maimon: "only *symbolic* knowledge is possible," p. 30.
4. Vaihinger, p. 101.
5. "All that is given to consciousness is sensation. By adding a Thing to which sensations are supposed to adhere as attributes, thought commits a very serious error." P. 167.
6. Vaihinger, p. 64.
7. Vaihinger, p. 73.
8. Vaihinger, p. 67.
9. Vaihinger, p. 84. See also p. 108. One wonders at the impulse which produced the word "really."
10. Vaihinger, p. 84.
11. Vaihinger, pp. xxx, xiii.
12. Vaihinger, p. 123.
13. Vaihinger, p. 171. He is distinguishing "understanding" from "knowledge."
14. *The Gay Science*, translated by Walter Kaufmann, p. 163. Note the difference from Vaihinger, who contrasted the truth of sensation to the errors of our understanding them. The final chapter of *The Philosophy of "As If"* is a detailed summary of Nietzsche's "will to illusion," tracing the theme through his works.
15. Nietzsche. In a similar list, he adds "divisible time spans, divisible spaces," p. 177.
16. Nietzsche, p. 203.

Notes to Pages: 226-229

17. Nietzsche, p. 330. Contrast with Vaihinger's statement that "The wish to understand the world . . . is a very stupid wish" Nietzsche's "the factual is always stupid." *Untimely Meditations*, p. 106.

18. Vaihinger, pp. 101f. Compare this lovely passage from his autobiographical preface, written much later than the book proper ("The world's work" at the end here would seem to be more than merely utilitarian):

> Experience and intuition are higher than all human reason. When I see a deer feeding in the forest, when I see a child at play, when I see a man at work or sport, but above all when I myself am working or playing, where are all the problems with which my mind has been torturing itself unnecessarily? We do not understand the world when we are pondering its problems, but when we are doing the world's work. (p. xiv)

19. *Consciousness Regained: Chapters in the Development of Mind* (Oxford and N.Y., 1984).

20. *Myths We Live By* (Chicago and London, 1980), pp. 4, 47, 49, 51, 27. I have altered or combined some of the examples.

21. Lakoff and Johnson, Chapters 4 and 6.

22. Lakoff and Johnson, Chapters 7 and 8. They include synechdoche, taking the part for the whole ("We need new blood in this organization.") as a type of metonymy, p. 36.

23. Lakoff and Johnson, p. 19.

24. Lakoff and Johnson, p. 119.

25. Lakoff and Johnson, p. 221.

26. Lakoff and Johnson, p. 117, also p. 5. What I am calling the rhetorical approach is, in my view, more appropriate for allegory and simile than for metaphor. See my *Tragedy and Innocence*, pp. 103ff.

27. Lakoff and Johnson, p. 60 and elsewhere.

28. Lakoff and Johnson, p. 234.

29. Lakoff and Johnson, p. 154.

30. The metaphor theory is too uniformly coherent and schematic in another way too, I think. The qualification suggested for the Whorf-Sapir thesis applies here as well (see Chapter 2, note 4). We understand both words and metaphors mythically in terms of what they do not say as well as in terms of what they do. When we hear them, we think of the bare reality they refer to as well as the way it is formulated. Although both cases are likely to have a significant influence upon our sense of truth, we may very well *misunderstand* them intelligently to different degrees according to our own wisdom. . . . The rhetorical view of metaphor seems usually to assume that the image is applied actively to a passive subject or experience, which it treats and interprets. (Giving it a free ride, if the image is a "vehicle.") Isn't it at least as likely that the subject reaches out for an image that can represent its salient features? Or, rather, that our minds are predisposed to find satisfaction in certain kinds of "fit" because of such cultural assumptions as materialism--what Lakoff and Johnson call appropriately "the objectivist myth"--and the consequent transcendence of the spirit, linearity of logic, and intransigence of fact. The metaphors and other linguistic forms that we find out and *live by* confirm such basic tendencies, perhaps, in a self-regulating way.

Notes to Pages: 229-231

31. Actually, both "submerged metaphors" and "mixed metaphors" may be regarded more properly as "blended metaphors," in which images overlay one another in such a way that their logical discordance is irrelevant. In a much discussed line of Sir Thomas Wyatt's, "They fle from me that sometyme did me seek, / With naked fote stalking in my chambre," the *suggested* presence of a deer overlays the remembered image of a woman, or a succession of women, "with naked fote." See my *Stoic in Love: Convention and Self in the Poetry of Wyatt* (University Microfilms, 1981), pp. 210f. and fn. 14, also 223ff.

32. When Lakoff and Johnson speak of ontology, they are concerned with the concrete existence one attributes to qualities or conditions, but the notion of myth as qualitative presence allows us to think of the reality that our acts of language take on in themselves. For a discussion of the creative, or constitutive, nature of symbolism, see "Conclusions" to Hazard Adams' *Philosophy of the Literary Symbolic*.

33. See Lakoff and Johnson, p. 39.

additional notes to chapter 4

30. Whorf, "Habitual Thought," p. 151.

31. Throughout the chapter "Sacred and Profane Time," in *The Sacred and the Profane*.

32. Gerardus Van der Leeuw, *Eranos Yearbook, 1949*, quoted by Gershom G. Scholem, *On the Kabbalah and its Symbolism* (N.Y., 1965; 1969), p. 117.

33. See Levi-Strauss, The Structural Study of Myth," *Structural Anthropology*, translated by Jacobson and Schoepf (London, 1968), pp. 209, 211. The source in Saussure is *Course in General Linguistics* (London, 1959), p. 81. He explains the contrast in terms of an "axis of simultaneities" and an "axis of successions," p. 80. In his usage, diachrony is the historical study of a topic through time, as in evolution or in biology. Levi-Strauss uses it to decribe the time-flow of a story.

34. Roland Barthes, *Elements of Semiology* (London, 1967), pp. 54f.

35. *The Raw and the Cooked*, translated by J. and D. Weightman (London, 1970), pp. 15f.

36. Lee, p. 139, my italics.

37. T.S. Eliot, from "Burnt Norton," *The Complete Poetry and Plays* (London, 1969), p. 173.

38. Whorf, "Habitual Thought," pp. 143f.

39. Eliade, *Myth and Reality*, p. 18.

40. *Myth and Reality*, p. 19.

41. Thomas Mann, "Freud and the Future" (1937), reprinted in *Myth and Mythmaking*, edited by Henry A. Murray (Boston, 1968), pp. 373f.

42. *Joseph and his Brothers*, translated by H.T. Lowe-Porter (Harmondsworth and N.Y., 1978), p. 3.

43. *Joseph*, p. 19.

44. *Joseph*, p. 32.

45. *Joseph*, p. 33.

46. Eliot, p. 173.

47. Van Gennep, p. 3.

48. Lord Raglan, *The Hero: A Study in Tradition, Myth and Drama* (1963; reprint N.Y., 1956), pp. 174f.

BIBLIOGRAPHY

ADAMS, HAZARD. *Philosophy of the Literary Symbolic.* Tallahassee: 1983.
ANONYMOUS. *The Mahabharata.* Vol. I. Translated by J.A.B. van Buitenen. Chicago and London: 1973.
ARONSON, ALEX. *Psyche and Symbol in Shakespeare.* Bloomington: 1973.
ARROWSMITH, WILLIAM. "Introduction" to *The Bacchae* in *The Complete Greek Tragedies.* David Grene and Richmond Lattimore, editors. Chicago: 1959.
BACHELARD, GASTON. *The Poetics of Reverie.* Translated by Daniel Russell. Boston: 1969.
BARFIELD, OWEN. "Language, Evolution of Consciousness, and the Recovery of Human Meaning." *Teachers College Record.* Columbia University: Spring, 1981.
⎯⎯⎯. *Saving the Appearances: A Study in Idolatry.* New York and London: 1957.
BARTH, JOHN. *Chimera.* New York: 1972.
BARTHES, ROLAND. *Elements of Semiology.* London: 1967.
⎯⎯⎯. *Mythologies.* London: 1972.
BATESON, GREGORY. *Steps to an Ecology of the Mind.* New York: 1972.
BAZIN, ANDRE. "The Ontology of the Photographic Image." *What is Cinema?* Berkeley: 1967.
BENJAMIN, WALTER. *Illuminations.* Translated by Harry Zohn. New York and London: 1968.
BERGSON, HENRI. *Creative Evolution.* Translated by Arthur Mitchell. London: 1911; 1960.
BETTLEHEIM, BRUNO. *The Uses of Enchantment: Meaning and Importance of Fairy Tales.* New York: 1975.
BIRENBAUM, HARVEY. "The Art of Our Necessities: The Softness of *King Lear.*" *The Yale Review:* 72.4. Summer, 1983.
⎯⎯⎯. "Between the Mirror and the Face: Symbolic Reality in *Richard II.*" In *Shakespeare and the Triple Play: From the Study to the Stage to the Classroom,* edited by Sidney Homan. Lewisburg, Pa.: 1987.
⎯⎯⎯. "Consciousness and Responsibility in *Macbeth.*" *Mosaic:* XV.2. June, 1982.
⎯⎯⎯. *Stoic in Love: Convention and Self in the Poetry of Wyatt.* University Microfilms, 1981.
⎯⎯⎯. "To Be *and* Not to Be: The Archetypal Form of *Hamlet.*" *Pacific Coast Philology:* XVI.1. June, 1981.
⎯⎯⎯. *Tragedy and Innocence.* Washington, D.C.: 1983.
⎯⎯⎯. "A View from the Rialto: Two Psychologies in *The Merchant of Venice.*" *San Jose Studies:* IX.2. Spring, 1983.
BLAKE, WILLIAM. *Complete Writings.* Edited by Geoffrey Keynes. London: 1957.
BLY, ROBERT. *Sleepers Joining Hands.* New York: 1973.

Bibliography

BOAS, FRANZ. *The Mind of Primitive Man.* 1911; revised edition, New York: 1938.
BOGEN, JOSEPH. "The Other Side of the Brain: An Appositional Mind." *Bulletin of the Los Angeles Neurological Societies.* Los Angeles: 1969. In ORNSTEIN.
BOHM, DAVID. "The Enfolding-Unfolding Universe and Consciousness." *Wholeness and the Implicate Order.* London: 1980.
BOLLE, KEES. *The Freedom of Man in Myth.* Nashville, Tenn.: 1968.
BROWN, CALVIN, ed. *Reader's Companion to World Literature.* New York: 1956.
BUBER, MARTIN. *I and Thou.* Translated by R.G. Smith. New York: 1958.
BURKE, KENNETH. *Counterstatement.* Second edition. Chicago: 1957.
———. *Language as Symbolic Action: Essays on Life, Literature, and Method.* Berkeley and Los Angeles: 1966.
CAMPBELL, JOSEPH. *The Flight of the Wild Gander: Exploration in the Mythological Dimension.* Reprinted South Bend, Ind.: no date.
———. *The Hero with a Thousand Faces.* New York: 1949.
———. *The Masks of God: Creative Mythology.* New York and London: 1968.
———. *The Masks of God: Primitive Mythology.* New York: 1959, 1970.
———. *The Mythic Image.* Princeton: 1974.
CAMUS, ALBERT. *The Myth of Sisyphus and Other Essays.* Translated by Justin O'Brien. New York: 1955.
CAPRA, FRITJOF. *Science and the Common Understanding.* Berkeley: 1975.
CASSIRER, ERNST. *An Essay on Man.* New Haven, Conn.: 1944.
———. *Language and Myth.* Translated by Susanne K. Langer. New York: 1946; Reprinted 1953.
———. *Philosophy of Symbolic Forms.* Vol. II, *Mythical Thought.* New Haven: 1954.
DIMOCK, EDWARD C., JR., and DENISE LEVERTOV, translators. *In Praise of Krishna: Songs from the Bengali.* Garden City, N.Y.: 1967.
DODDS, E.R. *The Greeks and the Irrational.* Berkeley, Los Angeles, and Cambridge: 1951.
EDINGER, EDWARD F. *Ego and Archetype: Individuation and the Religious Function of the Psyche.* New York: 1972; reprinted Baltimore: 1973.
EISELEY, LOREN. *The Immense Journey.* New York: 1946.
ELIADE, MIRCEA. *Myth and Reality.* Translated by Willard R. Trask. 1963; reprinted New York: 1968.
———. *The Sacred and the Profane.* Translated by Willard R. Trask. New York: 1959.
———. "The Yearning for Paradise in Primitive Tradition." In MURRAY.
ELIOT, T.S. "Burnt Norton." *The Complete Poetry and Plays.* London: 1969.
ELLIS, JOHN M. *One Fairy Story Too Many: The Brothers Grimm and their Tales.* Chicago: 1983.
ELLIS DAVIDSON, H.R. *Gods and Myths of Northern Europe.* Harmondsworth: 1964.
EVANS-WENTZ, W.Y., ed. *The Tibetan Book of the Dead; or, The After-Death Experiences on the Bardo Plane, According to Lama Kazi Dawa-Samdup's English Rendering.* Reprinted New York: 1973.
FELDMANN, SUSAN, ed. *African Myths and Tales.* New York: 1963.
FRANKFORT, HENRI, and MRS. H.A. *Before Philosophy.* Harmondsworth: 1949.

Bibliography

FRAZER, SIR JAMES GEORGE. *The New Golden Bough*. Edited by Theodore H. Gaster. Garden City, New York: 1961.
FREMANTLE, FRANCESCA, and CHOGYAM TRUNGPA. *The Tibetan Book of the Dead: The Great Liberation Through Hearing in the Bardo*. Boulder and London: 1975.
FREUD, SIGMUND. *The Interpretation of Dreams*. In *The Standard Edition of the Works of Sigmund Freud*, Vol. IV. London: 1953.
———. *Totem and Taboo*. Translated by James Strachey. New York: 1950.
FRYE, NORTHROP. *The Anatomy of Criticism*. Princeton: 1957.
———. "The Argument of Comedy." *English Institute Essays, 1948*. New York: 1949.
———. *Fearful Symmetry: A Study of William Blake*. Princeton: 1947.
———. *The Secular Scripture: A Study of the Structure of Romance*. Cambridge, Mass., and London: 1976.
FURTH, HANS G. *Thinking Without Language*. New York and London, 1966.
GADAMER, HANS-GEORG. *Truth and Method*. Translation edited by Garrett Barden and John Cumming. London: 1975.
GEERTZ, CLIFFORD. *The Interpretation of Cultures*. New York: 1973.
GIMBUTAS, MARIJA. *The Goddesses and Gods of Old Europe: Myths and Cult Images*. Berkeley, 1982.
GODDARD, PLINY EARLE, ed. *Kato Texts*. Berkeley: 1909.
GOMBRICH, E.H. *Art and Illusion: A Study in the Psychology of Pictorial Representation*. Princeton: 1960.
GRAVES, ROBERT. *Collected Poems*. London: 1975.
———. *The Greek Myths*, Vol. II.
GRIMM, JAKOB and WILHELM. *The Complete Grimm's Fairy Tales*. Translated by Margaret Hunt and James Stern. New York: 1972.
HARRISON, JANE. "Epilegomena to the Study of Greek Religion," (1921). *Epilegomena . . . and Themis*. New Hyde Park, New York: 1962.
HATHORN, RICHMOND Y. *Tragedy, Myth, and Mystery*. Bloomington, Ind.: 1962.
HEIDEGGER, MARTIN. *Poetry, Language, Thought*. Translated and edited by Albert Hofstadter. New York: 1971.
HENDERSON, JOSEPH L., and MAUDE OAKES. *The Wisdom of the Serpent*. New York: 1963.
HESIOD. *Theogony*. Translated with introduction by Norman O. Brown. Indianapolis and New York: 1953.
HEUSCHER, JULIUS. *A Psychiatric Study of Myths and Fairy Tales: Their Origin, Meaning, and Usefulness*. Springfield, Ill.: 1974.
HILLMAN, JAMES. *Re-Visioning Psychology*. New York: 1975; reprinted 1977.
HOLLIS, MARTIN. "Reason and Ritual." In WILSON.
HORTON, ROBIN. "African Traditional Thought and Western Science." In WILSON.
HUIZINGA, JOHAN. *Homo Ludens: A Study of the Play-Element in Culture*. Boston: 1950; reprinted 1955.
HUMPHREY, NICHOLAS. *Consciousness Regained: Chapters in the Development of Mind*. Oxford and New York: 1984.
JAMES, WILLIAM. *The Principles of Psychology*. Reprinted New York: 1950.
———. *The Principles of Psychology*. Cambridge, Mass., and London: 1981.
JANIK, ALLAN, and STEPHEN TOULMIN. *Wittgenstein's Vienna*. New York: 1973.

Bibliography

JARVIE, I.C. "Explaining Cargo Cults." In WILSON
JAYNES, JULIAN. *The Origin of Consciousness in the Breakdown of the Bicameral Mind.* Boston: 1976.
JUNG, CARL GUSTAV. *Aion: Researches into the Phenomenology of the Self.* Translated R.F.C. Hull. New York: 1959; reprinted Princeton: 1979.
———. *Memories, Dreams, and Reflections.* London: 1961.
———. "The Phenomenology of the Spirit in Fairy Tales." *Spirit and Nature,* Vol. I. Reprinted in *Psyche and Symbol,* edited by Violet S. De Laszlo. New York: 1958.
———. *Symbols of Transformation.* Translated by R.F.C. Hull. Princeton: 1956.
———. *Two Essays on Analytical Psychology.* Translated by R.F.C. Hull. 1953; reprinted Princeton: 1972.
KEEN, SAM, "The Art of Dreaming." *Psychology Today:* December, 1977.
KIRK, G.S. *The Nature of Greek Myths.* Harmondsworth and Baltimore: 1974.
KIRK, G.S., J.E. RAVEN, and M. SCHOFIELD. *The Presocratic Philosophers.* Second edition. Cambridge: 1983.
KOESTENBAUM, PETER. *The Vitality of Death: Essays in Existential Philosophy and Psychology.* Westport, Conn.: 1971.
KUHN, THOMAS S. *The Structure of Scientific Revolutions.* Chicago: 1962; revised 1969.
LAING, R.D. *The Politics of Experience.* London and New York: 1967.
———. *Self and Others.* London: 1961.
LAKOFF, GEORGE, and MARK JOHNSON. *Metaphors We Live By.* Chicago and London: 1980.
LANGER, SUSANNE K. *Feeling and Form.* London and New York: 1953.
———. *Philosophy in a New Key.* New York: 1942.
———. *Problems of Art.* London: 1957.
LEAKEY, LOUIS S.B., and ROBERT ARDREY. "Man, the Killer." *Psychology Today,* September 1972, pp. 73-85.
LEE, DOROTHY. "Codifications of Reality: Lineal and Nonlineal." *Psychosomatic Medicine:* 1950. In ORNSTEIN.
LEVI-STRAUSS, CLAUDE. *Myth and Meaning.* London: 1978.
———. *The Raw and the Cooked.* Translated by J. and D. Weightman. London: 1970.
———. *The Savage Mind.* London: 1966.
———. "The Structural Study of Myth." *Structural Anthropology.* London: 1968.
———. *Totemism.* London: 1964.
LEVY-BRUHL, LUCIEN. *The Notebooks on Primitive Mentality.* Translated by Peter Rivière. 1975; reprinted New York: 1978.
LORD, ALBERT B. *The Singer of Tales.* 1960; reprinted New York: 1965.
LUKE, HELEN M. *Woman: Earth and Spirit--The Feminine in Symbol and Myth.* New York, 1986.
LUKES, STEVEN. "Some Problems About Rationality." In WILSON.
LUTHI, MAX. *Once Upon a Time: On the Nature of Fairy Tales.* Translated by Lee Chadeayne and Paul Gottwald with additions by the author. New York: 1970; reprinted Bloomington and London: 1976.

Bibliography

MALINOWSKI, BRONISLAW. *Magic, Science, and Religion and Other Essays.* Garden City, New York: 1954.
MANN, THOMAS. "Freud and the Future." 1937. In MURRAY
_____. *Joseph and His Brothers.* Translated by H.T. Lowe-Porter. Harmondsworth and New York: 1978.
MASSEY, IRVING. *The Uncreating Word: Romanticism and the Object.* Bloomington and London: 1970.
MIDGELY, MARY. *Beast and Man.* Brighton: 1979; Cambridge: 1980.
MURRAY, HENRY A., ed. *Myth and Mythmaking.* New York: 1960; reprinted Boston: 1968.
MYERHOFF, BARBARA G. *Peyote Hunt: The Sacred Journey of the Huichol Indians.* Ithaca, New York: 1974
NEIHARDT, JOHN G. *Black Elk Speaks.* Lincoln, Nebraska: 1961.
NEUMANN, ERICH. *The Great Mother.* Translated by Ralph Manheim. New York: 1955.
_____. *The Origins and History of Consciousness.* Translated by R.F.C. Hull. 1954; reprinted Princeton: 1970.
NIETZSCHE, FRIEDRICH. *The Gay Science.* Translated by Walter Kaufmann. New York: 1974.
_____. "On the Uses and Disadvantages of History." *Untimely Meditations.* Translated by R.J. Hollingdale. Cambridge: 1983.
_____. *Twilight of the Idols* and *The Anti-Christ.* Translated by R.J. Hollingdale. Harmondsworth and New York, 1968.
ORNSTEIN, ROBERT E., ed. *The Nature of Human Consciousness: A Book of Readings.* San Francisco: 1973.
OTTO, RUDOLF. *The Idea of the Holy.* Translated by John W. Harvey. Second edition. London: 1950; reprinted 1977.
OTTO, WALTER F. *Dionysus: Myth and Cult.* 1933; reprinted Bloomington: 1965.
OTZEN, BENEDIKT, HANS GOTTLIEB, and KNUD JEPPESEN, *Myths in the Old Testament*, translated by Frederick Cryer (London, 1980).
OVID. *The Metamorphoses.* Translated by Horace Gregory. New York: 1958.
POLANYI, MICHAEL. *The Tacit Dimension.* London: 1966.
PROPP, VLADIMIR. *Morphology of the Folktale.* Translated by Laurence Scott. 1958; second edition revised by Louis A. Wagner, Austin and London: 1968.
RADIN, PAUL. *Primitive Man as Philosopher.* 1927; revised, reprinted New York: 1957.
_____. *The Trickster: A Study in American Indian Mythology.* Commentaries by Karl Kerenyi and C.G. Jung. New York: 1972.
RAGLAN, LORD. *The Hero: A Study in Tradition, Myth, and Drama.* 1936; reprinted New York: 1956.
REICHEL-DOLMATOFF, GERARDO. *Amazonian Cosmos: The Sexual and Religious Symbolism of the Tukano Indians.* Chicago: 1971.
RICOEUR, PAUL. *The Symbolism of Evil.* Translated by Emerson Buchanan. 1967; reprinted Boston: 1969.
ROTHENBERG, JEROME, ed. *Technicians of the Sacred.* Garden City, New York: 1968.
RUTHVEN, K.K. *Myth.* London, 1976.

Bibliography

SAGAN, CARL. *The Dragons of Eden: Speculations on the Evolution of Human Intelligence.* New York: 1978.

SARTRE, JEAN PAUL. *The Psychology of Imagination.* London: 1972

SAUSSURE, FERDINAND DE. *Course in General Linguistics.* Translated by Wade Baskin. Second edition, London: 1974.

SCHELLING, F.W.J. "Conclusion to *System of Transcendental Idealism.*" In *German Aesthetic and Literary Criticism: Kant . . . Hegel.* Edited by David Simpson. Cambridge: 1984.

SCHOLEM, GERSHOM G. *On the Kabbalah and Its Symbolism.* Translated by Ralph Manheim. 1965; reprinted 1969.

SPEISER, E.A., translator, "The Epic of Gilgamesh," in *Ancient Near Eastern Texts Relating to the Old Testament.* Edited by James B. Pritchard. Princeton: 1950.

SIMMEL, GEORGE G. *On Individuality and Social Forms: Selected Writings.* Edited by Donald Levine. Chicago: 1971.

SOREL, GEORGES. "Reflections on Violence." In MURRAY.

SPENCE, LEWIS. *The Outlines of Mythology.* 1944; reprinted New York: 1961.

THOMPSON, STITH. *Motif-Index of Folk-Literature.* 6 Vols. Copenhagen and Bloomington: 1955-1958.

_____. *Tales of the North American Indians.* 1929; Bloomington and London: 1966.

TOPITSCH, ERNST. "World Interpretation and Self-Interpretation: Some Basic Patterns." In MURRAY

TURNER, VICTOR, *The Ritual Process: Structure and Anti-Structure.* 1969; reprinted Ithaca, New York: 1977.

TURNER, VICTOR and EDITH. *Image and Pilgrimage in Christian Culture.* New York: 1978.

VAIHINGER, HANS. *The Philosophy of "As If."* Translated by C.K. Ogden. London: 1924.

VAN GENNEP, ARNOLD. *The Rites of Passage.* Translated by Monika B. Vizedom and Gabrielle L. Caffee. 1909; reprinted Chicago and London: 1960.

VICO, GIAMBATTISTA. *Vico: Selected Writings.* Edited and translated by Leon Pompa. Cambridge: 1982.

VON FRANZ, MARIE-LOUISE. *An Introduction to the Psychology of Fairy Tales.* Zurich: 1970.

_____. *A Psychological Interpretation of* The Golden Ass *of Apuleius.* Zurich: 1970.

WARD, DAVID. "Stepping out of Line." *The Guardian.* London and Manchester: December 22, 1978.

WATTS, ALAN. *The Joyous Cosmology.* New York: 1962.

_____. *The Two Hands of God: The Myths of Polarity.* New York: 1963; reprinted 1969.

WESTON, JESSIE. *From Ritual to Romance.* Garden City, New York: 1957.

WHEELWRIGHT, PHILIP. *Metaphor and Reality.* Bloomington: 1962; reprinted 1968.

_____. *The Burning Fountain: A Study in the Language of Symbolism.* Revised edition. Bloomington, Ind.: 1968.

WHORF, BENJAMIN. *Language, Thought, and Reality.* Edited by John B. Carroll. Cambridge, Mass.: 1956.

Bibliography

WILSON, BRYAN R., ed. *Rationality.* Oxford: 1970.
WITTGENSTEIN, LUDWIG. *Philosophical Investigatons.* Translated by G.E.M. Anscombe. Oxford: 1953; reprinted 1968.
YEATS, W.B. *The Collected Poems.* New York: 1956.
———. *Essays and Introductions.* London: 1961.
———. *A Vision.* New York: 1937; reprinted 1966.
ZIMMER, HEINRICH. *The King and the Corpse.* Second edition. Princeton: 1948; reprinted 1956.

INDEX

Actaeon 3, 21, 94, 137, 202, 248
Adams, Hazard 239, 257, 259
Adonis 29, 126
Aeneid 90
anima and animus 104, 105, 126, 130
Apollo *frontispiece* 71, 123, 136, 137, 150f., 176
Apuleius 113, 244, 247
Aronson, Alex 247
Arthur 3, 91, 213
Athene 2, 35, 71, 177
Attis 29, 30
Bachelard, Gaston 6, 232
Barfield, Owen 252
Barleycorn, John 120f.
Barth, John 147f., 164
Barthes, Roland 183, 249
Bateson, Gregory 36, 170, 236, 245, 253
Benjamin, Walter 248
Beowulf 130f., 134, 247
Bergson, Henri 193, 256
Bernini, Gian Lorenzo *frontispiece*
Bettelheim, Bruno 248
Bhagavad Gita 38
Black Elk 8-10, 12, 56, 81, 253
Blake, William xiv, 10, 38, 99-104, 117, 123, 204, 232f., 236, 243, 257
"Blind Men and the Elephant" 184
Bloom, Harold 237, 243
Bly, Robert 247
Boas, Franz 88, 232, 236, 248
Bogdanos, Theodore 257
Bogen, Joseph 20, 233, 234
Bohm, David 181f., 255
Bolle, Kees 238, 252
Brahma 68, 83, 176
Buber, Martin (see *I-Thou*) 44f., 48f. 93, 171, 238, 251
Buddha 4
Burke, Kenneth 20, 158, 235, 243, 251, 256
Burns, Robert 120f.
Cain and Abel 109, 119, 130

Campbell, Joseph 55, 114, 123, 154, 165, 245, 246, 248, 252
Camus, Albert 72, 211
Capra, Fritjof 178ff., 191, 255, 256
Carlyle, Thomas 34, 257
Cassirer, Ernst x, 20, 45, 52, 68, 79, 85, 111, 159, 169, 171, 201, 232, 235, 238, 239, 242, 251
Chamunda 144
charm 19
Chew, Geoffrey 180, 254
Cocteau, Jean 241
Codrington, R.H. 242
Coleridge, Samuel Taylor 234
collective unconscious 104, 107
Colombia 42, 173f.
communitas 47f., 122, 178
Demeter (Ceres) 80, 105, 122, 157, 173, 246
Desana Indians 157, 173f.
Dickens, Charles 88f.
Dionysius the Areopagite, St. 257
Dionysos 29, 47, 121, 157, 159, 166-67, 176-78, 254
Dodds, E.R. 247
dreams 5, 22f., 76, 79, 145
Dunne, John S. 246
Dying God (see *Adonis, Attis, Tammuz*) 87, 126
Edinger, Edward 244
Einstein, Albert 178, 180
Eiseley, Loren 110, 112
Eliade, Mircea ix, 55, 59f., 171, 238, 253
Eliot, T.S. xiv, 62-64
Ellis, John M. 239
Ellis Davidson, H.R. 253
Emerson, Ralph Waldo 246
endopsychic 79
Farb, Peter 251
fetishes 84, 161
fiddle-shaped figurines 84
fortunate fall 72
Frankenstein 39, 40, 130
Frankfort, Henri 45, 47, 238
Frazer, Sir James G. 34, 86

INDEX

Freud, Sigmund, 22, 24f., 64, 76, 79, 97, 109, 159, 217, 223, 235, 251
Frobenius, Leo 157
Frye, Northrop 36, 53, 79, 237, 239, 241, 248, 257
Furth, Hans G. 245
Gadamer, Hans-Georg 249
Gallagher David 210
Garuda 77
Gawain, Sir 105
Geb and Nut 129
Geertz, Clifford xi, 232
Gilgamesh 105, 126f., 129, 136, 165, 246, 247
Gimbutas, Marija 82, 124, 242
Goethe, J.W. von 169f.
Gombrich, E.H. 194f., 256
Goya, Francisco 127
Graves, Robert ix, 158, 164, 190, 251
Great Mother (see *Mother Goddess*) 29, 126, 131, 166
Grillparzer, Franz 255
Grimm, Jakob & Wilhelm 49, 72, 138-41, 239, 248
Hamlet 129, 247
"Hansel and Gretel" 138-40, 155, 247
Hariti 125
Harrison, Jane ix, 159, 251
Hasidism 145
Hathorn, Richmond 43, 155, 158, 238, 250
Heidegger, Martin 49, 143, 251
Heisenberg, Werner 180, 256
Helios 35f.
Heraclitus 3, 38
Herakles 3, 133, 134f., 172
Herder, J.G. von 238
Hesiod 236
Heuscher, Julius 245, 248
Hiawatha 162, 251
Hofstadter, Douglas R. 241
Hollis, Martin 251
Hopi Indians 17f., 59, 154, 161, 183
Horton, Robin 242
Huichol Indians 46, 172f., 242

Huizinga, Johan 156f., 251
Humphrey, Nicholas 227
Hymes, Dell 248, 252, 253
I-Thou 44-48, 57, 115, 157, 164, 167, 171, 201
Inanna 122
Ishtar 122, 126
Izanagi and Izanami 122
James, William 214, 216, 218, 255
Jarvie, I.C. 250
Jaynes, Julian 58, 233, 258
Jesus 39, 122, 125, 162
Johnson, Mark 227-31, 259
Jung, Carl G. xi, 19, 41, 57, 59, 79, 85, 97f, 104-9, 111, 113, 114, 115, 138, 154, 159, 166, 172, 176, 223, 232, 234, 237, 238, 239, 243, 244, 245, 253
"Juniper Tree" 49f., 69, 70, 76, 179f., 247
kachina 161
Kant, Immanuel 195, 225, 249
Keen, Sam 257
Kerenyi, Karl ix, 236, 243
Kirk, G.S. 250
Koestenbaum, Peter 118, 246, 258
Korzybski, Alfred 190
Kraus, Karl 257
Krishna 4, 83, 124, 127, 132, 176, 247
Kuhn, Thomas S. 191f., 256
Laing, R.D. 196, 232, 241
Lakoff, George 227-31, 259
Langer, Susanne 19, 20, 233, 243, 249
Lao Tzu 38
Latimer, Hugh 120
Leakey, Louis 111, 245
Leda 123
Lee, Dorothy 18, 58, 234
Lévi-Strauss, Claude ix, 26, 28, 53, 61, 86, 92, 108, 236, 241, 245, 246, 249, 255
Lévy-Bruhl, Lucien 169, 170, 172, 232, 251, 252
Lord, Albert 51, 239

INDEX

LSD 7
Luke, Helen H. 246
Lukes, Steven 233
Lüthi, Max 248
Mahabharata 73
Malinowski, Bronislaw 152, 154, 164, 249
mana 85, 86
Mann, Thomas 63f., 153
Marcel, Gabriel, 43f., 47, 68, 238
Marett, Robert R. 242
Maslow, Abraham 40
Massey, Irving 255f.
maya 199
McLuhan, Marshall 188
Mercator, Gerardus, 91f., 117, 182
Merlin 105
metamorphosis 80
metaphor 67, 68, 86
Midgley, Mary 176, 245
Miller, Henry 95
morris dancing 120
Mother Goddess (see Great Mother) 84, 122, 126, 134, 135, 139, 144, 160, 247
motif 49, 73
Myerhoff, Barbara 237, 239, 242
Nahua Indians 38
Narcissus 43, 80, 137
Neihardt, John G. 8, 232
Newmann, Erich 241, 244, 247
Nicholas of Cusa 237
Nietzsche, Friedrich 14, 187, 194, 226f., 233, 255, 256, 258
Novalis 183
Odin 3, 177
Oedipus 3, 35, 58, 69, 71, 72, 87, 92, 98, 137, 147f., 172, 202, 212
omphalos 56
Oppenheimer, Robert 255
Orpheus 72, 136
Osiris 29, 121, 157
Otto, Rudolf x, 252
Otto, Walter F. 177f., 254
Otzen, Benedikt 246
Ovid 80, 137, 253

Pacal 54
Parmenides 256
Parry, Milman 51
participation mystique 168
Parzival 72
Pearsall Smith, Logan 252
Persephone (Proserpine) 35, 105, 123, 135, 246
Perseus 105, 147
peyote 46f., 172, 239
Phaethon 136, 155, 244
Polanyi, Michael 256
Poseidon 2
Prometheus 3, 116, 119
Propp, Vladimir 51, 239, 241
Psyche 135f., 138, 244, 247
Punter, David 237
Quetalcoatl 4
Radin, Paul 82f., 84, 85, 238, 241, 242, 246, 249f., 252, 254
Raglan, Lord 65, 251
Raven 4, 7, 77, 81f., 246
Reichel-Dolmatoff, Gerardo 238
Ricoeur, Paul 211, 257
rites de passage
Robin Hood 120
Rousseau, Jean-Jacques 86
Ruthven, K.K. 237
Sabbatai Zevi 38f., 237
Sagan, Carl 233
Sartre, Jean-Paul 57, 193, 217, 256
Saussure, Ferdinand de 60, 257
Schelling, F.W.J. 232, 249
shadow 105, 109, 237
Shakespeare, William xiv, 67, 86, 145, 146, 247, 257,
Shamanism 169, 171, 253
shapeshifter 80
Shelley, Mary 39, 237
Scholem, Gershom 237, 242, 257
Shiva 83, 127, 128
Simmel, Georg 168, 186, 255
Sisyphus 72f.
Sophocles 58, 87, 148, 253
Sorel, Georges 188, 255
Structuralism 43, 60, 92, 257
Swift, Jonathan 71

270

INDEX

taboo 85, 88, 136
Tammuz 29, 122
Teilhard de Chardin, Pierre 1
The Golden Bough 34
"The Juniper Tree" 49
Theseus 99, 105, 133
Thompson, Stith 51, 243
Tibetan Book of the Dead 174-76, 254
Titian 94
Tom Thumb 139
Topitsch, Ernst 250
Trickster 81, 87-90, 248, 254
Trinity 83, 167
Trobrianders 18f.
Turner, Victor 47, 154, 245
Urizen 99-103, 117, 243
Usener, H.K. 239
Vaihinger, Hans 225-27, 258
van Gennep, Arnold 65, 239
Vico, Giambattista 232, 235
von Franz, Marie Louise 244, 248, 254
von Humboldt, Wilhelm 255

waste land 122, 242f.
Watts, Alan 7, 170, 172, 232, 235, 237, 253
Weston, Jessie 242
Wheelwright, Philip 25, 146, 158, 235, 236, 249
Whorf, Benjamin 16-18, 63, 154, 195, 233, 236, 250, 259
wise old man 105
Wittgenstein, Ludwig xiii, 232, 256
Wyatt, Sir Thomas 259
Xipe Totec 160
Yeats, William Butler 38, 87, 207, 237, 243
Zeus 29, 112, 123, 136, 138
Zimmer, Heinrich ix, 232, 243, 245
"zone of middle dimensions" 179, 181, 198
Zukav, Gary 254